CURRICULUM PLANNING

A Handbook for Professionals

David Pratt
Queen's University

Harcourt Brace College Publishers

Fort Worth Philadelphia San Diego New York Orlando Austin San Antonio
Toronto Montreal London Sydney Tokyo

Publisher	Ted Buchholz
Acquisitions Editor	JoAnne Weaver
Project Editor	Barbara Moreland
Production Manager	Cynthia Young
Art Director	Jim Dodson

Library of Congress Catalog Card Number: 93-80015

ISBN: 0-15-501098-0

Address for Orders:
Harcourt Brace, Inc.
6277 Sea Harbor Drive, Orlando, Florida 32887.
1-800-782-4479, or 1-800-433-0001 (in Florida).

Address for Editorial Correspondence:
Harcourt Brace College Publishers
301 Commerce Street, Suite 3700, Fort Worth, TX 76102.

For permission to use copyrighted material, the publisher is grateful to the Nobel Foundation. Permissions are continued on page 464 which constitutes a continuation of this copyright page.
Printed in the United States of America

4567890123 016 9876543210

Harcourt Brace College Publishers

▪ Biography ▪

David Pratt was educated in Britain, the United States, and Canada. Prior to specializing in curriculum planning, he worked for several years as a school teacher. Much of his understanding of curriculum comes from his work with teachers and from his three children, who were educated in four different countries. He has lectured and consulted on curriculum throughout the English-speaking world and is author of numerous publications in the field, including the widely used text, *Curriculum: Design and Development* (1980). His major interest is in how education can best contribute to human happiness. David Pratt is a professor of education at Queen's University, Ontario, Canada.

▪ Preface ▪

The human potential for life, liberty, and the pursuit of happiness has in many ways never been greater than it is today. Yet the obstacles to human well-being—personal, economic, social, and geopolitical—are formidable. What is the good life? How can we live it? How can we help others live it? Fifty million teachers around the world live these questions in their work every day. They constitute the only profession that is responsible for working with all the members of an entire generation, with the intent of enhancing the well-being of their students through the process of learning.

Schools, which a hundred years ago served a small elite, are now (second only to the family) the dominating institution for almost everyone from infancy to adulthood. While issues of cost and organization often loom large in the minds of both the public and educators, the justification for the existence of the school lies in its curriculum. What are schools teaching? How successfully? What are they failing to teach? These are the questions that need to be subject to constant inquiry and debate. These are questions central to the field of curriculum.

The study of curriculum and instruction has undergone radical transformation in the past twenty years. A generation ago, scholars professed that "schools make no difference," and that the field of curriculum itself was moribund. Today, the field of curriculum is fast-moving, optimistic, and above all, able to deliver practical and effective guidance to practicing educators.

There are many questions in curriculum that are not yet answered, many more that have not yet been asked. But now we do know the answers to many questions that were unsolved in 1970. In particular, we now have a very good idea what the conditions are under which most students can acquire most of the learning we want to teach them in the areas conventionally prized by schools and their clients, that is to say, in the development of knowledge and skills.

One loving, perceptive teacher is worth more to his or her students than all the educational theory in the world. But loving and perceptive teachers can benefit from attention to the evidence accumulated about teaching and learning over the past twenty years.

Much of what we have learned about effective teaching and learning has to do with planning, and this is the approach taken in this book. Curriculum planning is taken to include all aspects of decision making relating to student learning. The term "planning," then, encompasses not only the intentions of instruction, but also assessment of student progress, instructional content and strategies, identification of learning resources, program evaluation, and curriculum implementation. In describing what is known about effective ways of making these decisions, I have drawn heavily on the research literature, particularly that published since 1980, without, I hope, overburdening the text with references.

This book is intended to be a resource of information for everyone who plans educational programs. It is intended to meet the needs of classroom teachers and students in preservice education programs, as well as providing a resource for curriculum policy teams and educators involved in graduate education. Although most of the examples used in the text come from school contexts, the principles and processes described are also intended to be useful to instructors in colleges and universities, health and public services, business and industry, the armed forces, and recreational fields.

I wish to thank the many colleagues and students who, over the past years, have provided valuable feedback and suggestions on earlier drafts of this work. I have used their ideas extensively. I would also like to thank Ralph Westgarth, who invited me to look at the work of student artists, and the artists themselves for permission to use their work. I am grateful to the Nobel Foundation for permission to use the photographs of Nobel laureates. It has been a pleasure to work with the staff at Harcourt Brace. I particularly wish to thank JoAnne Weaver for her support of the project and Ruth Steinberg for her meticulous editing. I am grateful to Barbara Moreland for her dedicated work on the text and for her patience, which did not falter even when page proofs disappeared en route to me in Crete. I count myself fortunate in the many friends who have given me encouragement and whose company has enriched the period during which this book was written.

This book is intended to help educators make their instruction more effective and efficient. It is also a primary aim of this work to help them develop curricula that are more significant, humane, reflective, and meaningful to their students. To all those teachers who pursue this aim, this book is dedicated.

Contents

8. Specifying Learning Resources ———————— 256

9. Evaluating Curricula   296

10. Implementing Curriculum Change   320

CHAPTER 1

Curriculum and Human Well-Being

> *I continue to have the faith that schools . . . can actually contribute to the creation of a more loving, more just, saner world.*
>
> **David Purpel (1989, p. x)**

Amy pero   Age·6

Summary

The most important task of curriculum planners is to decide what is sufficiently significant to be worth teaching. This is a matter of determining priorities for curriculum. The concept of human well-being provides a point of reference for such decisions. Different schools of thought emphasize different priorities and avenues to well-being, such as cultural transmission, social transformation, individual fulfillment, and feminist pedagogy. Curricula need to be planned not only for the present, but for the future, which entails social and technical forecasting. Expertise in the art and science of planning curriculum makes an important contribution to the professionality and autonomy of teachers.

THE EDUCATIONAL CONTEXT ─────────────────

We live in an age of promise and an age of peril. While some of the international tensions of the cold war have relaxed, enough nuclear and chemical weapons remain stockpiled to destroy civilization many times over. In some countries the march of freedom seems inexorable. Yet, in many others, more political prisoners are jailed and tortured than ever before (Philip, 1989). Wars have ended in many parts of the world, but thousands continue to die daily in domestic violence, in civil strife, and in little-reported conflicts in remote parts of the globe. Agriculture has never been more efficient or productive, but millions of adults and children around the world are starving. New medicines save countless lives, but alcohol, tobacco, illicit drugs, and AIDS kill millions of people every year. Material well-being has never been so high, but neither have teenage suicide rates (World Health Organization, 1990).

This is the world that education inhabits, the world that education, in general, and curriculum, in particular, must address. In this world it is the role of education to enhance human well-being by promoting learning. That this is possible, and that it is desirable, must be the conscious or unconscious inspiration of every teacher. For who could long remain an educator without the belief that his or her actions will, in some way, improve the human condition?

In this chapter we shall look at some of the implications for curriculum planning of fundamental questions about our purposes in education. If you are anxious to read about the specific details of how to plan curriculum, then by all means go straight to Chapter 3. You can always come back and read this chapter later.

▪ What Is Significant? ▪

The first question that needs to be asked when planning a curriculum is not: How can we plan more efficiently or teach more effectively? It is: *What curricula are worth planning?* There is no point in doing more effectively what is not worth doing in the first place!

So let us step back, if only for a few moments, from our preoccupation with the teaching of sentence analysis—or the correct printing of the alphabet, or the division of fractions, or the periodic table, or French irregular verbs, or the causes of the French Revolution, or the origin of Halloween—and let us ask: What is significant?

Life and death are significant. That world population is increasing by ten thousand people *per hour* is significant. The extinction of dozens of animal and plant species from the world every day is significant. It is significant that the United States has seventy-three times as many killings per hundred men as does Austria ("Killings per hundred men," 1990). The fact that black men in Harlem have less chance of reaching the age of sixty-five than men in Bangladesh is significant (McCord & Freeman, 1990). The disappearance of at least one aboriginal language a year in North America is significant. So is the destruction of eleven million hectares of forest in the world each year. The ten million people rendered homeless in Africa by political, economic, and climatic disruption is significant. It is significant that in the age of cross-linked data banks, personal privacy has ceased to exist (Roszak, 1986). So is the fact that half of the world's scientists are engaged in the development of weapons (Capra, 1982). That forty thousand children below one year of age will die in the United States this year is significant (Sealing, 1989). So is the fact that the major cause of death of 10–14-year-old boys in Detroit is homicide by other children (McCaslin & Good, 1992). It is significant that the United Nations has reported that in many countries child slavery and the child slave trade continue to exist (Vichniac, 1988). It is tragically significant that industrialized countries spend as much on the military as on education; and that developing countries spend four times as much on military expenditures as they spend on education (Salam, 1989). So is the fact that Americans are, on average, spending half of all their disposable time watching television, and the more they watch, the more bored, tense, sad, lonely, and hostile they become (Kubey & Csikszentmihalyi, 1990).

And then again, the vast outpouring of generosity when famine or natural disasters strike is significant. The heroic work of international organizations such as the Red Cross, Amnesty International, OXFAM, and Médecins sans Frontières is significant. Significant also are the voices of women and men who speak out against injustice and oppression at great personal risk. So is the moral stature of individuals like Mahatma Gandhi, Martin Luther King, Jr., Aung San Suu Kyi, Rigoberta Menchú, Andrei Sakharov, Mother Teresa, and Jean Vanier.

But we do not need to look only to these public figures and events for significance. For most of us, significance lies primarily in the past and present of our lived experience. Loving or conflicted relationships, joyful or painful memories, deeply held commitments and aspirations, important values and principles, fond hopes and harsh anxieties, passionate interests or aversions: these are the chords that constitute the music of our lives. I know of a prison inmate, serving a life sentence, who spends his time making rocking horses that are given to needy children. That's significant. So is the artist who was badly abused as a child and who has made peace with her past sufficiently to paint works that glow with affirmation of life. I read recently of a woman whose son was murdered in his early twenties, and who since that time has devoted her life to campaigning against capital punishment. And I think of the eighty-five-year-old clergyman who said, "I feel as though I'd drunk the cup of life to the full, and all the sweetness is in the bottom of the cup."

Before we recycle, once more, last year's curriculum on calculating square roots by the formal method, we need to consider whether there are issues of greater significance to which we should first pay attention. It is to this question that writers on the subject of curriculum constantly return. The first, and still one of the greatest, textbooks on curriculum is Plato's *The Republic*, written in the fourth century B.C. In it, Plato devotes considerable attention to the question: What should be the curriculum for those who are to rule in the just society? The relative merits of such subjects as music, poetry, mathematics, and gymnastics are discussed in terms still interesting today. Bill Schubert (1980) argues that the first modern curriculum text was Claude Fleury's *The History of Choice and Method of*

Studies, published in France in 1686, which similarly focused on the relative significance of different curriculum elements. The same interest inspired Franklin Bobbitt, whose books *The Curriculum* (1918) and *How to Make a Curriculum* (1924) are often considered to have launched the study of curriculum development in the twentieth century. And very recently, curriculum scholars have returned once again to the one most crucial question for schooling: What should schools teach? (Eisner, 1990; McNeil, 1990; Rothman, 1989).

Herbert Spencer, whose famous essay entitled *What Knowledge Is of Most Worth?* was first published in 1861, was one of the first to recognize that, as time and other resources are limited, we must develop some grounds for determining the priority among different possible learnings. Spencer suggested that curriculum might be selected on the basis of a hierarchy of human needs. As the most basic need was survival, first priority should be given to knowledge and skills that could actually prevent premature death. This remains the rationale for such subjects as driver education, swimming, drug education, and safety education. Second, Spencer said, came occupational skills—in Victorian England you could starve to death if you were unable to earn a living. Today, involuntary unemployment, in addition to its economic consequences, remains one of the most personally devastating experiences (Ensminger & Celentano, 1988). Third, and a point we have yet to consider seriously, came the skills of parenting. It is hard to argue with Spencer's contention that it is in their role as parents that the present generation will do most to influence the future of our society. Fourth, Spencer placed learning to maintain healthy political and social relations, and fifth, the arts and leisure pursuits (Spencer, 1911).

We might argue with Spencer's hierarchy, but his was an attempt to place curriculum on a firmer foundation than mere tradition or prejudice. Such thinking is needed today as much as ever. Recently, curriculum scholars have begun to criticize themselves for "addressing everything except the most central of educational questions: What should be taught in schools?" (Eisner, 1990, p. 524). Curriculum tends to change by accretion; that is to say, as demands for new knowledge and skills arise, schools respond by adding new curricula. However, old curricula are not eliminated. Consequently, teachers and students feel harassed by too much content and too little time, too many demands and too few resources. Later in this book we shall suggest some strategies for dealing with this problem in terms of existing curriculum. At the design stage, what is needed is a focus or orientation that will serve as a reference point for establishing priorities. What are our basic commitments as educators and curriculum planners? This is the question to which we need to turn if we are to avoid drowning in a sea of different possibilities and demands.

▪ The Significance of Curriculum ▪

More young people today spend more time in school than ever before. In 1990 in the United States, 67.5 million people (27 percent of the total population) were either students in or employees of educational institutions (National Council for Educational Statistics, 1992). In this century youth and schooling have come to be co-identified. A century ago ten years of schooling was viewed as a high level of education. Today we lament the minority of students who leave school after "only" ten years.

Students who attend school full-time for twelve years invest well over two thousand days of their youth in school; at six hours a day, that is twelve thousand hours. They enter school as little more than infants and leave as young men and women. The school, for most of them, comes to shape their social life, their self-concept, their occupational future. Unlike other social organizations, such as the armed forces, churches, or prisons, the entire age group is legislated into schools and the schools must endeavor to accommodate all of them.

In this massive intervention by the state in the lives of individuals, it is easy to become distracted by questions of policy, finance, and administration. Certainly the cost is enormous: in 1984 the United States spent over three *trillion* dollars on formal education (Jorgenson & Fraumeni, 1990). But we need to remind ourselves periodically of the primary importance of what is taught and learned, and how it is taught and learned—in other words, of the importance of curriculum.

The original derivation of the word *curriculum* is from the Latin verb *currere*, "to run"; *curriculum*, a diminutive form, came to mean a "racing chariot" or "race track." Cicero applied the term metaphorically to speak of *vitae curriculum*, "the course of one's life," and *curricula mentis*, "the (educational) course of the mind." Only in the nineteenth century did the term come to be commonly used in educational discourse. The prevailing definition is usually similar to that coined by Hollis Caswell and Doak Campbell (1935) and repeated in successive editions of the American Educational Research Association's *Encyclopedia of Educational Research*, "all the experiences that a learner has under the guidance of the school" (Kearney & Cook, 1961, p. 358).

For our purposes this definition is a little too broad. It would, paradoxically, include within curriculum "extracurricular" activities such as the organization of school lunches, hallway traffic, sports clubs, and school dances. In this book our interest has a more specific focus on the content and processes of teaching and learning. Alan Tom defines curriculum succinctly as "a plan for teaching or instruction" (1984, p. 89). We shall use curriculum similarly in this book to mean "a plan for a sustained process of teaching and learning." The terms *program*, *course of study*, *course description*, *course outline*, and *syllabus* are approximate, albeit often incomplete, synonyms for curriculum. A policy regarding absenteeism is not a curriculum nor is a single lesson plan. Actual teaching and learning is not curriculum, for curriculum refers to *plans* for instructional acts, not the acts of instruction themselves. Curriculum is analogous to the set of blueprints from which a house is constructed. A curriculum can be viewed as a blueprint for instruction.

Before an architect begins to draw blueprints for a building, she or he must ask some basic questions about the uses and purposes of the building. Questions of basic purpose are helpful to architects and are equally helpful to curriculum planners. Perhaps the most general response we can give to such questions in education is that the function of curriculum is to enhance human well-being. What does this mean in practice?

▪ Human Well-Being ▪

It is, of course, a truism that educators are committed to human well-being. To what else could one be committed? But sometimes even the obvious is worth restating. As Robert Burns said two hundred years ago: "Whatever mitigates the woes or increases the happiness of others, this is my criterion of goodness; and whatever injures society at large, or any individual in it, this is my measure of iniquity" (1955, p. 32).

Let us examine the implications of this commitment. Human well-being may be advanced in two ways: by removing or preventing obstacles to future welfare and by directly enhancing people's welfare (promoting well-being).

Removing obstacles

Many obstacles to happiness are easily defined. To reduce an individual's illiteracy is, in almost every culture, to reduce a significant obstacle to that person's well-being; likewise to ameliorate a young person's social timidity. Certain ignorances are obstacles to well-being—not so much ignorance of the periodic table or the geography of Tibet as ignorance of how to learn, how to listen, how to choose a career, how to make friends, how to resolve conflicts, how to deal with anxiety, how to maintain a healthy body. But the absence of certain basic cognitions can also be damaging in direct personal terms. Consider the frustrations of this thirty-year-old adult who had difficulty with elementary number skills:

> To disguise his poor money skills, his usual procedure for going grocery shopping was to remove all bills smaller than $20 (he could recognize the values of paper currency) from his wallet before entering a store. When given the total by the cashier, he would reach into his wallet and pull out a "bunch" of bills and toss "them on the counter—with authority," hoping that there was sufficient money to cover his purchases. Unable to make use of the resulting change, he collected it in a large jar at home, and periodically took the change to a confectionery store during a quiet hour for an accommodating cashier to count. . . . Needless to say, he was a very frustrated person. . . . "I feel like a fool when I see eight-year-old kids that can do simple things that I can't, no matter how hard I've tried." (Hope, 1987, pp. 12–13)

There are worse starting-points for curriculum than the definition of critical ignorances.

Preventing obstacles

Preventing future obstacles is more difficult. I am thinking of tasks like persuading young people to wear seatbelts in cars, not to begin to smoke, and to take steps to avoid contracting sexually transmitted diseases. A 1987 survey of 11,000 eighth and tenth graders throughout the United States found that only 40 percent had worn a seat belt the last time they had ridden in a car, 33 percent had "seriously thought" about committing suicide, 14 percent had attempted suicide, and 25 percent did not know that using condoms is effective in avoiding sexually transmitted diseases. While three-quarters had completed a course in health education, fewer than half had received instruction on AIDS and other sexually transmitted diseases (American School Health Association, 1989). This task, the prevention of evil or misfortune, is truly heroic. The great heroes of history are not those who won wars, but those who prevented wars from occurring. History does not record their names, for it is blind to uncommitted evils. To take a mundane example: Years ago, the U.S. government accountants calculated the cost benefits accruing to various kinds of social intervention, from cancer screening to policing the use of helmets by motorcyclists. The most cost-effective of the actions they examined was increasing police enforcement of seatbelt legislation; the return was calculated at $1,351 for each dollar invested ("Putting a dollar sign on life," 1967, p. 87). This is almost certainly higher than the return on more glamorous police activities such as high-speed pursuit of bank robbers. The social costs of some preventable events, for example, the birth of seriously malnourished babies, is enormous. The educator whose work prevents a single case of AIDS—or an unwanted pregnancy, or long-term imprisonment, or lung cancer, or drug addiction, or quadriplegia, or suicide—has gone far towards justifying his or her entire career.

Promoting well-being

A purely preventive education, however, would be very limited in its outlook. Most educators are also interested in how to directly promote the well-being of their students. Such intentions may take the form of enabling graduates to discover the life work for which they are most suited and to prepare for it. Charles Givens points out that there are three strategies, all critical to people's future happiness, that are never taught in school: how to have a successful marriage, how to raise successful children, and how to build wealth successfully (1988). Given the significance to most people of their relationships, developing a capacity for loving and nonexploitive relations with others would appear to be a critical attribute.

Our subjective sense of well-being often derives from our senses. Homer's words of twenty-five centuries ago still ring true today: "Dear to us ever is the banquet and the harp, and the dance and change of raiment, and the warm bath and love and sleep." In his remarkable book, *The Seven Mysteries of Life*, Guy Murchie (1978) identifies thirty-two senses, including temperature sense, appetite, sense of humor, time sense, aesthetic sense, and psychic senses such as foreknowledge and telepathy. Yet school curricula rarely aim at education of the senses. Particularly neglected are the aesthetic senses. George Kennan, the American diplomat, said regretfully, "No one, to the day of my graduation, had ever taught me to look understandingly at a painting, or a tree, or the facade of a building" (1967, p. 16).

Narrow perceptions of relevance and utility have led us into the error of the bishop's housekeeper in *Les Misérables*, who commented that the bishop's flower bed was wasted because

"salads are more useful than flowers." "You are wrong," replied the bishop. "The beautiful is as useful as the useful." Then, after a pause, he added: "More so, perhaps." (Hugo, 1982, p. 3)

I am suggesting that as educators we need to articulate the unspoken and to make real our assumptions. In our teaching and our curriculum planning, we need to ask continuously, does this instruction help to remove important obstacles to well-being? Does it promote, in the best possible way, the future happiness of students and society? There is an additional question: Are we, at this moment, maximizing our students' well-being? This question obliges us to examine whether we are using curriculum content and instructional techniques that are the most interesting, enjoyable, and enriching for our students. Are we, in other words, providing an environment that, as experienced by students in the present moment, is an environment of joy rather than pain, interest rather than boredom? Fundamentally, we can live, not in the past or the future, but only in the present moment, a point often emphasized by John Dewey (1938). A curriculum that makes joy a conscious part of its agenda will provide opportunities for fun and play, for dreams and fantasy, for sharing and tenderness, all of which qualities are, in contemporary education, often conspicuous by their absence.

CURRICULUM PERSPECTIVES

Surprisingly, few curriculum theorists have discussed curriculum directly in terms of well-being and happiness. More commonly, curriculum is viewed as a vehicle for helping people construct meaning in their lives. This is salutary. Human beings are, first and foremost, meaning-makers, and a sense of meaning is a critical component in human happiness.

We will not attempt here a comprehensive survey of educational or curriculum philosophies. Each such philosophy has its distinct value commitments and its own view of the kinds of learning that are most meaningful. Almost all philosophies of curriculum agree (sometimes implicitly rather than explicitly) that the basis of education is helping learners to construct meaning in their lives. Where they disagree is with respect to the kinds of meaning that deserve priority.

Curriculum theorists have written diversely and at length about the classification of different schools of curriculum thought. Eisner & Vallance (1973) classified five "conflicting conceptions" of curriculum: technological, cognitive, self-actualizing, social-reconstructionist, and academic-rationalist. Schubert (1986a) defined three distinct schools: intellectual/traditionalist, social/behaviorist, and experientialist. Miller and Seller (1985) categorized curriculum models in terms of transmission, transaction, and transformation. The field of curriculum theory is a creative cacophany. Twenty years ago the late great Joseph Schwab declared the curriculum field moribund (1970). In a recent and masterful description of the field of curriculum, Philip Jackson epitomized it as confused (1992). This at least suggests some progress over two decades. Clearly any summary of so diverse a field will be selective. Let us, by way of example, limit our examination to four orientations:

1. Cultural transmission, which emphasizes the traditional academic disciplines;

2. Social transformation, emphasizing political and social change;

3. Individual fulfillment, emphasizing personal growth, relationships, and self-actualization;

4. Feminist pedagogy, emphasizing a more equitable balance among gender-related characteristics and interests.

These categories are neither exclusive nor exhaustive. They represent differences in focus, and there are strong interconnections among all of them. They will serve, however, to illustrate the range of outlook that different curriculum scholars bring to their subject.

▪ Cultural Transmission ▪

This strand of curriculum thinking has the longest pedigree, going back at least two thousand years. It views the role of curriculum, and of schools in general, as to transmit the best products of the intellectual culture. It is often associated with a belief in the generalizability of learning—that learning in one area will have beneficial effects in many areas. Plato, for example, maintained that training in mathematics "makes a slow mind quicker, even if it does no other good" (1941, p. 237). The school of cultural transmission tends to see curriculum in terms of a specific, and fairly limited, number of intellectual disciplines. The areas of learning most valued are those that tend toward abstraction and generalizability. Medieval scholars, treading in the footsteps of Plato, viewed education as consisting of the Quadrivium of four minor disciplines—Music, Arithmetic, Geometry, and Astronomy—and the Trivium of three major disciplines—Grammar, Rhetoric, and Dialectic—which together constituted the seven liberal arts.

Society constantly redefines the disciplines of importance. In the United States in 1885, the "Committee of Fifteen," under the leadership of William T. Harris, identified the five basic fields of knowledge, or "windows on the soul," as mathematics, biology, art and literature, grammar, and history. More recently, national reports in the United States, most notably The Paideia Proposal by Mortimer Adler (1982) and Horace's Compromise by Theodore Sizer (1984), have revived the demand that schools concentrate on cultural transmission by means of the traditional academic disciplines.

―――――――――― Déjà vu ――――――――――

What is more, even Grammar, the basis of all education, baffles the brains of the younger generation today. For if you take note, there is not a single modern schoolboy who can compose verses or write a decent letter. I doubt too whether one in a hundred can read a Latin author, or decipher a word of any foreign language. And no wonder, for at every level of our educational system, you'll find Humbug in charge, and his colleague Flattery tagging along behind him.

William Langland, *Piers the Plowman*, A.D. 1362 (1966, p. 190)

Because of its heavy reliance on cognition—that is, knowledge and intellectual skills—the kind of content advocated by these thinkers is relatively easy to teach and to test. Perhaps for that reason it has come to dominate school curriculum. The objectives stated in official curriculum guidelines focus almost exclusively on cognition (Klein, 1989; Pratt, 1989). Advocates of cultural transmission have sometimes claimed that cognition constitutes the only legitimate curriculum content (Hirst, 1970; Phenix, 1986).

Those who view cultural transmission as the primary purpose of the school have a number of beliefs in common: (1) that the role of the curriculum is primarily intellectual; (2) that all or most of what is intellectually significant is to be found in the traditional academic disciplines; (3) that the sources of education are essentially literary, to be found in words and symbols; (4) that the task of schools is to repair deficits or gaps in people's understanding; (5) that education is a didactic process whereby information is transmitted to the student by means of the spoken or written word; and (6) that particular studies will have general effects.

Few educators would deny the importance of teaching knowledge and intellectual skills. Many such learnings are critical to the well-being and successful functioning of human beings in society. Critics tend to attack not the idea that such learnings are necessary, but the idea that they are sufficient; that the traditional academic disciplines are the only legitimate curriculum content; that they should be emphasized to the exclusion of other types of human learning and aspects of human personality. They also suggest that an exclusively cognitive orientation casts the student in a passive role; that the issue of generalization is controversial; that what is accepted as a discipline at any point in history is the result of cultural and political forces; and that the curriculum itself "is a social artifact, conceived of and made for deliberate human purposes" (Goodson, 1989, p. 131). The historian Herbert Kliebard, noting their tenacity in curriculum, refers to the traditional school subjects as "the impregnable fortress" (1986, p. 269), while the philosopher Michael Scriven claims that the overwhelming majority of the traditional curriculum is either irrelevant or redundant (1975).

Missing in the emphasis on symbols of cultural literacy (memorized information) is the deeper rationale, implicit in the experientialist, for experiencing the great mysteries and for the liberating power of great ideas. The great works' emancipatory power to free people from the intellectual fetters of their day seems to be lost by many proponents of cultural literacy in the acceptance of tradition for its own sake. . . . Students should continually return to the questions of what is moral action in each situation encountered: What is right? What is good? What is worthwhile? This allows classrooms and families really to become sites of moral action, places where people, adults and children alike, are immersed in the wholehearted quest for a moral life, a life lived within a community where shared values and individual values are honored, a life of cooperation, harmony with nature, improvement, and possibility. It allows people to search for a world that is more caring, more peaceful, more meaningful, more beautiful, and more fair, and it creates a space for people to act on behalf of that search. It should become the organizing center of the curriculum itself . . . enabling and inspiring students to ask continuously: What is worthwhile? What is valuable to think about, study, do, be, and become?

William Ayers & William H. Schubert (1989, p. 364)

Social transformation

Another influential group of scholars views the school as a potential agent for the reform of society. Many view the school, as presently constituted, as an agent rather than an opponent of class oppression. Jean Anyon suggests that schools teach lower-class students to follow rules, middle-class students to give "right" answers, professional-class students to be creative, and executive-class students to manipulate the system (1980). Although not the first to advocate a socially activist role for the school, George S. Counts was for many years its best-known spokesperson. He summarized his beliefs in a book entitled *Dare the School Build a New Social Order?*, first published in 1932 (1969). This text and his other writings earned him a distinction shared by other great American writers such as Sinclair Lewis, Pearl Buck, William Faulkner, Ernest Hemingway, Tennessee Williams, Carl Sandburg, Truman Capote, Arthur Miller, Robert Frost, John Kenneth Galbraith, Norman Mailer, and John Steinbeck—an FBI dossier as a potential subversive (Mitgang, 1988).

While popular in the days of the New Deal, such radical views fell into disfavor after World War II, when the watchword became social adjustment rather than social transformation. But in the 1980s, the call for educators to play a role in the reform of society was made by several scholars. Educators, it was argued, must become advocates of those young people whose lives were increasingly blighted by poverty, malnutrition, homelessness, crime, violence, alienation, and

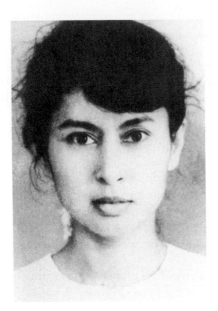

It would be difficult to dispel ignorance unless there is freedom to pursue the truth unfettered by fear. . . . Free men and women are the oppressed who go on trying and who in the process make themselves fit to bear the responsibilities and uphold the disciplines which will maintain a free society.

Aung San Suu Kyi (Burma), Nobel Prize for Peace, 1991. (Kyi, 1991, pp.180–81, 183)

drug addiction (McLaren, 1988; Van Til, 1989). Any purpose less than "the creation of a more loving, more just, saner world" (Purpel, 1989, p. x), it could be argued, is a trivialization of teachers' work (Apple, 1979; Giroux, 1983).

It is somewhat difficult in the Western world to find historical or contemporary examples of schools leading social change. But if curriculum seems unlikely to spearhead social or political revolution, it can, as innumerable adults

I am not against a curriculum or a program, but only against the authoritarian and elitist ways of organizing the studies [and] passive and silencing methods of transferring knowledge. . . . When I criticize manipulation, I do not want to fall into a false and nonexistent nondirectivity of education. For me, education is always directive, always. The question is to know towards what and which and whom is it directive. This is the question. I don't believe in self-liberation. Liberation is a social act. Liberating education is a social process of illumination.

Paulo Freire (Shor and Freire, 1987, pp. 21–23)

attest, have an impact on individuals. The process of *conscientization*, a term coined by the Brazilian educator, Paulo Freire, aims to liberate people by making them aware of the political, cultural, historical, and social assumptions of their society. The German philosopher, Jürgen Habermas (1974) termed the purpose of such education "emancipatory action." This is to be achieved not by transmission of information, but by dialectic and collaborative inquiry by teachers and students (Freire, 1970).

> We know that our arguments will not convince many. We know that our fundamental convictions that the only method of education is experiment, and its only criterion freedom, will sound to some like a trite commonplace, to some like an indistinct abstraction, to others again like a visionary dream.
>
> Leo Tolstoy (1967, p. 31)

The primary curriculum goal is liberation—developing in students maximum capacity for choice. Our liberation is incomplete as a result not only of social and economic constraints, prejudice, and discrimination. We are also oppressed insofar as we live with false information or incomplete understanding of ourselves and of the world. The education required to counter such oppression is not technocratic, but must in all its aspects be "consistent with values of human possibility and social justice" (Cornbleth, 1990, p. 198). It must have, in the words of Shirley Grundy, "a fundamental interest in emancipation and empowerment to engage in autonomous action arising out of authentic, critical insights into the social construction of human society" (1987, p. 19). The ultimate educational purpose is

> the emergence of people who know who they are and are conscious of themselves as active and deciding beings, who bear responsibility for their choices and who are able to explain them in terms of their own freely adopted purposes and ideals.   (Fay, 1987, p. 74)

Alan Webster, a New Zealand educator, has drawn a general outline of a curriculum for liberation. It would include the biology of liberation, which teaches the biological limits of consumption of energy and resources, since the future freedom of human beings depends on biological accounting. An ecology of liberation addresses the need to develop balance and interdependence in the ecosystem. A psychology of liberation is aimed at the maximization of personal competency. A sociology of liberation teaches the development of collective opportunity. A philosophy of liberation maximizes intellectual and moral autonomy in terms of freedom of thought and freedom of action. And a politics of liberation aims at the maximization of human equality, freedom, opportunity, and diversity. These various areas are seen as integrative rather than specialized. The purpose of all of them is to maximize understanding, anticipation, intention, and participation.

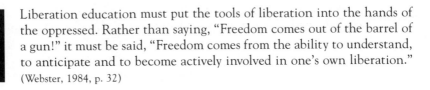

Liberation education must put the tools of liberation into the hands of the oppressed. Rather than saying, "Freedom comes out of the barrel of a gun!" it must be said, "Freedom comes from the ability to understand, to anticipate and to become actively involved in one's own liberation." (Webster, 1984, p. 32)

Individual fulfillment

A third orientation stresses the development of all aspects of the individual, as a means not so much to social change as to personal fulfillment or self-actualization. The roots of this approach are found in such sources as the romantic philosophy of Jean-Jacques Rousseau, the psychology of Abraham Maslow, and the pedagogy of A. S. Neill. Sometimes called humanistic, this orientation views people as essentially good and motivated by their own need for growth. Education is not a process of filling a vacuum or remediating a deficit, but of providing the conditions in which people can develop their full potential. The nurturance of self-concept is viewed as critical. It is seen as important to integrate the different aspects of being, including the social, the cognitive, the affective, the somatic, the aesthetic, and the spiritual. The primary vehicle for growth is human relations, and the preferred learning mode is direct personal experience (Pratt, 1986a).

The meanings of greatest interest to these thinkers are personal meanings. Personal meanings are so unique to each individual that they cannot be fully understood by anyone else. An individual's self-concept or gender identity or aesthetic responses—these are elements of personality that are subjectively lived and experienced rather than objectively articulated or formalized. The moment of illumination that may come to a child or adult while reading a work of literature is significant partly because it is often extraordinary and counter-cultural, estranging and liberating "from the normal and the endlessly normalized" (Greene, 1990, p. 253).

Most subjective of all, and most difficult to render into the verbal formulas beloved of Western thought, are spiritual meanings: the ways in which individuals conceive of their place in the universe and interpret the fundamental meaning of their lives. In the absence of spiritual meaning, writes Webster, we suffer "spiritual estrangement, defined as feeling apart from or broken and distant from both one's own deeper spiritual self and from any greater spiritual entity" (1984, p. 16). Spirituality weaves those strands of human consciousness that provide a sense of personal meaning, significance, harmony, or wonder. Perhaps because of a confusion in the minds of educators between spirituality and religion, such meanings are rarely addressed in school curricula.

But the consequences of an absence of a sense of personal meaning are all around us. Neurosis, alienation, false dependencies, meaningless delinquency and vandalism, violence, depression, suicide, and attempted suicide are often responses to a felt absence of personal meaning. Suicide rates have risen, especially among teenage males, to the point at which, in North America, they are now approximately twice as high as for the same group in Japan.

Table 1-1   *Suicide Rates in 1986 per 100,000 Persons in Selected Countries for Males Aged 15–24*

Japan	11.6
Sweden	19.5
United States	21.4
Canada	26.9

(World Health Organization, 1990)

Personal meanings are unlikely to be developed by purely cognitive teaching. They tend to rest on significant life experiences. If you reflect on the deepest meanings in your life and explore their origins, you will find that significant experiences, whether joyful or traumatic, played an important part in their formation. If we are interested in building in young people a sense of personal meaning in their lives, then we will need to plan curricula that make provision for significant experiences that allow students to grow as human beings. I am not thinking of courses in The Meaning of Life, but rather of teachers who would continually ask: Given this cognitively based curriculum, how can I use it to foster students' sense of personal meaning? What implications does it have for development of learners' self-concept and sense of identity? What significant experiences can I provide in the course of this program? How can I teach this subject in such a way as to enhance my clients' lives as social beings? This is what John Dewey recommended long ago: the teaching of all subjects so as to realize their social and personal potential (1902). To explore such questions is to find rich new possibilities even in conventional curricula. Mathematics, Welles Foshay argues, with its amazing intuitive and imaginative leaps, provides an opportunity for wonder and astonishment that can properly be described in terms of spiritual experience (1991). All of the sciences provide numerous possibilities for students to consider deeper meanings. Current thinking, for example, on the origin of the universe suggests that it consists of still-expanding debris from a primal explosion that took place some twenty billion years ago. Within the first second after the Big Bang, an immensely hot and dense fireball was formed, and all matter in today's universe is constituted from that first star. That includes all of the atoms that make up each of our bodies (Hawking, 1988). We are all star children! Learning for mastery is valuable for public meanings. For personal meanings, we need learning for mystery.

Humanistic educators focus not only on the personal, but also on the interpersonal. Paulo Freire opens one of his books with the words, "To be human is to engage in relationships with others and with the world" (1976, p. 3). The crucial importance of relationships to people's happiness, some would argue, makes it critical that schools assist their clients in developing the capacity to engage in enriching and nonexploitive relationships. As Mary Catherine Bateson writes, "In this society, we habitually underestimate the impulse in men, women, and even children to care for one another and their need to be taken care of" (1989, p. 140).

Like personal meanings, social meanings cannot be taught by cognitive means. Rather, they are developed as a result of what Martin Buber called "I-Thou" experiences (1970). Social meanings are crucial to people's happiness, particularly to that of young people. Aristotle recognized this more than two millennia ago, devoting more space to friendship than to any other topic (White, 1990). Adolescents, for whom friendship is primary, would likely agree with the words that Francis Bacon penned almost four centuries ago:

> It is a meere, and miserable *Solitude*, to want true *Frends*; without which the World is but a Wildernesse. . . . No Receipt openeth the Heart, but a true *Frend*; To whom you may impart, Griefes, Joyes, Feares, Hopes, Suspicions, Counsels, and whatsoever lieth upon the Heart, to oppresse it. (Bacon, 1985, p. 81)

The inclination and ability to make friends and to nurture friendship is, surely, more significant to an individual's future well-being than most of the cognitions we teach in school. Many people lack such abilities; in fact, "communication apprehensiveness" is more common in classrooms than all other handicaps combined (Hurt, Scott, & McCroskey, 1978). Making friends early in schooling, on the other hand, is a good predictor of positive attitudes toward school and gains in learning (Ladd, 1990). Shy children, by hesitating to become involved with others, may miss the experiences that are important in the development of social competence. Lacking this competence, they become "self-handicapped," withdraw still further, and are further excluded by peers. This pattern frequently becomes a lifelong condition, resulting in passivity and social isolation (Caspi, Elder, & Bem, 1988, p. 825).

The ability to function effectively and happily in relation to others, is, as it happens, also an important vocational attribute. Over 60 percent of job terminations are the result of a breakdown in personal relations. In surveys of business and industry, employers rate the importance of social skills and attitudes much higher than academic knowledge and skills (Frost, 1974).

Shyness is an insidious personal problem that is reaching such epidemic proportions as to be justifiably called a social disease. Trends in our society suggest it will get worse in the coming years as social forces increase our isolation, competition, and loneliness. Unless we begin to do something soon, many of our children and grandchildren will become prisoners of their own shyness. To prevent this, we must begin to understand what shyness is, so that we can provide a supportive environment where shy people can shed the security of their private prisons and regain their lost freedoms of speech, of action, and of human asssociations.

Philip Zimbardo (1977, p. 16)

This is not to suggest that the primary rationale for social meanings is utilitarian. Social meanings include such qualities as empathy and compassion. Many people would argue that we need to develop such characteristics in individuals if the next generation is to be able to contribute toward the solution of such worldwide problems as social injustice, the degradation of the environment, or imbalances in the distribution of food and wealth. Perhaps more importantly, we need these characteristics in order to lead, and to help others lead, lives that are joyful and fulfilling.

The humanistic orientation is criticized by academic rationalists as self-indulgent and undisciplined. Even friendly critics have pointed to the tendency of the humanists to become smug, anti-intellectual, and utopian (Farson, 1978). Critical theorists accuse humanistic educators of being naive and apolitical and of producing false consciousness. By aiming to make the classroom a place of joy and happiness, Henry Giroux claims, humanistic educators "in many cases unwittingly end up humanizing the very social and political forces they initially attempt to eliminate" (1981, p. 66).

Feminist pedagogy

The contributions of feminist thought to curriculum theory and practice are diverse, profound, and as yet neglected and underestimated by the wider educational community. It would be presumptuous to attempt a definitive description of this school of thought. Although feminist thinkers are united by a common interest, there is no single strand of feminist thinking. Liberal feminists differ in important respects from socialist feminists, who in turn are distinct from Marxist feminists. Furthermore, feminist thought is developing so rapidly that any description of the state of the art can be only temporary.

Feminist pedagogy is rooted in a feminist epistemology. Ever since Plato and Aristotle, it has been widely assumed, at least in Western cultures, that natural and human phenomena and events can be best understood by objective, analytical study. In such an epistemology, a knowing subject focuses upon an external object, uninfluenced by emotions, politics, or relationships. True knowing is viewed ideally as detached, dispassionate, and rational, an entirely abstract function of the mind. The mind, in turn, is sharply distinguished from the body or the emotions. Moral and ethical decisions are to be made in the same way as scientific judgments: by the application of general principles or rules to particular cases. These beliefs result in a view of the self "as autonomous, individualistic, self-interested, fundamentally isolated from other people and from nature"; of community "as a collection of similarly autonomous, isolated, self-interested individuals having no intrinsically fundamental relations with one another"; and of nature as "an autonomous system from which the self is fundamentally separated and which must be dominated to alleviate the threat of the self's being controlled by it" (Harding, 1986, p. 171). This long, rationalist tradition in Western philosophy reached its high point in the late nineteenth century, after which it came under increasing attack in philosophical circles. Rationalism, or positivism, however, continues to dominate the curricula of schools or universities, with their emphasis on scientific analysis and objective knowledge.

Feminist writers take issue with this dominant paradigm at many points. Madeleine Grumet (1988) has pointed out that Plato's elevation of ideas, which are eternal, over matter, which is transitory, inevitably devalues the physical, reproductive, domestic, and relational world. The abstract conceptual mode, Margaret Andersen (1986) argues, has more appeal to men than to women, and the prevailing abstract models used in the sciences and the social sciences are alien to women's experience. Curricula based on mainstream philosophical assumptions consequently "obliterate all that is personal in favor of whatever is general, all that is actual in deference to what is hypothetical, all that is moving in deference to all that is still" (Grumet, 1988, p. 173).

It is a concern of feminist writers on these issues that the limitations of traditional epistemology are disproportionately damaging to women. Belenky, Clinchy, Goldberger, and Tarule (1986), comment that "the care of children, or maternal practice, gives rise to maternal thought and particular modes of relating to the world" (p. 189). As Daphne Morris (personal communication, May 1991) puts it, "Women *are*, in many ways, their bodies, . . . reminded with regularity that control is neither possible, nor desirable. . . . And, at childbirth, the body and experience render one *humble*: in touch with, and in awe of nature." The modes of thought and action experienced by women, in contrast to those typical of men, are process- rather than goal-oriented, intuitive rather than rational, related rather than discrete, collaborative rather than solitary, cooperative rather than competitive, supportive rather than challenging, personal

Examine the recent national reports on education. You will find repeated demands for proficiency in the 3Rs, for clear, logical thinking and for higher standards of achievement in science, mathematics, history, literature, and the like. You will search in vain, however, for discussions of love of any kind. Why are there no calls for mastery of the 3Cs of care, concern, and connection? . . . Couldn't education develop intellectual virtues and also the feelings, emotions, values, and attitudes the future requires? . . . In defining the educated person as one possessing rational mind and construing this latter in intellectual terms, feelings, emotions and other so-called "non-cognitive" states and processes of the individual are ignored. . . . This idea also makes suspect the development of physical capacities, artistic talents, and effective moral action. The great irony of liberal education today is that it is neither tolerant nor generous. The liberally educated person . . . will have knowledge about others but will not have been taught to care about their welfare. That person will have some understanding of society but will not have been taught to feel its injustices or even be concerned about its fate.

Jane Roland Martin (1986, p. 7)

rather than impersonal, responsible rather than self-concerned (Belenky et al., 1986). "Objectivity is construed as truthfulness or fidelity to situated subjects, not as disinterest, separation or aloofness" (Noddings, 1992, p. 675). Failure to recognize a different reality, and failure to create harmony and synthesis among different realities, produces what Grumet calls a "crippling dichotomy of internal and external, dream and reality, body and thought, poetry and science, ambiguity and certainty" (Grumet, 1988, p. 155).

A feminine epistemology is matched by a feminine ethic. Traditional male ethics emphasize justice, based on an impartial application of rules. Carol Gilligan proposes an ethic of care, which views moral problems in contextual and relational terms: "While an ethic of justice proceeds from the premise of equality—that everyone should be treated the same—an ethic of care rests on the premise of nonviolence—that no one should be hurt" (1982, p. 174). Ethical theory is inadequate, Nel Noddings argues, unless the caring relation is viewed as ethically basic: "I am not naturally alone. I am naturally in a relation from which I derive nourishment and guidance. . . . My very individuality is defined in a set of relations. This is my basic reality" (1984, p. 51). While traditional, rule-driven ethics views moral acts as those that are performed out of duty, in conformity with principle, "an ethic of caring prefers acts done out of love and natural inclination" (1988, p. 219).

Recent feminist writers have suggested that the aim of replacing traditional male-dominated epistemology and ethics with feminine alternatives is insufficient, because it alters the priorities between the two positions while leaving the basic dichotomy intact:

> Many contemporary feminists . . . specifically advocate the adoption of a feminist epistemology, arguing that this contextual "feminine" understanding is superior to the abstract, rationalist "masculine" model. This position is anathema to a postmodern feminism for a number of reasons. Most significantly . . . their argument leaves the dichotomy that defines that inferiority intact. . . . If . . . we replace our dualistic, hierarchical epistemology with another one that is also based on the privileging of a particular set of concepts, in this case, the feminine, the result will be, once more, dualism and hierarchy. (Hekman, 1990, pp. 16, 161)

A number of feminist writers have advocated a view of humanity that embraces both what is traditionally feminine and what is traditionally masculine.

> Emotions are neither more basic than observation, reason, or action in building theory, nor are they secondary to them. Each of these human faculties reflects an aspect of human knowing inseparable from the other aspects. . . . The development of each of these faculties is a necessary condition for the development of all. (Jaggar, 1989, p. 165)

Ehrenreich and English call for "a synthesis which transcends both the rationalist and romanticist poles" (1979, p. 324). To avoid the continuation of stereotyping and exploitation of women, "an ethic of care should apply equally to men and women" (Erdman, 1990, p. 177).

What is the significance of these ideas and arguments for curriculum? First, they challenge the very basis on which curricula have traditionally been constructed, whereby "the experience, viewpoint, and goals of white, Western, elite males are taken as representing all of human experience" (Maher, 1987, p. 91), and "educational methods are determined by what works with males" (Martin, 1985, p. 22). Every academic discipline, together with its hidden curriculum, its form of inquiry, structures, and research base, becomes subject to new scrutiny. Jane Roland Martin uses examples of history curricula that exclude women from their narratives; psychology that generalizes about human beings on the basis of research with males; science curricula that employ a detached objectivity reflecting the cultural image of masculinity; philosophy that uses violent metaphors of dissecting or attacking an argument (1985). Phyllis Teitelbaum points to the hidden androcentrism of testing procedures that attempt to be value free, that separate knowledge into atomistic particles, that emphasize right-or-wrong dichotomies, that prefer what is quantitative to what is qualitative, and that reward individualism rather than collaboration (1989).

Next, they challenge schools to question the appropriateness—for both males and females—of curricula that emphasize only a narrowly construed model of intellectual development. Curricula need to change in the direction of "ecological and environmental integratedness of intellectual, affective, and physical domains" (McDade, 1987, p. 61). Instructional arrangements are needed in which students

> can resist the compulsion to become part of the dehumanizing forces of competition, elitism, and self-aggrandisement encouraged by patriarchal systems of education, and choose instead to reflect the different kinds of power and strength that exist—for instance, women's strong capacity to care for others—a quality often buried, diffused, misdirected or incorporated under patriarchy, but which redefined, contains the energy to in turn redefine human relationships.   (Thompson, 1983, p. 158)

Intrinsic to the thinking of these writers is the idea that education is a dyadic, not a transmissive, process. As such, curriculum must be responsive to actual students, constantly attentive to their needs (Tronto, 1989), and willing to change as they change:

> Curriculum is a moving form. . . . Considered apart from its appropriation and transformation by students, curriculum defined as design, a structure of knowledge, an intended learning outcome, or a learning environment, is merely a static form. . . . It is a curriculum that controls through mystification, encouraging placid passivity.   (Grumet, 1988, pp. 171–72)

> Feminist pedagogy begins with a vision of . . . the classroom as a liberatory environment in which we, teacher-student and student-teacher, act as subjects, not objects, . . . a classroom characterized as persons connected in a net of relationships with people who care about each other's learning as well as their own. . . . Feminist pedagogy strives to help student and teacher learn to think in new ways, especially ways that enhance the integrity and wholeness of the person and the person's connections with others. . . . Empowering pedagogy does not dissolve the authority or the power of the instructor. It does move from power as domination to power as creative energy.
>
> Carolyn Shrewsbury (1987, pp. 6–7)

The emphasis on the overriding importance of relationships is one that most teachers, it would be hoped, could support. Noddings writes:

> I do not need to establish a deep, lasting, time-consuming personal relationship with every student. What I must do is to be totally and nonselectively present to the student—to each student—as he addresses me. The time interval may be brief but the encounter is total. (Noddings, 1984, p. 180)

None of this is to suggest that interest in such qualities as caring is a monopoly either of feminists or of women, for to do so would be to stereotype both women and men.

What feminist pedagogy offers is not simply a curriculum that meets more justly the needs of women, but a curriculum that reflects more fully the nature of humanity. Until the curriculum gives place to the emotions, to intuition, to physical being, and to caring, it will remain inadequate for men as well as for women. A feminist ethic proposes instructional structures that are less hierarchical, less didactic, and less abstract. To adopt this project is to move towards an education that mitigates the separation between mind and body, theory and experience, the public and the private, the individual and the relational. Such an education holds promise for healing and liberation for both men and women.

▪ The Significance of Orientation ▪

The four orientations outlined above are not mutually exclusive. All see education as a potentially powerful means to desired ends. All are motivated by the desire for the well-being of the student and of society, but they have different visions of that well-being and of how it is to be achieved. Most educators do not fall neatly into one of the sharply defined categories. People are more various than that, more unexpected, inconsistent, idiosyncratic, and interesting. Most teachers share some of the concepts of each orientation, as well as of value systems other than the four described. Philip Jackson puts it this way:

> Few, if any people, living or dead, turn out to be occupants of these abstract positions, and for good reason, which is that the positions as usually presented are insufficiently contextualized and situated. In a word, they are too academic.   (Jackson, 1992, p. 18)

Practicing educators tend to conform to Joseph Schwab's injunction to be eclectic rather than doctrinaire (1969). Or, as a friend puts it, "Tao is realized . . . in the unity of these orientations. A year can be divided into four seasons and the four seasons make up a year" (Yang Chang, personal communication, September 1992).

It is the daily experience of the professional educator to become so enmeshed in the activities of teaching or administration as to lose sight of long-term goals. In this context, it is helpful now and again to reflect on basic goals and values, to examine our practice for its alignment with those ultimate intents, and, as the late James B. Macdonald urged, to clarify and profess our "grounding values of goodness" (1977, p. 21).

The examples of curriculum orientations described above do not exhaust the possible perspectives on curriculum. They are intended to suggest that as curriculum planners we should begin much further back than by asking such questions as: How can we incorporate whole language principles into the primary classroom? or, What new content is needed in the physics curriculum? or, Which novels will we use this year in the literature program? To begin with such questions is to run the risk of reducing curriculum planning to a technical and organizational exercise. Although it uses some technical procedures, curriculum planning is essentially not technical but philosophical. It is primarily concerned with values and priorities. However, even if we do begin the curriculum process with a particular discipline or content area, questions of orientation can still provide valuable insight: Given this novel, this century, this regional study, this scientific experiment, this foreign language—what are the crucial intellectual learnings to be derived? What political insights does the curriculum make possible? How can I structure the learning situation so as to enhance students' relational lives? What are the possibilities within this curriculum for memorable experiences and for growth of students as persons? Deliberation on such questions might be considered the hallmark of the reflective educator.

▪ Curriculum and the Future ▪

There is an additional complexity that we need now to consider. Like any other decision-making activity, curriculum development does not plan for the present or for the past, but for the future. Curriculum must certainly address the problems students are facing at the present moment, but the world in which our students will live, and of which they will try to make sense, is not the world of today. Nor is it the world of yesterday, upon which much curriculum focuses. Rather, it is a world which does not presently exist, but one which we must attempt to forecast, if our curricula are to be appropriate for students who are approaching this future at a rate of sixty minutes per hour. Educational systems can purchase immunity from change only at the price of irrelevance. This means that curriculum planners must be futurists.

> Americans look about ten minutes ahead while Japanese look ahead ten years.
> Akiro Morito, Chair of Sony (Parker, 1990, p. H5)

"To prophesy is very difficult," says the Chinese proverb, "especially with respect to the future." A recent review of the educational implications of occupational forecasting echoes this sentiment: "In the end, there are severe limitations to the usefulness of occupational forecasting for guiding educational reform" (Bailey, 1991, p. 11). As a field of inquiry, there are few areas as disreputable as futurism. It occupies the middle ground somewhere between astrology and *Trivial Pursuit*. Yet, hidden among the irresponsible sensationalism of much futuristic speculation are the sober forecasts of those futurists who make their living on the basis of a good track record of forecasting for clients in the public and private sectors. Such specialists have found certain guideposts to future developments. One is to visit research laboratories and to examine new patent applications to determine what products are currently in the early stages of development. Another is to monitor events in communities that tend to pioneer social and technological change.

Social futures

In North America many social changes are noticed first on the West Coast. Worldwide, it seems that Sweden is typically the first with social developments that ultimately spread throughout the Western world. Sweden, for example, has succeeded in achieving full participation of men and women in its economy, with an unemployment rate through the 1970s and 1980s of less than 2 percent. This is the result of decades of development that has produced an integrated system of governmental and social services, a high level of cooperation between the public and private sectors, and a commitment to principles of social equity. Despite periodic reports in the North American media that the Swedish social experiment is on the verge of collapse, an underlying consensus persists in Sweden that every adult has the right and the obligation to participate in the responsibilities and benefits of society. Barriers to employment of women have been reduced by antidiscrimination and pay equity legislation, by the provision of nine months of paid maternity or paternity leave, and by government-sponsored daycare from the age of eight months. (Swedish daycare centers are open from 7:00 A.M. to 7:00 P.M. and include three meals a day; parents pay about one-quarter of the cost, the government three-quarters [Hechinger & Hechinger, 1990].) Instead of funneling huge amounts of resources into supporting the unemployed, government puts the equivalent funds into retraining workers and assisting industry with the development of new products and processes (Milner, 1989). A more recent development in Sweden is successful advocacy of animal rights, resulting in legislation governing the housing, treatment, and killing of farm animals. We can anticipate similar movements in other developed countries over the next one or two decades.

Technical futures

Just as the invention and development of automobiles, television, computers, and nuclear fission has altered (and often come to dominate) our lives in the twentieth century, new technologies will further alter our existence in the twenty-first century. New modes of transportation and communication, new methods of power generation such as nuclear fusion, and new means of food production are likely to be among these developments. By way of illustration, let us look at one set of technologies: the technologies of life extension.

Specialists in longevity are now saying that the normal life expectancy should be thought of not as "threescore years and ten" but as 100 or 120 years. That is, if the

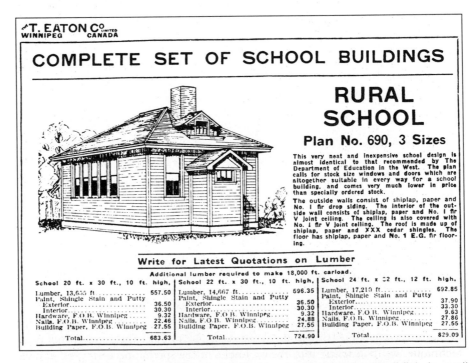

At one time it was possible to purchase a complete school building by mail order. This illustration is from the 1917–18 Eaton's of Canada catalog.

In 1967 I visited a Chicago vocational high school. As we entered the school, we passed a row of Platten presses—the ones that look like giant waffle makers. I asked why the students were being trained on such old-fashioned machines. "Oh," was the response, "there are plenty of small shops still using them." As we left the school, passing the same presses, I asked where they got spare parts for these ancient pieces of technology. "It's easy, there are plenty of shops closing down. We buy them for a song for spare parts."

Leroy Daniels (1991, p. 13)

individual consistently consumes the ideal balance of nutrients, including all desirable vitamins and minerals, in the correct quantities, avoids dangerous practices such as smoking or driving without a seatbelt, and takes the necessary daily amount of vigorous exercise, then a life expectancy of over 100 years is not unrealistic (M. Pratt, 1987).

Such an expectation is also facilitated by developments in conventional medicine such as improved surgery, drugs, immunizations, transplants, and artificial body parts. Very recently, two substances, Deprynyl and Human Growth Hormone, have shown remarkable effects in delaying aging and restoring or maintaining physical youthfulness and vigor (Rudman et al., 1990). With the exception of a few body parts such as the spinal column, the brain, and the intestines, almost all limbs and organs can now either be transplanted or constructed artificially. The final barrier, successful transplantation of a human brain, or development of true artificial intelligence, may be delayed for decades, but probably not forever.

All of these innovations, however, are unlikely to even double present lifespan, simply because our lifespan is genetically determined. Just as rabbits and daffodils have a certain expectation of life, so does the human species, and this is determined by the "time-clock" that exists in the DNA in every cell in our bodies. Geneticists are already on the trail of the chromosomes that control cellular senescence (Sugawara, Oshimura, Koi, Annab, & Barrett, 1990).

At this point the truly intriguing questions arise. Suppose we intervene in the DNA and change that time-clock by what is known as germ line intervention? It has been possible for many years to transfer genetic material from one species to another. For example, scientists have taken the genetic material known as luciferase that enables a firefly to illuminate itself and transplanted it into the cells or viruses of interest, which then become much easier to observe under a microscope (Rodriguez et al., 1988).

What appears to be on the scientific horizon is something like this: We take a human cell, say a newly fertilized ovum. Using a microlaser, we burn out the molecules of the DNA that control the aging process. Using a micro-injection technique, we then insert into the pronuclei of the sperm and ovum the equivalent genetic material from some longer-lived species, such as a redwood fir. The cell is then implanted in a foster-mother (or, by that era, perhaps, a test tube), and nine months later a baby is born, human in all respects but with the life expectancy of a redwood fir tree ("Biotechnology survey," 1988).

The implications of developments of this kind for curriculum lie more in the area of ethics and values than in the area of science. As a society we have some difficulty already with the more modest medical developments of the last twenty years. Consider the number of cases in which lifesaving medical technology, such as the respirator, the venous drip, or chemotherapy, has frequently come to be used not so much to restore people to health as to prolong their dying. There is considerable moral confusion surrounding such issues, not only among the general public, but also among health and legal professionals. How, then, are we going to handle questions such as a life expectancy of 100 or 800 years? How are we going to decide who is to be offered such a lifespan for their children? How will we respond to other parallel developments such as humans with entirely artificial bodies? Or human bodies with artificial brains? Or "humans" whose brains and bodies are both artificial?

To grapple effectively with the moral, social, legal, economic, and political consequences of such technical developments will require a public that has a somewhat more sophisticated moral outlook than is currently provided by high school civics courses and Sunday morning television programs. Schools have always claimed implicitly or explicitly to be committed to the development of right conduct in the young, but one looks in vain in official curriculum guidelines for serious attention to the development of moral judgment. How is it that the 2500-year-old discipline of ethics, or more broadly, that of philosophy, has been excluded from school curricula, at least in North America, for so long? In thirty years' time, those who are now our students will be the politicians and legislators, the judges and lawyers, the doctors and scientists, the clergy and journalists, and the general public who will be faced with ethical decisions of enormous complexity.

Unlike newspaper prognosticators, who are widely read and whose predictions are almost always wrong, genuine prophets are often unpopular people. According to Aeschylus, Apollo gave Cassandra the gift of foretelling the future, but when she would not return his love, he turned the gift into a curse by causing her always to be disbelieved. Colonel Billy Mitchell, who commanded over fifteen hundred aircraft at the end of World War I, must have felt like Cassandra. He forecast in 1925 that Pearl Harbor would be attacked by air by the Japanese. He described the attack and its consequences in detail. He was court-martialed, resigned from the army in 1926, and died ten years later. In 1946 Congress presented a special medal in his honor to his son (Lukasiewicz, 1992). His experience is reminiscent of that of Winston Churchill, who warned Britain in vain throughout the 1930s of the rising threat from Nazi Germany. Speaking in 1935, he said:

> Want of foresight, unwillingness to act when action would be simple and effective, lack of clear thinking, confusion of counsel until the emergency comes, until self-preservation strikes its jarring gong—these are the features which constitute the endless repetition of history. (Churchill, 1974, p. 5592)

But despite the political risks, there is no moral alternative to making our best estimate of what the future has in store. As Kenneth Boulding once said (where or when I cannot now discover), "The future is bound to surprise us, but we don't have to be dumbfounded." It is issues such as these that make the work of curriculum planning an intriguing challenge and responsibility.

CURRICULUM DESIGN

Curriculum design is not so much a unique activity as an extension of normal everyday behavior. All human beings are designers. Victor Papanek is a designer and sometime-dean of the School of Design at the California Institute of Arts. He is celebrated for his inventions on behalf of the developing world through such organizations as UNESCO and the World Health Organization. It is Papanek's view (personal communication, December 1992) that design, when conducted in the service of others, is a spiritual activity:

> All that we do, almost all the time, is design, for design is basic to all human activity. The planning and patterning of any act towards a desired, foreseeable end constitutes the design process. . . . Design is the conscious effort to impose meaningful order.   (Papanek, 1971, p. 3)

From the point in history, about two million years ago, when *homo sapiens* first began to fashion stone tools, human beings have survived and prospered (and blundered) by their ability to design their environment rather than merely adapt to it. We plan almost constantly, by giving forethought to our actions, predicting consequences, weighing alternatives. This is part of what it is to be a human being. It is also an integral part of being a professional. Herbert Simon, the polymath who won the 1978 Nobel Prize for economics, writes as follows:

> Everyone designs who devises courses of action aimed at changing existing situations into preferred ones. The intellectual activity that produces material artifacts is no different fundamentally from the one that prescribes remedies for a sick patient or the one that devises a new sales plan for a company or a social welfare policy for a state. Design, so construed, is the core of all professional training; it is the principal mark that distinguishes the professions from the sciences. Schools of engineering, as well as schools of architecture, business, education, law, and medicine, are all centrally concerned with the process of design. . . . The professional schools will reassume their professional responsibilities just to the degree that they can discover a science of design, a body of intellectually tough, analytic, partly formalizable, partly empirical, teachable doctrine about the design process. . . . The natural sciences are concerned with how things are. . . . Design, on the other hand, is concerned with how things ought to be. . . .   (Simon, 1969, pp. 56–58)

There are approximately one billion elementary and secondary school students around the world, taught by some fifty million teachers. These fifty million people constitute the only profession dedicated to the human development of all the members of an entire generation. All of these teachers are curriculum planners. Regardless of the detail prescribed in official curriculum documents,

> teachers do not serve merely as instructional technicians, rigidly implementing a highly detailed curriculum exactly as it has been given to them. Instead, they become active participants in the formulation of curriculum by further defining and detailing it in light of specific contextual variables with which they are most intimately familiar. (Comfort, 1990, p. 397)

Teachers plan what is to occur in the next few moments, the next day, or the next year. Whether they view their immediate purpose as to enhance human happiness, liberation, meaning, or other qualities of life, how successful they are depends to a great extent on the quality of their planning.

> Traditionally, teacher planning has been regarded as static. . . . However, planning is a much more fluid process. Instruction begins with a plan of teachers' intentions; however, as soon as a lesson begins, teachers modify the plan to accommodate students who, in the process of interpreting instructional information, create their own meanings. Effective teachers respond to students' restructured understandings by modifying their plans. . . . Planning . . . is not a script to follow but a blueprint from which teachers make adjustments in response to students' emerging understandings.
>
> Dole, Duffy, Roehler, & Pearson (1991, pp. 252–53)

There is much we still do not know about human learning. But in the past twenty years we have discovered a great deal about the conditions that facilitate learning. Despite its long pedigree, the field of curriculum had, by about 1970, very little to offer to practicing educators that was worth their listening time. Indeed, the mood of researchers at that period was one of defeat and despair, reflected by the slogan "schools make no difference." This belief was abetted by sociological research concluding that "schools bring little influence to bear on a child's achievement that is independent of his background and general social context" (Coleman et al., 1966, p. 325). In the past twenty years, this picture has changed remarkably. We now have at our behest an array of curriculum strategies, each of them more powerful than a student's social class or family background. Ineffective schools still make no difference, but we now know some of the factors that do make a difference, and it is the task of the curriculum planner to design conditions of learning that will incorporate these factors.

Curriculum planning might be defined as "the art and science of planning the conditions of learning." These conditions include such considerations as identification of the learning needs to be met; selection of the modes of evaluation to be used; determination of entry characteristics of learners; selection of instruction content and methods; provision for individual differences; and logistical issues such as choice of materials, equipment, facilities, personnel, time, and cost.

Most curricula, whether produced by nations, states, districts, or schools, resemble houses that look attractive from the outside. But when you go inside, you find there is no wiring or plumbing. The floors are not level; the angles are not true. Doors won't close, and windows won't open. The chimney doesn't draw, and water leaks into the basement. The designers had an idea of how a house should look, but that was about all. An exaggeration? Frances Klein, in a study of American curricula, found that 41 percent of state curricula contained no details on evaluation, 23 percent said nothing about teaching methods, 76 percent ignored individual differences, and 41 percent did not deal with materials (1980). Ten years later, in a study of Canadian curricula, I found a similar situation. Thirty-five percent of provincial curricula contained no rationale, 41 percent contained nothing on evaluation, 89 percent made no suggestions for slow learners, 86 percent said nothing about instructional equipment, 99 percent omitted any reference to instructional software (Pratt, 1989).

In the short term, good design costs very little more than bad design. In the long run, it costs much less. This is not a book about how to design half-finished curricula. To return to our analogy, it is about how to design houses fit to live in—where the wiring and plumbing are sound and safe; where all the angles are true; where the walls and doors are weatherproofed; where the woodsmoke draws sweetly up the chimney—a house that is comfortable and sound, and serves the needs of those who live in it.

THE HIDDEN CURRICULUM

This book is about the *overt curriculum:* the blueprint for teaching and learning that is publicly planned and adopted. The term *hidden curriculum* refers to conscious or unconscious intentions reflected in the structure of schools and classrooms and the actions of those who inhabit them. If official curricula call for commitment to democracy, but the governance of a school is autocratic, there is a disjunction between the overt and the hidden curriculum. A classroom full of desks in rows gives the lie to a curriculum proclaiming decision making by consensus. A teacher's arbitrary or unreasonable behavior toward students will contradict an official curriculum aim of developing in students a capacity for reasoned problem solving.

What is taught and learned in schools has, over the last century, been the subject of considerable study. A less studied but intriguing field is what is *not* offered in school curricula; this is sometimes called the *null curriculum* (Flinders, Noddings, & Thornton, 1986). The null curriculum of elementary and secondary schools typically includes such established disciplines as philosophy, psychology,

Russian, and Japanese. It usually includes such crucial intellectual areas as how to study, how to learn, and how to think, and practical topics such as financial management, parenting, and making friends. Yoga, Tai Chi, meditation, and relaxation are rarely found in official curriculum documents.

Changing the official curriculum may not be easy, but it is simple compared with the task of changing the hidden curriculum. Those who work in schools need at all times to reflect on these questions: What are my most basic commitments? How are they reflected in the way I work? How can I better communicate them through the structures I establish? The written curriculum is only one component in the socially and politically complicated world of the school. It can, however, be a powerful component, especially in the hands of educators whose curricula reflect their lived beliefs. To explore its potential is the purpose of this book.

THE ART OF CURRICULUM DESIGN

Most great artists are also great designers. Scholars have revealed how Renaissance masters such as Leonardo da Vinci used geometrical principles to design paintings that achieved balance and harmony (Bouleau, 1963; Kemp, 1990). Even in abstract painting or in jazz improvization, a design is apparent that typically rests on years of dedicated study and practice. In the creative field of architecture, mathematics and physics are essential components to the realization of an aesthetic vision in a form that will be stable and enduring. In the design of fabrics, intricate patterns and embellishments are achieved by conformity with the design ideas of the makers. Design, in fact, could be said to be a crucial component in all art forms, whether we consider ballet, poetry, pottery, landscape gardening, sculpture, theater, interior decorating, flower arranging, dressmaking, or music.

It is not that artists simply impose a design on reluctant material. They seek equally to identify and reveal designs or structures that are inherent in nature itself. The "golden proportion," a rectangle of dimensions 1:1.6 was beloved by Classical Greek artists and architects. This proportion, related to the Fibonacci series (1, 2, 3, 5, 8, 13 . . .), is found in the structures of plants, shells, ocean waves, human anatomy, musical intervals, and in fact throughout the world of nature and art (Vajda, 1989).

In seeking general principles for education, we could do worse than look to the arts. When we do so, we find meticulous design united with a high degree of dedication and discipline. The fluency and elegance of many a work of art can conceal the hundreds of hours of blood, sweat, and tears consumed by its planning and execution.

Hemingway rewrote some of his work more than forty times. Dylan Thomas would often redraft a poem a hundred times. The brilliant lyricist, Alan Jay Lerner, worked on the title song of the musical, *On a Clear Day You Can See Forever*, three hours a day, seven days a week, for eight months, in the process writing and discarding ninety-one complete lyrics (Lerner, 1978). As Konstantin

Stanislavski, the guru of twentieth-century theater, said, "There are no accidents in art—only the fruits of long labor" (Moore, 1976, p. 14).

Teachers are sometimes concerned that a commitment to design may inhibit innovation and creativity in the classroom. But we are unlikely in curriculum ever to approach the intense degree of design found, for example, in a musical composition. A composer specifies every note, every change of tempo, and every accent. Yet musicians do not feel inhibited by playing to such detailed instructions. Rather, the music they follow is the vehicle for the expression of their own musicianship. At the same time, there is a risk in overplanning. We need to provide enough flexibility in our curriculum plans to allow for deviation from and amendment to the plan by teachers. Teachers, classes, and individual students need opportunity and provision for the free play of their intuition and imagination to allow for the serendipitous, the interests of the moment, the unexpected question, the unanticipated interruption, the opportunity for exploration, discovery, and play. The curriculum should be a springboard, not a straightjacket. Teaching is an art, and so is curriculum planning. Together, they can reinforce one another to the extent that they reflect the dedicated expression of an inner vision.

"And then, of course, there's the possibility of being just the slightest bit too organized."

THE PLANNER AS PROFESSIONAL

Planning is a key role of the professional. Art and professionality meet in what Donald Schön calls "practical competence and professional artistry" (1983, p. vii). This competence and this artistry are both reflected and enhanced by engagement in curriculum planning. More than fifty years ago, the authors of a high school curriculum commented that "the chief value of curriculum revision does not lie in the product made, but in the process of the making. In the construction of the courses of study the outstanding benefit has been the rekindling of the intellectual life of all those who have participated in the enterprise" (quoted in Winters, 1990, p. 5).

The costs of curriculum development are considerable. A recent analysis of curriculum development in (formerly West) Germany revealed that there were more than 1,500 separate curricula for general education, and that the total time involved in development averaged 15,000 person-hours per curriculum (Haft & Hopmann, 1989). In the United States each of the fifty states typically develops all of its own curricula. While the total annual cost of curriculum development in the United States might not buy a single Stealth bomber, it is substantial enough that we are under an obligation to develop curricula as professionally as possible. These costs do not include the most pervasive and significant kind of curriculum planning: the daily decisions made by every teacher as he or she converts general state or district guidelines into instructional plans. Yet the art and science of curriculum planning is rarely taught to beginning teachers, and still more rarely taught well.

As a recent text on instructional design says, "All teachers design instruction . . . and all instructional designers teach" (West, Farmer, & Wolff, 1991, p. 1). Those who design and teach well do so with maximum economy. All people who are skilled in a craft are a pleasure to watch, whether they are carpenters or philosophers, bricklayers or violinists, because they have learned economy. They achieve excellence with a minimum of effort, a minimum of waste. Such economy is the essence of elegance, of style, of mastery. The same is true of curriculum planning. Doing it well means not only doing it better, but also doing so more fluently and economically.

The benefits are to be found in a greater likelihood of success if our instructional actions are planned rather than improvised. A clearly thought out plan allows better communication with students, parents, other teachers, and the public. And perhaps most important is growth in professional autonomy. A number of recent curriculum scholars have written of the "deskilling" that is inflicted on teachers when their work is dictated by rigid curricula, purchased materials, and standardized tests (Apple & Jungck, 1990; Giroux, 1988; Pinar, 1989). So long as we feel able only to follow the plan of some outside authority, we lack professional autonomy and degenerate into what Stanley Aronowitz and Henry Giroux call "high-level clerks implementing the orders of others within the school bureaucracy" (1985, p. 36). The purpose of this text is to subvert this insidious process of deskilling by *reskilling* teachers. We need to return much of curriculum power to the place it belongs—to the individual teacher working directly with students. By providing working teachers with the knowledge necessary to conduct every stage of curriculum planning, one can hope, in at least a small way, to rescue them from the forces of bureaucratization, alienation, and disempowerment. To the degree that we can take curriculum guidelines, general or specific, and adapt them to reflect our educational vision and the needs of our students, to that extent we become autonomous and authentic professionals.

■ Learning as a Moral Achievement ■

In planning curriculum, we are engaged in a task of ultimate significance. Learning is often thought of as an intellectual achievement. But we could think of learning in a different way, as a moral achievement. It is a moral achievement when people develop the capacity to choose new ways of thinking, feeling, and acting. It is a moral achievement whenever people choose to search for their own truth rather than to accept the assumptions of others. It is a moral achievement when people choose altruism rather than self-interest, reconciliation rather than conflict, excellence rather than mediocrity, effort rather than complacency, justice rather than oppression. Such moral achievements give people their essential nobility. This nobility, so evident in human beings as they struggle to make meaning of their existence, as they anchor themselves in human networks, exists in everyone, even in those most damaged, most angry, most discouraged, most convinced that they are ignoble. It is the principal task of all educators to plan learning experiences that will support and nourish this nobility, in all of their students and in themselves.

■ SELF – ASSESSMENT

1. Why is the major criterion for curriculum selection *relative value* rather than *absolute value?*

2. In addition to driver, drug, and safety education, what other curricula could be considered "survival curricula" in the sense of helping people avoid premature death?

3. What are some reasons why the present happiness of learners cannot be the *only* criterion for selecting curriculum content?

4. You want to introduce a ten-hour unit on prenatal nutrition into your high school health curriculum. What arguments could you use to support this innovation?

5. Some "academic rationalists" argue that the principal criterion for selecting curriculum should be centrality to intellectual traditions. On what other grounds might curriculum also be selected?

6. A colleague asks your advice about revising her grade seven social studies curriculum to concentrate on Africa rather than Canada. What are some suggestions you might give?

7. What are some of the curriculum implications of the fact that most people in our society watch more than twenty hours of television a week?

8. Why do curriculum planners need to be forecasters?

9. A teacher says, "I don't believe in curriculum planning because education is an art, not a science." While rational argument rarely affects such beliefs, what rebuttals could you make?

10. A principal says, "My teachers don't need to know how to plan curriculum, because the school board does that for them." How might you respond?

For feedback, see Appendix F.
If you felt that you were able to make good responses to eight or more of these questions, you have a good grasp of the basics of curriculum outlined in this chapter. If not, spend some more time thinking, reading, and talking about basic curriculum issues.

CHAPTER 2

Identifying Learner Needs

Good schools are places where students are seen as people worthy of respect.

Sara Lightfoot (1983, p. 350)

Summary

There is general, though not universal, agreement among educators that curricula should be based on learner needs. We may define a need as a discrepancy between a present and a preferred state. Needs assessment is a set of procedures for gathering information about human needs. These processes include consultation, collection of social indicators, and task analysis. Specialists, clients, and gatekeepers should be consulted. Telephone interviews are an effective means for reaching respondents. Other steps to be taken before beginning the design of new curricula include reviewing existing curricula and research, conducting a feasibility analysis, and obtaining the necessary human and material resources for curriculum planning.

NEEDS AND NEEDS ASSESSMENT

For teachers, and for curriculum planners, there is no substitute for rigorous and creative thinking. The previous chapter outlined some of the important questions and issues curriculum designers need to consider. Solitary reflection, however, important as it is, has its limitations. When we plan curriculum, we are planning not only for ourselves, but also for other people. We are making proposals for the ways in which human and material resources, such as energy, time, and money, are to be spent. The risk in this activity is of making unwarranted assumptions about how other people think and feel. How can people who are well fed understand people who are hungry? One answer is that we can ask them. A corollary is that we listen to their answers with respect. Not to do so is to pretend omniscience. To take the position that "We know better than you what your needs are—without even asking you," which is the position tacitly taken by most curriculum developers, is the very essence of paternalism.

Pope John XXIII spoke of paternalism as "a caricature of paternity." Nadine Gordimer, the South African writer who received the 1991 Nobel Prize for literature, speaks of "the shameful impotence of paternalism" (1976, introduction, np). With its undertones of condescension and dismissal, paternalism is not only repugnant in principle, it also does not work well in practice. This is illustrated by some development projects in the Third World that fail to take into account the needs and values of the people they are intended to serve. A development aid worker comments that many maternity buildings constructed by Western aid programs in Africa ignored traditional African birthing practices and consequently never saw a birth: "When travelling around the villages, we quite often spend the night in a rural maternity building built by some well-meaning foreign government; nobody bothered to consult the villagers, who use the building for storing hay and for sleeping visitors" (Lacville, 1990, p. 24). Tom Peters, the management scientist, has often written of the importance to corporations of staying "close to the customer." The successful corporation, he says, becomes "obsessed with listening":

> Listen to customers—end users, reps, distributors, franchisees, retailers, suppliers. Listen frequently—listen systematically—and unsystematically. Listen for facts—and for perceptions. Listen "naively." Use as many listening techniques as we can conjure up.   (Peters, 1988, p. 144)

The philosopher Robin Barrow (1988) suggests that there are three alternative ways of deciding what constitutes an educationally worthwhile curriculum— philosophical inquiry, democratic consensus, and empirical assessment of needs. But these three approaches are not mutually exclusive. The previous chapter argued for the importance of curriculum planners reflecting on and clarifying their philosophical orientation. This is a necessary, but not a sufficient, basis for building a curriculum. It is a critical feature of genuine democracy that those affected by decisions have both the right and the opportunity to be heard before such decisions are made. A clearly thought-out and articulated philosophical orientation on the part of the planners is a good start. But this orientation needs to be tested against and informed by the real and felt needs of other participants, and by hard evidence from the outside world. These are the functions of needs assessment.

▪ The Concept of Need ▪

At a tacit level, there seems to be general agreement even among widely differing curriculum philosophies, that the justification for a curriculum resides in a human need. In fact, this is a statement of the obvious because of the overlap between the meanings of the terms *justification* and *need*. Those who promote the primary significance of cultural transmission share with those who advocate personal development the belief that the curricula they propose are needed by the learners.

The term *need*, however, requires definition. It is clearly not the same as a desire, or a want, or a demand. McKillip defines a want as "something people are willing to pay for" and a demand as "something people are willing to march for" (1987, p. 16). You may *want* a cigarette, but we might argue whether you actually *need* it. Similarly, you may need vitamin D without consciously wanting it. Wants, according to Scriven (1983), are the object of market research, not needs assessment. Scriven and Roth (1978) define need as anything without which the individual's state would be significantly less than satisfactory. This definition leaves unresolved the question of how we decide, or who decides, what is a satisfactory state. Clearly, however, the term need is intended to imply some requirement based on firmer evidence or argument than individual whim or impulse. For our purposes, we will use the term *need* to mean "a discrepancy between a present and a preferred state." In terms of curriculum, the gap between where the learner is now and where we (or the learner, or some other person) would wish the learner to be constitutes the need. Use of the word "preferred" indicates that we are defining need in terms of values.

Although we are dealing in this chapter with empirical processes for gathering information about learner needs, it would be a serious error to assume that we could reduce the issue of needs to an empirical question. This false assumption has engendered much criticism by philosophers towards the way in which the concept of needs has been used in curriculum planning (Komisar, 1961). Boyd Bode addressed this issue half a century ago. The claim that needs could somehow be revealed by a process of empirical research, he described as "academic bootlegging" (1938, p. 67). What was needed, he suggested, was a dialectical or educational process that would enable people to discover or clarify their own needs.

Suarez (1991) defines *needs assessment* as "an information-gathering and analysis process which results in the identification of the needs of individuals, groups, institutions, communities, or societies" (1991, p. 433). Needs assessment can be viewed as a kind of evaluation study, except that unlike most program evaluations that look back to the question, What has the program achieved?, needs assessment looks forward and asks, What goals should a program pursue? (Stufflebeam, McCormick, Brinkerhoff, & Nelson, 1985).

The formal practice of needs assessment was first introduced in the United States in the early 1960s by government departments seeking to ensure that proposals for funding from communities were based on verified local needs. Needs assessments are often conducted on a large scale by corporations (where they are typically called market assessments), states, or large school districts. This has led to the common belief that needs assessments can be conducted only by wealthy agencies. This belief is one of many that helps to disempower teachers. In this chapter we are concerned with small-scale needs assessments that can and should be conducted prior to curriculum revision by schools or individual teachers.

Considering that needs assessment was first invented in the 1960s, it has remained less sophisticated than one might have hoped. As Hall points out, it is sometimes "considered a stepchild of educational research methodology" (1982, p. 3). Major weaknesses are lack of definition of the term *need*; a misplaced belief that needs assessment is an empirical, rather than a philosophical, exercise; failure to transcend existing curricular assumptions, existing curricula, and accompanying achievement data; and over-reliance on public opinion and on questionnaires for its assessment. A further weakness is the belief that needs assessment must necessarily be expensive and conducted on a large scale. In fact, modest but viable needs assessments can and should be conducted periodically by classroom teachers without heavy requirements for outside resources.

▪ First Steps in Needs Assessment ▪

Careful planning is as necessary for a needs assessment as for other aspects of curriculum development. Stufflebeam, McCormick, Brinkerhoff, and Nelson (1985), in a detailed guide to educational needs assessment, outline basic questions that should be addressed early in the process. Some of these are: What is the purpose of the needs assessment? How is the concept of need understood? What is the value base of the needs assessment? What questions will it address? Who is asking that the needs assessment be conducted? Who is the audience for the needs assessment? Who is sponsoring the needs assessment? Who else's sanction and support is required? Who will conduct the study? What staff, budget, training, and other resources will they need? How will fairness and objectivity be maintained? How will the needs assessors avoid being coopted by the respondents or sponsors? How will the public and the sponsors be kept informed? What information will be collected? How will samples be drawn? How will the information be collected and analyzed? Who will write and edit the final report? To whom will it be presented?

In the following discussion, we shall focus primarily on sources of information and the means that may be used to access them in a needs assessment. There are four main information sources that are of greatest interest. There are opinion surveys, task analyses, social indicators, and test and research data.

■ Opinion Surveys ■

The basic reasons for conducting a needs assessment prior to beginning to plan a curriculum are informational, ethical, and political. To meet these ends, three main groups of respondents may be consulted—specialists, clients, and gatekeepers.

Specialists

Our need for information requires that we ask the opinion of specialists. (The word specialist is preferred here to the term expert, the expert having become the Tyrannosaurus Rex of the late twentieth century.) For example, if we are about to plan a new curriculum in mathematics, we would want to speak with some competent mathematicians, particularly those interested in the underlying principles and philosophy of mathematics. This group would no doubt include university professors, but it would also be desirable to include mathematicians working in government, business, and industry. It is important that curriculum planners do not allow themselves to be overawed by the expertise of subject specialists. Nevertheless, specialists are important, because many of the other correspondents consulted in needs

The most important human endeavor is the striving for morality in our actions. Our inner balance and even our very existence depend on it. Only morality in our actions can give beauty and dignity to life. To make this a living force and bring it to clear consciousness is perhaps the foremost task of education.

Albert Einstein (Germany/Switzerland/USA), Nobel Prize for Physics, 1921.

(Dukas & Hoffmann, 1979, p. 95)

assessment will tend to be conservative in their orientation, their views of the subject often biased by their own school experience, perhaps decades previously. Specialists in the discipline may also be conservative, but of all groups they are the most likely to have a sense of the future development of the field, and they should be asked their opinion of such developments. Unfortunately, curriculum committees in chemistry will typically include teachers of chemistry but no professional chemists; a curriculum committee in music will contain music teachers but no full-time musicians. An example of the consequences of ignoring professionals is shown in a study by Larry O'Farrell. He consulted 145 practicing playwrights about important aspects of the teaching of their craft. They were in agreement that the essence of playwriting lay in producing an entire play and rewriting many times; the only legitimate evaluation was performance before an audience. In contrast, drama curricula, written by teachers of drama, recommended that students write small pieces of a play and submit them for evaluation based on reading by the teacher (O'Farrell, 1990).

For any given curriculum, there will be many specialists who might be consulted. Who would not want to consult Ernest Hemingway about literature curricula or Albert Einstein about a science curriculum? The telephone is a wonderful instrument. Why not use it to call a successful athlete about the new physical education curriculum, a poet to talk about the poetry curriculum, a world traveler to discuss the geography curriculum? The late Isaac Asimov said that people were simply not listening:

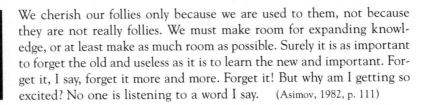

> We cherish our follies only because we are used to them, not because they are not really follies. We must make room for expanding knowledge, or at least make as much room as possible. Surely it is as important to forget the old and useless as it is to learn the new and important. Forget it, I say, forget it more and more. Forget it! But why am I getting so excited? No one is listening to a word I say.   (Asimov, 1982, p. 111)

Another important group of specialists are found in the classroom. It is essential that we consult teachers who not only have substantial successful experience in teaching, but who have reflected deeply on the purposes and meanings of the subjects they teach. Social scientists, such as sociologists, anthropologists, and psychologists, may provide further specialist input.

Clients

The most obvious clients of curriculum are *students*. Consultation with students about the curriculum is an appropriate mark of respect. Students are no more omniscient than curriculum planners. They are, however, experts in at least one sense: they are expert at being students and (if young) at being young people. "There are philosophers in schools," writes Roland Barth (1990a, p. 515), "usually the 5- and 6-year-olds." We have sufficient evidence to show that children in the

> There is, finally, a humanistic principle which might lead us to take student participation in curriculum decisions more seriously than we commonly do at present. In its simplest form, the principle is that what we do for people we must as far as practicable do with them.
>
> Malcolm Skilbeck (1985, p. 265)

earliest grades can provide perceptive insights into what and how they are taught (Nicholls & Thorkildsen, 1989; Stodolsky, Salk, & Glaessner, 1991).

There is no other place to begin instruction than where students already are. Ascertaining their background, their interests, their aspirations and motivations, their preferences and aversions, their histories of success and failure, is essential if curricula are to meet their needs rather than those of teachers or curriculum planners. This has been recognized as a central principle of andragogy (the teaching of adults) (Knowles, 1984). Typically, adults in educational programs will "vote with their feet" if their life experience is ignored or discounted. Like most principles of andragogy, this turns out simply to be a sound educational principle that needs to be adopted also in situations where students are a captive audience.

When surveying potential students, it is worth asking questions not only about what they want to learn, but also how they prefer to learn. This became clear in a study conducted in a business setting of weight reduction programs for male employees. Men traditionally do not attend weight reduction workshops. A needs assessment of employees in high-technology companies showed that the format men preferred for learning about being overweight was a self-help package—a teaching workbook and access to a dietitian as a resource person (Reid & Dunkley, 1989). Without such information, a planned program may fail, however pertinent the information it teaches.

In some ways even more valuable as sources of information than current students are former students, both *graduates* and *dropouts*. These are clients who have experienced existing programs and are now in a position to judge their subsequent usefulness. I find myself bemused by conferences on dropouts where people who know the least about dropping out—educators who have completed high levels of schooling—debate the issues without the presence or the input of those who have the most direct experience of the subject—the dropouts themselves. We need to listen to observations like this one from an illiterate former dropout:

> You want to experience what illiteracy is like? Go into a restaurant and ask a waitress to read the menu to you. Go to the supermarket and ask for a particular brand when standing right next to the display. Go to any government office and say you can't fill out the form. Ask the phone company for a waiver in directory assistance charges because you can't read the phone book. That will give you some idea. But you can never feel the frustration, the anxiety.   (Frontier College, 1991)

> Let's start with the really important question first. What should children learn in schools? Think about that. I have asked that question across the nation of school board members, legislators, captains of industry, parents, superintendents, principals, teachers and students. Their answers are remarkably similar. Coming high on each list are the following attributes and skills: Learning to learn, problem solving, ability to use information, a broad sense of history and the world, communication skills, responsibility, a sense of self-worth, respect for others, cooperative skills, a knowledge base, and survival skills. Never . . . not in *one* case did anyone list higher scores on achievement tests, nor did any group list basic skills near the top of the list.
>
> Jane Stallings (1987, p. 1)

Parents are also clients of school systems. Some U.S. legislation, such as Public Law 94-142, the Education for All Handicapped Children Act, mandates the involvement of parents. A number of British government reports have also recommended involvement of parents in educational policy and practice (Bullock, 1975; Plowden, 1967). A majority of parents believe that they should have more influence on curriculum and that at present they have little or none (Elam, 1990). The curriculum philosopher, Joseph Schwab, suggested that in every school, curriculum should be directed by a committee which would include both students and parents, the latter being experts on their own children (Schwab, 1983).

Misunderstandings between schools and parents often occur. Naama Sabar (1990) suggests that while administrators consider parents to be merely indirect clients of the school, parents view the school as an extension of the education given their children at home, and consider it to be primarily responsible to them. Parents tend to underestimate the commitment teachers have to their students, just as teachers tend to underestimate the commitment parents have to their children. Parents are eloquent about the needs of their children. Here is an immigrant mother from El Salvador talking about her child:

> I say to that teacher Maria tries hard . . . she study study at night. Could you help her extra? She need help, she try hard and she cries. . . . She need extra help. That teacher she told me no. "I have Grade Three class to teach. I am a Grade Three teacher. . . . I don't give special help. I teach all the childrens." I try to talk to that teacher. She no help me. She no help Maria. . . . Who will help her here? We cannot go on like this. (Tocher, 1991, p. 75)

Teachers are also clients of the school system, not merely its servants. They have a right to be consulted about curriculum changes that may affect their work and their environment. Teachers do not feel the same way about many issues as the general public. For example, fewer teachers than members of the general public would want their own children to become teachers (43 percent vs. 58 percent). Teachers feel that of the major professions, they contribute most to the general good of society, but have the lowest professional prestige (Elam, 1988).

Employers are dependent on the schools for the competencies with which people enter their employ. Curriculum planners often consult employers when planning curricula in electronics or welding. But why not in English and mathematics? Employers tend to be critical of the caliber of school graduates. A majority of executives surveyed in one study reported that their companies suffered from problems of schooling (Bradley, 1989). The chair emeritus of Boeing commented scathingly on the remedial work his company had to provide for graduates "who don't know how to use an alarm clock" (Dolan, 1990, p. R20). A survey of 1,283 personnel officers showed that the qualities that they rated most important in hiring secondary school graduates were dependability (94 percent), attitudes about work (84 percent), teamwork (74 percent), rapid learning (57 percent), and reading ability (57 percent) (Crain, 1984).

The *community* itself needs to be regarded as a major player in the curriculum development process. It is desirable to consult community members as widely as possible, rather than relying on only a few "key informants" (DeVillaer, 1990). Some of the most effective curriculum development today is taking place in Native American communities in North America. In the Yukon and Northwest Territories in Canada, curricula are being developed in collaboration with elders and native communities. Science curricula incorporate both Western science and native legend. Health curricula deal with both Western and traditional native medicine. The developers of a recent program to train childcare workers for native communities in Ontario started with the assumption that the first priority of the communities would be quality childcare. Consultation with native elders and communities, however, revealed that while this was important, a principal expectation of the native communities was that childcare centers would develop programs aimed at preserving and protecting native culture (Ron Common, personal communication, April 1990). In a community in Alaska, teachers decided to precede development of a curriculum on native culture by conducting a survey in the village. Lipka reports what happened:

> As soon as students began interviewing parents throughout the village, concerned community members got on the CB and warned everybody not to fill out the questionnaire. . . . They felt that "if kass'at (white people) teach our culture to the students, then what is left for us? Our culture belongs to the community." (Lipka, 1989, p. 223)

Other clients of schools include subsequent educational institutions and the general public, and these should also be consulted as appropriate. The annual Phi Delta Kappan Gallup poll provides interesting data about public attitudes toward schools. For instance, about half of the general public have some direct contact with the school system each year. In 1991, 21 percent of the public gave the public schools a grade of A or B; 42 percent gave an A or B to schools in their community, and 73 percent of parents gave an A or B to the school their child attended. Eighty-nine percent of the 1,500 adult respondents believed that it was "very important" to develop the best education system in the world; fewer Americans considered it very important to develop the most efficient industrial system (59 percent) or the strongest military force (41 percent) (Elam, Rose, & Gallup, 1991).

The process of consultation is particularly important if the clients are not represented on curriculum development committees. Studies in the United States and other countries show that it is very rare for curriculum development committees to include anyone other than professional educators. Parents, students, and other members of the public are systematically excluded unless they happen also to be professional educators (Haft & Hopmann, 1989; Klein, 1980; Orpwood & Souque, 1984; Pratt, 1989).

Worth listening to

Bill Moyers quotes the following letter received in response to a PBS series based on Mortimer Adler's book, *Six Great Ideas* (1981):

> I'm writing in behalf of a group of construction workers, mostly, believe it or not, plumbers who have finally found a teacher worth listening to. While we cannot all agree whether or not we would hire you, Adler, as an apprentice, we can all agree that we would like to listen to you on our lunch breaks. We've been studying your books for over a year now and put together a sizeable library of your writings. We never knew a world of ideas existed. The study of ideas has completely turned around our impression of higher and lower education. We only wish we had not wasted 25 to 35 years in the process. But we have to thank you for the next 35 to 40 years that we have before us to study and implement the great ideas into our lives and into the lives of the community.
>
> Bill Moyers (Finn, Lightfoot, Greene, & Noah, 1989, p. 29)

Gatekeepers

A competent needs assessment not only places curriculum on a sound foundation, it also helps to ensure successful implementation of curriculum change. Needs assessment is a vehicle for disseminating information about areas in which change is being considered, and for demonstrating interest in people's judgments in those areas. It allows us to identify changes that will be welcomed and those that will meet resistance. It may also enable us to identify potential supporters and opponents of the change. Supporters may be recruited at some stage in the development of the project. Opponents can be consulted to ascertain points of opposition. Compromises may be possible; if not, rebuttals can be prepared.

Gatekeepers are individuals who have the power to affect the implementation of decisions. Gatekeepers typically include members of the school board, the state department of education, the legislature, and committees of these bodies; district superintendents and other influential administrators and educators; community opinion leaders such as clergy, newspaper editors, and columnists; officers and members of parent-teacher associations; leaders of teacher organizations; university admissions officers; chambers of commerce, chief executive officers, and personnel directors.

It is generally fatal, particularly in the case of controversial curriculum, to plan programs without taking account, from the very beginning, of the views of significant members of the community. Perhaps the best-known, most expensive, and most scholarly-based social studies program ever developed was "Man, a Course of Study." Formulated on the pedagogical ideas of Jerome Bruner, supported by the National Science Foundation, and using much anthropological material on Inuit culture, the program ran afoul of conservative opinion in the United States, which attacked its "cultural relativism" and depiction of "immoral behavior" (Boyd, 1978). These attacks eventually resulted in funding cuts and hastened the program's demise. With hindsight, it is clear that early discussions with potential opponents of the program might have enabled designers to avoid the problems that occurred.

Programs in sex education developed during the same period underwent a similar experience. Those curricula that were implemented smoothly in school districts were the work of curriculum committees that had consulted continuously with members of the local medical and ministerial communities. Those committees that neglected this vital step created for themselves months and years of conflict and recrimination, and often, in the end, nonimplementation of the curricula they developed (Kenney & Orr, 1984).

Teachers fall into all three categories: they are clients, specialists, and gatekeepers. This is why it is crucial to stay in close contact throughout the entire process of curriculum development with the teachers who will eventually implement and use the new curriculum. The advocates of "school-based curriculum development" urge that curriculum improvement is most likely to succeed if it is localized to the individual school, and the change is devised and implemented by those teachers who will be most affected by it (Holt, 1987; Walker, 1988). There is clearly much truth in this position. One of its important implications is that school-based curriculum development can be successful only if individual teachers have had the opportunity to develop expertise in curriculum planning.

The academic tendency toward specialization has tended to separate the study of curriculum development from the study of curriculum implementation. As a consequence, the belief has grown that we first develop curricula and then try to find effective ways of implementing it. It is more logical to think from the beginning in terms of *developing implementable curricula*. We will look more closely in the final chapter of the book at the evidence showing that the approval of teachers is critical to implementation. One of the best ways of obtaining that approval is by ensuring that we include teachers among those we consult before, during, and after development.

Administrators are also gatekeepers, and as Wutchiett et al. (1984) point out, they are quite capable of ignoring the results of needs assessments. For this reason, if resources or implementation of change depend on their approval, this should be obtained prior to embarking on the needs assessment. In large-scale needs assessments an advisory committee is sometimes appointed to oversee or advise on the project, and key decision makers can be included in its membership. Alternatively, the views of specialists, clients, and gatekeepers can be accessed by meetings with individuals and groups to assist in the design of the survey (Galluzzo, 1990).

■ Methods for Collecting Opinions ■

Questionnaires

The standard method for accessing public opinion is by means of questionnaires. Questionnaires appear to be cheap, fast, and easy to design. Unfortunately, they have so many drawbacks that research based on questionnaires must often be treated with skepticism. This is particularly the case when questionnaires are

"I have no answers, man
—only questions."

designed by people without substantial training and experience. Questions may be unconsciously biased; the language may not be understood by respondents; "social desirability response set" may distort answers; people may not be prepared to be honest in their responses; respondents may not really be sure what they think on certain issues; response rate may be too small to ensure a random sample. Even questionnaires designed by experts and scholars often show deficiencies. Over 44,000 secondary school students were asked in a questionnaire whether they agreed with the statement, "Homosexuality is acceptable today" (King, 1986, p. 29). Eleven percent of males and 27 percent of females agreed. The ambiguity of the question makes the data difficult to interpret. Are students being asked whether *they* find homosexuality acceptable or whether they think *other people* think it is acceptable? Bias is often a problem in questionnaires. A distinct Western cultural bias is apparent in the following statements, with which respondents were asked to agree or disagree, as an index of "modernity" in a World Bank study in Tanzania: "It is usually better to meet familiar people than new people"; "Happiness is more important than success"; "The only people one can really trust are one's own family and relatives"; "There is no sense in worrying about the future"; "I would like to live in another country for some time"; "I am more ambitious than most of my friends" (Psacharopoulos & Loxley, 1982). One wonders how predictive of actual behavior was the British survey in which 58 percent of men surveyed said that for one million pounds they would withhold information concerning a murder, 35 percent said they would sell drugs, and 8 percent said they would abandon their families (Clements, 1991).

The least a planning team should do if intending to use questionnaires is read some of the literature on questionnaire design (e.g., Fink & Kosecoff, 1985; Fowler, 1988; Wolf, 1990).

When Levi Strauss & Co. asked students which clothes would be popular this year, 90 percent said Levi's 501 jeans. They were the only jeans on the list. . . . "There's good news for the 65 million Americans currently on a diet," trumpeted a news release for a diet-products company. Its study showed that people who lose weight can keep it off. The sample: 20 graduates of the company's program who endorse it in commercials. . . . Kiwi Brands, a shoe-polish company, commissioned a study earlier this year on the correlation between ambition and shiny shoes. The study found that 97 percent of self-described "ambitious" young men believe polished shoes are important. . . . There are at least four widely publicized studies on diapers that explore the issue of whether disposables are disproportionately responsible for burdening U.S. landfills and fouling the environment. Two studies were sponsored by the cloth-diaper industry and conclude that cloth diapers are friendlier to the world; two others, sponsored by the paper-diaper industry, conclude the opposite.

Cynthia Crossen (1991, p. D5)

Telephone interviews

Face-to-face interviews are time-consuming and expensive to conduct. Consequently, the telephone interview has now become a standard method for opinion research. It is relatively fast and cheap, and with up to six call-backs, over 99 percent of the sample can usually be reached. It provides respondents with greater anonymity and more control (as they can always hang up) than in face-to-face interviews. Evidence also suggests that deception is rare in telephone interviews. Interviews can also be conducted from a central location, where continuous supervision and support is available to interviewers. James Frey, director of the Telephone Survey Center at the University of Nevada, in a book full of practical advice on the design of telephone surveys, suggests that January–April are the best months for such work (surveys during the summer months tend to miss people who are on vacation), Tuesday–Thursday the best days, and 6–7 P.M. the best hour. The elderly and homemakers are more easily reached during the day, and students between 3:00 and 7:00 P.M. on weekdays (or at school) (Frey, 1983; Lavrakis, 1987).

It is preferable if callers are not employees of the organization conducting the study, for example teachers, as this can bias the results. Often, volunteers from the community can be used. Some basic training in telephone interviewing should be provided. The University of Illinois Survey Research Laboratory (1982) has developed a training manual for telephone interviewers. Random-digit dialing can help to ensure a random sample. The gender of the respondent can be prescribed to obtain equal numbers of male and female respondents. As far as possible, callers should be typical of the people being called, especially with regard to language and ethnicity. It is a common experience that actual interviews last longer—typically by about 50 percent—than expected (Galluzzo, 1990; Noble, 1986). By 1986, 95 percent of American households had telephones (ranging from 100 percent in California to 82 percent in Mississippi). Working-class, inner-city, minority, and female subjects are more likely to have unlisted telephone numbers (half of the households in Chicago have unlisted phones), and this must be taken into account in the survey design (Lavrakis, 1987).

Paul Lavrakis (1987) outlines the main steps in preparing for a telephone survey as follows: (1) determine the sampling design; (2) choose a method to generate a pool of numbers; (3) produce a call-sheet for each call; (4) develop a draft introduction and fall-back statements in response to common interviewee questions (such as,"How did you get my number?"); (5) recruit interviewers and screen them by phone; (6) conduct a pilot test of the survey; (7) print the survey and other forms; (8) train interviewers and supervisors; (9) have each interviewer conduct 25–50 supervised practice interviews; and (10) make a written agreement with each interviewer.

In interview research, the quality of the data collected depends on the quality of the questions asked. Do not underestimate your respondents! If you ask serious questions, you will get serious answers. The questions to be asked should be carefully worked out beforehand. It is a good idea to enlist the advice of individuals and groups of specialists, clients, and gatekeepers in planning the questions and

Needs Assessment: Opinion Survey

Check whichever of the following you might contact.

Contacts	Number
Clients	
Students/clients in program	_____
Students/clients in other programs	_____
Graduates	_____
Dropouts	_____
Future students	_____
Parents	_____
Employers	_____
Other clients (specify)	_____
Total clients	_____
Specialists	
Specialists in subject	_____
Specialists on future trends	_____
Specialists in instruction	_____
Instructors in subject	_____
Instructors in other subjects	_____
Specialists in curriculum	_____
Other specialists (specify)	_____
Total specialists	_____
Gatekeepers	
Administrators	_____
Colleagues	_____
Community & opinion leaders	_____
Professional associations	_____
Government officials	_____
Licensing bodies	_____
Advisory committee members	_____
Board members	_____
Other gatekeepers (specify)	_____
Total gatekeepers	_____
Total contacts	_____

issues to be raised in the needs assessment. Questions will vary with the nature of the study and with the respondents. In a needs assessment preceding the revision of a curriculum in modern world history, for example, questions such as these might be asked: Do you believe that all school graduates should have some knowledge of world history? For what main reasons? Are you familiar with the present world history program? What do you think are its good points? Its weaknesses? What countries' histories should students be knowledgeable about? Can you think of any skills that students should learn in a world history program? What kinds of ideas would you like students to develop through studying world history? Did you study world history yourself at school? What were the main things you learned from that program? What were its main faults? and so on. If you take seriously the mission of the school in personal and social areas, do not fail to ask questions in these areas. For example: What should we be doing in this and other school programs to develop students' social attitudes? How do you think the study of history can make students better people? How could it be taught so as to increase their sense of meaning? How has your own understanding of history affected the way you look at the world?

The interviews can be pilot-tested with a small sample, then revised before the main survey is begun. Note that it is better to get responses from 100 percent of a small sample than from only 50 percent of a much larger sample (Posovac & Carey, 1989).

Hearings and briefs

Public hearings, or community forums, and invitations to submit briefs can also be used both to gain access to public opinion and to raise public interest. One of the largest such enterprises ever undertaken was in New Zealand in 1984–85. A new government, determined to embark on reform of the school system, assigned twenty-nine people to fan out through the country visiting communities, holding public hearings, and encouraging groups and individuals to submit briefs to the Committee to Review the Curriculum for Schools. They made particular efforts to reach people who are often ignored in such processes, such as inhabitants of Maori villages, Pacific islands, and prisons. The assistance of radio, television, and newspapers was enlisted for publicity. McDonald's of New Zealand even printed special placemats urging its customers to send in briefs and giving the address of the commission. The outcome was that, from a country of $3\frac{1}{2}$ million people, the government received 21,000 briefs. An initial report was prepared, further briefs in response were invited, and another 10,000 were received. On the basis of this input, the New Zealand school system and curriculum were radically revised (New Zealand Department of Education, 1987).

■ A Cautionary Note ■

The great strength of well-conducted opinion surveys is that they show that the curriculum planners respect the views of those persons consulted. But a word of caution is in order. The curriculum planners need to be clear about where responsibility for curriculum decisions lies. There are contexts in which it is appropriate to delegate the planning of curriculum to a community, which then becomes the curriculum planning agent. More commonly, care must be taken in a public survey to make clear to respondents that the purpose of the exercise is to seek information and advice, not to conduct a referendum. Education is more than merely a part of the market economy, with curriculum to be dictated solely by the current demands of consumers. If the public feels that it is being asked to determine curriculum policy, it will be legitimately aggrieved if its judgments are not reflected in the curriculum that ultimately emerges. A curriculum based exclusively on public opinion—itself subject to the vagaries of fashion and media emphasis—will be vulnerable as soon as public opinion changes. Yesterday's bandwagon can easily become tomorrow's hearse. The responsibility for making curriculum decisions ultimately belongs to curriculum developers. If these are major curriculum decisions, they will eventually be subject to approval by public representatives such as Boards of Education. The purpose of needs assessment is to ensure that these decisions are informed, but not determined, by the opinions of all of those concerned.

▪ Task Analysis ▪

Important as is direct interaction with the school's various constituencies, "needs cannot be determined merely by asking people what they need, no matter how insightful, honest, wise, and mature the target group may be" (Kuh et al., 1981, pp. 11–12). Other methods are needed to corroborate the subjective data produced by respondents in interviews, hearings, or surveys. One such method is task analysis. Its function is to identify the important components of tasks that will in turn become significant elements of the curriculum. This approach is often used in the development of training programs in employment contexts, but its applications are wider than this. In a text on task analysis, Jonassen, Hannum, and Tessmer assert their "belief that task analysis is the single most important component process in instructional systems design" (1989, p. vii).

There are normally two elements of task analysis. The first is task identification by direct observation of task performance: trained observers, for example, might follow employees through an entire day to monitor the nature, purpose, scope, frequency, sequence, and importance of tasks performed. Observers might also note what information, skills, and attitudes are used on the job; what training and supervision are relied on; what tools are used; and the extent to which tasks involve interaction with data, people, and things (Jonassen, Hannum, & Tessmer, 1989). The second element is task evaluation. Specialists such as workers, supervisors, and trainers are given the list of tasks and asked to rate the importance of each and add any omitted tasks. Table 2-1 illustrates a task analysis of wilderness survival, such as might be completed during the planning of a wilderness survival course.

Task analysis has uses beyond vocational contexts. In fact, one of the earliest works on curriculum planning, Franklin Bobbitt's *How to Make a Curriculum*,

Table 2-1   *Task Analysis: Wilderness Survival*

Task	Conditions	Equipment	Time	Probability of Use	Consequences of Incompetence	Importance
make fire	wind & rain	2 matches, saw	40 min (to boil 1 liter water)	90%	disastrous	critical
build shelter	wind & rain	30-m line, 2 × 3-m polythene	1 hr	60%	serious	critical
obtain food	winter	2 hooks, fish-net, hatchet, cooking pot	7 hrs	50%	significant	important
obtain water	summer, no open water	cooking pot, polythene	24 hrs	10%	serious	critical
first aid	any	first aid kit		10%	serious	critical
find direc-tion	cloudy, dense bush	compass	1 min	90%	disastrous	critical
navigate on foot	rough terrain	compass	2 km/hr	100%	serious	critical
signal	day & night	whistle, ground-to-air symbol sheet, 3 flares		10%	serious	critical
choose equip-ment			1 hr	100%	disastrous	critical
maintain morale	alone or group			100%	serious	critical
solo	wilderness	all of above	24 hrs	100%	significant	important

(Adapted from Pratt, 1980)

attempted to define curriculum by task analysis of the activities of people who were experts in "high-grade living." His catalog of human abilities ended up looking slightly absurd:

> Ability to care for the teeth; ability to care for the eyes; ability to care for the nose, ear and throat; . . . ability to sharpen, adjust, clean, lubricate, replace worn or broken parts, and otherwise keep household and garden tools and appliances in good order and good working condition. (Bobbitt, 1924, pp. 14, 28)

More recent efforts in this direction have produced useful results. A number of studies in mathematics have observed people, in employment and nonemployment situations, in an attempt to understand and describe the kinds of mathematical operations that people use and need in their daily lives. These studies tend to show that the mathematics taught and learned in schools is little valued or used by adults (Advisory Council for Adult and Continuing Education, 1982; Capon & Kuhn, 1979). Sometimes the inadequacy of shoppers' mathematical background is vividly apparent. In one British study, about one-third of the sample questioned in a supermarket thought that all percentages were meaningless, including such expressions as 10 percent ("You've got me there."). Many adults reported feelings of anxiety, helplessness, fear, and guilt when asked to perform some apparently straightforward number skill (Advisory Council for Adult and Continuing Education, 1982). Studies of shoppers in supermarkets show that while a great many adults cannot perform relatively simple unit price calculations, most of them do employ some kind of arithmetic comparison-shopping procedures (Murtaugh 1985). Carraher, Carraher, & Schliemann (1985) found that young children in Brazilian open-air markets could perform much more sophisticated calculations than would be expected from their achieved level of formal education. Studies of employees show that many of the operations taught in school mathematics are not used on the job (Hiscox 1980; Pirie, 1981). On the other hand, inability to perform such tasks as repricing items at half price could lead to the dismissal of an otherwise satisfactory employee (Hiscox, 1980). John Bishop (1990a) has shown that mathematical competence is not usually rewarded in the paycheck of employees, even though it does contribute significantly to their productivity.

Interesting and significant as they are, studies of this kind have not yet made a great impact on mathematics curricula. This has less to do with their importance than with the politics of curriculum planning, the expertise (or its absence) of planners, and the stranglehold of tradition on school curricula. Task analyses are more likely to be effective if they are conducted by curriculum planners themselves as part of their preparatory work. In such circumstances, it would be illuminating to research the use that people made in their daily and working lives of many curriculum areas, such as reading, writing, geography, physics, sex education, or philosophy.

■ Social Indicators ■

Other kinds of empirical data that have value in needs assessment are social indicators. Like task analysis, research on social indicators balances the more subjective information obtained in opinion surveys. Industrial hygienists are usually consulted as a result of subjective complaints about the environmental quality of the workplace. Such complaints, however, do not in themselves prove that there is a problem or a need. The World Health Organization expects that 20 percent of workers will normally have complaints about their workplace environment. In order to establish whether there is a need for change, it is necessary to collect much hard data, by means of studies of worksite layout and drawings, a walkthrough survey, and epidemiological research, in addition to an analysis of specific employee complaints (Bickis, 1992).

Social indicators are not opinions but relatively "hard data," such as statistics on births and deaths, unemployment rates, housing, consumption, family income, and so on. The social indicators required will depend on the nature of the curriculum being designed. Planners of a curriculum in physical fitness may want to know about actual fitness levels of potential clients and local utilization of sport facilities. Developers of a curriculum in poetry may want to determine utilization of the poetry collections in the school and public libraries, attendance at poetry readings, and numbers of people writing poetry in the community. Much demographic and economic data, based on census information, can usually be obtained from data banks such as those maintained by the National Center for Health Statistics, the National Institute of Mental Health, and by state and federal governments.

Public opinion and social indicators are complementary types of data. They have complementary benefits and complementary problems. While public opinion may be fickle, official statistics may be unreliable. Criminal statistics are a case in point. If an inefficient chief of police is replaced by a more vigilant officer, the crime rate may appear to go up, as more crimes are detected and reported and more arrests are made. Or crimes may be committed, but no one may be aware of them. For instance, if a butcher sells short weight, his victims may eat the evidence. Or those aware of crimes may not report them to the police. (Many instances of computer fraud by employees are so embarrassing to the employers that they go unreported.) Or the police may not identify the offender or may decide not to press charges. Or the accused may be discharged before trial, or may be tried and acquitted. Rossi, Freeman, and Wright (1979) concluded on the basis of interviews with victims of crime that the standard statistics prepared by the FBI—the Uniform Crime Reports—underestimated the actual number of crimes committed by a factor of about four.

■ Tests and Research Data ■

In principle, test results should be helpful in needs assessment, for they should provide hard evidence on the extent to which those needs reflected in curriculum objectives are currently being met in schools. They should not, however, be relied on as the sole source of data for needs assessment. Sometimes tests are based on narrow conceptions of learning, and sometimes their validity is questionable. But if valid tests are used, the data can be valuable to curriculum planners. This is especially the case if test data is disaggregated—that is, if it provides data on achievement broken down by gender, ethnicity, age, social class, and so on. Without disaggregation, the educational disadvantage of certain groups may be obscured by the reporting only of average achievement.

In recent years, interest has increased in comparisons of student achievement among different nations. Better communications and increasing international economic competition fuel this interest. Here are a few of the results from national and international studies conducted during the 1980s:

Eighty-two percent of 17-year-olds are in full-time schooling in the United States, compared with 92 percent in Japan and 17 percent in Britain.

The 1 percent of U.S. high school seniors taking their second chemistry course knew less chemistry than the 25 percent of Canadian 18-year-olds taking chemistry.

Proportionately five times as many 17-year-old students take algebra in Hungary as in the United States.

Twice as many American parents believe their school is "doing an excellent job" than do parents in Japan or Taiwan.

Ninety-five percent of Taiwanese and 63 percent of American fifth graders have their own study desk at home.

In Australia teachers earn about the same as scientists; in the United States, teachers earn less than half as much.

Japanese senior high school students average 19 hours of homework a week; American students average 3.8 hours.

American students average 19.6 hours of TV a week, Canadians 10.9 hours, and Norwegians 5.9 hours.

(Bishop, 1990b; Hanna, 1989; McKnight et al., 1987; Stevenson, Lee & Stigler, 1986)

Another important research activity involves examining the available evidence on instructional aspects of the curriculum. A curriculum development team in beginning Spanish, for example, would be well advised to read some of the research on such questions as: How effective are conventional Spanish programs? What seems to be the best age for introduction of second-language learning? What are the comparable effects of "core" and "immersion" language programs? What is the optimal number of minutes per day for second-language learning? Do language programs have different effects on students from different backgrounds? What is the effect of second-language learning on development of first-language abilities? There is substantial research on such issues as these, and it is unwise to proceed in ignorance of it. The following would make quite useful starting points for such research:

The *Curriculum Handbook*, published by the Association for Supervision and Curriculum Development (1992), is actually a subscription service with periodic updates and a quarterly newsletter.

The *Handbook of Research on Curriculum* is published by the American Educational Research Association (Jackson, 1991).

The *International Encyclopedia of Curriculum* (Lewy, 1991a).

The Educational Resources Information Center (ERIC) database, which contains over 730,000 documents and journal articles. The database is accessible via CD-ROM retrieval systems at some 3,000 sites, and the articles and documents are available on microfiche at some 900 sites around the world. (Stonehill, 1992)

SMARTLINE (Sources of Materials and Research About Teaching and Learning for Improving Nationwide Education), an electronic information system under development by the Office of Educational Research and Improvement to provide parents and educators with quick, jargon-free answers to educational questions. SMARTLINE will eventually be accessible from 75,000 school libraries and 15,000 public libraries, as well as from home computers. It will link the user with other networks and databases and provide information on research and evaluation findings; statistical data; innovative, exemplary, and demonstration programs; opportunities for funding; and teacher fellowships (Office of Educational Research & Improvement, 1992a).

Curriculum journals that regularly publish research on curriculum issues, such as *American Educational Research Journal, Curriculum Inquiry, Educational Leadership, Elementary School Journal, Journal of Curriculum Studies, Phi Delta Kappan, Review of Educational Research,* and the many journals that focus on particular curriculum subject areas.

EXISTING CURRICULA

It is always desirable, in principle, to conduct a needs assessment prior to developing a curriculum. But it is not always necessary to develop a new curriculum. For one thing, the needs assessment may show that the existing curriculum is working sufficiently well that only minor revisions are needed. Or it may indicate that there is insufficient support for a new curriculum to have much hope of implementation.

Of equal importance is the fact that a perfectly good curriculum may have been developed elsewhere. During the 1960s the United States spent over $100 million

developing new science curricula. Some of these were successfully adapted for use in other countries. The Biological Science Curriculum Study (BSCS), for example, was translated into twenty-one languages and adapted for use in over forty nations. The Soviet Union adapted BSCS, giving Russian scientists more coverage. Some "second-generation" adaptations were also developed. The Colombian version of BSCS was the basis for the Puerto Rican version, while the West Indian SCIP (Science Improvement Project) was adapted for use in Africa (Blum & Grobman, 1991). These examples, however, are exceptions rather than the rule. It is more customary for every jurisdiction to develop its own curricula more or less from scratch. While there may be some benefits in terms of generating a local sense of ownership, this approach is enormously wasteful. So once the needs assessment is complete, the next step is to review other curriculum documents in the same field.

There are a number of ways of doing this. Some state departments of education and some university schools of education maintain collections of curricula. The ERIC system contains over 80,000 state, district, and provincial guidelines. For any curriculum related to health issues, the MEDLINE system should also be accessed. Or state and district curriculum offices can be contacted directly. Another source is the Kraus Curriculum Development Library (Millwood, N.Y.).

Chicago and Beijing

A comparative study of mathematics achievement at Grade 1 and Grade 5 by children in Chicago and Beijing was published in 1990. Pupils in two classrooms at each grade level were studied in twenty schools in Chicago and eleven schools in Beijing. All Beijing pupils were Chinese. Chicago pupils were 55 percent white, 24 percent black, 15 percent Hispanic, and 4 percent Asian. Mean income of the parents was $32,500 in Chicago and $778 in Beijing. Mean educational level of mothers/fathers was 12.8/13.5 years in Chicago, 10.2/11.5 in Beijing. All Chicago teachers had bachelor's degrees, and 37 percent had master's degrees. Sixty percent of Chinese teachers had attended a 2- or 3-year teacher training college; 37 percent had completed only high school.

On twenty-four comparisons of test scores in mathematics, the Beijing students were significantly superior in twenty-two. Beijing students solved $1\frac{1}{2}$ to 3 times as many problems as the Chicago students. Ninety-eight percent of the Beijing students scored higher than the average Chicago student.

Here are some examples of questions on the tests:

Grade Level	Question	Percentage of Students Answering Correctly	
		Chicago	Beijing
1	There were 15 bunnies. Nine hopped away. How many bunnies were left?	30.1	95.8
1	Chris has 26 toy cars. Mary has 19. How many do they have in all?	13.1	84.7
5	A stamp-collecting club has 24 members. Five-sixths of the members collect only foreign stamps. How many collect only foreign stamps?	43.5	91.6
5	Ten cans of pop cost $1.50 at one store. I can get 5 cans for 80 cents at a second store. Where is the pop cheaper, the first or the second store?	38.0	80.7

Nine percent of Chicago teachers and 34 percent of Beijing teachers considered math the most important subject they taught. Thirty-five percent of American and 13 percent of Chinese mothers thought their children were doing "very well" in math. Chicago parents said they would be satisfied with scores in the 70s; Beijing parents wanted their children to score in the high 80s or 90s.

Harold Stevenson et al. (1990)

This company offers for sale a microfiche collection of over 5,000 curriculum guides in more than twenty subject areas, to which it adds 300 annually. Curricula from the ten Canadian provinces can be obtained on microfiche through ONTERIS (the Ontario Educational Research Information System, Toronto, Ont.). Whatever the source, it makes obvious sense to review the work of other developers prior to beginning one's own.

■ Small Is Beautiful ■

So far, the process of needs assessment may look formidable. Where could anyone find the time to do this? But needs assessment does not require a million-dollar budget. It is a process that is within the capacity of every classroom teacher. Suppose that a physical education teacher, Ms. Brown, is interested in reviewing the curriculum in physical fitness. She is willing to devote two lunchtimes and three evenings to a needs assessment. It would be possible within that time frame to speak in person with one coach, two athletes, three colleagues, four students, and the school principal. By phone, she talks with the manager of a fitness center, a physician who runs marathons, a sports physiotherapist, a sporting goods retailer, a member of the school board, an exercise physiologist at the local university, two dropouts, two graduates, four parents, and an official with the State Department of Education. Two of her students agree to research as a course project the findings of recent fitness surveys in the community. She conducts a task analysis with another class by asking them to keep a quarter-hourly log of physical activities performed for a week. She also reviews student scores on the fitness knowledge subtest of the previous year's examinations.

For the investment of a few hours of her time, Ms. Brown could obtain a great deal of useful information about the interest of respondents in the school in general, and in fitness programs in particular. In the process she might also identify individuals in the community who are willing to assist with the school physical education program. She will develop new skills in herself and her students. She may obtain some new ideas for the design of the revised program. She will almost certainly develop increased confidence that her curriculum reflects the needs of students and the community and that it will ultimately be implemented.

RESULTS OF NEEDS ASSESSMENT

Pinchas Tamir (1990) reports an exceptionally thorough needs assessment conducted in connection with revision of the electricity curriculum in Israeli technical schools. Table 2-2 shows the constituencies consulted.

What made Tamir's study of particular interest was that he conducted a controlled experiment on the effects of providing six different curriculum planning committees with varying amounts of information from the needs assessment, ranging from committees receiving no information to those who were provided with all the information obtained from the 1,206 respondents shown in Table 2-2.

Table 2-2   *Electricity Program Needs Assessment*

Students in electricity programs	641
Students in other programs	201
Graduates of electricity programs	94
Teachers in electricity programs	18
Teachers in other programs	181
Chairs of electricity departments	9
University electricity teachers	6
Electrical engineers	27
Employers of electricity graduates	13
Technical school principals	10
School inspectors in electricity	6

(Tamir, 1990)

This enabled him to monitor the effects of receiving such information on the discussions that ensued in the curriculum planning committees. His findings give strong support to the use of needs assessment in program design. He found that those committees that received full data, as compared with those receiving less information:

> spent less time exchanging opinions about subject matter;
>
> spent more time discussing learners, teachers, and the environment in which graduates would apply their learning;
>
> spent more time on the translation of subject matter into learning experiences;
>
> had greater ability to determine planned curriculum outcomes; and
>
> showed greater facility in identifying significant curriculum problems and the curriculum revisions needed to solve them.

It seems that the overall effect of needs assessment is to make the process of curriculum planning more reflective, more inclusive, and more professional. Unfortunately, curriculum committees working at the state and district level frequently continue to establish priorities not on the basis of empirical needs assessments, but on the basis of tradition and political pressure. Indeed, Belle Ruth Witkin, author of an authoritative text on needs assessment, concludes that "the most simplistic and least valid methods of deriving priorities are those in widest use in educational systems" (1984, p. 206).

The experience of those conducting needs assessments suggests some of the results that can be anticipated:

1)   Respondents will be remarkably supportive. No one likes having supper interrupted by a telephone salesperson, but, as a perceptive individual once commented, we all admire the wisdom of those who come to us for advice. In one community survey which had allocated fifteen minutes per telephone interview, the average interview lasted twenty-three minutes, so eager were respondents to express their views on the local school system (Noble, 1986).

2)   Researchers will learn new skills: skills of interviewing and skills of planning, conducting, analyzing, and reporting research. Needs assessment is an educative process.

3)   The results themselves will contain surprises. This is, in fact, the best reason for conducting any research, which would be largely redundant if results were predictable.

4)   The processes of surveying community opinion may also identify individuals who are competent and willing to become involved in the projected program as volunteers (Becker et al., 1989).

5)   Because the process is, in part, political in nature, the curriculum planners can now proceed with greater confidence, being reasonably confident that their work will not be disregarded on completion.

6)   Involvement in needs assessment reflects and builds commitment to the process of curriculum change. In an empirical study of school improvement in New York City, Clark and McCarthy (1983) found that the reaction of a school to a needs assessment was one of the clearest indicators of its readiness to continue with the improvement process.

7)   At the end of the exercise, the organizers have a new sense of confidence in the curriculum work on which they are embarking. They have a good grasp of public and professional opinion and know the areas in which they can count on strong support. They feel that the curriculum to be developed will reflect student need more surely than if based merely on their own subjective judgment.

FEASIBILITY ANALYSIS

Feasibility analysis involves ensuring that the task to be undertaken can be successfully completed. This is essentially a matter of weighing resources against constraints. Constraints are factors such as amount of time and money available, teacher and student competence, facilities, community opinion, official curriculum policy, external examinations, and so on (Sosniak, 1991). Constraints are typically difficult to change.

Resources are those capabilities that can be used to achieve intentions. They tend to fall into the same categories as constraints: time, money, personnel, political support, and so on. The needs assessment should have indicated whether or not there is the necessary political support to proceed. The curriculum developers need to ascertain at this point that there are sufficient competent people to develop the curriculum and subsequently to implement it; or, alternatively, that in-service training can be satisfactorily delivered to generate the necessary competence. The necessity of conducting a feasibility analysis looks perfectly obvious. That it is not is shown by the high proportion of new curricula that never leave the drawing board.

ORGANIZING FOR CURRICULUM DEVELOPMENT

By this point the curriculum developer or developers, if not already exhausted, are ready to begin the work of curriculum development. But before the journey begins, a word about planning the trip. For the individual teacher, planning for his or her own classes, this is straightforward. At and above the school level, it is usual to form a curriculum committee. If this seems desirable, it is best to establish the committee early enough that it can be involved in planning and conducting the needs assessment. There is some evidence that seven is the maximum number of people who can work together effectively as a productive team. Whatever the number, the curriculum team should contain all of the critical expertise needed for the task. This includes expertise in the curriculum subject, in curriculum planning, in pedagogy, and in measurement and evaluation. Skill in writing, political acumen, and leadership and membership skills are also important assets on a committee.

For political reasons it may be necessary to include on the curriculum committee some of the same stakeholders surveyed in the needs assessment, such as representatives from the university community, teachers' professional associations, and the state or district Department of Education. However, representativeness is sometimes counterproductive in the formation of action-oriented committees. It is often preferable to form a separate advisory committee for this purpose. A good Advisory or Curriculum Development Committee, that has the confidence of the community and is able to develop cohesion and consensus among its own members, is the best defense against community criticism of new curricula (Lohrmann, 1988).

Curriculum planning is not a task that can be easily carried out in people's spare time. Nor is it a task that should take years and millions of dollars. Curriculum planning teams require some basic resources, including time, funds, access to good advice, and access to the decision makers in the system. If these resources cannot be provided, then Marilyn Winters (1992) suggests that it is better just to give teachers good textbooks and in-service education in how to use them.

Before it begins work on constructing a new curriculum, a curriculum committee needs to review its resources, organize its budget, plan liaison activities with gatekeepers and future users, allocate tasks, set deadlines by which phases of the project will be completed, and plan for the most effective use of its time. We are now ready to begin developing a curriculum.

▪ SELF – ASSESSMENT

1. Which of the following steps should curriculum planners take first?

   A   specify the objectives of the curriculum
   B   determine government curriculum policy
   C   develop a strategy to meet people's needs
   D   attempt to analyze and predict people's needs

2. What is a characteristic of a properly conducted needs assessment?

   A   it shows respect for the viewpoint of the clients
   B   it allows the public to determine school curricula
   C   it takes at least five years and costs at least $500,000
   D   it can be conducted only at the state or national level

3. Which of the following definitions of "need" is used in this chapter?

   A   a gap between a present and a preferred state
   B   anything wanted or desired by an individual
   C   the gap between objectives and test results
   D   an empirical and objective determination of the ideal state of an organism

4. Needs assessment seeks the opinions of three main groups. What are they?

   A   students, parents, and teachers
   B   specialists, clients, and gatekeepers
   C   specialists in the school, the workforce, and the government
   D   people in favor of, opposed to, and neutral about the innovation

5. In the past, which group has typically been allowed the least direct participation in planning curriculum change?

   A   the clients
   B   the teachers
   C   central office personnel
   D   elected educational officials

6. What method for gathering public opinion best combines a reasonable degree of validity and efficiency?

   A   public hearings
   B   telephone interviews
   C   face-to-face interviews
   D   mail-out questionnaires

7. What advantage do mail-out questionnaires have over personal interviews?

   A   they are more valid
   B   they are faster and cheaper
   C   they are less likely to be misinterpreted
   D   it is easier to obtain a satisfactory return rate

8. What democratic principle is reflected in needs assessment?

   A   one person, one vote
   B   no taxation without representation
   C   curriculum issues should be decided by public referendum
   D   those affected by decisions should have the right and the opportunity to make input into those decisions

9. When beginning their work, how should curriculum planners view questions of implementation?

   A   consider questions of implementation from the beginning
   B   obtain approval to implement the new curriculum before it is developed
   C   first develop an excellent curriculum, then work out the best way to implement it
   D   have curriculum specialists develop the curriculum and administrators deal with questions of implementation

10. What is feasibility analysis?

   A   another name for needs assessment
   B   a review of curricula similar to that being planned
   C   formulation of a budget for curriculum development
   D   a process in which resources are weighed against constraints

For answers, see Appendix F.
If you answered nine or ten correctly, you understand the material in this chapter.
If you answered seven or eight correctly, reread the relevant sections of the chapter.
If you answered six or less correctly, reread the chapter carefully.

CHAPTER 3

Articulating
Curriculum Intentions

**Trust the true voice of feeling and it
will create its own vocabulary.**

Sylvia Ashton-Warner (1979, p.354)

Summary

There is no fixed sequence for planning the elements of curriculum. But at some
point planners need to clarify the intentions they hold for student learning. An
overall aim expresses the essential purpose of the curriculum. The curriculum rationale justifies the commitment of resources to the pursuit of this aim. Objectives
are more specific statements that guide actual instructional decisions. Educators
range from those who prefer to express objectives in terms of outcomes to those
preferring to express them as experiences. Six main types of objective are knowledges, skills, somatic objectives, attitudes, process objectives, and experiences. Objectives are best articulated as states rather than as behaviors. An important step
for planners is to identify priorities among objectives.

6 types

WEAVING CURRICULUM

The process of developing a curriculum is not linear. It is not a matter of moving from one phase to the next in strict sequence. It is not so much like bricklaying as like weaving; it is less a technology than an art. It is a task for poets rather than bureaucrats. In designing a curriculum, we typically need to shuttle back and forth from one activity to another, creating, correcting, embellishing, adjusting. This chapter is about writing curriculum aims and objectives. There is a certain logic in embarking on this process early in curriculum development, but I am not convinced that it is essential to do so. Studies of teachers show that in their daily work they rarely think consciously about aims or objectives. They tend to think much more in terms of planning instructional activities and organizing instructional materials (Brown, 1988; Bullough, 1987). In planning a curriculum, it seems reasonable that one might begin with favorite instructional activities and then ask questions about the intentions that underlie them. Or one might begin the process of development with specific teaching materials, as many literature teachers do when they focus on *Romeo and Juliet* or *To Kill a Mockingbird* as the core of their curriculum, for example.

So it is partly for reasons of convenience that we are addressing the issue of curriculum intentions at this point. But while its location in the development sequence may be varied, the importance of articulating intentions needs to be emphasized. I am using the word "intentions" at this point to delay introducing terms like "goals" and "objectives." A misbegotten movement in the 1960s, known as "behavioral objectives," resulted in widespread suspicion among teachers of any discussion of objectives and in the corruption of the term itself.

THE BENEFITS OF CLARITY

When President Kennedy launched the Apollo program in 1961, he summarized the "mission definition" in a single sentence: "This nation should commit itself to achieving a goal, before this decade is out, of landing a man on the moon and returning him safely to the earth." It seems to be a sign of institutional health when an institution can agree on a clear, succinct statement of mission or vision. One Minnesota school is admirably concise: "We care, we share, we dare" (Barth, 1990b, p. 176). Conversely, a symptom of institutional sickness is confusion or division about the purposes of the institution. Effective principals are clear about the goals and priorities for their schools; effective school districts place emphasis on the statement and pursuit of clear curriculum goals (Coleman & LaRocque, 1990; Murphy & Hallinger, 1988).

The process of curriculum planning is a process of clarification and articulation of meaning and significance. It is characteristic of human beings that they are conscious of purpose. People manifest immediate purpose in their actions and seek transcendent purpose, or meaning, in their lives. Actions can be understood or justified only in terms of their purposes or goals. As the philosopher Abraham Kaplan said, "Acts that are not in some sense goal directed are precisely those, it seems to me, that are designated as meaningless" (1964, p. 363). Zigmunt Bauman makes a similar point: "Men and women do what they do on purpose. . . . To understand a human act, therefore, [is] to grasp the meaning with which the actor's intention invested it" (1978, p. 12).

In curriculum planning, there is a discipline that develops and is imposed by forcing oneself to state clearly intentions that one at first grasps only vaguely. There are risks in this activity, risks of trivialization on the one hand and verbosity on the other, but there are greater risks—of confusion and ineffectiveness—when we fail to articulate our intentions. The process of articulating curriculum intentions is a learning process, sometimes a frustrating one. Often it will take many drafts and much discussion before a satisfactory statement emerges.

Business and industry discovered the necessity decades ago of clearly stated intentions (Bryan & Locke, 1967, Hamner, 1974). Peter Drucker was explicit:

> It is not possible to manage . . . unless one first has a goal. It is not even possible to design the structure of an organization unless one knows what it is supposed to be doing and how to measure whether it is doing it. (Drucker, 1969, pp. 190)

Industrial psychologists concluded that a clear goal, understood and accepted by employees, was more effective than any other incentive (Steers & Porter, 1974). One of the keys is clarity. The other is acceptance. If there is no commitment to the goal, it remains an empty formula (Latham & Yukl, 1975). As Peters and Waterman put it, "People must believe that a task is inherently worthwhile if they are really to be committed to it" (1982, p. 72). Two decades earlier, the famous psychiatrist and writer Frantz Fanon (from an ideological stance as different as it is possible to imagine from that of American corporate management) said something similar:

> The time taken up by explaining, the time "lost" in treating the worker as a human being, will be caught up in the execution of the plan. People must know where they are going, and why. The success of the struggle presupposes clear objectives. . . . Neither stubborn courage nor fine slogans are enough. (Fanon, 1965, pp. 108, 154)

Clarity of intent appears to be equally important in the classroom. Frances Klein, in her study of effective and ineffective elementary schools, found that children in the effective schools tended to agree with the statement, "Our teacher tells us ahead of time what we are going to be learning about." The students in the ineffective schools, on the other hand, agreed that "Many students don't know what they're supposed to be doing during class" (1989, p. 148). A summary of the research evidence indicates that advising students of the objectives of instruction raises their achievement significantly (about 0.30 of a standard deviation, the equivalent of raising a student's performance from the fiftieth to the sixty-fifth percentile) (Cohen, 1987; Kulik & Kulik, 1989).

But clarity alone is insufficient. More important is that goals are recognized as worthwhile by participants, and as attainable by them. If either of these factors is missing, no investment of effort can be expected (Feather, 1982; Meece, Blumenfeld, & Hoyle, 1988). The importance of goal acceptance takes us back to the significance of clarity about student needs. It is unlikely that students will commit themselves to an instructional goal if they do not think it addresses any of their significant needs. There are two ways to enhance the match between curriculum and learner needs. One is to negotiate the intentions of a curriculum with the learners. How this might be done in practice is described through a number of case studies in a book entitled *Negotiating the Curriculum* by the Australian educator Garth Boomer (1982). There is much to recommend the process of discussion with learners about their interests and priorities. But while each learner and each classroom is unique, if the needs assessment has been thorough and thoughtful, the judgments of students will already have been canvassed by this stage. And that will include not only present students, but also graduates, dropouts, and other constituencies.

The process of defining curriculum intentions is not simple. We are asking basic questions about what we consider desirable for a generation, and hence for the future of our society. We must look with suspicion on any statement arrived at without controversy and debate. The individual teacher planning curriculum for his or her own classes must struggle with basic questions at this point, questions of what is worthwhile? what is significant? what is enduring? what is urgent? As soon as more than one planner is involved, we enter the world of educational politics, where stable decisions can be achieved only through much discussion, negotiation, and compromise. The outcome should be goals that can command wide support and that are persuasive to students. In his study of 10,000 classrooms, John Goodlad found that this was the exception rather than the rule:

> In general, our observers had grave difficulty gathering evidence regarding what teachers were endeavoring to accomplish in the classroom apart from coverage of topics selected largely from courses of study and textbooks. If there were central concepts or children's needs and interests guiding the selection of specific learning activities, they escaped our attention.   (Goodlad, 1974, p. 78)

Even when asked, it is my experience, and that of others (Gross, Giacquinta, & Bernstein, 1971), that teachers often cannot identify the essential purpose of the curriculum they are teaching. This literal "aimlessness" cannot bode well for the learning experienced by students. Just as significantly, it deprives teachers of leadership and autonomy, leaving the task of goal definition to the makers of textbooks, standardized tests, and official curricula.

> Where the educational experience offered to pupils is unsatisfactory, the problem may lie, not simply in clumsy or unskilled performance, but in the lack of any sense of what the point is in teaching a particular lesson, a particular subject, or, indeed, in the educational enterprise as a whole.
>
> Colin Wringe (1988, p. 4)

CURRICULUM AIMS

I shall use two terms in describing curriculum intentions: *aims* and *objectives*. An *aim* may be defined as "a general statement of intent for a curriculum," and *objectives* as "specific intents derived from the aim."

Many curricula contain a large number of aims, or perhaps a lengthy paragraph discussing aims. It is my experience working with many hundreds of teachers developing curricula that there are few disciplines more beneficial than being required to state the intention of a curriculum in a single sentence. This is particularly so when a team of developers collaborates in the exercise of drafting and redrafting, reflecting, paraphrasing, expanding, condensing, polishing, and elaborating an aim. This is not a technical task, but a literate and philosophical endeavor. It sets the stage for the kind of rigor and reflection that takes place throughout the development of a curriculum.

The curriculum aim is typically placed at the beginning of a curriculum, and it will influence the reader's feelings about the curriculum as a whole. (I recall once seeing, behind the counter at McDonald's, a reminder to staff: "You never get a second chance to make a first impression.") Three criteria will assist in the writing of a good curriculum aim: it should be *significant*, it should be *clear*, and it should be *concise*. Of these three criteria, the most important is significance.

If the purpose of a curriculum is not significant, no amount of technical expertise or quality can make that curriculum anything but a waste of time. The worth of a curriculum, expressed in its aim, must be apparent to everyone, including students. We are not speaking here of narrow relevance, but of basic *meaningfulness*. Meaningfulness does not apply only to learning for which students can find immediate practical utility. As Kieran Egan points out, it can also be interpreted in terms of its relation to students' imaginative lives (Egan, 1991). Children and adolescents are passionately interested, says Egan, in the mythic, the legendary, the heroic, the transcendent, and the romantic. Curriculum that is concerned with the growth of students as whole persons needs to pay as much attention to these dimensions as to the practical, vocational, and utilitarian aspects of learning.

A curriculum aim is *clear* if it can be understood by its readers, including students, without further explanation. As Ludwig Wittgenstein said, "Everything that can be thought can be thought clearly. Everything that can be put into words

---

Curriculum aims

The instrumental music program of the Elmira City School District endeavors to provide every child with the opportunity to experience musical growth through the acquisition of specific knowledge, skills, and attitudes that will contribute to lifelong enjoyment of music. (Elmira City School District, *Instrumental Music Program*, 1987, p. 3)

The purpose of Social Studies is to prepare students to become humane, rational, knowledgeable and participating citizens in a diverse society and in an increasingly interdependent world. (Phoenix Union High School District, *World History/Geography Curriculum Guide*, 1990, p. ii)

Geology 12 and Earth Science 11 are intended to provide secondary school students with the background and the desire to investigate their earth, its materials and its processes. (British Columbia: *Geology; 12*, 1976, p. 1)

The Kelso physical education program is designed to enhance students' self-image, to promote social growth, and to develop personal goal achievement for leisure and wellness. (Kelso Public Schools, *Physical Education Curriculum Guide*, 1990, p. 4)

To enable students to respond sensibly to the impact of law on daily life. (Nova Scotia, *Law in High School*, 1978, p. 1)

To create the environment necessary for students to become caring physicians, responsive to the needs of their patients and of contemporary society. (Queen's University Medical School, *Strategic Plan, 1991–1995*, p. 3)

I see *the facilitation of learning* as the *aim* of education. (Rogers, 1969, p. 104; his italics)

---

can be put clearly" (1961, p. 26). This means avoiding jargon, highly specialized terms, obfuscation, and verbosity in writing curriculum aims.

We could arbitrarily define an aim as *concise* if it states the basic intent of the curriculum in fifteen words or less. A curriculum aim that requires half a page suggests that the curriculum developers were not really clear about the aim. Curriculum guidelines often contain no single statement of the curriculum aim, but nine or so separate aims. Nine may be the most frequent number because it appears to be the average number of people on a curriculum development committee (Pratt, 1989). Reconciling competing conceptions of a curriculum aim in a development committee is a hard but crucial task.

Fragmentation is a real and present danger in curriculum. There is always too much material for teachers to cover, too many disparate elements for students to master. One function of the aim is to act as a kind of unifying theme and hence to enhance the conceptual integrity and structural unity of the curriculum. This means that the curriculum aim must be well enough thought out and articulated that it can provide a reference point for the objectives, content, resources, and other curriculum elements (Pratt & Short, in press).

Writing a curriculum is a process of articulating what we value. Peters and Waterman urge managers to:

> Figure out your value system. Decide what your company stands for. What does your enterprise do that gives everyone the most pride? Put yourself out ten or twenty years in the future: what would you look back on with greatest satisfaction? (Peters and Waterman, 1982, p. 279)

Peter Block makes a similar proposal in his book, *The Empowered Manager:*

> The core of the bureaucratic mind-set is not to take responsibility for what is happening. . . . Autonomy is the attitude that my actions are my own choices and the organization I am a part of is in many ways my own creation. . . . Creating a vision forces us to take a stand for a preferred future. . . . Once we have created a vision and communicated it to the people around us, it becomes a benchmark for evaluating all of our actions.
>
> Pick an important project about which you care. . . . Ask why you care so much about the project. . . . Keep asking Why? until you hear statements that come from the heart. . . . The dialogue about vision should strive to achieve three qualities: depth, clarity, and responsibility. Depth is the degree to which the vision statement is personally held. Clarity comes from insisting on specific images. Vagueness is a way of not making a commitment to vision. Responsibility involves moving from helplessness to active ownership. (Block, 1987, pp. 6, 123)

THE CURRICULUM RATIONALE

Early in a curriculum document—and immediately following the aim is as good a place as any—the reader should be able to find the rationale for the curriculum. The final draft of a curriculum rationale cannot be written until the curriculum is completely developed and the developers know exactly what it is they are rationalizing. However, the work that has been done on needs and aims will make it possible for a draft to be written at this point.

The purpose of the curriculum rationale is not to restate the aim and say *what* the curriculum is intended to achieve, but to say *why* the aim is worth achieving. Any curriculum document is a proposal for the expenditure of resources. The primary resource consumed in education is people's time, and this resource is uniquely finite. We all have only a limited amount of time on this earth. I believe it was Blaise Pascal who said that life is a moment of time between two eternities. To use up students' time is to use up part of their lives. It is never enough to argue that the need for a curriculum is "perfectly obvious." Yesterday's perfectly obvious truth has a way of finding itself in today's shredder. Herbert Kliebard outlines the importance of justification of curriculum choices:

> Curriculum development includes justifications for why certain things should be studied in school rather than others. Despite, possibly, a naive assumption that we take the subjects of study for granted and that curriculum planning merely involves finding ways to teach these subjects effectively, the curriculum developer must constantly assume a critical posture on what is taught and must examine the assumptions, implicit and explicit, that underlie including these studies in the school curriculum. . . . The questions that are central to the curriculum field . . . are all value questions. Curriculum development requires sophistication, judgment, and intelligence and only secondarily technical skill.
> (Kliebard, 1989, pp. 4–5)

It is an aspect of treating our clients with respect to tell them, and others, exactly why this particular curriculum is worthwhile—how it contributes to their present and future well-being. This involves articulating the principles on which it is based and the needs it is intended to meet. If a needs assessment has been conducted, its results can be referred to in the rationale.

Rationale: Driver and traffic safety education

Most people drive a vehicle. Driving is a task that requires considerable skill and involves decision-making. The primary consideration of this course is to provide students with the skills and attitudes that will make them safe drivers. The saving of life and limb and the reduction of accident rates in our streets and highways is a worthy objective. At a time when automotive registrations are increasing each year, and with them the number of drivers on the road, the risk of accidents also increases. This alone establishes a need for a course which will equip our young people to meet the challenge that faces them when they drive a motor vehicle.

Alberta Education (1978, p. 69)

The rationale is essentially a brief essay that endeavors to persuade the reader of the significance and importance of the curriculum. It should be eloquent, but exaggeration should be avoided, as should unnecessary diffidence. The rationale should be written for an audience that includes unmotivated students and skeptical parents as well as sympathetic colleagues (Pratt, 1991a).

Although the need for a good rationale may seem fairly obvious, not every teacher can readily frame a sound and articulate argument supporting his or her teaching. The chair of a high school mathematics department once asserted matter-of-factly to George Posner that "everybody knows that the only reason to take math is to prepare you to take more math" (Posner, 1992, p. 2). All too often, the first attempts of teachers to justify what they teach rely heavily on clichés, slogans, platitudes, unsupported assertions, and circular arguments (Pratt, 1983a). It is greatly beneficial for teachers to work out the justification for what they teach. But they do not have to do this alone. The professional literature can be of considerable assistance. In the area of mathematics, for example, a number of recent national reports by leading mathematicians and mathematics educators provide compelling rationales for the teaching and learning of mathematics in schools (American Association for the Advancement of Science, 1989; National Council of Teachers of Mathematics, 1989a, 1989b; National Research Council, 1989; National Research Council, Mathematical Sciences Education Board, 1990).

■ Definitions ■

The rationale is a suitable point in the curriculum document to define any specialized terms. A curriculum in dental hygiene, for example, would probably need to define such terms as *acarious, adentulous, dental caries, dentulous, gingivitis, periodontal disease,* and *plaque*. A curriculum on light, or optics, might define such terms as *angle of emergence, angle of reflection, diffuse reflection, incident ray, principal axis, refraction,* and *vertex*. The Philadelphia School District's Science Grade 3 Curriculum (1989) contains a "third grade science vocabulary list" that defines, for teachers and pupils, such words as *food chain, habitat, life cycle,* and *population*. The

term *total health* is used in the Wisconsin Department of Public Instruction's Guide to Curriculum Planning in Health Education and is defined early in the document:

> *Total health* refers to the lifelong interdependence, constant interaction, and balance of the physical, emotional, social, and intellectual dimensions of human growth and development.   (Wisconsin Department of Public Instruction, 1985, p. xii)

CURRICULUM OBJECTIVES

The curriculum aim provides a sense of purpose and direction at a general level. At some point, this general intention must be stated in terms of intentions specific enough to guide instructional decisions. In employment training, this process often involves job description and task analysis, systematic methods for describing and detailing the operations involved in particular occupational performance. In most educational situations, the analytical process of breaking an aim down into its component parts requires creativity and imagination. Suppose

---

School Improvement in Pittsburgh

Here's how it works: we pull together a group of teachers—English, math, science, and so forth—and we ask them to tell us the 20 most important learning outcomes in their academic disciplines at each grade level. We ask for 20—not 220—because I've learned over the years that teachers can manage effectively only about 20 objectives a year, give or take a few. Once we have achieved reasonable consensus among that group, we ask all the other teachers whether or not they agree with their colleagues that these are the most important learning outcomes in math or whatever, so we involve everybody. . . . When we have consensus on what the most important learning outcomes are, we dismiss that group and convene another group. We say to them, "Your colleagues say these are the most important learning outcomes. Your job is to develop what you're willing to accept as evidence that these outcomes have been achieved. . . . Then we dismiss that group and call in another group of teachers and say, "Okay, your colleagues say that these are the outcomes, these are the measures; now you take a look at the instructional materials you have and tell us whether these materials are adequate to the task that's been laid out. If not, we want you to find materials that will help teachers teach to these objectives. . . . This, by the way, reflects a very strong bias of mine: you figure out what your goals ought to be, you move immediately to criterion outcomes, and then you look at how you get from here to there. Eventually our syllabus-driven examination system will be the way we judge how well our kids are being educated.

Richard Wallace, Superintendent, Pittsburgh Public Schools (Brandt, 1987, p. 42)

we have written as an aim, "The student will appreciate theater as an art form." We now need to ask, What does this mean? What understandings will we have to develop in learners? What skills? What values? If we accomplish all of these specifics, will the aim have been achieved? If not, what else is implied? What have we missed? What other educational opportunities does this aim present? In this way, we arrive at a list of objectives that collectively comprehend the meanings implied by the aim.

As a general rule, objectives should be written in conceptual terms, as capabilities or states of mind—states of skill, knowledge, attitude, and so on—rather than in terms of actions, behaviors, learning activities, or test items. Confusion on this point led to the long and pointless "behavioral objectives" debate a few decades ago, discussed in more detail below.

The box on page 76 shows the objectives derived from the aim, "Students will be able to use the telephone efficiently and courteously." This might be used as a unit in a course in Grade 4 Communications, or as part of a program for recent immigrants, or within a foreign-language program. Note that some of the objectives are quite broad. If we were to "unpack" the objective, for example, "Students will be able to use telephone directories efficiently," we would find that the "teaching points" would include at least the following:

use the white, yellow, and blue pages

be able to use "800" directories

be able to find area codes

be able to follow the instructions for international calls

be able to calculate time differences between time zones

To write each of these as a separate objective would result in scores of objectives for the curriculum, which would be counterproductive. Purposes at that level of detail are better treated as "teaching points" and outlined at the instructional stage. Note also that some necessary knowledges and skills are not included as objectives because they would be treated as prerequisites. These would include such skills as alphabetization, ability to read a map (for area codes or time zones), recognition of a phone, how to hold the receiver, and so on. The determination of prerequisites is discussed in Chapter 5.

A useful principle in writing curriculum objectives (and aims) is: *Aim for maximum transfer*. For instance, a teacher of literature might write as an objective, "Students will be able to identify the subplot of *The Merchant of Venice*." While this objective is not without value, there is not much point in teaching students to identify the subplot in one work of literature unless this capability has some subsequent and permanent value for them. A more significant objective is, "Students will be able to identify subplots in works of literature." This difference in wording of the objective will make a difference in the nature of the curriculum. In the first case, the teacher is likely only to focus on teaching the subplot of the one play,

─────────── **Using the Telephone** ───────────

Aim: Students will be able to use the telephone efficiently and courteously.

∎ Objectives ∎

Knowledge

1. Students will know the approximate costs of telephone use and ways to minimize costs. (Important)

Skills

2. Students will be able to use telephone directories. (Critical)

3. Students will be able to make operator-assisted calls. (Critical)

4. Students will be able to make local and long-distance direct dialing calls. (Critical)

5. Students will be able to deal with harassing calls. (Important)

6. Students will be able to make calls from a pay phone. (Critical)

7. Students will be able to make emergency calls. (Critical)

Attitudes

8. Students will develop courteous telephone habits. (Important)

9. Students will develop confidence in their ability to use the telephone. (Important)

Process

10. Students will each make three supervised "live" telephone calls. (Important)

Experience

11. Students will visit a telephone exchange. (Important)

essentially as an item of knowledge; in the latter case, the teacher is more likely to have students practice identifying subplots in a number of works, in order to facilitate generalization and transfer of the skill. Although there is debate among scholars about the extent to which transfer of learning can be taught, examples such as this suggest the truth of the position of Clark and Voogel (1985) that transferability of learning is often more important than mastery of knowledge.

As the process of identifying objectives proceeds, curriculum developers often discover that the aim itself is inadequate. Objectives may surface that are important, but not comprehended in the original aim. In this way, a dialogue between the aim and the objectives takes place, with both being subject to revision.

> The fear of many educators that the detailed specification of objectives forces us to work with only simple behaviors which can be forced into measurable and observable terms is, indeed, an incorrect notion. The situation rather is, that if we do not attempt to specify the complex processes we want to see in the student, then we are in danger of omitting them and following the path of least effort toward teaching more easily observable and trivial behavior.
>
> Robert Glaser (1967, p. 2)

▪ Outcomes versus Experiences ▪

The curriculum field, as befits any discipline that is either youthful or vigorous, is fractured by many disputes. One of these concerns the nature and place of objectives, in general, and whether they should identify outcomes or experiences. Some educators want to write only objectives that refer to outcomes. For example:

■ *Given a hand calculator and ten 5-digit subtraction problems, the student will correctly solve at least 9 problems in 2 minutes.*

This might be called a *preordinate* approach—that is, one in which the objectives to be achieved are identified before instruction begins. This was the position advocated by Ralph Tyler, who wrote in his famous handbook, *Basic Principles of Curriculum and Instruction* (1949): "We are devoting much time to the setting up and formulation of objectives because they are the most critical criteria for guiding all the other activities of the curriculum-maker" (1949, p. 62). Other curriculum thinkers, especially but by no means exclusively those working with pupils and teachers at the early elementary level, advocate a *nonpreordinate* approach, in which we provide rich experiences for the learners, but do not try to dictate in advance what particular outcomes should result. These educators prefer objectives that refer primarily to learner experiences. For instance:

■ *The learner will experiment in the production of sound with many different kinds of material.*

Clearly this aim implies an intention, having to do with sound or music, but the possible specific outcomes are quite open-ended. This kind of intention is discussed more fully in the section on "process objectives."

The position an educator takes on issues of curriculum intentions has roots that are philosophically profound. Western traditions tend to emphasize the importance of taking responsibility for the outcomes of our actions. Eastern philosophies, on the other hand, prefer that we perform all actions with full awareness and attention, but without attachment to particular outcomes.

Table 3-1   *A Continuum of Approaches to Objectives*

Preordinate end of the continuum		Nonpreordinate end of the continuum
Educators preferring to state objectives as outcomes only	Educators including as objectives both outcomes and experiences	Educators preferring to state objectives as experiences only

Debate on this issue has often become divisive, with inappropriate amounts of understanding and dismissal on each side. Models of curriculum have been developed that exclude one or the other school of thought. Curriculum models, however, are of limited usefulness if they exclude large numbers of educators. I prefer a different approach, a pluralistic approach that welcomes diversity and sees not a dichotomy but a continuum, a model generous and spacious enough to accommodate diverse orientations.

▪ Types of Objectives ▪

Ever since Benjamin Bloom and his colleagues published *The Taxonomy of Educational Objectives: The Cognitive Domain* (Bloom, Engelhart, Furst, Hill, & Krathwohl, 1956), it has been customary for curriculum designers to identify their objectives by type—for example, as knowledge, skill, or attitude objectives—and often by level of complexity as well. Bloom et al. identified three domains: cognitive, affective, and psychomotor. Within the cognitive domain, they distinguished among knowledge, comprehension, application, analysis, synthesis, and evaluation. Robert Gagné (1977) developed a taxonomy of cognitive activity consisting of the categories information, concrete concepts, defined concepts, principles, problem solving, and cognitive strategies. Many other taxonomies exist (De Landsheere, 1991).

The types of objective we consider important will reflect those aspects of human experience that we value. We shall use here a classification that attempts to reflect the importance in human life of *knowing, thinking, acting, feeling, growing, experiencing,* and *being.* The pedagogical purpose of classifying objectives is to indicate to teachers the different objectives requiring different instructional approaches. To take a straightforward example: An objective that is primarily knowledge implies presentation methods of teaching; an objective that is primarily skill requires practice by the learner. Modes of assessment will also vary with different kinds of objective. A written test will usually serve to assess achievement of knowledge objectives; it is rarely an effective means of assessing change in attitudes. In classifying objectives, therefore, we are writing reminders to the user regarding appropriate modes of instruction and evaluation. Table 3-2 summarizes the types of objective used in this discussion.

Table 3-2   *A Typology of Curriculum Objectives*

Knowledge

Description: Knowing, remembering, understanding, or comprehending something.

Example: Students will understand the nature of the cell.

Skill

Description: The capacity to perform some mental or physical operation.

Example: Students will be able to read music.

Somatic ‒ cellular Physical Ed.

Description: A bodily, physiological, cellular change in a person.

Example: Students will develop healthy teeth.

Attitude

Description: A predisposition or orientation with positive or negative effect.

Example: Students will develop increased confidence in their mathematical ability.

Process

Description: An instructional activity considered educative but without predetermined outcomes.

Example: Students will write and read a story to their Grade 1 reading partners.

Experience

Description: An intrinsically valuable, meaningful, significant, memorable experience.

Example: Students will take part in a live theater production.

Knowledge objectives

Knowledge is the basis of almost all human learning, and almost all curricula include some knowledge objectives. I am referring here to what philosophers call "knowledge that," or "propositional knowledge," not "knowledge how to," or skill (Ryle, 1949). Low-level knowledge, simple "facts" and information, is quite easy to teach and to test. Much knowledge can be taught merely by presenting it in oral or written form, and it can be tested by asking learners to reproduce it in writing. Unfortunately, in many classrooms, many textbooks, and many examinations, rather low-level knowledge, in the sense of trivial information, is almost the sole focus. One study found that of 60,000 questions asked in school textbooks, 96 percent concerned low-level information (United States Department of Education,

1987). Research in elementary schools in England showed that over a three-year period of observation, teachers devoted only 1 percent of classroom time to questions requiring problem solving (Mortimore, Sammon, Stoll, Lewis, & Ecob, 1988). And Francis Klein's analysis of 269 state and district curriculum guides showed that their objectives were "very traditional, subject-based, and exclusively cognitive" (1989, p. 28). Such an approach has the support of some eminent authorities, including the former British Prime Minister, Mrs. Thatcher, who in a parliamentary debate on a proposed revision of the history curriculum in English schools, proclaimed it to be "absolutely right" to return to a system of learning by heart dates and lists of kings and queens (Kettle, 1990, p. 21). Knowledge, we might say, is a necessary foundation of all learning, but if we do not build on it, we are going to spend our lives living in an intellectual basement.

Knowledge by itself is insufficient, but it is necessary. Knowledge is power, and ignorance is powerlessness, more so than ever in the information age. Those who prescribe the knowledge to be taught in the curriculum exercise power over a generation. For knowledge does not remain inert and external to the knower; when internalized, it shapes our personality and our perception of the world.

Writing curriculum requires careful use of language, and nowhere more so than in writing objectives. Consider the difference between: "Pupils will *know* the process of photosynthesis" and "Students will *understand* the process of photosynthesis." The first statement appears to encourage role learning of certain verbal formulas. The second clearly calls for a more sophisticated comprehension. As compared with the word "know," which is often interpreted as merely ability to recall, the word "understand" "involves apprehending the meaning or significance of what is known" (Ackoff & Emery, 1972, p. 46). Note that we do not say, "The student will *describe* the process of photosynthesis." We may well ask the student to describe it at some point, but this is only in order to find out whether he or she understands it. The understanding is what we are really interested in; description has to do with assessing the understanding, which is a separate, and later, step.

At a more subtle level, compare "Students will *understand that* green plants produce food by photosynthesis" with "Students will *understand how* green plants produce food by photosynthesis." The first is a single proposition that could be memorized; the second implies an understanding of a complex process and its internal relationships. As with the writing of aims, the process of writing objectives is an arduous but healthy process of clarifying one's thinking and intentions.

Here is a final example from a science curriculum:

> *At the completion of this unit the student should be able to . . . define the terms atom, proton, neutron, electron, ion, isotope, atomic number, atomic mass, and molecule.* (Dennis-Yarmouth Regional School District, *Introductory Science*, 1986, p. 4)

There are three problems with this objective: (1) Students will tend to study and learn in the way they think will be rewarded. This objective suggests that students will be rewarded for memorizing the definitions of nine terms in physics. In fact, we are hardly ever interested in students merely memorizing definitions; almost always, what we want is for students to understand concepts. (2) The phrase "be able to define" suggests a skill in defining, but in fact this is not a skill, but a knowledge objective. (3) The objective prevents the developers or teachers from adding additional terms that may be found significant during instruction. All of these defects could be easily corrected by changing the objective to:

> The student will understand some basic concepts in physics, such as atom, proton, neutron, electron, ion, isotope, atomic number, atomic mass, and molecule.

Skill objectives

Unlike knowledge, skills cannot be taught only by presentation methods, for they have requirements for speed, coordination, and integration that can be developed only by practice. For curriculum purposes, the requirement for practice is the mark that distinguishes knowledge from skill. This is true of intellectual skills like "The student will be able to solve simple equations." It is also true of motor skills like "The student will be able to swim," and of sensory skills like wine-tasting. The term "be able to," which has the meaning of "have the skill to," is appropriate for all skills objectives and is best used only for skills objectives.

The development of skills in learners can be seen as a process of empowerment. Any literate individual who lives close enough to a medical school can learn how to use MEDLINE and the Index Medicus. Using these databases, a few hours of research will quickly give her or him more information about a particular health condition than is possessed by most general practitioners. Most parents, similarly, could learn how to use the ERIC database of educational research. In this way, the disempowerment that patients and parents experience in the presence of professional expertise can be replaced by a sense of confidence and responsibility. Tom Peters reports on the success of the Pacific Presbyterian Medical Center in San Francisco, which encourages its patients to read their medical records, to learn how to use the medical library, and to research their own condition and the drugs they are taking (1988).

When we have a new skill, new choices are available to us, and this expansion of human choice is the ultimate purpose of education. The importance of clearly identifying skills in a curriculum is to help persuade teachers to go beyond the presentation of knowledge, and to prompt them that practice will be necessary for this part of the curriculum. People like myself, who teach in schools of education, are persistent offenders in this regard whenever we delude ourselves into believing that we can develop pedagogical skills by lecturing to students.

Somatic objectives

A word needs to be said at this point on behalf of a rather unusual and much-neglected educational area: physical development. A somatic objective (from the

---

Some objectives from the Grade 11 Biology Curriculum

The pupils should know:

> the definition of the concepts of the biosphere, anabolism, catabolism, and photosynthesis;
>
> substance circulation and energy flow in the biosphere;
>
> the role of basic inorganic substances in the cell;
>
> the principle of DNA replication;
>
> the chromosome theory of heredity;
>
> the need to protect the natural environment against mutagenic pollution;
>
> the deleterious effect of alcohol consumption and smoking upon human heredity.

The pupils should be able to:

> apply various methods of plant propagation;
>
> use a microscope; prepare and examine microscope slides;
>
> conduct rudimentary cytological and genetic experiments;
>
> ascertain the basic components of a cell;
>
> work independently with all the components of the textbook; compile outlines and reviews of popular science articles; prepare and deliver briefings.

Chief Directorate of Schools, USSR (1987, pp. 58–60).

Greek *soma*, "the body") is an objective by which we are interested in changing not the student's mind, but his or her body. Examples would be:

> *To increase the flexibility of the lumbar spine.*
>
> *Students will develop improved cardiovascular fitness.*
>
> *An objective of the dental hygiene unit of the Grade 8 Health Program is to have students develop healthy teeth and gums.*

Typically, this kind of objective is pursued by weight-reduction clinics, spas, and gyms. The amount of money that people spend on diets, health club memberships, and universal gyms, let alone on the entire medical system, should be a clue to educators that this area is important.

Most Western educational systems have fallen into the trap (set, some philosophers would say, by Platonic dualism) of treating students as disembodied minds. Certainly when we read official curricula, they are highly "mentalistic"— they deal only with cognitions, as though students were people without aesthetic senses, friends, genders, souls, or bodies. But in fact what happens to our bodies is of fairly major concern to most of us:

> Our bodily dimension is integrally involved in most aspects of our existence—not least in the establishment of a meaningful relationship with the world around us. Taken from this viewpoint our body and its motility can be seen to have an equal claim for attention in education alongside our other attributes which give life its meaning. (Whitehead, 1990, p. 3)

A century from now, today's patterns of early schooling may be viewed as a particularly pernicious form of child abuse. We take young children, whose natural habitat is the open air, whose natural social context is the mixed-age play group, whose natural activity is almost constant locomotion; we place them inside sealed buildings, segregate them into one-year cohorts, squeeze them into ill-fitting furniture, and deprive them of fresh air, sunshine, and physical movement. Under these conditions, it is likely that children will be at their healthiest and fittest the day before they enter school. This state of affairs is unlikely to change until curriculum thinkers begin to give it their attention.

The first step is to recognize that the curriculum needs to include students' bodies as well as their minds within its legitimate responsibility. This is not likely to happen so long as systems of educational objectives exclude the somatic from their field of responsibility. For every curriculum, teachers need to ask: How can this curriculum enhance students' personal sense of meaning? How can it help students to develop as social beings? They might also ask, is there any way that this curriculum can help to protect and develop students' physical integrity?

Attitude objectives

Bruno Bettelheim put it in a nutshell: "Our hearts must know the world of reason, and reason must be guided by an informed heart" (1960, p. viii).

Schooling invariably contributes to the development of attitudes. Unfortunately, the attitudes developed in school are not always positive. Graduates and dropouts who claim to be "hopeless at languages" or "unable to do math," or even more generally, "not intelligent," are usually reflecting attitudes they have learned in school. Ninety percent of elementary school students believe that science will be valuable to them in the future, but only 75 percent of seventh graders, and only 20 percent of young adults, feel this way (Yager & Penick, 1986). But if negative attitudes can be developed in school, so can positive attitudes. They cannot, however, be taught (or measured) in the same way as knowledge and skills. This has been amply demonstrated by many generations of experience with the failure of the hectoring-and-lecturing approach to teaching attitudes. Innumerable are the failures of courses in nutrition education, smoking education, driver education, environmental education, and sex education, that despite inculcation of much relevant information, have proved ineffective in changing typical voluntary behavior. This is beginning to be realized among AIDS educators. Traditional cognitive programs have been found ineffective (Flora & Thoresen, 1988). David Ostrow, M.D., writes that "changing the voluntary interpersonal behaviors linked to the transmission of the HIV virus is the only 'cure' for AIDS" (1989, p. 229).

The same is true even in more "cognitive" areas. Orr and Flein comment on the inefficacy of conventional cognitively based programs in critical thinking. What is needed, they argue, is development of a "critical spirit":

> . . . the development of thoughtful people who habitually avoid capricious analyses of situations, who exhibit a questioning orientation in various domains of life, and who are willing to examine situations creatively and flexibly. . . . These traits must be present if the educational enterprise is to proceed, even minimally, not simply because they are morally admirable, but because their absence constitutes a corruption of teaching and learning. Schools have a responsibility to promote such traits. (Orr & Flein, 1991, p. 132)

'We're rather worried about William'

Educators of professionals also assert the importance of affective development. Recommendations adopted by the Council on Medical Education in 1982 included the following statement:

> If medicine recognizes that certain "dehumanizing" factors have an influence on the education of a physician, medical educators can ameliorate this influence by increasing the emphasis placed on personal qualities essential to the best practice of medicine. These include warmth and personal concern and, even more important, integrity in both academic and interpersonal relationships.   (Council on Medical Education, 1982, p. 3227)

Attitudes do not normally develop from the information people receive, but from the significant experiences they undergo. The following anecdote illustrates how attitudes and knowledge can be confused:

> In my first school administrative position in Ohio, I received a notice that two free trips to our national capital, Washington, D.C., would be awarded to the winners of a contest to be held state-wide on "The Harmful Effects of Alcohol and Narcotics." A 32-page pamphlet was furnished on the subject, which contained questions and answers to the questions that would be covered in a final test. I announced the competition to my 12th grade students and asked if any were interested in a free trip to Washington, D.C. Several responded that they were. I suggested that they memorize the answers to the questions given in the pamphlet. One young lady did just that, and made a perfect score in our school, at the county level, and at the state level; she went to Washington. She graduated at the end of the year, married, had children, and died before she was 30 years old —from alcoholism! She literally drank herself to death.   (Wood, 1990)

Attitudes have to do with people's feelings. Self-concept is an attitude toward oneself. Values are those things toward which we have a positive attitude. Habits are practices that attitudes have rendered consistent. When planning curriculum and day-to-day instruction, it is important that teachers ask such questions as: What feelings about themselves does this curriculum allow me to strengthen in these students? How can tomorrow's lesson be used to develop students' social relations and consciousness?

Careless use of language can lead to confusion in this area. "Students will appreciate the connection between deforestation and soil erosion" is not an attitude, but an understanding, and is better stated simply, "Students will understand the connection between deforestation and soil erosion." If we want to develop an attitude, we need to be explicit, for example, "Students will develop a personal commitment toward protection of the environment."

Because knowledge and values are inseparable in human action (though they may be separable for purposes of analysis and discussion), and because the educative process is a form of human action, it is clear that anyone who teaches addresses values. Sometimes the values taught are explicit, but more often they are implicit; sometimes moral deliberation is engaged intentionally and vigorously, other times morality is embodied in a kind of hidden curriculum. In either case, educators in both families and schools teach values. Sometimes they teach by precept and instruction; always they teach by example, personality, social context, and the life they create as educators or parents or, simply, persons. Thus the central question that emerges is: On what basis are the knowledge and values we deem worthwhile for students selected?

William Ayers and William H. Schubert (1989, p. 357)

Two of the attitudes that will be implicit in most curricula are *an interest in the subject being taught* and *a sense of confidence in one's abilities* in that area. Such objectives illustrate the interrelatedness of attitudes and learning. There is no point in developing misplaced confidence! American children are actually much more confident of their ability in mathematics than are Chinese or Japanese children, but this confidence is not based on higher attainment (Stevenson, Lee, & Stigler, 1986). We should work consciously to develop positive attitudes in students toward their own abilities and towards learning; but we should seek to place such attitudes on a firm foundation of significant attainment. The importance of stating such attitudes explicitly, in addition to making them available to public scrutiny and discussion, is that they are more likely to be achieved if teachers keep them consciously in view.

It is appropriate to approach attitude objectives with a lighter touch than knowledge and skills. The purpose is to give students maximum opportunity to develop the attitudes we value, without becoming too attached to particular attitudinal outcomes. If, after our best efforts, the student does not develop an interest in science or an enjoyment of history, then no one has really failed. We need to respect, rather than regret, informed student choice.

How, then, does Dewey achieve the transition from what we have called the morality of the task to the task of morality? His answer—original for his time and still largely disregarded—is to teach *all* subjects in such a way as to bring out and make focal their social and personal aspects, stressing how human beings are affected by them, pointing up the responsibilities that flow from the inter-relatedness.

Sidney Hook (Dewey, 1975, p. xi)

Process objectives

To believe that all of our purposes for an educational situation can be specified in advance is both dogmatic and restrictive. We all know in practice that as we engage in activities, new insights arise that we want to pursue—new questions that demand answers, new opportunities that can be seized. Many of the activities teachers choose for their pupils are chosen precisely because their results are multiple and diverse; different students learn different things from their interactions and encounters, and some of these learnings are unpredictable. William Doll puts it this way:

> Goals arise in and from action. . . . They are not set (except in the most general, broad, and "fuzzy" manner) prior to action. Process becomes not a precursor to product but an all-encompassing frame in which many products, moments, or events exist. Important as these "ends" may be they are but turning points in a larger process frame. (Doll, 1989, p. 13)

Here are some examples of process objectives:

> *Each student will read for 15 minutes daily to his or her reading partner.*
>
> *Students will conduct a community survey of attitudes toward recycling.*
>
> *In pairs, students will construct a battery sufficiently powerful to drive an electric clock, using a fruit or vegetable as the power source.*

Eliot Eisner coined the term *expressive objective* in an article first published in 1969, which is worth quoting at length:

> Expressive objectives differ considerably from instructional objectives. An expressive objective does not specify the behavior the student is to acquire after having engaged in one or more learning activities. An expressive objective describes an educational encounter: it identifies a situation in which children are to work, a problem with which they are to cope, a task in which they are to engage; but it does not specify what from that encounter, situation, problem, or task they are to learn. An expressive objective provides both the teacher and the student with an invitation to explore, defer, or focus on issues that are of peculiar interest or import to the enquirer. An expressive objective is evocative rather than prescriptive.
>
> The expressive objective is intended to serve as a theme around which skills and understandings learned earlier can be brought to bear, but through which those skills and understandings can be expanded, elaborated, and made idiosyncratic. With an expressive objective what is desired is not homogeneity of response among students but diversity.

> In the expressive context the teacher hopes to provide a situation in which meanings become personalized and in which children produce products, both theoretical and qualitative, that are as diverse as themselves. Consequently the evaluative task in this situation is not one of applying a common standard to the products produced but one of reflecting upon what has been produced in order to reveal its uniqueness and significance. In the expressive context, the product is likely to be as much of a surprise to the maker as it is for the teacher who encounters it.   (Eisner, 1969, pp. 15–16)

In this passage, Eisner outlined what was to become, over the subsequent two decades, a central approach to the teaching of young children. The role of the teacher in this approach is to establish a rich learning environment and then to allow children to explore, experiment, and discover, "to move from spot to spot, being helpful but never consciously prompting or directing" (Hawkins, 1965, p. 6). It may be that this kind of unobtrusive structure can be achieved only on the basis of substantial classroom experience on the part of the teacher. The approach tends to be thematic rather than subject-based, child-centered rather than teacher-centered, activity-oriented rather than objectives-oriented. Such an approach recognizes that knowledge is dynamic and ambiguous, not static and unequivocal. Questions, theories, and mysteries are as important as facts and right answers (Goodman, 1986). The orientation has blossomed particularly in the whole language approach to literacy. Process objectives describe experiences or sets of experiences in which learners are to engage, not as ends in themselves, but with a view to results which are diverse, unconstrained, and not wholly predictable.

Experience objectives

Kurt Hahn, the refugee from Nazi Germany who founded the Outward Bound schools, declared that "It is the sin of the soul to force young people into opinions—indoctrination is of the devil—but it is culpable neglect not to impel young people into experiences" (Schoel & Stratton, 1990, p. 134). Educators who have difficulty with process objectives are likely to have even more difficulty with experience objectives. These objectives are "ends in themselves"; they have no "ulterior motive"; they are experiences that are "intrinsically valuable" and provided "for their own sake." In *Nicomachean Ethics*, Aristotle identified such activities as the essence of happiness:

> If some activities are necessary, and desirable for the sake of something else, while others are so in themselves, evidently happiness must be placed among those desirable in themselves, not among those desirable for the sake of something else; for happiness does not lack anything, but is self-sufficient. Now those activities are desirable in themselves from

Occasionally in life there are these moments of unutterable fulfillment which cannot be completely explained by those symbols called words. Their meanings can only be articulated by the inaudible language of the heart. Such is the moment I am presently experiencing.

> Martin Luther King (U.S.A.), Nobel Prize for Peace, 1964,
> Nobel lecture, 11 Dec 1964. (King, 1965, p. 246)

which nothing is sought beyond the activity. . . . Everything that we choose we choose for the sake of something else—except happiness, which is an end.   (Aristotle, 1947, pp. 530–531)

It is a characteristic of intrinsic experiences that, unlike most school activities, they focus not on the past or the future, but on the present moment. We cannot appropriately prepare students for the future by depriving them of their present, as John Dewey pointed out in his book, *Experience and Education:*

The ideal of using the present simply to get ready for the future contradicts itself. . . . We always live at the time we live and not at some other time, and only by extracting at each present time the full meaning of each present experience are we prepared for doing the same thing in the future. This is the only preparation which in the long run amounts to anything.   (Dewey, 1938, p. 48)

The Italian novelist, Ignazio Silone, strikes a similar note:

> All our life is lived provisionally. . . . We get ready to die, still complaining that we have never lived. Sometimes I am obsessed with the idea that we have only one life, and spend the whole of it living provisionally, waiting for real life to begin. And thus the time passes. Nobody lives in the present. Nobody has any profit from his daily life. (Silone, 1937, p. 31)

Schools, however, are driven almost entirely by instrumental thinking, that is, the belief that an action is justified only if it is a means to some end. Some historians of ideas blame this orientation on the Protestant Reformation, others on the Industrial Revolution. Be that as it may, there is a dichotomy between normal human behavior and the expectations of schooling. Normal human beings "do things for fun." Indeed, they work hard and save money assiduously to this end— the ski trip, foreign travel, a visit to the theater or the ball game. It is recognized that what is really important in life are the significant experiences.

Yet in schools there is a sense that it is somehow not legitimate to "do things for fun." Although teachers in certain curriculum areas, such as dramatic arts, are nobly resisting this mindset, official curricula are virtually devoid of references to fun, enjoyment, play, or fantasy. Our curricula are not aesthetic; they are anaesthetic (the Greek meaning of which is "non-feeling"). Although many teachers might be well disposed toward activities that are justified primarily by enjoyment, they feel defensive and apologetic about them. Thus the class trip to the theater must be followed by an essay or quiz to show that it was not just for fun. But let us beware! We cannot have one philosophy for our personal lives and a diametrically opposed philosophy for our professional lives. This is fundamentally unhealthy and inauthentic; it is schizophrenic.

The term "peak experience" was coined by Abraham Maslow (1959). Maslow, who is regarded as "the father of humanistic psychology," regarded peak experiences as a form of "self-actualization," a state of fulfillment that he considered attainable by all, and a necessary part of normal human health. He described the peak experience in these terms:

> The peak experience is felt as a self-validating, self-justifying moment which carries its own intrinsic value with it. That is to say it is an end in itself, what we may call an end-experience rather than a means-experience. . . . My subjects . . . describe these experiences not only as valuable intrinsically, but as *so* valuable that they make life worthwhile by their occasional occurrence. . . . The peak experiences are for my subjects ultimate goals of living and the ultimate validations and justifications for it. . . . In these moments the person is outside of time and space subjectively. . . . Not only does time pass . . . with a frightening rapidity so that a day may pass as if it were a minute but also a minute so intensely lived may feel like a day or

> a year. It is as if they had, in a way, some place in another world in
> which time simultaneously stood still and moved with great rapid-
> ity. . . . The experience is intrinsically valid and the experience is
> perfect, complete, and needs nothing else. It is sufficient to itself. . . .
> The emotional reaction in the peak experience has a special flavor of
> wonder, of awe, of reverence, of humility and surrender before the ex-
> perience.   (Maslow, 1968, pp. 79–88)

Often, the origin of such an experience is aesthetic. One work of art that has
deeply affected many who have seen it is Michelangelo's statue of Moses in the
church of St. Pietro in Vincoli in Rome. The statue depicts Moses at the moment
when, on descending the mountain where he has received the tablets of the Law
from Jehovah, he sees the Israelites worshipping the golden calf. Freud was fasci-
nated by this statue, spending days studying it (Yerushalmi, 1991). Welles Foshay
describes his own experience:

> I was with a busload of sightseers in Rome. We stopped at an elegant
> small church to admire the building. At one side of the altar, and a bit
> to the rear of it, was Michelangelo's Moses.
>
> I was transfixed. The statue suddenly became my entire universe. I
> lost all sense of time and place; I was utterly absorbed in the wonder of
> the statue. Moses looked in rage at his people; the tablets fell from his
> hands. He was experiencing the shock of human frailty, having just
> come from God. For me, the experience transcended the place, the craft
> of the sculptor, the fact that, after all, I was looking at stone.
>
> I don't know how long I stood there. When I 'came to', the touring
> group had left and I was alone. The majesty, the awesome presence, the
> intensity of that moment, have remained with me to this day.   (Foshay,
> 1991, p. 280)

Foshay records an archetypal experience of the transforming effect of great art.
Subjects such as drama, literature, visual art, and music lend themselves readily to
the provision of experiences whereby "perspectives may open in unpredictable directions; they may disclose the unthought, the unacted upon . . . the territory
that lies beyond" (Greene, 1990, p. 261). A subject like history need not be
thought of as the inculcation of myriad historical facts, but as an opportunity to
involve young people vicariously and imaginatively in those experiences that have
been significant in the development of our identity as a community, a nation, a
civilization.

Many years ago, Benjamin Bloom conducted a small survey of eighty college
students. He asked them to describe any "peak learning experience" from their
formal schooling; any occasion on which they found themselves totally absorbed
and engaged in some activity that was intrinsically interesting or enjoyable. The
students had, among them, over 1,200 years and 1,000,000 hours of formal schooling. Altogether, they could recall a total of only sixty such experiences (1981).

However, those experiences that were reported were clearly of great significance in the students' lives:

> The peak learning experiences were described in such a manner that they appeared to be "moments of truth" for the student. Whatever set of ideas or way of thinking the student glimpsed in the peak learning experience was seen as a fundamental truth. The student regarded the experience as valuable in its own right rather than as a means to some learning task or as useful for other purposes. . . . Frequently, descriptions suggested that the peak learning experience was essentially an aesthetic experience which was seen as true, beautiful, and valuable—whether or not it had some effect on the learning of a subject or had value for other learning. . . . They had experienced it fully at the time, while organizing, analytic, and application types of thinking were temporarily suspended. The peak learning experience was good in its own right at the time— only later was it seen as useful and valuable for other learning purposes. (Bloom, 1981, p. 195)

Interestingly, Bloom also found that such experiences were as a rule not accidental, but the result of some deliberate planning by a teacher. Also, if the experience was powerful for one student in the class, it was typically powerful for all. Although the critical feature of peak experiences is the experience of the moment as lived, such events do have aftereffects. They are typically vividly remembered; they can alter a person's view of him or herself, of others, and of the world; they often give people an increased sense of the value of living. It is experiences more than anything else that are the foundation of attitudes. If we want to change students' attitudes to the environment, we would be well advised to abandon much of the propagandistic approach to environmental education, and instead have students spend one full day a year—Arbor Day—out of doors in the sunshine planting trees, for the nurture of which they would then take responsibility. Experiences of success are particularly important for students—whether children, adolescents, or adults—both because they are significant in themselves, and because they contribute to the development of a healthy self-concept.

The creation of peak experiences in the classroom requires imagination and commitment on the part of teachers. But such experiences are not hard to find. Because of light pollution in our cities at night, many young people will never really see the night sky. It is necessary to go many miles from most urban areas before the stars become clearly visible. But the experience of seeing millions of brilliant stars on a clear and moonless night in an inky blue-black sky is one that is both memorable and within the organizational ability of most teachers.

Here is an example of a project that became a significant experience for a group of preservice technical teachers. From a hobby shop they obtained a kit for the construction in cardboard of a small model dinosaur skeleton, Tyrannosaurus Rex. They transferred the blueprints to acetate, blew them up on an overhead projector, and copied them (allowing for the parallax effect) at ten times the original scale. They then built the dinosaur skeleton out of ³/₄-inch plywood, laminated into two thicknesses. Beautifully finished with many coats of clear varnish, the ten-foot-long skeleton now stands in the main foyer of the building where I work. A future project that I have in mind would involve collaboration between history and technical teachers. Using historical drawings, students would sketch and draw plans for a huge medieval catapult. Obtaining timber from a wrecker (and appropriate liability insurance), they would construct and operate a working model big and strong enough to hurl boulders, tree trunks, and old cars the length of a football field.

The following are examples of objectives that might be provided principally for their experiential value:

Students will watch a live performance of Romeo and Juliet.

Students will participate in a religious ritual in a faith different from their own.

Students will have the experience of being restricted to a wheelchair for half a school day.

Students in the senior biology course will visit the city morgue and attend an autopsy.

In the last session of the history course, the room will be darkened and three Roman oil-lamps, borrowed from the local museum, will be lit for the first time in 2000 years.

Students will play before an audience a piece of music of their own composition.

Students will have a direct experience of scientific experiment and discovery.

Students will spend three days camping and participating in an archaeological dig at a Navajo site.

> All experience educates, and our social personality forms underneath our vanishing experiences like layers of chalk under a rain of dying protozoans.
> Northrop Frye (1988, p. 30)

■ The Function of Classification ■

Scratch a knowledge and you find an attitude. There are dangers in trying to separate knowledge and skill, attitudes and experience. Human beings are complex, and interaction between different kinds of learning takes place all the time. The proper function of a typology of instructional intentions is not to establish hard and fast distinctions, but simply to provide some focus and emphasis to guide the planning of instruction. There is no rule that every kind of objective must be reflected in every curriculum. One curriculum might be built solely on process objectives. Another might address only knowledges. Different typologies can also be constructed, to include, for example, social and psychological objectives. What is important is that the planner and the teacher be consciously aware of what it is they are attempting to do.

Nor are there rules about how many objectives a curriculum should contain. A rule of thumb is to divide a curriculum for a year or a semester into units of manageable length—typically not much more than ten hours of instruction—and then endeavor to limit the number of objectives for each unit to ten or twelve. It is just very difficult for teachers and students to keep their minds on more than twelve objectives (some teachers would say more than two) at any one time. This prevents objectives from becoming too detailed. Thus an objective in a Driver Education unit on safety might be: "The student will understand the causes, symptoms, effects, and means of avoiding carbon monoxide poisoning." It would not be: "The student will know that carbon monoxide poisoning may be insidious and produced by inhaling small amounts of carbon monoxide over a long period." The latter is better seen as a "teaching point." We may have thousands of teaching points, but it is impossible to manage a curriculum that has thousands of objectives.

To be scientific, a classification system should provide categories that are both mutually exclusive and collectively exhaustive. The typology described in this chapter is neither. It is not scientific, but suggestive. Not only is there obvious overlap between categories, but because we are continually learning more about human capacity, it is probably not exhaustive either. Where would telepathy fit? In the twenty-first century we will no doubt discover not only new knowledges and new skills, but new areas of human capacity that are distinct from either knowledge or skill.

One basic thesis underlies all of the above discussion. This is the belief that it is salutary for teachers to ask themselves periodically—and to ask intelligently, reflectively, and seriously:

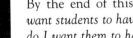

By the end of this lesson/unit/course/program: *What knowledges do I want students to have? What skills do I want them to have? What attitudes do I want them to have? What experiences do I want them to have had?*

■ Behavioral Objectives ■

To those readers familiar with the "behavioral objectives" orientation to curriculum, it will be clear that this is a different approach. Readers neither aware of, nor interested in, this issue are invited to skip this section.

The behavioral objectives approach to goal-setting developed in the 1960s. It was an offshoot of behavioral psychology pioneered by such psychologists as J. B. Watson and B. F. Skinner. Advocates insisted that curriculum objectives be "operationalized." As understandings, skills, and attitudes were within the "black box" of the human mind and could not be directly observed, objectives should describe only observable behaviors on the part of the learner. Thus, an objective such as "Students will understand Pythagoras' theorem" was regarded as meaningless. What was needed was a statement such as, "Given the dimensions of two sides of each of five right-angle triangles, the student will correctly calculate the length of the third side in ten minutes without error."

What occurred was a confusion between *the intent of instruction* and *the criterion for assessment*. The qualities of an adequate statement of intention (i.e., significance, clarity, conciseness) are quite different from those for an assessment instrument (validity, reliability, efficiency). The first consequence of this confusion was that objectives began to be written that were neither good intentions nor good evaluative measures. The second consequence was that as behavioral objectives were typically highly specific, each curriculum tended to contain hundreds, sometimes thousands, of objectives, and the system began to collapse under its own weight (Eraut, 1991; French et al. 1957). The third consequence was even more damaging. Teachers were told, "Don't state an objective unless you can measure its achievement." This terrorized teachers into not stating any objective unless it could be assessed by the (alas) limited measurement techniques at their disposal, which usually meant by simple written tests. That wholesale trivialization of the curriculum did not invariably result was not thanks to behavioral objectives, but to the fact that most teachers wrote the objectives as required, submitted them to administrators (in triplicate), and then went on with their work as though nothing had happened.

James Popham summarized some of the consequences:

> Perhaps the most serious shortcoming of behavioral objectives, however, was not widely recognized. . . . That shortcoming stems from the common tendency to frame behavioral objectives so that they focus on increasingly smaller and more specific segments of learner post-instructional behavior. The net effect of such hyper-specificity is that the objectives formulator ends up with a plethora of picayune outcomes. . . . The typical set of narrow-scope behavioral objectives turned out to be so numerous that decision-makers would not attend to evidence of objective-attainment. (Popham, 1990, p. 190)

It is important to recognize that the purposes of education are never behaviors, but always states. That is, our fundamental purposes are always to develop in learners not one-shot actions, but ongoing states of mind (or of body, in the case of somatic objectives). These may be knowledge states, or skill states, or attitude states. Sometimes these are temporary states of significant experience (although these will leave permanent and important memories). And sometimes the states are diverse and unpredictable, and, as with process objectives, we specify only the conditions that we will establish for them to grow. In all cases, we are primarily interested in the development of capacities and potentials, not behaviors. The objectives generate a universe of possible behaviors, and to assess, we sample from that universe and then make an inference about the overall state. The error of behavioral objectivitsts was to elevate such samples into the purposes of education. The remedy, as Popham pointed out, was (a) to separate objectives and performance standards, and (b) to define curriculum in terms not of innumerable specific behaviors but of a manageable number of broad-scope objectives (1986).

Despite the reservations of scholars, a behavioral orientation continues to flourish in official curriculum documents. Klein comments on her findings in an analysis of 269 curriculum guides: "The strong emphasis on . . . behavioral objectives was reflected very clearly in the guides. Any controversy about their desirability and usefulness, although present in the research literature, was not acknowledged in these guides. Indeed, the desirability of behavioral objectives was clearly endorsed and never questioned" (1989, p. 25). Here is an example, from a Vernon, Connecticut, curriculum. An objective is: "Students will . . . state that skin has two parts, an epidermis and a dermis, and identify the function of each" (Vernon Public Schools, 1986, np). However, if one reflects on this learning, it seems apparent that *stating* is not really the intent; *understanding* is. So this objective would be better written something like: "Students will understand the structure and function of the skin." Later, when we come to assess the student's understanding, then we will ask for some kind of statement from the learner.

In the approach advocated in this book, we first become clear about the direction in which we want to move our learners. The focus is very much on the identification of what is meaningful, significant, worthwhile. Then, when we have become clear about what is most worthwhile (and only then), we begin to think about the best possible ways of assessing student attainment. There may be areas in which the measurement questions are very difficult. But we cannot allow measurement considerations to constrain us at the intentions-setting stage. What is worth attempting is worth attempting whether or not we think we can measure its achievement precisely.

▪ Priorities ▪

We have now established an appropriate level of clarity regarding our curriculum intentions. The final stage in this process is to establish priorities among our intentions. It is recommended that each objective be identified as *critical, important,* or *desirable.*

The point of reference is to the curriculum aim. If a particular objective is not achieved, can the aim still be realized? If the answer is no, then that objective is critical. In other words, *an objective is critical if its non-achievement jeopardizes achievement of the aim.* In addressing the question of priority, we need to ask about each objective, How probable is it that students will need this learning? and How serious are the consequences of not mastering this learning? If the answers are "very probable" and "disastrous," then the objective is almost certainly critical. If the answers are "improbable" and "negligible," the objective is trivial, arcane, or eccentric, and should probably be thrown out of the curriculum (Kane, Kingsbury, Colton, & Estes, 1989).

The key to this stage is the identification of the critical objectives. These are the objectives we are willing to bleed for. They are the experiences students *must* have or the things they *must* learn. It follows that we let students know (or negotiate with them) which objectives have priority. When we identify an objective as critical, we are telling students that we are prepared to do our best to ensure that all of them master that objective and that their success is dependent on its mastery. We then put our best efforts into developing instruction that does enable all students to attain these objectives successfully.

This is not a new idea. It was not invented by Benjamin Bloom, or even by Ralph Tyler. Effective teachers have probably always practiced it, right back to Neanderthal parents teaching their children to make spears or clothes. The earliest explicit statement I have found in modern educational writing is by Carleton Washburne, the great superintendent of the Winnetka schools in the 1920s. He wrote in 1925:

> The common essentials, by definition, are those knowledges and skills needed by everyone; to allow many children, therefore, to pass through school with hazy and inadequate grasp of them, as one must under the class lock-step scheme, is to fail in one of the functions of the school.   (Washburne, 1925, p. 79)

This is a somewhat different approach from that found in most educational institutions. Conventional practice is to teach, set a task for assessment, grade the submissions from excellence to failure, return the work, and proceed to the next piece of instruction. Some students will have mastered some objectives, some others. On particular objectives, some students will have learned very well, some very badly. But we proceed regardless. If we wanted to spread out student achievement, to ensure that we would have many failures as well as successes, this is the best way to do it. But if we want all students to achieve certain crucial learnings, then we do not embark on the next unit of instruction until all students have mastered the critical learnings in the previous unit.

This is not only a prescription for curriculum, but for a minimum level of social justice. There are learnings without which the individual in today's society has limited chances of developing a sense of self-worth or personal fulfillment. There are also learnings that are prerequisite to continued success in education, and in the absence of which students are likely to fail and to drop out of school mentally or physically. Basic literacy is one obvious example. We know enough about the destructive effects of unemployment on mental health to accept learnings that are essential to employability as a critical area. My personal bias is to include understandings, abilities, and appreciations in such areas as music, poetry, and the visual arts high up on the list of qualities essential to human happiness.

Establishing priorities helps to solve two other persistent curriculum problems. One is the diversity of aptitude in any classroom. We shall deal with this problem at greater length in Chapter 7. At this point, we need only observe that student diversity is such as to make it unrealistic to try to teach all students everything we would like them to learn. Once we have identified the learnings in a curriculum that are critical, we can try to ensure that all students master these learnings, and that the more able learners also master important and desirable learnings. ("Critical" does not mean "boring." The critical objectives may be the most fun. If they are not, the methods used to teach them should be.)

The second problem is that of overcrowded curricula. Official curriculum guidelines, at the state, provincial, or district level, tend to be politically influenced. Many pressure groups seek to ensure that their favorite topics are included. The response to this by decision makers at higher levels is often to include them all. The consequence is that curricula are constantly growing. As every topic has its advocates, nothing is ever eliminated, and perhaps for the same reason, priorities are rarely shown. Teachers feel under constant and growing pressure. Every year there are more new programs, more new skills to teach, and the curriculum implies that all teachers will successfully teach all of them to all of their students. As teachers know this to be impossible, the curriculum itself loses its credibility. We would be well advised to heed what Anthony Cave Brown calls "a fundamental military law: to try to be strong everywhere is to be weak everywhere" (1975, p. 275).

When a teacher or a team of teachers in a school receives a new mandated curriculum, the first step is to avail themselves of an inexpensive piece of modern technology called a highlighter. The teachers read through the curriculum, highlighting those objectives, experiences, or topics that they consider critical. This may be 10 percent of the curriculum, or it may be 50 percent, but it will rarely be 100 percent. The task ahead immediately becomes more manageable, the teachers more confident, the students less harassed.

ASK FOR WHAT YOU WANT

The field of family therapy holds many insights for educators. A family comes into therapy, most frequently, when it sends one of its members, the "identified client," to a therapist to be "cured." Family therapists, however, view problems within families as systemic, that is, as the product of the whole complex of interactions among all members of the family. They therefore commonly decline to work with a family until all its members are present (Satir, 1967).

Let us imagine a typical first session with five people—the therapist, two parents, and a teenage son and daughter. After a period of small talk or uncomfortable silence, the teenage daughter states what it is that has been bothering her about her family. She talks about frustrations and unmet needs. When she has finished, the therapist asks the parents whether they were aware that their daughter felt this way. They say they had no idea. The therapist then asks the daughter whether she had previously spoken in this way to her parents. The answer is a classic in family therapy, and it goes something like this: "Of course not. If they loved me, they would know what I wanted without my having to ask." On this shoal perhaps more than any other, human relations shipwreck themselves.

One of the functions of family therapy is to help people discover what it is they really need. Another is to give them the confidence to ask for it. As this seems to work in family relationships, one is inclined to suppose that it will work in other relationships, such as those that exist in classrooms. In educational contexts, we hope to base objectives not on teacher needs, but on the needs of learners established either by dialogue with them or by needs assessment. In stating objectives, we are not entering legal contracts or writing guarantees, we are simply trying to establish clarity and agreement about what it is we want.

■ SELF – ASSESSMENT

1. What kinds of questions are primarily involved in specifying curriculum intentions?

   A   literary questions
   B   technical questions
   C   questions of values
   D   questions of bureaucratic regulations

2. Which of these statements is most clearly a question about curriculum aims or objectives?

   A   whether academic students should learn keyboard skills
   B   which novels should be studied in the English curriculum
   C   how underachievement can best be remediated in mathematics
   D   what proportion of the science budget should be spent on equipment

3. "Children will understand grasshoppers." What is wrong with this aim?

   A   it is not concise
   B   it is not measurable
   C   the significance is not clear
   D   the age of the children is not stated

4. What is the best place in a curriculum to mention outcomes that are "hoped for" rather than actually intended?

   A   the aim
   B   the content
   C   the rationale
   D   the objectives

5. Which of the following should be included in the rationale for the curriculum?

   A   imaginative suggestions for instructional strategies
   B   clear and precise statement of the curriculum objectives
   C   convincing argument that the curriculum meets a significant need
   D   detailed budget showing that the curriculum will not be expensive

6. Which of the following is *not* a good reason for stating objectives clearly?

    A   to guide the teacher
    B   to help motivate the students
    C   to describe the teaching methods
    D   to aid in determining the effectiveness of the curriculum

7. What will teachers tend to do if they try to state all of their objectives as measurable behaviors?

    A   they will write better objectives
    B   they will specify many intangible objectives
    C   they will develop more skill in measurement techniques
    D   they will omit some important objectives from the curriculum

8. What is necessary if aims and objectives are to enhance student learning?

    A   they must be written in behavioral terms
    B   they must be established by subject-matter experts
    C   they must be significant to the learners
    D   they must be determined by the learners themselves

9. Activities can be classified as "means to ends" or as "ends in themselves." Which objectives are by definition primarily "ends in themselves"?

    A   somatic objectives
    B   attitude objectives
    C   knowledge objectives
    D   experiential objectives

10. An objective is *critical* if and only if

    A   it is an important learning outcome
    B   its non-achievement jeopardizes achievement of the aim
    C   failure to achieve it could make a life-or-death difference
    D   it encourages students to criticize social or intellectual conventions

For answers, see Appendix F.
If you answered nine or ten correctly, you understand the material in this chapter.
If you answered seven or eight correctly, reread the relevant sections in the chapter.
If you answered less than seven correctly, reread the chapter carefully.

CHAPTER 4

Assessing
Student Learning

We must constantly remind ourselves that the ultimate purpose of evaluation is to enable students to evaluate themselves.

Arthur L. Costa (1989, p. 2)

Summary

A curriculum plan needs to include a plan for assessment. Assessment of student learning serves many purposes, but if inadequately conceived or conducted, it can be damaging to learning and teaching. In selecting appropriate approaches to assessment, a wide variety of possibilities should be considered, taking into account the criteria of humanity, validity, reliability, efficiency, and frequency. It is often helpful to assign a performance criterion to each objective, and particularly to each critical objective. Expectations tend to determine level of achievement and should be explicit, realistic, and challenging. Assessments need to be carefully planned and conducted and subject to ongoing analysis, evaluation, and improvement. Student grades should reflect the learning priorities established in the curriculum.

THE USES AND MISUSES OF ASSESSMENT

In productive learning environments, both students and teachers experiment, try out ideas, take risks, tackle and puzzle over problems, think, reflect, listen, discuss, ask questions, look up information, surprise themselves and each other. Such environments are distinguished by multiple channels of feedback. Participants seek, receive, pay attention to, and respond to messages of inquiry, encouragement, confirmation, and correction. Such feedback is assessment in its broadest sense. At its least formal, and in some ways its best, it is unobtrusively woven into the fabric of classroom activity and interaction. At its most formal, and in some ways its worst, it is separated from the classroom environment and activities and conducted in ways that are ritualistic and intimidating. Curriculum planners are well placed to influence the assessment choices of teachers. To do this effectively, they need to consider the entire array of options available for the assessment of student learning.

Madaus and Kellaghan (1992, p. 120) define assessment as "an activity designed to show what a person knows or can do." Students view assessment as a basic source of the power of teachers and of stress and disempowerment for themselves. As students move through the grades, they become more dissatisfied with and cynical and suspicious about assessment practices, increasingly viewing them as unfair and as a means of distributing rewards and punishments (Evans & Engelberg, 1988; Paris, Lawton, Turner, & Roth, 1991). Assessment similarly looms large in the memories that adults carry of their schooling (Rafferty, 1985). For that matter, teachers themselves do not particularly enjoy being assessed. Michael Scriven uses the term "valuephobia," which he describes as "a pervasive fear of being evaluated, which I take to be a part of the general human condition" (1983, p. 230). The results of assessment can decisively affect the academic and occupational future of students. In the form of reports, they are one of the main means of communication between school and home. Formal and informal assessment activities consume a significant proportion of classroom time. Very often, the nature of assessment dictates the curriculum, rather than vice versa. It is estimated that over 100 million, and possibly as many as 320 million, standardized tests are administered in American classrooms every year, at a cost of at least $387 million a year, consuming 20 million school days in taking the tests and perhaps 10–20 times as many days in preparing for them (Bullough, 1990; Madaus & Kellaghan, 1992; National Commission on Testing and Public Policy, 1990; Paris, Lawton, Turner, & Roth, 1991). Educators are beginning to question the value of this investment. The Association for Supervision and Curriculum Development (ASCD) surveys an international panel of five hundred educators annually. In 1990 ASCD reported:

> For the third year in a row, members of ASCD's International Polling Panel identified tests and testing as the number one negative instructional trend in education. . . . Members also thought that most tests measure "discrete low-level" basic skills and promote the use of rote, drill, practice, and lecture as the primary modes of instruction. (Hodges, 1990, p. 6)

Measurement-driven instruction, comments Edmund Short, (1990, p. 202) "is, and always has been, devastating to both the curriculum breadth and teaching flexibility needed to ensure high quality education." The problems associated with "high-stakes" standardized tests are well known. They tend to drive out of school curriculum any subject matter that is not tested. This often includes not only such subjects as art and music, but also higher-order thinking skills, nonverbal, non-mathematical areas that may not be tested, and non-mainline topics on which individual teachers are experts. This problem deprives teachers of the freedom to make curriculum choices, both about content and method, that they consider to be in the best interests of their students. Tests often encourage excessive reliance on drill and lecturing by teachers and cramming by students. Such tests may also result in teaching practices that are ethically questionable. These include drilling students on content known to be on a test, or on items similar to those on a test; using commercial test-boosting preparation packages; dismissing low-achieving students on testing day to raise scores; discouraging low-achieving students from taking challenging courses; increasing the number of students retained in grade; and various forms of cheating, such as illegally increasing testing time and presenting items verbatim from the test to be given. All of these practices pollute the test results and corrupt the inferences drawn from them about student attainment (Berk, 1988; Haladyna, Nolan, & Haas, 1991; Madaus, 1991; Madaus & Kellaghan, 1992; Smith, 1991a; Smith, 1991b). Such criticisms go back more than a century (White, 1888).

Measurement-driven instruction may also fail basic tests of justice. Suppose that a mandated test is based on announced curriculum objectives, but a student achieves poorly because the teacher has not taught all of the relevant material?

This was the scenario debated in the Florida Fifth Circuit court in *Debra P.* v. *Turlington* in 1981. The court ruled that in such circumstances the test results were unfair and should be set aside. Clearly any summative assessment measure should be administered only after the students have had a genuine opportunity to master the relevant material. Ideally, curriculum intentions, assessment, and instruction are all parts of an integrated whole.

In this book, however, we are less interested in systemwide assessment than in the use of assessment by teachers in their classrooms. Assessment by teachers generally has more positive effects on student learning than do standardized tests (Madaus & Kellaghan, 1992). Standardized tests provide information that educational policy makers need to evaluate or to justify programs. The information that teachers need is often quite different. They need information from curriculum-embedded tests to tell them about student learning in their classrooms and to provide a basis for feedback and grading decisions. Teachers recognize the importance of assessment in their work, but often feel inadequately trained in this area (Stiggins & Bridgeford, 1985). They receive little help either from their initial teacher education or from official curricula, which rarely provide clear guidance to teachers on the development of appropriate means of assessment (Klein, 1989; Pratt, 1989).

Terms such as measurement, evaluation, assessment, and grading are often used rather loosely in educational discussion. Here, we shall attempt to use each term in a specific sense. By *measurement* is meant "the assignment of numbers to objects or events according to rules" (Stevens, 1951, p. 22). The distinction between assessment and evaluation used in the *International Encyclopedia of Educational Evaluation* (Walberg & Haertel, 1990; Choppin, 1990c) and the American Educational Research Association's *Handbook of Research on Curriculum* (Jackson, 1992; Madaus & Kellaghan, 1992) will be adopted here. *Assessment* will be used to refer to "judgments about people, and in particular about students' learning." *Evaluation* will be used to refer to "judgments about instruction, curricula, policy, programs, and institutions." *Grading* will be used to refer to "the process of classifying students (for example, into letter, percentage, or pass-fail categories) on the basis of assessment data." In this chapter, we are primarily interested in the process of assessment.

In planning assessment, we are concerned not only with formal tests and examinations, but with all the means by which we might gather information about how students are learning and have learned. This includes pretests as well as posttests, informal observation as well as more formal tests and examinations. Assessment can serve many functions and often does serve several at the same time. The nature of the assessment will vary depending on the purpose to be served, and the purpose depends on the individual. The information needed by the student is different from that needed by the teacher, which is also different from the information needed by the principal. In recent years, much educational assessment has become dominated by the politically driven information needs of state bureaucracies and politicians, which often have little to do with, and may in fact run counter to, the needs of teachers and pupils.

The following, several of which overlap, are some of the main purposes of assessment. Some apply more to formal than to informal assessments, and some apply to both.

1. **As an integral part of instruction.** A piano teacher says, "That's not quite right. Try being a little lighter with the left hand. Listen, I'll play it." A teacher is passing back students' creative writing assignments, "I like the images you've used in your first paragraph, Jane. They're effective because they're surprising." A math teacher notes in the margin of a pupil's quiz, "You forgot to change the sign when you removed the brackets!" A French teacher says, "In English, the O and the R in 'Bordeaux' are one sound, but in French each sound is pronounced: 'Bo-r-deaux': try it." A kindergarten teacher says, "Andy, crayons are for drawing, not for stuffing up your nose." The pervasive observation, monitoring, and transaction that takes place in classrooms is the most prevalent and important kind of educational assessment. In some learning contexts, usually combined with some systematic record-keeping, it is the only kind of assessment required.

2. **To provide feedback about the success of the program.** Curriculum and instruction can improve only if there is a flow of meaningful information about the program available to those responsible for its revision and delivery. Like all living systems, educational systems need feedback in order to maintain equilibrium, to survive, and to grow. This is true at the micro-level of a classroom; it is also true at the macro-level of a school district or a state system of education. Consistent and valid data about achievement can help a system identify pockets of underachievement. Individual states, districts, schools, or classrooms may contain an unacceptable number of students who are being educationally disadvantaged. This is in fact the case in North America. In the 1990 National Assessment of Educational Progress, the difference in mathematics achievement between the highest and lowest performing states was greater than the national average difference between Grade 8 and Grade 12 (Office of Educational Research & Improvement, 1991). In the absence of valid information, such problems may go undetected, and hence unremediated. Information from the assessment of student learning is one kind of data utilized in program evaluation, a topic dealt with more fully in Chapter 9.

3. **To report individual student achievement.** Several constituencies have a legitimate interest in the achievement level of students, and they are entitled to accurate, adequate, and timely assessment information: first, the students themselves; their parents; other educational institutions to which they may apply for admission; potential employers; and occupational and professional licensing boards.

4. **To diagnose the student's learning.** It is usually insufficient to know simply whether or not a student has reached a certain standard. We also need to know our learners' areas of strength and weakness, so that we can plan instruction that will build on the one and remediate the other. Such "formative" assessment may be conducted formally or informally.

5. **To consolidate students' knowledge prior to moving to the next unit of instruction.** Assessment soon after studying a topic tends to enhance long-term

retention, and moderately frequent assessment results in gains in student performance (Madaus & Kellaghan, 1992). A summative test may allow a student to syn-
thesize and consolidate the understandings acquired over a period of instruction.

6. **To direct students to instructional priorities and to influence their approach to learning.** Tests, examinations, and informal teacher questions indicate
to students which parts of the curriculum have priority. If the tests examine only
trivial information, students will adopt learning strategies aimed at factual recall
(following the test, this material can be safely forgotten); if tests call for "deep
learning," students will change their approach to the material accordingly (Crooks,
1988). That the word "studying" has become largely synonymous with last-minute
cramming for a test is an indication of the extent to which assessment has tended to
trivialize education.

7. **To enhance students' self-concept and sense of efficacy.** This benefit will
occur only if instruction is designed to produce real success. Under this condition,
frequent assessment will stimulate student confidence and willingness to engage
in learning. As Terence Crooks puts it:

> The main mechanism for building self-efficacy in a particular domain ap-
> pears to be experiencing repeated success on tasks in that domain. . . .
> To foster self-efficacy, evaluations of task performance should emphasize
> performance (task mastery) rather than task engagement. . . . This is
> crucial for the less able students, who might otherwise receive little posi-
> tive feedback.   (Crooks, 1988, pp. 462–63)

8. **To guide decisions about the learner.** The better our diagnostic and
achievement data, the more appropriate the guidance we will be able to give to
learners about their learning, and about their future academic and occupational
choices.

9. **To provide organizing targets for learners.** Most people seem to organize
their activities more purposefully if they know that at a particular future date they
will be asked to perform to a certain standard. This is true of concert pianists,
competitive athletes, and actors, as well as of students at every level. This is not to
legitimize the use of examinations as instruments of terror and control. Assessment activities that are perceived by learners as a means of controlling their behavior, rather than providing feedback on their progress, have a negative effect on
student motivation (Ryan, Connell, & Deci, 1985).

10. **To provide symbolic significance.** All institutions develop rituals, and
assessment provides some of the primary rituals in educational institutions. A
teacher's question to an individual student in class is a spotlight, making that student for an instant the center of attention. Tests and examinations act as quasi-
ritualistic points of demarcation in a student's career. In the same way, such public
events as the district track and field meet, the solo flight for a pilot's license, and
the public piano recital are symbolically significant milestones in the development
of an individual's career, and particularly important in the development of giftedness (Bloom, 1981). Students facing examinations develop a sense of solidarity

with one another, and graduates achieve a shared sense of identity. The huge gymnasium with its hundreds of geometrically arranged desks; the rules and regulations regarding what may be brought into the examination hall; the imposition of silence; the watchfulness of proctors: all of these elements add to a ritualistic sense of awe. (At Oxford University, students are required to wear a kind of comic-opera outfit for final examinations—"sub-fusc": black and white only, with academic gown and mortar board.) The fact that much of this symbolism and ritual may well be dysfunctional is an important reason for educators to reflect on their assessment practices.

DIMENSIONS OF ASSESSMENT

The field of assessment is as diverse as that of curriculum. The many debates that are carried on both in academic journals and in school staff rooms are indicative of a field that is growing and vigorous. Here we shall look at six dimensions on which educators hold a range of views. These dimensions will serve to indicate the array of assessment devices available to practitioners.

Naturalistic versus formal assessment

Educators vary in their taste for formality. Some educators regard as the only valid assessment a highly formal examination under controlled conditions. Others see assessment as meaningful only if it is an integral part of the continuing learning situation. Debate between these schools of thought tends to harden positions into polarized dichotomies. But we can view the spectrum of opinion as a continuum, as shown in Table 4-1.

Such words as "test" and "examination" conjure up, for most people, archetypal memories of assessment: huge and intimidating examination halls; heads bent over papers in silent classrooms; a feeling of tension in the pit of the stomach. It is characteristic of such formal types of assessment that they are quite distinct from daily life in or outside of classrooms. Examinees typically

Table 4-1   A Continuum of Approaches to Assessment

Formal or "objective" end of the continuum		Informal or "naturalistic" end of the continuum	
The formal examination separate in time, place, and substance from the learning situation.	Formal tests conducted in the class setting.	Informal quizzes, assignments, homework, and seat work.	Teacher observation of children's learning, recorded by checklists, descriptions and anecdotal comments.

respond to questions and perceptions posed by teachers. Decisions that are made on the basis of such measures are primarily inferential: we examine a student's performance under artificial conditions and infer abilities to act in certain ways under other conditions.

Naturalistic assessment, by contrast, makes learners' perspectives the primary focus. It attempts to understand the performance of learners in the ordinary context of the classroom, or of their out-of-classroom lives. It asks, as noncommittally as possible, "What is going on here?", and it may utilize as data almost any of the events that occur in the setting. The naturalistic assessor observes, listens to, and reflects on what learners do and say, engages in planned interviews and impromptu conversations, records and uses the actual words of learners, and takes an interest in expressed feelings as well as thoughts (Dorr-Bremme, 1990).

Naturalistic assessment is particularly appropriate in primary-level classrooms. It is similar to the kind of assessment of a child's growth in walking, talking, or other aspects of development carried out by parents and grandparents, using constant observation, interaction, and participation. But this is not to suggest that the value of naturalistic assessment is limited to either elementary or to language classrooms. Probably assessment would be improved at every level if naturalistic data were included in the record of achievement.

Preordinate versus nonpreordinate assessment

These two rather cumbersome terms define two different approaches to assessment. Classical test theory is mainly preordinate, that is, we define or "preordain" certain objectives that we want the learners to attain, and we then determine the measures to help us decide how far they have attained them. Critics have pointed out that if we engage only in preordinate assessment, we will miss all of the unanticipated effects of the curriculum, both positive and negative. Nonpreordinate assessment endeavors to discover what and how students are learning, without reference to specific anticipated outcomes. The question asked in preordinate assessment is: How well has the student mastered X, Y, and Z? The questions in nonpreordinate assessment are: What are students learning? What insights are they developing? In what ways are their perceptions maturing? How are they responding to the learning environment? Such assessment is less likely to use formal tests than it is to use systematic or unsystematic observation. It is the kind of assessment of choice when the objectives themselves are nonpreordinate, as is the case with process objectives, which define a learning context or opportunity, but not a specific outcome.

Formative versus summative assessment

A useful distinction has developed over the past two decades between assessment intended to provide feedback into an ongoing instructional situation and assessment intended to provide a final judgment on a learner. Airasian distinguishes between the two kinds of assessment in this way: "Formative assessment provides data about how students are changing . . . summative assessment is concerned with how students have changed" (1971, p. 78). I believe it was Robert Stake who provided the useful metaphor: "When the cook tastes the soup, that's formative assessment. When the guests taste the soup, that's summative assessment." Another way of putting it is that the purpose of summative assessment is to prove learning, while the purpose of formative assessment is to improve learning.

> Trying to impose a measurement-based view of assessment on a whole-language philosophy is a little like trying to fit a nut onto a bolt that has a different thread; it can only be done with force and even then the fit is dysfunctional.
>
> Brian Camborne and Jan Turbill (1990, p. 339)

The same instruments can be used for both formative and summative assessment. In fact, the same test may be so used. Let us suppose a teacher gives a 10-item quiz on a Friday. Those students who score 8 or more are told they have passed the unit. For them, the test was summative. The students who have scored less than 8 are given some advice regarding how to prepare over the weekend for a retest on Monday. For them, the test was formative. Many formative measures are less formal. Experienced teachers monitor student responses by observing body language, by engaging students in discussion, by asking questions, and by looking at seatwork, homework, worksheets, and assignments.

By definition, marks are not given for formative assessment. To do so would be to permanently penalize students for the errors they make in the natural process of learning. Any test from which permanent marks are recorded is by definition summative. Summative tests should be given only after the students have had an adequate opportunity to learn. In summative tests students are typically told only their total score, or which items they answered correctly. Much of the value of formative tests lies in the feedback given to students. "Right or wrong" feedback is ineffective; learning takes place when students are guided to the correct answer (Bangert-Drowns, Kulik, Kulik, & Morgan, 1991).

Formative assessment plays a crucial role in the management of learning, and particularly in maintaining student achievement. It will be discussed more fully in Chapter 7. In this chapter, we are mainly concerned with summative assessment, but many of the principles of summative assessment also apply to formative assessment.

Norm-referenced versus criterion-referenced assessment

An important distinction has been made by assessment experts since early in the century (Thorndike, 1919) between norm-referenced and criterion-referenced assessment. Norm-referenced assessment compares students with one another and is usually a form of ranking. It is typically competitive, as there is only one "first place." Norm-referenced measures tend to spread students out along a distribution. "Marking on the curve" is an example of norm-referenced assessment. School policies limiting the number of high grades, or the number of failures, or the mean class score, are essentially norm-referencing policies. Admission to law school, a political election, the 100-meter dash, and becoming the dominant male in a baboon troop are all instances of norm referencing.

Criterion-referenced assessment seeks to discover what students have learned, or whether they have learned, or how much or how well they have learned, in relation to a set of well-defined competencies, but without reference to the achievement of other learners. The question is not, Where does the student stand in relation to other students? but Where does the student stand in relation to these objectives and these criteria? Examples of criterion-referenced assessment are the driving test, the Congressional Medal of Honor, and the age qualification to vote.

Norm-referencing and criterion-referencing often concern the way in which evaluative data is treated, rather than the nature of evaluative instruments themselves. The same test may be either norm-referenced or criterion-referenced. If it is criterion-referenced, students will be graded according to their reaching one or more specific cutoff points. If it is norm-referenced, students will be graded in terms of their rank order of achievement on the test.

Although both norm-referenced and criterion-referenced assessment have their advocates, among assessment experts the proponents of criterion-referencing have been more numerous in recent years. In part, this reflects some of the negative consequences of competition for grades that is apparent in the norm-referenced classroom. Under criterion-referenced evaluation, every student can reach the announced standards and become a winner. Under norm-referenced assessment, for every winner there is at least one loser—what is known as a "zero-sum game." Criterion-referenced assessments allow all students to show that they have learned and to experience success. But on norm-referenced tests, half of the students will score below the median and are likely to feel unsuccessful, however good their actual achievement. Norm-referencing consequently tends to work against the self-image of those students whose self-confidence is already low.

An interesting study by Herbert Marsh has shown that norm-referencing may also injure the self-concept and learning of high achievers. Using data on 14,825 students in 1,015 American high schools, Marsh showed that attendance at a high-achieving high school actually tended to suppress student achievement: "There is no support whatsoever for any positive benefits associated with attending higher-ability schools" (1991, p. 471). The critical factor appears to be not the caliber of the school or its students, but the policy of norm-referencing. Marsh suggests that the effect in such schools of constant comparison among and ranking of students in terms of their achievement often has the effect of diminishing the self-concept and educational aspirations even of competent students.

Snapshot versus continuous assessment

Snapshot assessment has some of the limitations of photography. The picture that looks natural may in fact be posed. The camera may catch the subject at a particular advantage or disadvantage. Few people like the way they appear in photographs. One-shot evaluations, such as the conventional examination, suffer similar limitations. They usually involve artificial situations not encountered outside of schools; much depends on students' test-anxiety level or how they are feeling on the examination day; and a single test may not do justice to a student's competence. Often it is preferable to build a cumulative record of pupil performance. The "writing folder," for example, containing all the pieces of writing completed during a year or a semester, like the art portfolio, will provide a much fuller account of a student's writing abilities than could any one-shot assessment.

Continuous assessment is truer to the cumulative and integrative nature of learning. The question of interest if often not, Has the child achieved this criterion? but Where is the child on this continuum? Human learning tends to proceed through a series of phases, as learners become able to accommodate more elements of information, build relationships among the separate elements, and ultimately construct abstract concepts or general rules (Biggs & Collis, 1982). In skills training, we are often interested not simply in whether a person can perform a skill, but at what level: for example, only with assistance, with occasional assistance, without assistance, or at an independent and superior level. Once the continuum is understood and described, benchmarks can be identified that will help to locate and track each student's progress.

Assessment by teachers versus assessment by learners

Assessment is usually viewed as a major responsibility of teachers. However, teaching students to assess one another's work not only shares the heavy load of marking, but also helps students to learn and to take responsibility. It utilizes a potentially rich source of feedback that is always available, though usually neglected, right in the classroom. It is necessary that the criteria be discussed with students and be as clear as possible. In awarding marks to the work of peers, students tend to be cautious and use rather a narrow range of marks. Peer assessment is particularly valuable for formative assessment. Sometimes a successful division of labor can be established by peers identifying good and bad points and teachers awarding marks. If the assessment is summative, the teacher must be certain that the marks awarded can be justified. Note that in some jurisdictions peer assessment is prohibited by privacy legislation.

In self-assessment, this process is taken one stage further. The aim of education is to produce autonomy, not dependency, and it is therefore not only legitimate but important that students become able to evaluate their own work. The more students understand and internalize criteria for assessing their own progress,

the less arbitrary will assessment—and education—seem to them. Furthermore, inviting students to evaluate their own work shows respect for them as responsible people (Falchikov & Bond, 1989; Gorman, 1989).

FIVE CRITERIA FOR ASSESSMENT

If assessment has a bad reputation particularly among those who are assessed, it is often because the assessment instruments used are in fact deficient. By deficient I mean that they violate one or more basic criteria. Let us consider five criteria that are crucial.

Humanity

Validity is usually considered the primary criterion for assessment. I propose, however, that the first order of priority should be humanity. Is a test, examination, measure, or performance criterion humane? Does it help the learners to thrive and grow as persons? Does it develop learners as social beings? Does it avoid causing unnecessary anxiety, pain, humiliation, or self-doubt? Regardless of how valid and reliable an assessment may be, if it is inhumane it is inappropriate for use with human beings.

Validity

In the assessment context, a test is usually defined as valid if it measures what it purports to measure (Zeller, 1990, p. 251). However, educational tests, unlike tape measures or weigh scales, rarely measure anything directly. Instead, they provide measures, based on a limited sample of behaviors, that allow us to make inferences about learners. As Windham and Chapman put it: "Items on a test are only a sample of the universe of possible items that might have been asked. The claim, based on a test score, of what participants have learned is actually an inference to that universe of items of which the test is but a sample" (1990, p. 199). The inferences of interest are those concerning the learner's achievement of the objectives. So we might better define an assessment as valid *if it allows us to make correct and useful inferences about the student's learning* (Messick, 1989).

Inferences are one of the pitfalls of testing. We find, let us say, that it is difficult and time-consuming to test a child's ability to write good prose. So we conduct experiments with true/false questions to see if any of them *predict* children's ability to write prose. Sure enough, after several hundred tryouts, we eventually identify twenty true/false questions which the good prose-writers consistently answer correctly and the poor prose-writers consistently answer wrongly. Now instead of having children and evaluators spend a lot of the time writing and reading prose, we can simply have children answer true/false questions, and then make inferences about their prose writing. Alas! The argument is all too seductive, and its consequences are played out annually in thousands of classrooms. The first thing that happens is that teachers, recognizing the nature of the tests, stop teaching children how to write prose and instead have them practice answering true/false questions. What the tests then begin to predict is not good prose-writing but good test-coaching.

A study by Swamy (1987) provides a typical example. Swamy found that 97 percent of a sample of chemistry students solved gas-pressure problems correctly. But in interviews, only 3 percent actually revealed understanding of gas pressure.

Now, this is not to say that indirect assessment is necessarily invalid. We use a fuel gauge in our car, which is an indirect measure, rather than a dipstick in the gas tank, which would be direct. But it does seem desirable that the measures we use in educational assessment as far as possible consist of the actual tasks that we want students to learn. William McGaghie makes this point about examinations in accountancy. To become a certified public accountant in the United States, a candidate must pass a test that consists predominantly of multiple-choice questions. The qualifying examination for chartered accountants in Canada, however, consists of

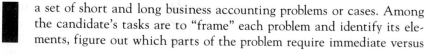

a set of short and long business accounting problems or cases. Among the candidate's tasks are to "frame" each problem and identify its elements, figure out which parts of the problem require immediate versus delayed attention, formulate a problem solution in terms of a series of accounting practices, exercise judgment in developing and evaluating alternatives and proposing practical solutions, communicate effectively with users (write letters and memos), and respond to users' needs. This is just the sort of work that real accountants do when they show up for work. Just like physicians, accountants do not spend their time answering multiple-choice questions at the office.   (McGaghie, 1991, p. 7)

The term "authentic assessment" is beginning to be used for tests that faithfully reflect the intended learning (McLean, 1990; Shepard, 1991). That is, rather than using proxies or predictors, they ask students to display the actual knowledge and skills intended in the curriculum under the conditions in which the learning is normally applied. Writing skills are assessed not by multiple-choice tests, but by collecting samples of students' day-to-day writing. Children's ability to deal with the arithmetic of money is tested not by worksheets but by simulations of purchasing, making change, or budgeting. "A good assessment makes a good teaching activity, and a good teaching activity makes a good assessment" (Shavelson, Baxter, & Pine, 1992, p. 22).

Validity, or authenticity, can be violated in many ways. It is very frequent to encounter classroom tests that assess recall of *course content* rather than achievement of the announced objectives. A teacher may say that his aim is to teach students to adopt responsible attitudes toward environmental conservation. But his assessment consists entirely of questions asking for recall of scientific facts. Another teacher says that she is trying to develop discriminating taste in literature; her tests are composed of factual questions about the plots of Shakespeare's plays. A team of teachers of Spanish announces several objectives having to do with effective oral communication in Spanish; they evaluate this entirely with written tests. A teacher of the learning disabled says she wants to develop good work habits in her students; her assessment of achievement of this attitude consists of deducting five marks for each absence. In all such cases, one would have doubts about the congruence of the measure with the announced curriculum intention.

Reliability

Next in importance to humanity and validity is reliability, which in assessment terms means consistency. More technically, the issue of reliability concerns the question of generalizability, or "how accurately a test sample represents the broader universe of responses from which it is drawn" (Thorndike, 1990, p. 260). A measure cannot be valid unless it is also reliable. A steel measuring tape is, for practical purposes, completely consistent; longer and shorter items will consistently measure longer and shorter, regardless of the attitude of the measurer, the day of the week, or the weather. But in educational practice, contrary examples abound. The same essay is assessed by two teachers: one awards it an "A," one a "C." In a large university course, four students, as an experiment, submit identical essays, each in a different handwriting. The grades range from "A" to "D." Ten principals in a workshop assess a videotaped lesson. The most impressed gives the lesson an "A"; the least awards it an "F." Reuven Feuerstein, a renowned Israeli educator, once worked with an epileptic boy whose IQ was reported as 63. He turned out to have an IQ of 158 (Goldberg, 1991). Most readers of this book will have first-hand knowledge of similar experiences.

Reliability is a major problem inherent in any measure relying on human judgment. In the Olympics, certain events have highly reliable measurement, such as electronically timed track events. Others, such as diving or gymnastics, require a measure of subjective judgment. The problem of reliability is reduced, for example in figure skating, by using seven judges and ignoring the highest and lowest scores. There is a law of measurement that *reliability increases as a function of the number of observations.* The scoring of essays is notoriously unreliable, but if you could have each student essay graded by ten judges and average their scores, the measure might have adequate reliability.

Efficiency

The fourth major criterion is efficiency. Bear in mind the rule that reliability is a function of the number of observations. This means there is always a tradeoff between reliability and efficiency. As in medicine, testing in education should be as quick and painless as possible. And as in medicine, we should use the smallest sample that will provide a reliable measure. If your physician decides to have your blood tested, she or he does not drain all the blood from your body! Ten milliliters would usually be adequate. Similarly, if we want to find out whether students can spell correctly the most common 1,000 words in the English language, it is not necessary to test them on all 1,000; a random sample of 50 would be plenty. Instructional time is sacrificed if a forty-minute test is used when a five-minute quiz would yield results just as useful.

Frequency

Frequent small tests, both formative and summative, are more effective than widely spaced major examinations. Frequent opportunities to demonstrate success, practice skills, receive feedback, and focus on learning priorities all contribute to higher achievement and more favorable student attitudes (Bangert-Drowns, Kulik, & Kulik, 1988). These findings suggest the desirability of assessing student achievement once instruction on each objective is complete, rather than (or in addition to) assessing several objectives after a prolonged period of instruction.

TYPES OF ASSESSMENT INSTRUMENTS

There are many different ways of assessing student learning. These may range from having a beginning piano student play a Clementi sonatina to observing a surgical intern remove an appendix. Here, we will limit our comments to seven main kinds of assessment instruments.

Observation

Experienced teachers use observation a great deal. They are constantly aware of which students are having difficulty or are becoming distracted. Often, particularly in the early grades, they maintain a logbook in which they record observations on students' work habits, their reading progress, and so on. A self-adhesive notepad carried in the teacher's pocket is a useful medium for recording observations on children which can later be stuck on their record. ("2/11/93: I asked Jimmy to point to a 2 and he pointed to a 5.") Table 4-2 shows an example of such anecdotal comments. A tape recorder, a Polaroid camera, or a videocamera are also very useful for capturing children's active and interactive performance, particularly when working in groups. There is no need to try to be a full-time photographer: simply assign each child the task one day a month. Such records are particularly valuable on parents' evenings. Children and older students can also be encouraged to maintain a journal in which they record their main daily learning activities and experiences.

Portfolios and records of work

Portfolios are a standard mode of assessment in visual arts such as painting and photography. The "writing folder" is a file in which a student's written work, or the best examples of it, are kept. It can readily be seen how a portfolio could be used to build a record of students' lab reports in science, and how it would also have relevance in such subjects as drafting, mathematics, history, or geography.

Table 4-2   *Example of an Anecdotal Record*

Observation Records

2/15   Observed during retelling activity. A's predictions were good, his actual retelling well-sequenced, sensitive, some good vocab., no punct!!!

2/22   Observed while working on activity involving information for "Stone-Age Man" task. Skim-read for information. First time I knew he knew how to do it.

2/25   Had brief reading conference with A. Reading *First Fleet*. Nonfiction. Says he enjoyed the illustrations, says he chose it for the humor.

4/02   Observed during SSR. A is fully engaged when reading and is covering fiction/nonfiction/poetry. His comprehension so far has been very sound.

(Camborne and Turbill, 1990, p. 346)

Portfolios provide a cumulative record of performance that shows pupil progress over time and is much richer in detail and substance than a mere list of scores. They do not need to be restricted to written material, but can also include such items as tape recordings of children's reading, and of conversations and interviews with the teacher and other learners. Experimental evidence shows that teachers are able to make much more specific instructional plans and recommendations on the basis of portfolios than of standard test scores (Garcia, Rasmussen, Stobbe, & Garcia, 1990).

Portfolios are particularly useful for describing students' progress to parents. A large portfolio can easily be made from two sheets of cardboard taped along three sides. A transparent pocket can be attached to hold the student's photograph. It is a good idea to keep a date stamp handy for dating student's work. A chair or desk turned upside down provides a convenient rack for storing the portfolios. When passed on to the pupil's next teacher, portfolios provide valuable insight into pupils' status as they begin a new year or course.

Oral questions and interviews

Classroom questions are a teaching strategy rather than an assessment instrument. However, insofar as they provide feedback to the teacher, they are a form of assessment. It is known that questions before, during, and after instruction, all assist students' learning. Research indicates that most classroom questions tap only low levels of knowledge. Students learn more if classroom questions are thought-provoking. A question such as "When did Lincoln deliver the Gettysburg address?" requires only recall. The question, "What does Lincoln's Gettysburg address tell us about the differences in American society between 1863 and today?" requires deeper thought on the part of students. "What is the area of a rectangle 3 m × 4 m?" requires simple multiplication. "What is the maximum perimeter of a rectangle of area 12 m²?" requires more sophisticated thought. Because there is a natural tendency to ask more questions of more able students, teachers should take care that their questions are evenly distributed among the learners in a class. It has also been shown that pausing between the question and naming a student—for example, "How would our mathematical system be different if humans had twelve fingers? . . . [3-second pause] . . . Tracey?"—increases the quality of student thought and response (Tobin, 1987).

The oral examination has a long tradition and is still widely used, often as the final hurdle in graduate degrees and advanced medical qualifications. It is also often the method of choice in such areas as assessment of oral fluency in a foreign language. The main weaknesses of oral examinations are (1) they are labor-intensive, because each student must be examined separately; (2) it is difficult to ensure consistency from one examination to another; and (3) there are many ways in which subtle and unconscious bias can interfere with the validity of oral examinations.

The interview constitutes a particular kind of oral examination. It is a standard method in assessing candidates for employment and for professional training. Over 90 percent of American medical schools, for example, employ the interview as part of their selection process (Puryear & Lewis, 1981). The value of preadmission interviews for predicting success in training or in practice is not particularly high—correlations average around .30—but even so it is one of the more predictive measures in an area where prediction is difficult (Pratt, 1987). The interview has generally been shown to be more valuable if (1) the interviewers are trained, (2) the assessment criteria are clear, and (3) the interview conditions and questions are standardized (Mitter, 1990).

Questionnaires

The use of questionnaires in student assessment is largely limited to assessment of attitude. Some of the problems of validity and reliability that afflict questionnaires were outlined in Chapter 2. Despite their known limitations, questionnaires should not be despised as sources of information. Several years ago, the U.S. Air Force found that the best predictor of adjustment of military personnel to service in Alaska was their answer to the single question, "Do you like cold weather?" (Gottman & Clasen, 1972, p. 157). More recently, Drs. Idler and Kasl (1991) found

Table 4-3 *Questionnaire for Self-Assessment in Small-Group Discussions*

Small-Group Discussion: Self-Assessment

Use the following responses to answer each of the questions:

A = Always
S = Sometimes
N = Never

Did I contribute information or ideas to the discussion?	——
Did I show willingness to have my ideas questioned without being defensive?	——
Did I take my fair share of "air time"?	——
Did I encourage other members of the group to contribute to the discussion?	——
Did I question the ideas of others in a friendly way?	——
Did I help the group get back on topic when necessary?	——
Did I ask questions when necessary to ensure I understood what others were saying?	——
Did I modify my views when faced with new or conflicting evidence?	——
Did I show respect for the ideas of others?	——

(Adapted from Cornfield et al., 1987)

that people's answer to the question, "Is your health excellent, good, fair, or poor?" was a better predictor of their mortality than in-depth physical examinations with extensive lab tests.

Questionnaires are rarely used as a basis for awarding marks, and they are often more useful for generating data connected with program evaluation—for example, to find out about student opinion of a course. However, they can also be used to stimulate students to think about their learning. Table 4-3 shows a questionnaire designed to help students reflect on the processes they use in working in cooperative groups.

Checklists

Checklists are an extremely valuable and underutilized resource for teaching and learning. They are of particular value in the assessment of complex skills. Often teachers who begin with observational techniques find that they can eventually formalize some of their expectations into checklists, thus facilitating the process of collecting information. Table 4-4 shows a checklist that might be used in a primary-level language arts program.

Checklists are valuable for students as well as for teachers. They have the virtue of making criteria public, so that learners are clear about exact expectations. Once students receive and understand an assessment checklist, they can become their own evaluators. Table 4-5 shows a checklist for parallel parking. A student driver, armed with this instrument, can assess his or her own competence with little dependency on the instructor.

Table 4-4   Checklist for One Area of Language Development

Confidence in Using Language

	Yes	No
Willingness to share information during sharing/discussion sessions	☐	☐
Willingness to volunteer comments and/or answer questions during sharing sessions	☐	☐
Willingness to question others during sharing/discussion sessions	☐	☐
Willingness to respond to questions and criticisms about own language products (pictures, written text, oral text)	☐	☐
Willingness to attempt new language tasks	☐	☐

(Adapted from Camborne and Turbill, 1990, p. 347)

Table 4-5	*Checklist for Parallel Parking*

Checklist for Parallel Parking

Directions: A check in the appropriate box indicates that the student has satisfactorily demonstrated the procedure indicated.

	Yes	No
1. Uses correct signals throughout	☐	☐
2. Uses mirrors and shoulder-checking throughout	☐	☐
3. Avoids unduly obstructing traffic	☐	☐
4. Stops with rear bumper level with rear bumper of car ahead of space	☐	☐
5. Turns wheel to reverse at 45-degree angle	☐	☐
6. Reverses until front bumper has cleared rear bumper of car ahead of space	☐	☐
7. Turns wheel and backs into space	☐	☐
8. Pulls forward and stops in middle of space	☐	☐
9. Stops with inside wheels within 20 in (50cm) of curb	☐	☐
10. Turns wheels correctly for gradient	☐	☐
11. Engages parking brake	☐	☐
12. Avoids touching other cars or curb	☐	☐
13. Pulls out of space without hitting car or obstructing traffic	☐	☐

Essay-type questions

Essay questions belong to the class of assessment instruments known as "constructed-response questions." These are instruments in which the examinee is asked to create a response, as contrasted with "selected-response questions," in which the student selects a response from a given list of alternatives, as in a multiple-choice question.

Constructed-response questions can yield rich information about a student's thinking and learning. Assessment of a learner's ability to organize information, to think through a problem, to marshal an argument, to write descriptive prose, to paint a watercolor, to design an experiment, to troubleshoot a malfunctioning carburetor, or to write a poem demand some kind of constructed response on the part of the learner. Much research has suggested that students' performance on selected-response tests is generally a good predictor of their performance on constructed-response tests, and an effect of this research has been to reduce the use of essay tests in standardized testing programs in the United States and other countries. More recently, however, researchers have challenged these findings, pointing to the decline in students' writing skills, and proposed a return to wider use of constructed-response tests (Quellmalz, 1990).

Constructed-response tests, however, suffer from some significant disadvantages. We shall discuss these problems in terms of the student essay, which throughout the world and throughout history, is probably the single most widely used assessment instrument. The first problem has to do with unreliability of scoring. Such factors as writing speed, student's name, verbal fluency, student test anxiety, examiner familiarity with the examinee, and other sources of examiner bias can seriously distort the mark awarded (Fuchs & Fuchs, 1986; Harari & Mc-David, 1973). Scannel and Marshall (1966) showed that essay grades will be adversely affected by errors of punctuation, spelling, or grammar, even when markers are specifically instructed to disregard such errors. The same is true of handwriting (Markham, 1976). Agreement among markers of essay tests is notoriously low. It can be improved by lengthening the test and increasing the number of markers. But this may not be feasible. The designers of the Advanced Placement Examination in American History calculated that a score reliability of .90 could be obtained with an eleven-hour essay test containing fifteen questions, each marked by a different rater (Coffman, 1971).

On the other hand, an extended piece of writing, such as an essay, is the only really authentic way to judge a student's prose-writing ability. The essay allows an insight into the learner's abilities of organization and self-expression, understanding, and orientation difficult to achieve by means of a selected-response test. For these reasons, essays are particularly useful for formative assessment, where, because no marks are recorded, reliability of marking is not a critical issue (Stake, 1983).

In any assessment, it is necessary to ask, What real-world capability is being assessed? The formal essay test requires learners to produce, from their internal resources, quality prose under timed conditions. While this may be a valuable skill for journalists and diplomats, it is one that will rarely be used by most adult citizens. The argument that essays test higher-order thinking is plausible. But analysis of university examinations shows that the great majority of essay questions require simple recognition and memory of facts, with some ability to apply factual information in fairly routine ways (Beard & Pole, 1971). Furthermore, essays are relatively inefficient: they can assess only a few areas of learning per hour of assessment time and therefore may not validly sample a student's learning (Lorber & Pierce, 1990).

A number of steps can be taken to increase the value of essays as assessment instruments: (1) The problem of unreliability of marking can be offset by using essays primarily for formative assessment, where the purpose is to obtain insight and to comment on the learner's progress, rather than for summative assessment, in which marks are awarded and recorded. (2) The skills, concepts, or principles that are to be assessed should be clearly defined for examiners and students. (3) Essays are inefficient for testing knowledge; they should be used for assessing higher-order understandings and intellectual skills. (4) The essay question should be precise and clear: "Discuss inflation" is not as clear as, "In 1–2 pages, describe the relationship between unemployment and inflation." (5) The scoring criteria should be explicit for both examiners and students. (6) The mode of discourse required of students should be indicated. Is it, for example, to describe, to summarize, to express, to inform, or to persuade? (7) Several short essays will sample the learning more adequately, and hence provide a more reliable score than a few long essays (Quellmalz, 1990). (8) Ideally, each essay should be read by at least two judges. (9) The examiner should write a model answer to each essay before beginning to score essays: This both sharpens criteria and enhances empathy. (10) Holistic evaluation is often more valid and efficient than itemized marking scales (Scriven, 1983). (11) In any large-scale testing program, raters should be trained and periodic checks made to ensure comparability of judgments. (12) If students perform poorly on essay questions, they may need instruction specifically on essay-writing and examination skills.

The question of authentic assessment is particularly germane to the use of essay tests. If nurses are being taught "how to give an intramuscular injection," it is more appropriate to have them demonstrate this skill on one another, using injections of distilled water, than to have them write an essay on intramuscular injections. In preparing an assessment of students' abilities in such a subject as history or English, we need to ask, in what ways will our students use these knowledges and skills in the real-world (or the after-school world) context? When this question is asked, the ritualized formal essay examination in the school gymnasium often begins to appear bizarrely inappropriate. Sometimes its only defense is that it is preparation for the same kind of questionable ritual at the university level. People do use essay-type skills in their private and occupational lives: when writing letters, memoranda, and reports. But typically they have the opportunity to draft and revise several times, with considerable time flexibility, and with access to human and reference resources. In such circumstances, the take-home essay will be a more appropriate measure than an essay examination under timed and artificial conditions.

Selected-response questions

Selected-response questions include multiple-choice, true/false, matching questions, and any other question in which the student selects an answer from a restricted list of alternatives.

It is harder to write good selected-response questions than good essay questions (and that is not easy). The prevalence of defects in selected-response tests has given them a bad reputation among teachers and students. It is not true that selected-response questions can assess only trivial knowledge (Choppin, 1990a). But it is the case that most such questions used in classrooms test little else. The quality of selected-response tests can be safeguarded to a considerable extent by avoiding certain common errors.

1. **Avoid internal clues.** Often the correct answer is more detailed or longer than distractors. Test-wise students quickly learn that choices including the words

A good many years ago I visited a school . . . and picked up the composition book of a 9-year-old boy. In it I read a composition entitled "My real father." The subject set to the class had been "My father," and the author of this particular composition had asked whether he might be allowed to write on his *real* father. I mention this circumstance because it shows that the teacher did receive a warning that the subject had some special significance for the child. The composition was as follows:

> My father is on the broad side and tall side. My father was a hard working man and he had a lot of money. He was not fat or thin. . . . His age was about 30 years when he died, he had a good reputation, he is a married man. When he was in hospital I went to see him every Sunday afternoon. I asked him how he was going on, he told me he was getting a lot better. My father was very kind to me and gave me and my cousins cigarette cards. He likes doing woodwork, my father, for me, and he likes a little game of cards now and then; or a game of darts. He chops the wood and saws the planks and he is a handsome man but he is dead. He worked at the rubber works before he died.

The comment that the teacher had thought fit to write at the foot of this intensely moving and, in its way, beautiful piece of writing, was: "Tenses. You keep mixing past and present."

John Blackie (1963, pp. 15–16)

"always" and "never" are usually wrong. Patterns of correct responses need to be avoided; many students use the rule "when in doubt, select choice C." The following question contains an obvious grammatical clue:

A polygon of eight sides and eight angles is called an:

A   octagon

B   pentagon

C   hexahedron

D   cube

2. **Avoid "all of the above" and "none of the above."** There is a systematic tendency for such choices to be right rather than wrong, which acts as an internal clue. They also have a more serious defect. Consider the following question:

Which of the following poets wrote his or her best poetry before the age of 35?

A   *John Keats*

B   *Alan Seeger*

C   *Sylvia Plath*

D   *All of the above*

In this question, "All of the above" is correct. But in fact, choices A, B, and C, are each correct, and it would be unjust to penalize a student for choosing one of them.

3. **Avoid long confusing stems.** The following question does not test knowledge so much as the logical skills of understanding complex prose:

Considered from an economic viewpoint, which of these proposals to maintain world peace derives the least support from the military potentialities of atomic energy?

A   *An international police force should be established.*

B   *Permanent programs of universal military training should be adopted.*

C   *Sizes of standing military forces should be increased.*

D   *The remaining democratic nations of the world should enter into a military alliance.*   (Ebel, 1972, p. 199)

4. **Avoid negatives in item stems or responses.** Questions such as the following involve logical skills in untangling the double negatives:

Which of the following was not a major cause of the First World War?

A   *Britain and Germany were competing in naval power.*

B   *Germany did not expect the United States to intervene.*

C   *France resented German possession of Alsace-Lorraine.*

D   *Russia could not await a German declaration of war before mobilizing.*

5. **Use a complete question in the stem, followed by four answers.** A sentence-completion format is more difficult to understand.

6. **Avoid questions to which the "correct" answer depends on agreeing with the examiner's bias.** I was not at first aware that a standard question I used to use in a curriculum planning quiz contained a cultural bias:

Effective classroom discussion requires eye contact.

True ❏

False ❏

When I taught the course to a group of aboriginal teachers, one of them pointed out to me that in an aboriginal cultural context, prolonged eye contact with a teacher would be viewed as defiance on the student's part (Merle Pegahmagabow, Personal Communication, October 1992).

7. Avoid questions that test trivialities.

Which play did Shakespeare write in 1599?

A   *The Tempest*

B   *Romeo and Juliet*

C   *Macbeth*

D   *Julius Caesar*

Such questions bring multiple-choice questions into disrepute. They also send a distinct message to students. The message is: This test is trivial, this course is trivial, I am trivial, and I consider you trivial!

Thoughtful students, especially those who are divergent thinkers, often feel disempowered by selected-response questions. They may read complexities into a question that have been overlooked by the test designer. For example, what is the answer to this question?

Water freezes at 0°C.

True ❏

False ❏

The more thoughtful student may realize that the answer is "False" if the water is salty or not at sea level.

One technique that helps offset student frustration with selected-response questions is to invite students to write justifications for their responses, as shown below:

What is the minimum students should do before they are awarded credit for a course or unit?

A   *Master all or almost all of the content*

B   *Master at least half of the objectives*

C   *Master all the critical objectives*

D   *Score 50% or more on the final exam*

Justification _____

Not all students will respond to the invitation, and few will write many justifications. But this procedure does give students an option that they value; it makes them feel more comfortable and, in their view, makes assessment more of a learning experience (Gorrell & Cramond, 1988).

> One fool can ask more questions in a minute than twelve wise men can answer in an hour.
>
> Lenin (Lockhart, 1974, p. 245)

PERFORMANCE CRITERIA

Our interest in this chapter is in those aspects of assessment that need to be considered during curriculum planning. The approach is based on the assumption that the purpose of curriculum is not to help students prepare for tests, but to help them meet significant needs. In other words, curriculum should drive assessment, not vice versa. For this reason, our main interest is in discovering the progress students are making with respect to the learnings we consider important. This means that we are interested in assessing not on a calendar basis, at the end of each year, semester, or month, but on a curriculum basis. *The appropriate point for summative assessment is when the student has had an adequate opportunity to learn something.*

Several different kinds of objectives were described in Chapter 3. Let us focus for the moment on the assessment of "preordinate" objectives, that is, on objectives determined in advance of instruction, typically in the knowledge and skill areas. If a learning is important enough to write into an objective, then it is important enough to find out whether students have learned it. Knowledge, skill, and attitude objectives are generally written in terms of states of mind rather than behaviors. These states are internal to the knower and not visible to another person. So in order to ascertain, or rather, to infer their existence—for example, to determine whether the learner knows or is able to do something—we need to ask for some kind of behavior that we can assess. The term *performance criterion* will be used to refer to such behaviors.

The purpose of a performance criterion is to provide clear guidance to teachers and students about the means by which realization of an objective will be assessed. Suppose we are teaching a course in personal finance to a group of teenagers. One of the objectives is:

■ *Students will be able to maintain an accurate record of their bank balance.*

We might, after some thought, arrive at the following performance criterion:

> *Given a calculator and a check register showing five credits and ten debits up to a maximum of $1,000, the student will correctly calculate the balance for each line without error in a total time of five minutes.*

Such operational definitions are empowering to both students and teachers. Students warmly appreciate this kind of clarity regarding expectations. They can now practice the skill independently and are in a position to judge their own competence. When they are assessed, dispute is less likely about the grade awarded. Assessment is an area that often produces tension between teachers and students. The less teachers tell students about assessment, the more helpless, anxious, and dependent students become. Statements so frequently heard in classrooms—"Will this be on the test?" "Are we responsible for this?" "Could you tell me if I am doing this right?" "I don't understand why I've lost marks here." "What exactly is it you want?"— are all indications of a high and unhealthy level of student dependency. So long as the criteria for assessment appear hidden within the teacher's mind and inaccessible to the students, so long will assessment seem arbitrary and students will be dependent, helpless, and alienated.

By contrast, take the case of a student who has been told exactly how he or she will be evaluated.

Objective: *The student will be able to use the Pythagorean theorem.*

Performance criterion: *(1) Given drawings of three right-angled triangles with the length of two sides shown, the student will calculate correctly in each case the length of the third side. (2) Given the dimensions of five triangles, the student will correctly identify the two that are right-angle triangles. (3) Using pencil, ruler, unruled paper, and compasses only, the student will use the ratio 3:4:5 to construct a right-angled triangle. The right angle must be between 89 and 91 degrees. Time allowed: ten minutes. Accuracy: maximum of one error.*

Students still require someone to check their work. But their autonomy is greatly increased by the detail provided in the performance criterion. To a degree, they become their own instructors and their own evaluators. Responsibility and autonomy replace dependency.

Note, however, that performance criteria of this kind, designed in advance of instruction, are not appropriate in all areas. It may be desirable to negotiate performance criteria with the class or with individual students. If the intent of instruction is to have students develop their own capabilities or their own image of the world in their own idiosyncratic ways, then the performance criteria must be relatively unrestrictive.

Assessing knowledge

Knowledge is generally the simplest kind of learning to assess. Probably for this reason, most educational assessment examines only knowledge, and often rather low-level knowledge at that. This is particularly true of teacher-made tests (Gullickson, 1982). An analysis of more than 60,000 questions in teacher guides, student workbooks, and tests for nine history textbooks showed that more than 95 percent were devoted to factual recall (Trachtenberg, 1974). An analysis of 8,800 test questions from various grade levels and subjects found that almost 80 percent were at the knowledge level (Fleming & Chambers, 1983). The same is apparently true of examination papers at the university level (Beard & Pole, 1971; Black, 1968). Benjamin Bloom and his colleagues published the *Taxonomy of Educational Objectives: Cognitive Domain* (Bloom et al., 1956), partly to show teachers that there was more to knowledge than mere cognitive recall. Twenty years later, Bloom commented wryly:

> After the sale of over one million copies of the *Cognitive Taxonomy of Educational Objectives,* and twenty years of use of this domain in preservice and inservice teacher training, over 95 percent of test questions that our students are expected to answer deal with little more than information. Our instructional material, our classroom teaching methods, and our testing methods rarely rise above the lowest category of the taxonomy—knowledge.   (Bloom, 1981, p. 146)

Here is a practical example of assessing knowledge. A teacher writes the following objective:

> *The student will know the basic multiplication facts for all pairs of numbers from 1 to 10.*

The teacher's first draft of a performance criterion is:

> *Students will write the correct product of at least 18–20 number combinations in 3 minutes.*

However, reflection shows that this criterion might merely show that students have the skill of multiplication rather than knowledge of the multiplication facts. If these facts are truly known, an answer should be immediately forthcoming. So a time constraint is introduced that is stringent enough to inhibit the use of multiplication skills:

> *Students will write down the products of twenty pairs of digits from 1 to 10, dictated at 4-second intervals (i.e., "Four times seven"). At least 18 of the 20 responses must be correct.*

Here is an example of a more complex understanding:

Objective: *The student will understand the use of metaphor.*

Performance criterion: *The student will submit three examples of metaphor, each from a different genre or medium, e.g., prose, poetry, film, television, radio, conversation, visual art, etc. The student will submit a written paragraph explaining the comparison implied by the metaphor. At least two of the three examples must, in the judgment of the teacher, show a good understanding of the concept of metaphor and of the example chosen.*

Knowledge may be assessed in many different ways, including essays, oral questions, observation of student activity, and asking students to demonstrate their knowledge by creating and performing an improvisation on the subject. For the benefit of students whose learning styles differ, it is important to use varied forms of assessment. Whatever form is chosen, care should be taken that the assessment is not trivial. Trivial assessment encourages trivial learning.

Assessing skills

The typical written test is often suitable for assessing knowledge, but not always for assessing skill. Whereas knowledge can be stated, skills must be demonstrated. Ideally, the demonstration asks students to show that they can use the skill in as realistic a situation as possible. Let us suppose you have written an objective:

Students will be able to distinguish statements of fact from statements of opinion.

An appropriate performance criterion might be something like:

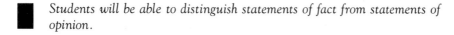

Given an editorial from the local newspaper, containing at least 5 statements that are clearly statements of fact and 5 statements that are clearly statements of opinion, the student will correctly identify, by underlining and labelling, at least 4 of each kind.

Whether the skill to be evaluated is an intellectual skill or a motor skill, the same requirement applies: the student must demonstrate the skill, and the performance criterion must indicate the criteria that will be used to judge the adequacy of the demonstration. Here is an example from a photography course in color printing:

Objective: *The student will be able to recognize and troubleshoot common processing/printing problems.*

Performance criterion: *When shown a set of 10 color prints, each exhibiting one processing/printing error, the student must correctly identify the error* *and describe the corrective action to be taken to remedy the problem for at least 8 of the prints.* (Perrins, 1991, p. 3)

Assessing somatic objectives

Objectives in the area of physical development are usually assessed either by performance or by some biometric measure. Heart-lung capacity, for example, might be measured by a stress electrocardiogram, or by a standard test such as the Harvard step test, or by a specifically designed test involving some suitable activity such as running, bicycling, or swimming. "Sit-ups" are often used to test the strength of abdominal muscles. A curriculum developed by the Wichita public schools spells out this requirement in detail:

Lying on back, hands behind neck and knees bent. Examiner holds the feet down. . . . "Curl" up into a sitting position. . . . Child performs one sit-up, keeping hands clasped behind head. (Wichita Public Schools, 1987, p. 38)

Assessing attitudes

Attitudes are the most difficult kind of objectives to assess. Indeed, most social psychologists would hesitate to claim that any attitudes of an individual person could be validly and reliably assessed. For this reason, attitude assessment is more useful for program evaluation than for assessing individuals. Awarding marks to students for manifesting desired attitudes is particularly problematic.

Suppose a teacher has specified this as one of the objectives of a poetry unit: *"Students will enjoy poetry."* It would seem to be quite useless to ask students to fill in a questionnaire with questions like:

Do you enjoy poetry?

very much ❏

somewhat ❏

not at all ❏

Such an approach suffers from all the problems of questionnaires. Even if the questionnaires are anonymous, the answers may depend not on whether the students enjoy poetry but on whether they like the teacher. A more valid method might be to use what is known as *"unobtrusive observation"* —observing typical and voluntary behavior, which is what attitudes actually describe.

Human behavior is in one way like subatomic particles: It is difficult to observe it without altering it. If a person's normal behavior is subject to the conscious attention of another person, it may cease to be normal. Because attitudes are reflected in normal, voluntary, or habitual behavior, any evaluation of them must normally be unobtrusive.

Garbologists are great unobtrusive observers. A recent book on the "archaeology of garbage" shows that while people may not always be truthful to pollsters, garbage rarely lies. Analyses of garbage show that people generally claim to consume much more cottage cheese, liver, tuna, and skim milk than is actually the case, and far less sugar, candy, bacon, and ice cream. Rich people throw out more gardening products, and poor people more auto-care products (Rathje & Murphy, 1992).

Let us explore further the case of the teacher who is interested in finding out to what extent her students have developed an appreciation for poetry. The teacher could invite a local poet to give a reading one lunch hour, and without putting pressure on students, see how many showed up. Or she could check the library for withdrawals of poetry before and after the unit. Or see how many students submit poetry in response to the course requirement to submit a piece of creative writing. Each of these is a serious effort to determine whether the students' voluntary behavior corresponds to what we would expect of someone who appreciates poetry.

Assessing process objectives

In the activity-based classroom, where not all objectives are preordinate knowledges or skills, but are more often planned encounters, experiences, and opportunities, assessment depends heavily on observation and recordkeeping. Naturalistic methods, described earlier, are particularly valuable when assessing process objectives. Observation, anecdotal comments, quotations, checklists, interviews, photographs, audio and video tape recordings, journals, work samples, writing folders, and portfolios are useful techniques for the assessment of process objectives. Here is an example:

Objective: Students will interact daily with their reading partners.

Performance criterion: Each Grade 9 student will be assigned a reading partner in Grade 4 or Grade 5. For 15 minutes each day, each Grade 9 student will meet his or her partner, to read the partner, listen to the partner read, or help the partner with story-writing. The teacher will monitor the interactions to ensure and encourage appropriate interaction and will read students' journals on a weekly basis. The process will be considered successful if there is any evidence of student growth in communication skills, psychological insight, empathy, social development, student enjoyment, or any other significant area.

Assessing experiences

It will be recalled from the previous chapter that experiential objectives are those experiences that we provide that are intrinsically valuable, or worthwhile in themselves. An example might be a class trip to a live performance of *Romeo and Juliet*. It is important for two reasons not to fall into the "follow-up" trap— requiring the students on their return to answer a quiz or write an essay about Shakespeare. The first reason is that students' knowledge that there is to be some kind of assessment will interfere with the quality of their experience. The second is that if your purpose in organizing the trip is to have students learn more about Shakespeare, it is not an experiential objective, but simply a learning strategy: a means to an end, not an end in itself. What would be valid would be some attempt to assess the quality of the students' experience: a class discussion, review of students' journals, and attention to remarks they make about the experience. The entry in the curriculum might read like this:

> **Objective:** *Students will see a live performance of* Romeo and Juliet *at the Festival Theater.*

> **Performance criterion:** *This objective will be achieved by all students who participate in the class trip to the Festival Theater. The nature and quality of their experience will be monitored by the teacher by means of conversations during and after the trip, and entries in the journals students are required to keep during the course.*

ESTABLISHING EXPECTATIONS

One of the most consistent findings of the school effectiveness research is that teacher expectations have considerable power in determining student performance. This should not be a surprise. Our day-to-day behavior reflects to a great extent the expectations of others. How we behave in our families responds to the expectations of family members. Our work is continually affected by the expectations of colleagues and superiors. It seems to be a natural human response to conform to the expectations of others. It follows that to set low standards for some students, particularly for disadvantaged students, is one of the worst things we could do. What influences attainment is not the teacher's expectations, but the teacher's actions that result from those expectations (Goldenberg, 1992). Once we label certain students as "slow learners," or group them in a "nonacademic" track, or stop asking them difficult questions in class, or require them to repeat a grade, or reward them with marks for effort when they do not achieve marks for attainment, we are setting expectations for continued failure.

One of my graduate students, who taught high school mathematics, became interested in the question of expectations. He had noticed over the years that although few students failed to achieve the 50 percent required for credit in his mathematics courses, there was frequently a cluster of students at the end of the year who had scored about 51 percent (in the jargon, this is called "strategic minimalism"). He asked for and was granted permission by the school principal to raise the passing grade in his Grade 12 math course from 50 to 70 percent. He did not change any other significant element of the course: the texts, exercises, subject matter, and examinations remained as in previous years. You can already guess the result: At the end of the year there were no failures, but there was a cluster of students who had scored 71 percent.

I had to work very hard, but I did it because I wanted to. That's the real key to happiness.

Rosalyn S. Yalow (USA), Nobel Prize for Medicine, 1977. (Current Biography, 1978, p. 460)

There is a mass of empirical evidence on the issue of expectations. It indicates that, up to a point, higher standards lead to greater student efforts and participation. It suggests that the criteria for mastery that we establish are probably some of the strongest determinants of the actual level of achievement reached by students (Kulik & Kulik, 1986; Millman, 1989; Natriello & Dornbusch, 1984). However, unrealistically high standards will be counterproductive, as students will give up when they perceive targets as unattainable.

Setting standards

One of the benefits that results from writing clear performance criteria is the guidance it gives to students regarding the standard of achievement expected. A key question is, How high should the standard be? There is no fixed answer to this question. There is a myth that excellence in education can be achieved by raising all pass marks to 80 percent. But this is as arbitrary as the convention that 50 percent should always be considered a pass. Any skillful test designer can construct a test on which everyone will score at least 80 percent, and another on which no one will score more than 50 percent. There is good evidence, in fact, that teachers do manipulate the difficulty of tests in order to bring test results into line with administrators' expectations for class medians (Wilson & Rees, 1990). Unless we know the nature of the assessment instrument, scores alone are meaningless. Gene Glass, in particular, has criticized the decontextualized setting of standards as "pseudoquantification, a meaningless application of numbers" (1978a, p. 238). He points out that standard-setting must always consider the context of the learners and the learning, citing as an example a study in which Grade 7 pupils averaged 86 percent on vertical addition, but only 46 percent on horizontal addition (1978a).

Some assessment specialists recommend that standards should be set by co-operative deliberation among test designers, teachers, parents, students, and subject matter experts (Hambleton, 1978; Norcini, Shea, & Kanya, 1988). Both the nature of the learners and what is to be learned need to be taken into account. This may be suggested as a general principle: *Set minimum standards as low as is compatible with effective use of the learning*. Thus, in a course on European cultural history prior to a school trip to Europe, a knowledge of 50 percent of the material might well be enough to enhance the quality of the experience in Europe. On the other hand, a child who can play a piece of music on the piano, and plays only 90 percent of the notes correctly, would take or give little satisfaction in the performance. Ability to identify by country 50 percent of the wines in a blind test at the end of a wine tasting course could be regarded as reasonable success. Ability to spell only half of the words correctly in a university English paper—or to land a plane safely half the time—or to know half of artificial respiration—would not.

As a general rule, standards will be higher when

a) the learning is critical, or

b) the learning is prerequisite to subsequent learning, or

c) the consequences of inadequate mastery are serious, or

d) the probability of use of the learning is high, or

e) the student is allowed multiple attempts to reach the standard.

A corollary to this discussion is: *Avoid setting standards that approximate mediocrity*. There are several reasons for this. One is that we can usually do much better than mediocrity with a little planning and effort. A more important reason is that when an educational experience leaves students with a mediocre level of achievement, they may begin to believe that their abilities are mediocre. To confirm this, ask most of the population about their abilities in foreign languages or

---

The pursuit of excellence is healthy.
The pursuit of perfection is neurotic.
The pursuit of mediocrity is unnecessary.

(Poster in school hallway, October 1992)

mathematics—mediocrity in these areas is made, not born. I believe it was Lee Sechrest who once remarked that mediocrity is so easily achieved, there is not much point in planning for it!

Setting the passing grade on a test

Many students are socialized at an early age to believe that a score of 50 percent on any test represents a passing grade. Clearly a passing grade of 50 percent on a true/false test would be absurd, because this could be obtained by blind guessing. An attempt is sometimes made to compensate for guessing by deducting the number of questions answered wrongly from those answered correctly. This practice is generally frowned on by test experts (Choppin, 1990b). The arithmetic assumptions are false if each question has more than two possible answers, the practice is generally resented by students, and the purpose can be better realized by raising the passing mark to an appropriate level.

Generally speaking, passing scores on tests are set too low to be sure that they represent competence. Suppose we plan a test of 20 items on which we want the students to be competent "at the 80 percent level." A score of 16 out of 20 sounds quite rigorous; but in fact, 16/20 yields a probability of only 0.44 that a student is competent at the 80 percent level. We would need to raise the standard to 18 out of 20 before the probability would exceed 0.80 that the student was competent at the 80 percent level (Davis & Diamond, 1974).

Individualized standards

There are occasions when a standard needs to be fixed, and there are other situations when it needs to vary with the student. The public generally seems to support the idea that the driver's test maintain a fixed standard of competence. The idea that schools should at least aim at a certain minimal level of literacy in their graduates is rooted in an ideal of social justice. It is in students' interest to ensure that all of them have reached a minimal level in their ability to solve simple equations with a high level of accuracy before encouraging them to embark on calculus.

On the other hand, there are many contexts in which we seek to monitor individual achievement rather than impose a common standard. This is the case for much of the learning in the early grades. It may also apply in later grades. Let us look at weightlifting as a simple example.

Objective: The student will be able to perform the curl.

Performance criterion: The student will curl a 30-kg barbell 10 times.

This performance criterion takes no account of different levels of strength on the part of students. A rough adjustment might be made by compensating for body weight:

Performance criterion: The student will curl a barbell one-third of his or her body weight 10 times.

However, this criterion does not take into account that some students may have been able to perform at this standard before entering the course. To deal with this factor, we might say:

Performance criterion: The student will be pretested on the curl. On the post-test he or she will perform 10 curls of a barbell at least one-third of his or her body weight and at least 10 percent heavier than that curled on the pretest.

ASSESSING PROGRESS OF STUDENTS WITH SPECIAL NEEDS

It is the task of professional educators to work effectively with all their students. The students whom teachers encounter in classrooms are becoming more diverse as the practice of mainstreaming becomes more widespread. Chapter 7 is devoted to the issue of adapting curriculum for individual differences. At this point, some observations may be made about planning assessment for special students.

The points made earlier regarding clear criteria and expectations in most cases apply at least as strongly with regard to special students. However, there are many kinds of exceptionality. In the case of giftedness or hearing impairment, it may be unnecessary to make any change in written testing materials. In the case of visual impairment or reading disability, assessment instruments involving reading and writing may be replaced by having another student read questions orally or by using a tape recorder for questions or answers.

More important are the issues raised by learning disabilities. As a general rule, we have set realistic objectives and performance criteria that we believe almost all pupils can attain. We have decided what prerequisites are critical. But what of the 5 percent, or the 1 percent, or the one-tenth of 1 percent of students who cannot attain these standards? What if school policy dictates the admission into our program of learners who lack the critical prerequisites? Here are some ideas.

1. **Don't give up too easily.** Try everything else before you decide that the critical objectives cannot be mastered. Try to find an adult volunteer who can tutor the student. Try peer tutoring. Try different instructional strategies, particularly those using tactile or kinesthetic approaches. Try interviews, oral questions, or observation of classroom work rather than written assessment. Critical objectives are crucial to the learner's welfare or educational progress. Once we lower our expectations, they may become self-fulfilling prophecies that further stigmatize and stereotype the disabled learner. Don't demean students by "giving away" marks. Take heart from educators such as Kaare Bolgen, whose article, "There Are No Hopeless Children" (1970) reports his experiences teaching profoundly disabled children how to do such things as read and ride a bicycle.

2. **Try to find special strengths.** Use and review pretest data. Interview parents. Don't underestimate these students. The learners may be disabled in certain areas; that does not mean they are disabled in all. They may have special gifts or interests in music, in visual arts, in constructing three-dimensional objects, or in making friends. Emphasize the positive. Plan modes of learning and assessment that use these strengths. Recognize student effort and growth (in addition to, not instead of, achievement). Plan successful experiences, praise student success to their parents, celebrate achievements.

3. **Provide the disabled learner with more time to learn and to demonstrate learning.** Provide students with examples of and practice with forms of assessment (Lundenberg & Fox, 1991). Provide frequent informal feedback. Allow multiple attempts at achieving standards without penalty. In assessing, concentrate on the positive. Evaluate in informal ways to avoid stimulating test anxiety. Ensure that instructions are clear and understood. Focus on the concrete rather than the abstract; for example, test the student's ability to make change by having him or her make change, not by written answers to mathematical or word problems. If necessary, focus only on the critical learnings and sacrifice the noncritical.

4. **In testing, emphasize the progress, achievement, and quality of work of the student, not comparison with other learners or merely handing work in.** Give feedback in the form of positive comments rather than numerical or letter grades. If appropriate, announce that test scores will be used only to raise grades, not to lower them (Barth, 1990a).

5. **Pay special attention to the development of learning and study skills in learning-disabled students.** As these students are likely to have had a history of school failure, it is especially important to develop their self-concept by providing them with experiences that lead to success. It may be appropriate to use some strategy such as allowing students to bring to a "closed-book" test as much written material as they can fit on one sheet of paper. In preparing a "crib-sheet" of this kind, students will develop notetaking and paraphrasing skills; they will also learn most of the requisite material.

6. **Ask yourself what really is critical for these learners.** It may be that developing some learning skills, work habits, a greater degree of self-control, or an enhanced self-concept is critical for them, rather than particular knowledges or cognitive skills.

TEST CONSTRUCTION

Up to this point, we have discussed assessment in terms of assessing objective by objective. Sometimes an individual objective will require a small formal test. Sometimes a formal test is considered desirable to evaluate achievement of several objectives at once or to assess the students' integration of the learning of a course or unit as a whole. The first question to ask is always, is a formal test needed? If student achievement on each objective has already been assessed by means of performance criteria, then a comprehensive test may be redundant. The reason often given for end-of-year tests, that students will otherwise forget material as soon as they have satisfied the performance criterion, seems fatally flawed; in that case, they will surely forget it after the final test.

Published tests

Thousands of tests are published annually by publishers and testing agencies. These tests are designed by experts in testing and in the subject matter and have usually undergone extensive field testing and revision. *The Mental Measurements Yearbook* (Mitchell, 1985) contains information on over 1,400 published tests. Other sources of information on published tests are *Test Critiques* (Keyser & Sweetland, 1984–1986); *Tests: A Comprehensive Reference for Assessments in Psychology, Education, and Business* (Sweetland & Keyser, 1984); and *Tests in Print* (Mitchell, 1983). Clearly, caution is needed in the selection and use of published tests, which may have been developed for use in a different curriculum context. Nevertheless, if a satisfactory published test is available, it is wise to review it before embarking on designing a homemade test.

Curriculum planners can be of great service to teachers by developing good assessment materials and including them in the curriculum document. In the absence of time and expertise, the tendency is for teachers to produce tests that trivialize learning. The construction of tests that assess significant learning in significant ways requires time, dedication, and competence—and is therefore a highly appropriate activity for curriculum planners. This is especially the case if the assessment materials need to contain graphics, as may often be the case with such subjects as science, geography, or visual arts. The Phoenix Union High School District *World History/Geography Curriculum Guide* (1990), for example, contains a large number of assessment instruments of different kinds that are photocopier-ready for use by teachers.

Planning a test

If a suitable published test is not available, it will be necessary to design your own test. It is most important that the test reflect the emphases of the course. Unless you have advised them otherwise, students will expect that those topics that you have indicated as critical and those dealt with at greater length will be given proportionately greater emphasis on the test. With this end in view, a "Table of Specifications" is constructed. Table 4-6 shows an example.

In addition to ensuring a balance of content, it is also wise to ensure a balance between questions that assess recall and those asking for higher-order thinking. If this is not done, there is a danger that the test will consist almost entirely of recall questions, which are much easier to construct. Even professional test designers are prone to write items primarily measuring recall of information (Frederiksen, 1984).

Table 4-6   *Table of Specifications*

Topic	Emphasis in Course	Total Questions
Political history	10%	5
Social history	40%	20
Economic history	20%	10
International relations	10%	5
Historical interpretation	20%	10
Total	100%	50

Planning the administration of tests

The purpose of a test is to allow all students to perform at their best. For this reason, the conditions of testing should be well controlled. For conventional written examinations, a wall clock should be visible to all examinees. Attention should be paid to physical comfort, with comfortable chairs and adequate work space, lighting, and ventilation. Outside noises, telephones, bells, and interruptions via the public address system should be eliminated. Questions raised by students should be answered "without disdain, sarcasm, or impatience, no matter how trivial or redundant the questions may appear" (Airasian & Terrasi, 1990, p. 120).

Test instructions are very important. They should give students all the relevant information they need about how much time they have, how marks will be allotted to different parts of the test, what to do if they have a question, and so on. The following instructions might head an essay examination:

Answer three of the questions on this page. You have two hours from the time the examination begins. Each essay will be marked out of 20. The following criteria will be used.

Did you state both points of view?
Did you establish your point of view on each issue?
Did you use supporting evidence?
Did you indicate why other points of view were less satisfactory?
Is your argument organized, clear, logical, and convincing?
(Adapted from Cornfield et al., 1987, p. 129)

Cheating

Although it falls within the realm of practice rather than planning, a word needs to be said about cheating. Studies show that most students admit to having cheated on tests at some time or other (Calabrese & Cochrane, 1991). Obviously,

Answer five questions in all. Answer at least two from Section A and at least one from Section B. Your other two questions may be chosen from any of the three sections. Answer at least two questions from this Section and not more than four. Choose questions on at least two Topics. Answer at least one odd-numbered question and at least one even-numbered question. Do not answer more than two questions on any Topic.

Instructions heading the Advanced Level examination in Latin of the General Certificate of Education, England, 1986 (Hadaway, 1986, p. 13)

a test on which students cheat loses much of its validity; it becomes a test not of successful learning but of successful cheating. Cheating tends to occur when anxiety and alienation are high and preparation is low, and it is something of a barometer of these factors. Children are more likely to cheat if they have low self-esteem and a high need for approval (Lobel & Levanon, 1988). Females are less likely than males to cheat, and more likely than males to do so to help another student than to succeed personally (Calabrese & Cochrane, 1991). It is perhaps more useful to find out what cheating is telling us about the curriculum than simply to condemn and punish it. Students are less likely to cheat if (1) they find the learning intrinsically interesting, valuable, or significant; (2) the material has been effectively taught; (3) they have had successful experiences in previous assessments in the course; (4) they have been advised how to prepare for the test; and (5) they have acquired effective study and examination skills.

Cheating is only one result of high test anxiety. Another consequence of test anxiety is lowered achievement. In severe cases, test anxiety may result in the use of tranquilizers, hospitalization, and even suicide. For humane as well as for educational reasons, teachers should seek to avoid stimulating such anxiety in students. Excessively high standards, sudden changes in test dates or content, difficult or unexpected questions, rigid time limits, unfamiliar or uncomfortable test formats or conditions, lack of information about the nature of examinations, inadequate preparation, punishing parents, pressure to maintain high academic marks, inferior examination skills, and social comparisons (i.e., norm-referencing) will all tend to provoke test anxiety, alienation, and a sense of helplessness (Blishway & Nash, 1977; Crooks, 1988; Weir & May, 1988).

Test-wiseness

Some students perform well on tests, not because they are knowledgeable or hard-working, but because they have honed their examination skills. They have learned how to read internal clues in badly constructed questions; how to write convincing arguments in the absence of information; how to figure out what the examiner wants to hear. One of the main effects of test-wiseness is to reduce the scores of students who are not test-wise. As there is adequate evidence that test-wiseness can be taught to all levels of student (Sarnacki, 1990), the best solution to this problem is to teach the skills of test- and examination-taking thoroughly to all students. For example, there is a widespread idea that when students change their initial answer to a multiple-choice question, they usually change it from a right to a wrong response. But this is a myth. In fact, by changing answers students tend to gain approximately one-and-a-half to three points for every point lost (Geiger, 1991; Weich & Leichner, 1988). The intent of teaching test-wiseness to students is not to provide them with an unfair advantage, but rather to enable all students to perform at their best, unimpeded by their lack of examination skills. This is one way to reduce test anxiety, particularly for low achievers (Naylor, 1990).

TEST ANALYSIS

Test analysis is an important step in test improvement. One kind of test analysis is qualitative: you examine and reflect on student answers and "debrief" the test with students to find out how they felt and thought about the questions. It is also a useful practice to ask students when writing the test to make a note (e.g., by putting an asterisk next to the item number) of any item they consider unduly difficult, trivial, biased, or unfair.

Another kind of analysis is quantitative and is known as "item analysis." It is a useful procedure, developed several decades ago, but still not widely used by teachers. It is a procedure for examining the quality of test items on the basis of information from student responses. The method cannot be readily applied to constructed-response questions, but there are simple applications of it for selected-response items. The calculation of two indices, item difficulty and item discrimination, will be described.

You can begin an item analysis as soon as you have marked all the tests. First, rank the scores from top to bottom. If you have a class of between thirty and forty students, take the top ten papers and the bottom ten papers (technically you should choose the highest and the lowest 27 percent of scores; if you have ten in each group, the arithmetic is simple). You now have a "high" group of papers and a "low" group of papers.

Here is how you calculate item difficulty. *Item difficulty* is defined as "the percentage of students answering a question correctly." (Logically, it should be called item easiness.) To work out the statistic: (1) calculate the percentage of students in the high group answering the question right (e.g., 8 out of 10 = 80 percent); (2) calculate the percentage of students in the low group answering the question right; (3) add these two figures together and divide by two to give the average, as shown in Table 4-7. If, as is usually the case, the scores are normally distributed, the proportion of the high and the low group answering a question correctly turns out to be a very close estimate of the proportion of the total class answering correctly. The item difficulty index may be expressed as a percentage or a decimal.

Item difficulty is a useful statistic. Items that every student answered correctly may be redundant or too easy. But not necessarily: you may simply have

Table 4-7   *Calculating Item Difficulty*

Item Number	High Group (% correct)	+ Low Group (% correct)	÷ 2 = Difficulty
1	90	50	0.70
2	70	60	0.65
3	100	100	1.00
4	60	70	0.65

taught the material very well. You can obtain further data on this issue by giving the question to a group of students who have not received the instruction. If an item seems to be very difficult—for example, if more than half the students got it wrong—you need to examine the item carefully. Was it badly written or confusing? Did it ask for information that had not been taught? Or did the result suggest that the relevant instruction needs to be improved? Teachers need information on item difficulty in order to build fair tests.

Item discrimination may be defined as "the extent to which an individual item discriminates between those who score highest and lowest on the test as a whole." It is chiefly an index of the homogeneity of a test. It has great practical usefulness in test improvement. The same data is used to calculate item discrimination as item difficulty, but this time instead of adding the percentages of high and low scorers answering correctly, calculate the difference by subtracting the low figure from the high figure, as shown in Table 4-8. The discrimination index is normally shown as a decimal. Classical test design sought as high discrimination as possible, as it item number 5 in Table 4-8. But this produces a difficulty of 0.50, which is not compatible with the principles of mastery learning. So on a post-test, the ideal pattern is something like item number 6, where 85 percent of the students answer the item correctly but the discrimination is still a respectable 0.30.

Table 4-8   *Calculating Item Discrimination*

Item Number	High Group (% correct)	− Low Group (% correct)	= Discrimination
1	90	50	0.40
2	70	70	0.00
3	100	100	0.00
4	60	70	-0.10
5	100	0	1.00
6	100	70	0.30

The discrimination statistic is particularly useful for identifying items that work in reverse—that is, items that penalize the most knowledgeable students. Item number 4 in Table 4-8 is such an example; more of the low group got it right than the high group. If there is no obvious reason, such as the marking key being wrong, such items are best abandoned.

It is quite simple to perform item analysis procedures by hand, but computer programs are available for this purpose. After each item analysis, good items can be kept, weak items revised or eliminated. Each item, together with a record of its use, difficulty, and discrimination, can be stored for future reference. As your "item bank" grows, you will be able to use progressively more of the items stored in it. This means that your items, and hence your tests, will in the course of time become fairer, more useful, and more predictable.

Some simple test statistics

Test results are typically reported in statistics that can confuse the nonspecialist. A few of these statistics are worth understanding. We shall look at mean, median, mode, percentile, and standard deviation. None of these are particularly terrifying.

The *mean* of a set of scores is the average. If you add the scores and divide by the number of scores, you have the mean. The mean of 1, 2, and 3 is $(1 + 2 + 3)/3 = 6/3 = 2$. The mean of 1, 2, 3, and 4 is $(1 + 2 + 3 + 4)/4 = 10/4 = 2.5$.

The *median* is the middle score of a group of scores. The median of the scores 1, 2, and 3 is 2. The median of 1, 2, 3, 4, and 5 is 3. The median of 1, 2, 3, and 4 is 2.5 (midway between 2 and 3).

The *mode* is the most frequent score. If five students score 6, 7, 8, 8, and 10, the mode is 8.

A *percentile* tells us where a score falls relative to other scores. A student whose achievement is reported as being at the 90th percentile scores higher than 90 percent of the other students and lower than 10 percent of the others. Percentiles are illustrated in the figure below.

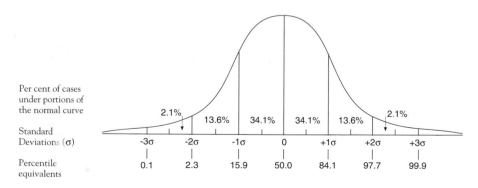

Per cent of cases under portions of the normal curve

2.1% 13.6% 34.1% 34.1% 13.6% 2.1%

Standard Deviations (σ)

-3σ   -2σ   -1σ   0   +1σ   +2σ   +3σ

Percentile equivalents

0.1   2.3   15.9   50.0   84.1   97.7   99.9

The Normal Curve: Percentiles and Standard Deviations

The *standard deviation* is a measure of the dispersion or variability of scores. Statistical calculators normally carry a function for this calculation. If you want to work it out yourself, the procedure is as follows (if you are number-phobic, skip the next five lines): (1) Calculate the mean for the total group of scores; (2) subtract the mean score from each raw score to find the deviation score; (3) square each deviation score; (4) add together all the squared deviation scores; (4) divide the sum by the number of scores to obtain the average; (6) find the square root of this average.

It is more important to understand the meaning of the standard deviation. In a normal distribution, 68 percent of scores fall within one standard deviation above or below the mean. Thus a student who scores "one standard deviation above the mean" is scoring better than 50% + 34% of students, or at the 84th percentile.

GRADING AND REPORTING STUDENT PROGRESS

Grading is the last formal step in the assessment sequence, the point at which some formal summative judgment is made on the student's achievement to that point.

The first question the planner should ask is, Do we need formal grades? Making judgments about people is not something to do unless it is essential.

If the answer is affirmative, the next question is, What form should grades take? Very often, this will be determined by institutional policy. Grading systems differ from one another primarily in the number of grading categories. Percentage

---

A study conducted in Jerusalem, Israel, by Ruth Butler (1988), suggests that task-focused comments enhance student interest and attainment, but that numerical grades damage the performance of students, particularly of low achievers. Butler had low- and high-achieving fifth and sixth grade students perform a series of three tasks, such as constructing words from the letters of a longer word. The 132 pupils were randomly assigned to one of three groups so that they received either (a) written comments, such as "You thought of quite a few correct words; maybe it is possible to think of more short words," or (2) a numerical grade between 40 and 99, or (3) a combination of comments and grades. Butler found that students receiving comments outperformed both the students receiving grades and those receiving grades and comments. In fact, the low-achieving students receiving comments outperformed the high-achieving students receiving grades. Children receiving comments maintained a high level of interest, whereas the interest of the other groups declined over time. The interest level of low-achieving students seemed especially responsive to comments.

grading provides a theoretical 101 categories, from 0 to 100. Letter grading normally has five categories, and pass/fail grading has two. Another type of grading, often very appropriate in the early years, is anecdotal grades, where a teacher's comments constitute the "grade."

Grades should reflect the priorities established by the curriculum. Thus, passing grades should be available only when students have mastered all the critical objectives. Factors such as attendance should not enter into grading decisions unless related to the announced objectives (many U.S. courts have ruled on this issue). Grading decisions are public judgments that can affect the lives of people. They should be able to "stand up in court." A recent study compared the actual achievement of students in an urban school district (measured by curriculum-referenced tests) with the course grades they received (awarded by teachers). The study found that male students and economically disadvantaged students received consistently lower teacher grades than their actual attainment merited. The researchers concluded that the teacher grades were responding to student behavior rather than attainment (Farkas, Sheehan & Grobe, 1990). A minimal requirement of grades is that they be based on thoughtful professional judgment about students related to the overall purposes of the curriculum.

The somewhat thankless task of recording and calculating grades has been made easier and more interesting by the development of software for use with personal computers. Most of these programs enable teachers to create customized spreadsheets, calculate grades and such factors as attendance rapidly, and produce class means, medians, and standard deviations at the touch of a key. Data can be presented in numerical or graphic form, for the whole class, for groups, or for individuals.

There should be more to a school report, however, than numerical grades and "canned" comments. The school report is one of the main interfaces between the school and parents. Some parents want to know about the skills and knowledge their children have acquired. Rather more parents, themselves products of schools

Table 4-9 *Example of an Inadequate Grading System*

If a passing grade is 50, students can pass the course without achieving critical objectives.

Objective	Importance	Value	Cutoff
1	critical	25	20
2	critical	25	20
3	important	15	10
4	important	15	10
5	desirable	10	5
6	desirable	10	5

that ranked their students, want to know where their children stand relative to others of the same age. Some parents also tend to demand quantitative rather than qualitative data. It is a reasonable expectation that school reports contain both kinds of information—a checklist of attainments and an indication of relative standing. Relative standing, however, is more useful if the standard of comparison is a large group—for example, all people of that age in the district, state, or nation—rather than merely a specific classroom which may itself be quite atypical. If our aim is to have students internalize standards of excellence and to take responsibility for their learning, it is appropriate to include space on the official school report for students' own self-evaluations.

News from Grade 2

Dear Carol-Ann*

Good for you for having a perfect record on the final spelling dictations. You are studying your words. I also want you to read out loud every day at home so that you learn to recognize more words. You are reading in a choppy way. With practice you will be a smoother reader. I see a large improvement in your storywriting.

You are a terrific leader at the math centers. Your pattern block designs during the sorting and classifying tubs were used as models for the other children. You are able to name, create, reproduce, and extend patterns. Your measuring activities show a tremendous effort. Well done!

Thanks for being such a dependable researcher. You brought information on monarch butterflies, frogs, owls, bats, moose, and beavers. Your folder about apples was gorgeous. You have a superlative sense of color and design. I can hardly count how much outstanding artwork you have up!

Personal Report Card

(Ralph Westgarth, personal communication, March 1992).

*not actual name

It is a good practice, when writing reports, to spread out the student's work, from portfolios, notebooks, assignments, and so on, and to base the report on immersion in this material rather than on vague and general recollections. If a student has failed to attain objectives but has worked hard, say so. Avoid using jargon in reports to parents. Accentuate the positive, but be candid about failures. A teacher who fails to discuss student deficiencies with parents creates subsequent difficulties for any succeeding teacher who does so.

Parents' evenings and interviews are a major opportunity for communication with the community. Prepare for parent interviews by reviewing the students' work and by having the course outline, objectives, students' records, work folders, and examples of work available. To inspire confidence, you must be superorganized and show detailed knowledge of each student's progress. Parents need to know that you care about teaching and about their child. Don't waffle or use jargon, and don't tell parents you are experimenting with their children! Be candid about underachievement, and tell parents what they can do to help. Try to ensure that the interview setting is as congenial as possible. Displays of students' work add a dimension to marks, and photographs of student activities (on a bulletin board or in a photo album) provide a vivid record. Even better is a videotape or slide presentation with an audiotaped narration made by the students.

Teachers often observe that the parents who most need to attend parents' evenings are those who are absent. But there are many other ways of maintaining contact with parents. The ideal situation was described to me by a teacher in a northern aboriginal community in Canada: The day after every parents' evening, she gets on her snowmobile and visits all the parents who did not attend (Janet Slaney, Personal Communication, August 1992). Completed work can be sent home with laudatory comments. Congratulatory messages such as "happygrams" can be used. Ideally, you should telephone the parents of each of your students once a semester or year. When doing so, emphasize the positive to overcome the tradition that a telephone call from the school means trouble.

Swedish schools have introduced an interesting innovation. This is a meeting twice yearly between the teacher and the student to review achievement in all areas, including both the academic and the personal (Hargreaves, 1989a). This would seem to be an appropriate way of acknowledging respect for the primary client of the school.

■ SELF - ASSESSMENT

Match the statement on the right with the appropriate term on the left.

1. ____ Constructed-response test

2. ____ Criterion-referenced assessment

3. ____ Formative assessment

4. ____ Item analysis

5. ____ Mean

6. ____ Median

7. ____ Norm-referenced assessment

8. ____ Reliability

9. ____ Summative assessment

10. ____ Validity

A.   A technique for the evaluation of individual test items by examination of the pattern of responses.

B.   The extent to which a measure enables an observer to draw correct, meaningful, and useful inferences about the learner.

C.   The average of a set of scores.

D.   A test in which examinees have considerable freedom of choice in response, for example, to write an essay in their own words.

E.   The consistency of a test score when factors other than quality of student response are altered.

F.   The middle score of a set of scores.

G.   Assessment conducted during the course of instruction, primarily to diagnose, monitor, and provide feedback on student learning and/or the instruction.

H.   Assessment based on comparison of learner attainment against fixed criteria.

I.   Assessment at the end of an instructional sequence, intended to judge student attainment and provide a mark or grade.

J.   Assessment based on comparison of a person's attainment with that of other people.

K.   A method of studying typical or voluntary behavior by observing the actions of people who are unaware that they are being observed.

For answers, see Appendix F.
If you answered nine or ten correctly, you understand the material in this chapter.
If you answered seven or eight correctly, reread the relevant parts of the chapter.
If you answered less than seven correctly, reread the chapter carefully.

CHAPTER 5

Describing the Learners

The major developmental task is to become a human being.

Elliot Eisner (1989)

Summary

Instruction must take the initial status of the learner as its starting point. This involves ascertaining such student characteristics as background in the subject material, level of intellectual development, and preferred learning style. Prerequisites help to ensure that the learner can benefit from instruction. Pretests may be used to identify those students who require remediation in the prerequisites, and those for whom the instruction would be redundant. Pretests can also provide information that helps teachers to personalize instruction.

WHAT THE LEARNER ALREADY KNOWS

"Where are we going?" has been the theme of this book up to this point. "How do we get there?" is the theme of the next chapter. Before we can address that question, however, we must look at another: "Where are we now?" There is only one legitimate starting place for instruction: the learner's present status. Determining this status is a crucial step in planning a curriculum.

David Ausubel earned an M.D. and then specialized in psychiatry. Subsequently, he acquired a Ph.D. in psychology and became a licensed clinical psychologist, eventually specializing in educational psychology. Toward the end of a distinguished career, he summarized a lifetime's learning:

> If I had to reduce all of educational psychology to just one principle I would say this: The most important single factor influencing learning is what the learner already knows. Ascertain this and teach him accordingly. (Ausubel, 1968, p. vi)

Typically a curriculum guideline will indicate only that the curriculum is intended for students at a particular grade level. This is insufficient guidance for either curriculum developers or for teachers. The purpose of the learner description is to describe those characteristics of the learners for whom the curriculum is intended that are of importance in planning appropriate instruction. This includes both common factors and the range of diversity among the students.

Not all kinds of diversity are relevant. We are not interested, as a rule, in students' eye color or height. We are interested in such factors as their educational background, their intellectual and social development, and their motivation. The fine detail of these factors will need to be ascertained when an actual class of students is selected, but whether we are dealing with kindergarten students or a third-year medical class, we can always make some descriptive predictions based on previous experience.

Educational background

We can find out "what the student already knows" by means of pretests, and we can, if we wish, dictate it by means of prerequisites. Study of curricula and programs that students have previously taken will tell us what they are supposed to have been taught, if not what they have actually learned. Equally important is the question, What was the quality of the students' prior experience? Have their experiences been predominantly of failure, of mediocre learning, or of success? Of interest, or of boredom? Recent studies in New Zealand and the United States indicate that the most important predictor of children's academic self-concept is their reading achievement early in their schooling; this factor is more significant than, for example, the intelligence, emotional state, or socioeconomic status of their parents (Chapman, Lambourne, & Silva, 1990; Juel, 1989). Previous teacher

---

What do American 17-year-olds know?

100 percent can add and subtract two-digit numbers.

100 percent know everyday science facts.

100 percent can carry out simple, discrete reading tasks.

99 percent know simple historical facts.

53 percent can identify a cause of the "greenhouse effect."

51 percent can compute with decimals, fractions, and percents.

46 percent understand basic historical terms and relationships.

27 percent can identify likely areas of soil erosion using maps of elevation and rainfall.

6 percent can solve multistep mathematical problems and use basic algebra.

5 percent are able to interpret historical information and ideas.

What do our 17-year-olds know? (1990)

---

evaluations are a major determinant of learners' academic self-concept in specific subjects (Hope, Smit, & Hanson, 1990). Parents and peers also help to determine students' educational attitudes and aspirations (Bank, Slavings, & Biddle, 1990; Hossler & Stage, 1992).

Prior academic experience is a crucial factor. As Adele Gottfried puts it, on the basis of her studies of young elementary-school children, "achievement appears to be a more consistent predictor of motivation than the reverse" (1990, p. 537). In other words, the way to raise academic motivation is to work on building success and confidence in academic skills. The prior academic experience and success of the learners needs to be ascertained, so that they can be taken into account in the design of instruction. This can be done by review of student records or by questionnaires administered before or at the beginning of a course. If students have previously experienced a good deal of failure in, let us say, mathematics, then the first part of the math curriculum must involve them in experiences that lead them to significant, worthwhile success.

Level of intellectual development

Research on cognitive development is useful for the curriculum planner. A substantial amount of teacher and pupil failure might be avoided if curricula were planned more carefully with regard to the developmental level of the learners. Classical Piagetian theory identifies four stages through which people move in their intellectual development: the sensorimotor stage, the preoperational stage, the stage of concrete operations, and the stage of formal operations.

The sensorimotor stage characterizes the first two years of life. In this stage children respond to information from their senses, with only the beginning of symbolic thought. The preoperational stage typically accompanies the development of language and allows children to perceive relationships, while egocentrism begins to give way to socially directed thought and action. Some children will still be at the preoperational stage upon entry to school, but others will have arrived at the stage of concrete operations. At this stage children can classify objects and are developing greater social competence and an understanding of the relativity of viewpoints, but they are still solving problems in terms either of application of rules or of direct experience.

The characteristics of the child in K-8

a. Diverse backgrounds in aesthetic experiences and social experiences.

b. Visual expression is varied, some in the "scribble" stage and some in the "symbol" stage.

c. Visual communication is an important means to express needs, desires, and excitement.

d. Naturally spontaneous to creative activity.

e. Approaches activities in a solitary and egocentric way.

f. Teacher and parent are important influences on his/her life.

g. Limited attention span.

h. Enjoys imaginative play and make-believe.

Burlington, MA, *Art Curriculum, Grades K–8* (1985)

The stage of formal operations, typically occurring during adolescence, allows individuals to manipulate abstract ideas and deal with purely verbal problems. Piagetian theory claims that only when individuals have arrived at the stage of formal operations can they think about thinking, imagine possibilities, think in terms of multiple causation, develop theories and intellectual systems, make explanatory judgments, become interested in and understand ideologies, grasp simile and metaphor, and "come to control . . . hypothetico-deductive reasoning and experimental proof based on the variation of a single factor with the others held constant" (Inhelder & Piaget, 1976, p. 335). Questions having to do with philosophy, society, economics, politics, ethics, or history are typically highly abstract and therefore have little meaning to individuals who have not reached the stage of formal operations. This is not a matter of intelligence: before the age of 11, even children with an IQ of over 160 can hardly ever solve formal operations problems (Webb, 1974).

Some researchers claim that a considerable proportion of adults in our society—estimates vary from 30 to 90 percent—never reach this stage (Case, 1973).

The development of a gradient of increasing sophistication of thought has been noted in several different cognitive areas. Young children have difficulty conceptualizing large spaces and their representation in maps (Rhys, 1979). Children's conceptions of the earth move fairly consistently from the idea that the earth is flat, through the idea that people live on top of a sphere in space and that objects fall to the surface of the earth, to the adult notion that people live around the sphere and objects fall toward the center of the earth (Sneider & Pulos 1983). Certain sequences in human learning appear to be unchangeable. For example, "a child will always learn the conditions under which weight remains constant before he learns the conditions under which displaced volume remains constant and after he learns the conditions under which number and amount remain constant" (Case, 1973).

Children's understanding of historical time may serve as an example of intellectual development. At the preoperational stage, the concept of historical time has not developed; few five-year-olds can discriminate between what happened five years ago and five hundred years ago. History is little more than isolated stories and unrelated events. In the stage of concrete operations, although children may know the superficial meaning of words such as "century," they have difficulty understanding long periods of time or ordering events in historical sequence. Prior to the age of 9, many children will answer this question wrongly: "Robin Hood lived in 1187; would your grandmother be alive then?" (Jahoda, 1963). Many 13-year-olds believe that when we move our clocks forward an hour in the spring, we instantly become an hour older. (When in 1548 Europe changed from the Julian to the Gregorian calendar, which meant moving the calendars forward ten days, there were riots everywhere by people who wanted their ten days back!) It is only in late adolescence that the concept of time as an interval scale becomes fully developed.

The development of historical thought has been researched in detail by British scholars. Work carried out in the 1960s and 1970s appeared to confirm classical Piagetian theory, except that abstract thought in history appeared to develop even later than in other areas—typically at about $16\frac{1}{2}$ years (Hallam, 1970; Peel, 1967). Experiments suggested that development of this stage could not be accelerated by deliberate instructional efforts (Shemilt, 1980). It seemed to follow from this that it was wasteful, if not counterproductive, to teach history prior to about Grade 11; learners would simply become bored and frustrated, able only to memorize facts and dates for examinations.

Recent research is more optimistic. Scholars have pointed out that all of Piaget's experiments in the development of formal operations used scientific problems employing logical-mathematical reasoning, which were not necessarily appropriate for investigating historical reasoning (Booth, 1987; Egan, 1983a). It was necessary to construct a picture of the development of historical thought that was true to the discipline, rather than one adapted from a scientific paradigm. This was achieved as a result of the research of several scholars who conducted extensive classroom studies and in-depth interviews with learners.

The picture that emerges is very informative. At the earliest stage, *Stage 1*, predominant in early adolescence, and still apparent in many 14- and 15-year-olds, knowledge of the past is taken for granted—it is given in a book or by the teacher. Pupils say, "I just don't know. . . . I've never thought about it. . . . Teacher always tells us. . . . All the information is written down; you've just got to find the answers in the book" (Shemilt, 1987, pp. 42–43). At this stage, people in the past are seen as, in a sense, mentally defective, and their actions as unintelligible. "The further back we go, the more stupid (primitive, ape-like) people can be expected to be. Patently, people in the past were not as clever as us anyway, because they lacked airplanes and television, thought the world was flat, and had inadequate standards of hygiene and medicine" (Ashby & Lee, 1987, p. 68).

At *Stage 2*, evidence is seen as something to be discovered, and the role of the historian is thought to involve the identification of accurate pictures of the past. Pupils begin to understand the problem of bias and to accept "that there may be more than one possible answer to questions of fact and interpretation" (Shemilt, 1987, p. 48). At *Stage 3*, historical evidence is viewed as being worked out by a rational process whereby conclusions are drawn by inference. Ideas about how evidence is used to test hypotheses are still naive. But the past is no longer viewed as providing direct answers, and a conception of history is emerging that transcends commonsense constructions of everyday experience. At *Stage 4*, "history is beginning to be recognized as no more than a reconstruction of past events, a reconstruction, moreover, which makes visible connections and continuities, moralities and motives, that contemporaries would not have perceived, nor perhaps have understood" (Shemilt, 1987, p. 57).

Equally important in these studies are the findings regarding pedagogy. Ashby and Lee write:

> Children often reach higher levels of understanding when arguing out a problem among themselves than they would achieve on their own, provided the problem is one they have some strategies for tackling. And . . . provided the teacher is prepared to tolerate error, value the various contributions of all pupils, and refrain from early intervention with corrections or the 'right' answer. . . . An instructional and didactic approach is relatively ineffective.   (Ashby & Lee, 1987, p. 86)

While the recent studies of development of historical thought are more encouraging than earlier research, they generally confirm the suspicion that elementary school age children could spend their time more usefully than in the study of history. The danger, which will vary with the sophistication of the teacher, is that children will sit docilely learning names and dates or listening to stories that have little significance or personal meaning. They may reproduce the factual data correctly on tests, and this may be mistaken for historical understanding. The main learning from such experiences is that history is boring and meaningless.

Obtaining a clear perception of the developmental range of the pupils to be taught is an important task for the curriculum planner. At a more basic level, it is one of the tasks of the planner not only to understand what children most need to learn, but also in what order and at what stage they are most ready to learn it.

Why teach a subject at a stage at which success is unlikely? If history is introduced too early, foreign languages are probably being introduced too late. There is substantial evidence that children's linguistic and metalinguistic abilities are highest between approximately 4 and 8 years of age (Safty, 1988). Many parents can attest to the uncanny ability of children at this stage to imitate accent and intonation. Why wait to begin a second language until this ability has diminished?

It is probably time to move on from the narrow, science-based developmental schema of Piaget to construct alternative models of human development that address the particular demands of different areas of the curriculum. A model that is more likely than Piaget's to appeal to teachers of language arts and humanities is Kieran Egan's. He views children's development as proceeding through four stages: the mythic, the romantic, the philosophic, and the ironic (1983a). In a recent work, Egan (1991) outlines some ways in which teachers can capture the interest and imagination of early adolescents. He suggests some interesting ways to revive the woeful state of social studies, the least favorite subject of most elementary school children (Klein, 1989). He points out that, contrary to the arguments of many educators, adolescents are not motivated only by relevance in terms of practical utility. Rather, they are attracted to the legendary, the heroic, the romantic, the exotic, the bizarre, and the extreme. They tend to collect things compulsively, read everything they can about a single topic, keep secret and imaginative diaries often filled with perceptive insights. Egan suggests that teachers should not engage in the hopeless endeavor of trying to make the Middle Ages relevant to such an age group. Instead, they could teach it in a way that responds to the romantic imagination of adolescents. This would involve attention to dramatic stories, such as the assassination of Thomas Becket and the humiliation of the Emperor Barbarossa; the great themes of ideological conflict and schism among religious and secular powers; the enormous popular appeal of personalities like Francis of Assisi and Peter Abelard; details of the differences from our own age, shown by such simple particulars as typical foods and eating utensils; the waning of medieval ideas with the onset of the Black Death and the Inquisition; and the plethora of "strange, exotic, and wonderful events, characters, and inventions of the period" (Egan, 1991, p. 69). Whereas conventional curriculum content often discourages students by its disconnectedness from their lives, teaching of the kind advocated by Egan captures, affirms, and enriches the imaginative life of students.

Learning style

Not everyone learns in the same way. Some people learn best by hearing, some by seeing. Some people study best in low illumination, some under bright lights. Some people learn best in silence, some with music in the background (Dunn, Beaudry, & Klavas, 1989). Three decades ago, Gladstein (1960) described the different classroom behaviors of students with both high and low levels of anxiety. The high-anxiety student sits at the front of the class, takes assiduous notes, recopies

them every evening, listens to the teacher's every word, memorizes material for examinations, and resents other students raising questions or initiating discussion. The low-anxiety student sits at the back of the class (likely with the chair tipped or feet on the desk in front), makes no notes, is not unduly concerned about examinations, and delights in arguing points with fellow students or with the instructor. It is possible to convert an entire class into high-anxiety students, for example, by weighting examinations heavily and providing no guidance to students to help them prepare for exams. Experiments show that students learn best when their learning style is matched by the teacher's teaching style (Cafferty, 1980), but the typical class contains a wide array of different student learning styles. A teacher using a single style will disadvantage many of his or her students. Student variety must be matched by instructional variety.

Gender

Recent years have seen much discussion of and research into the effects of gender on learning, particularly in science and mathematics, but also in such areas as language arts and athletics. Much debate has focused on the question of whether apparent differences are due to biological or environmental factors. A recent, large-scale research synthesis, summarizing the data from many studies in several different countries, involving a total sample of over three million students, shows that differences between the achievement of men and women in mathematics are small and have decreased over the past three decades. Girls outperform boys in computation in elementary and middle school. Differences favoring men emerge in high school; they are generally small and are most apparent in complex problem solving and in highly precocious populations (Hyde, Fennema, & Lamon, 1990).

It seems probable that in some schools subtle social pressures continue to work against high achievement by females in science and mathematics. One of these pressures is the attitude of teachers, which in many studies has been shown to influence students' attitudes and self-concepts in math and science (Baker, 1990; Karp, 1988). Newman and Goldin (1990) found that girls were more reluctant than boys to seek help for problems in learning mathematics. This may account for the fact that some female students appear to achieve better in single-sex environments (Lee & Marks, 1990). To counteract these tendencies, some schools have been successful in offering workshops for teachers and students aimed at providing classroom experiences in science and mathematics that are directed at the interests of women as well as men. Other effective approaches are to bring successful women scientists and mathematicians into schools as role models and to provide practical career information for women interested in careers in mathematics and science (Mason & Kahle, 1988).

Between friends

Marc: I know I'm doing wrong, but I can't control it. I need it. You know I need it so much that I can kill, just to get the money to buy drugs. [Pause] Drugs is one of the biggest problems in school.

Friend: I know it's a big problem and I want you to know that I hope you know what you're doing and, you know, I was gonna let you talk, let you express your feelings. This is what I'm talkin' here for, so you could have somebody to talk to. [Pause] Anytime you want to talk to me you could just talk to me.

Marc: I wanta always have the attitude I had before, you know before I was not using drugs. I know you're a real friend, and I [pause, crying] . . .

Friend: Okay Marc, you don't, Marc, um [pause] you don't have to cry. [Pause] I'm [pause] Marc, okay, that's all right, Marc [pause] stop crying. [Pause] It's all right, don't worry, I'll be with you. I'll pull you through, don't worry about it. You'll pull through this problem, Marc, all you need is a little self-confidence, that's it, and with that self-confidence, you could go anywhere. I mean just think of this, if you wanta become a basketball player, if you wanta become a singer, if you wanta become an actor, you need to fix up your life. [Pause] I'm in back of you. If you fall down, I'll pick you up.

Farrell, Peguero, Lindsey, & White (1988, pp. 495–496)

Student characteristics as resources

Student characteristics should not be viewed merely as constraints. Every student brings unique characteristics and talents to an instructional situation. Some students—gang leaders, for example—have a talent for leadership, some for membership. Some have particular skills in human relations, some in particular areas of expertise. The more of these talents we can identify and allow to flourish constructively in the classroom, the more educative the classroom will become. It is not surprising that peer tutors are among the most effective kind of teachers, and peer counselors the most effective kind of counselors.

PREREQUISITES: BASIC PRINCIPLES

The preceding description of the learner is purely *descriptive*: we are merely writing down the characteristics of students who are likely to find themselves in the program. Prerequisites are *stipulative*: here we are determining the qualities that we want to ensure students will have before they embark on the program. The principle of "moderate novelty" is based on the idea that learning involves two processes: assimilation and accommodation. New learning needs to be similar enough to what is already known that assimilation is possible. But it needs to be sufficiently different from previous learning to force the learner to grapple with it and bring about accommodation (Rabinowitz & Schubert, 1991). Neither assimilation nor accommodation is possible if critical prerequisites are lacking.

As with many other aspects of curriculum, prerequisites often become the subject of political debate, notably between egalitarians and elitists. Egalitarians want to give everyone a chance to succeed, to admit as many people as possible to every program. Elitists want to be selective and to allow into programs only the few most likely to benefit. Some large jurisdictions are openly elitist or egalitarian. California, where over 80 percent of students now enter postsecondary education and 20 percent enter the University of California, is one of the most egalitarian jurisdictions. Many developing countries, by contrast, cannot afford universal secondary education and, consequently, must be selective in choosing students who will continue their education beyond elementary school.

Ideally, a prerequisite is intended neither to reduce numbers nor to produce homogeneity. Its purpose, rather, is to ensure that the learner can benefit from the instruction. Sometimes the numbers we can admit are restricted by factors outside our control. This is the case in professional schools, where there may be ten eligible applicants for each place. In this case, admission becomes competitive, and we have to seek admissions criteria that will best predict professional success—a continuing problem in such areas as medicine and teacher education. But in most public education contexts, the only people we want to exclude, or more probably dissuade, are those whom prior evidence suggests will probably not, at this stage, be able to benefit from the program.

It is seductively simple to make assumptions about necessary prerequisites. Is it necessary, for example, to complete high school mathematics before beginning university-level mathematics? Johns Hopkins University has taken many mathematically gifted students from Grades 7, 8, and 9 and placed them in university mathematics programs with great success (Stanley, 1976). Is it necessary to be literate to obtain a job? A McDonald's hamburger chain official in California declared that he was not concerned about the quality of public education because "we find we can train high school students who can't read or write as easily as we can train those who can" (The "Sign of the Times Award," 1981, p. 26). Is normal hearing necessary as a prerequisite for a course in jazz dance? Jazz dance is one of the most popular and successful courses at Galaudet College, a college for those with profound hearing loss. Finally, is it necessary to have good college grades to be a successful teacher? The average correlation between undergraduate grades and success as a teacher is approximately zero (Pratt, 1987). One might reasonably ask, What are the appropriate prerequisites for professional practice? Frank Damara, known as "The Great Imposter," practiced successfully as a surgeon in the Canadian Navy during the Korean War, although his formal education ended in Grade 10 (Crichton, 1959).

Anecdotal evidence is provocative rather than conclusive. Consider the following examples of the nonpredictiveness of prerequisites:

Charles Darwin, naturalist, dropped out of medical school.

Thomas Edison, inventor, had only three months of schooling.

Albert Einstein, physicist, failed in his first attempt to gain admission to the Zurich Polytechnic.

Marchese Marconi, inventor of the radio, had no formal training in physics.

Gregor Mendel, geneticist, twice failed the qualifying examination to become a teacher.

Auguste Rodin, sculptor, failed three times to enter art school in Paris.

Leo Tolstoi, novelist, dropped out of the University of Kazan.

Werner von Braun, rocket scientist, failed high school mathematics and physics.

Emile Zola, novelist, scored zero in literature at his lycée in Paris.

The process of defining prerequisites requires both logic and empirical data. It seems logical to require that children master addition before we teach them multiplication, that we teach regular verbs in French before we teach irregular verbs, that we teach velocity before we teach acceleration, that piano students master the scale of C before learning the scale of D, and that photography students learn darkroom techniques before specializing in portrait photography. We can verify our prerequisites now and again by allowing eager students to advance without them and judging how well they succeed. For fighter pilots restrictions apply

---

A letter to the Coca-Cola Corporation

There is something that has been bothering me. Our precalculus class at Eisenhower High School was given the problem of finding the can that would hold 12 fl. oz and would use the least amount of aluminum. Much to our surprise, the can we discovered is much different from the one you chose! Our calculations show that a can with a radius of approximately 3.8367 cm and a height of approximately 7.667 cm would use less aluminum than yours and still hold 12 fl. oz. Please explain why you still choose to use more aluminum than is necessary. I doubt that you want to lose money, and I hate to see valuable resources go to waste.

Matt Barker, Junior at Eisenhower High School, Tacoma, Washington

(Crosswhite, Dossey, & Frye, 1989, p. 519)

not only to health and eyesight, but also to height, owing to the physical constraints of cockpit size.

More commonly, a prerequisite identifies knowledge or skill that is critical to subsequent learning. To decide that "History 201 is prerequisite to History 301" is less satisfactory, unless we can show that all those, and only those, students who have completed History 201 can be successful in History 301.

Prerequisites: Practicalities

Using prerequisites in program planning presents different problems in secondary and in elementary schools. At the elementary level, the most effective approach lies in continuous liaison between teachers of successive grade levels. Thus the Grade 3 teacher is in close touch with the Grade 4 teacher; the learnings and experiences that the Grade 4 teacher would like to be able to take for granted in the incoming children—that is, the critical prerequisites for Grade 4—can then be considered critical objectives of the Grade 3 program. Facilitating this kind of professional discussion and "vertical liaison" is an important role for elementary school principals.

At the secondary level, such liaison is also desirable. In addition, prerequisites can be indicated in the course calendar or outline that is made available to students when they select their program for the following year or semester. Pretests, if necessary, could even be offered some months before the beginning of the course, so that students lacking prerequisites would have time to remedy their deficiencies or to choose a preparatory course.

The worst scenario is for a teacher to discover at Christmas that a student has not understood any of the previous three months' work on account of lack of prerequisite learning. So the minimum that should be done is to administer a prerequisite test on the first day of the course and provide prompt remediation at that point. Such "prerequisite enrichment," as might be expected, has been found to have a significant effect on subsequent student achievement (Bloom, 1976).

A Ph.D. student registered at a certain midwestern university filled out an application form and indicated her first languages were Arabic, Armenian, English, French, and Turkish. Later, when the second language requirement for the Ph.D. had to be satisfied—an educational objective intended to guarantee that the student could read work written in another tongue—she was told that since all of these were first languages she must take a second language. Undaunted, she pointed out that computer languages could count and she knew both COBOL and FORTRAN. Equally undaunted, bureaucracy said that they did not count because she had studied them as an undergraduate. So she had to study and pass an exam in German!

David Mitchell (1981, p. 9)

Pretests

Not every course requires prerequisites, nor does every course require pretests. But pretests can serve a number of useful functions.

1. To identify students who lack prerequisites. Once identified, these students can be provided with appropriate guidance or remediation. In a tightly designed and logically sequenced program, the post-test in a previous course may serve as a pretest for the subsequent course.

2. To identify other students who are at risk. It is critical that school programs and their teachers be sensitive to the students whom they serve. Sometimes students who are under extreme emotional stress are not recognized or acknowledged, even when suicidal (Wolfle, 1988). (Teachers need to be aware of the warning signs of suicide, including depression, irritability, delinquency, addiction, academic deterioration, physical slowness, sleepiness, rule-breaking, avoidance of peers, dropping out of sports and clubs, giving away possessions, themes of death in writing or artwork, and self-destructive talk [Frymier, 1988; Martin, Kocmarek, & Gertidge, 1987].) At the same time, the boredom and frustration of some students with precocious academic gifts are not recognized because these gifts are masked by either docility or misbehavior (Stanley, 1976). A few pertinent questions on a preassessment should help to identify some of these students.

3. To identify students who do not need the program. Some students may have already achieved the objectives of the course you are about to teach. For them, the program might well be redundant, boring, and frustrating. (So much so, that they might end up failing it!) For them, it would be a waste of time, and to waste people's time is to waste their lives, which is perhaps the ultimate educational sin. To identify such students, the pretest should contain a mini–post-test. Alternatively, students may be invited to "challenge for credit"—to take the post-test for any course at any time, and if successful, to receive credit for the course. This policy was at one time in effect at the University of Chicago, and it enabled Lawrence Kohlberg, later a distinguished psychologist, to complete his B.A. there in one year (Rest, Power, & Brabeck, 1988).

4. To provide a baseline of achievement. The average score of my class on the post-test is 85 percent. I congratulate myself on this success. As I didn't pretest, I'm unaware that, had my students taken the test at the beginning of the program, they would have averaged 90 percent! Most teachers are as interested in pupil growth as they are in learners achieving specific standards of achievement, and to monitor growth accurately, we must obtain a clear picture of the entering status of our students.

5. To describe the learners. A pretest may be used simply to gather information about students' knowledge, skills, and attitudes, in order to help the teacher

United Nations Declaration of the Rights of the Child

1. Every child shall be entitled to these rights, without distinction or discrimination on account of race, color, sex, language, religion, political or social origin, property, birth or other status . . .

2. The child shall enjoy special protection, and shall be given opportunities and facilities . . . to enable him to develop physically, mentally, morally, spiritually and socially in a healthy and normal manner and in conditions of freedom and dignity . . .

3. The child shall be entitled from his birth to a name and a nationality.

4. The child shall . . . be entitled to grow and develop in health. . . . The child shall have the right to adequate nutrition, housing, recreation and medical services.

5. The child who is physically, mentally or socially handicapped shall be given the special treatment, education and care required by his particular condition.

6. The child, for the full and harmonious development of his personality, needs love and understanding. He shall, wherever possible, grow up in the care and under the responsibility of his parents, and in any case, in an atmosphere of affection and of moral and material security . . .

7. The child . . . shall be given an education which will promote his general culture, and enable him, on a basis of equal opportunity, to develop his abilities, his individual judgment, and his sense of moral and social responsibility, and to become a useful member of society . . .

8. The child shall in all circumstances be among the first to receive protection and relief.

9. The child shall be protected against all forms of neglect, cruelty and exploitation. . . . The child shall be protected from practices which may foster racial, religious and any other form of discrimination. He shall be brought up in a spirit of understanding, tolerance, friendship among peoples, peace and universal brotherhood, and in full consciousness that his energy and talents should be devoted to the service of his fellow men.

Yearbook of the United Nations (1959, pp. 192–199)

learn more about the students and design instruction that is appropriate for them. An experimental prekindergarten guide developed by the New York City Board of Education recommends that a questionnaire be completed by parents of children entering prekindergarten, if possible at a parent-teacher conference. The questions deal with such issues as the children's favorite foods, stories, and toys, and whether they know their home address and can button their coats and tie their shoes (New York City Board of Education, 1986). If we were planning a curriculum in language arts for pupils in the middle grades (Grades 6–8), then a questionnaire would be designed to ask such questions as: What newspapers does your family read? what magazines? How often do you read the newspaper? What is your favorite kind of reading? How many books have you read in the last year? Which one did you enjoy most? How many hours of television do you watch each day? What are your two most favorite programs? What is the best movie you have seen? Do you ever write letters? Do you keep a journal or diary? Have you ever written a poem?

This kind of questionnaire can easily be expanded to provide more detailed information about pupils, by asking such questions as: What sports do you play? What hobbies do you enjoy? Have you ever been overseas? to which countries? Do you have any pets at home? What are they? What is your favorite food? What do you want to be when you grow up? What is your favorite subject at school? Why? To what places have you traveled? What do you think is the biggest problem facing the world today? Such information serves several purposes. It helps the teacher come to know the pupils and their interests and to use this knowledge in the classroom. Asking, "What kinds of fruit grow in the Caribbean?" is different from asking, "Sheila, you visited Jamaica last summer with your family; what kinds of fruit did you notice growing there?" The latter lets the pupil know she is recognized as a unique individual.

Visits are more labor-intensive than questionnaires, but they are also likely to provide richer and more illuminating information. Appointments can be made to visit prospective kindergarten children and their parents at home prior to entry to kindergarten. There, information can be gathered regarding languages spoken in the home, typical leisure activities, children's responsibilities, daycare or summer camp experiences, children's special needs, and health problems. This is also an opportunity to describe the kindergarten program to parents and to answer their questions. The children who are in daycare can also be visited in these settings; this provides an opportunity to meet daycare staff, discuss the program, and observe the children's level of learning and socialization. The principles underlying these approaches also apply at later levels. Secondary school teachers would benefit from visiting their elementary feeder schools. It is even conceivable that university teachers might occasionally visit secondary schools.

6. *To offset stereotypes and assumptions.* It is all too easy for educators, like other people, to make assumptions about students based on personal experience.

For instance, as Dick and Carey (1990) suggest, a teacher may make assumptions about fourth grade boys' interest in baseball based on his own interests or those of his own children. Assumptions and stereotypes about student potential can become self-fulfilling prophecies. This can be particularly damaging to disadvantaged students. The best safeguard is direct information collected from students themselves.

7. To serve as an advance organizer for instruction.   Pretests give students a foretaste of some of the topics that will be introduced in the course. David Ausubel invented the term "advance organizer" to describe strategies that focus the learner on the essence of what is about to be taught (Ausubel, 1978). There is some evidence that use of advance organizers increases student learning, although the magnitude of the effect is controversial (McEaney, 1990).

The theme of this chapter is simple: Time spent in getting to know your students is time well spent.

People, especially young people, need compliments and admiration. We must give them a sense of their importance and dignity, and we must encourage them to use and develop all their talents. If ever I have children, I'll certainly do so. I'll tell them outright that they're important and that they're beautiful.

Mairead Corrigan (Northern Ireland), Nobel Prize for Peace, 1976
(with Betty Williams). (Deutsch, 1977, p. 47)

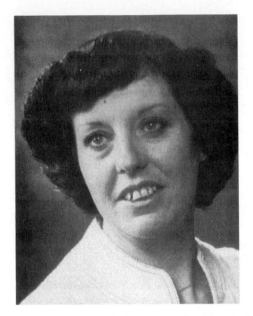

All I want to do is to take a bomb out of a kid's hand and put a tennis racket in it.
Betty Williams (Northern Ireland), Nobel Prize for Peace, 1976
(with Mairead Corrigan). (Opfell, 1986, p. 54)

CONTEXT

This is an appropriate point to mention the curriculum context. This is a usually brief section describing the "frame factors" of the curriculum. It answers such questions as: How does the curriculum fit within the program of which it is part? What precedes it and what follows it? Which department is responsible for it? How does it fit with district or state curriculum guidelines? What is the institutional, social, and community context? What other audiences could benefit from

---

Aboriginal Medicine: Context

This curriculum is planned as part of the unit on Aboriginal Communities in the Grade 7 History curriculum, which deals with Early North American Communities. It would normally be taught in the second part of the fall semester and would follow an introduction to aboriginal culture. It conforms to the principles enunciated in the *History and Contemporary Studies Curriculum Guideline, 1991*. With some adaptation, it could be modified to form part of a history curriculum for older students, or a curriculum in multiculturalism or health.

this program? What other institutions might be able to use this curriculum, with or without adaptation?

■ SELF – ASSESSMENT

Answer the following questions as True or False.

1. _____ In describing the learners for whom a curriculum is intended, it is sufficient to indicate their age and grade level.

2. _____ Learners are so varied that it is pointless to try to describe them in a curriculum.

3. _____ Even brilliant children generally have difficulty with complex abstract problems prior to about age 11.

4. _____ Almost everyone reaches the stage of "formal operations" by age 18.

5. _____ One of the functions of curriculum planning is to identify the optimal stage at which to introduce particular concepts, skills, or subjects.

6. _____ The most effective teachers consistently use the pedagogical style that is most consistent with their own learning style preference.

7. _____ Elitists want to minimize the probability of admitting a student who may subsequently fail; egalitarians want to minimize the probability of excluding a student who might succeed.

8. _____ The main purpose of prerequisites is to help ensure that the learner can benefit from the instruction.

9. _____ Prerequisite enrichment is an effective way of raising the average achievement of a class.

10. _____ Pretests may be used to check attainment of prerequisites but not of objectives.

For answers, see Appendix F.
10 correct: you understand the material in this chapter.
9 correct: reread the relevant parts of the chapter.
8 or less correct: reread the chapter carefully.

CHAPTER 6

Planning Instruction

The mind is not a container to be filled, but a fire to be ignited.

Plutarch

Summary

Instruction refers to curriculum content and teaching strategies. Major break-throughs have occurred in the past twenty years in this area. A belief that almost all students can learn successfully has replaced a belief that the role of the school is simply to sort strong from weak learners. Studies of effective schools and classrooms have provided an empirical base for understanding what works in schools. A new statistical technique, meta-analysis, increases our ability to summarize the effects of available research. Twelve principles of effective instruction are outlined. They involve time on task, motivation, mastery learning, high expectations, reading and study skills, planned lessons, an orderly environment, instructional variety, cooperative learning, computer-assisted instruction, school ethos, and parent involvement.

CURRICULUM AND INSTRUCTION

The terms *curriculum* and *instruction* are often used as if they shared a common meaning. In this book, we shall use *instruction* to refer to "one part of curriculum: the *content* or subject-matter we teach, and the *methods* or strategies we use to teach it." Despite the emphasis by curriculum theorists on objectives and evaluation, it has long been known that practicing teachers think about their teaching first and foremost in terms of content and classroom activities (Bullough, Knowles, & Crow, 1989; Clark & Yinger, 1980; Doyle & Ponder, 1978).

In both official curriculum guides and in the individual planning of teachers, this aspect of curriculum planning is generally the most fully developed. Almost all curricula contain lists of subject-matter topics. Some, in fact, contain little else, and much so-called curriculum reform consists only of changing subject matter or altering its sequence.

We have already discussed several of the issues that instructional designers consider important in their work. These include clear objectives (Chapter 3) and criteria of performance (Chapter 4); expectations and feedback (Chapter 4); and specification of prerequisites (Chapter 5). These issues provide a frame for the focus of this chapter: What and how do we teach? In this chapter we will look at evidence on this question and draw some implications for teachers and curriculum planners.

BREAKTHROUGHS IN THE STUDY OF INSTRUCTION

It is now becoming difficult to remember the period before 1970 when the mood among researchers in curriculum and instruction was largely one of defeat and despair. Fifty years of research had produced few findings that merited the attention of classroom practitioners. Experiment after experiment had yielded "no significant differences," or if a significant difference was found in one study, it was disconfirmed by the next study. "Schools make no difference" and "Teachers make no difference" became the profoundly alienated slogans of a field that was discouraged and disempowered.

> Instruction can be characterized as a process in which teachers attempt to make learning sensible and students attempt to make sense of learning.
>
> Dole, Duffy, Roehler, & Pearson (1991, p. 255)

Casting around for explanations for a half-century of failure, many curriculum workers were attracted by sociological explanations. Schools could not make a difference because the distribution of power and privilege in society prevented them from doing so. And many studies, notably a massive study headed by James Coleman entitled *Inequality in Education* (Coleman et al., 1966), did appear to demonstrate that it was social background, rather than the work of schools and teachers, that determined educational achievement. The beliefs fostered by this and many other similar studies did enormous damage as teachers began or continued to set lower expectations for disadvantaged learners. These lower expectations became self-fulfilling prophecies, diminishing a generation of teachers and their students.

Times have changed dramatically. We can now provide classroom teachers with an array of strategies that can have more impact on the achievement of learners than does their social class. Three main movements have contributed to this change: (1) An orientation that emphasizes success for all has replaced a belief that the role of schools is to sort students into successes and failures. (2) Studies that compare effective and ineffective schools and classrooms have provided many insights into the ingredients of instructional effectiveness. (3) A new statistical technique, meta-analysis, enables researchers to make judgments based on a synthesis of the best available research on a given question.

A SUCCESS ORIENTATION

Throughout history, great educators from Plato to Erasmus to Montessori have always seen success as the goal of education. Informal education has almost always been success-oriented. A child is expected to learn to walk successfully. A cabinetmaker expects an apprentice to learn to make a dovetail joint very well. A violin teacher expects a student to play all of the notes in a piece of music correctly, not 51 percent of them. But institutionalized schooling has often fallen into a habit of mind that assumes that only a minority of students can be really successful, while a majority will fail or perform at a mediocre level.

An early attempt to base school programs on a doctrine of success for all was made by Clayton Washburne, who was superintendent of the Winnetka, Kansas, public schools in the 1920s (Washburne, 1925). But the necessary theoretical and empirical support for the belief that almost all pupils could achieve real success had to wait another forty years, for the work of Benjamin Bloom.

It was Benjamin Bloom, a professor of education at the University of Chicago, who reformulated the principles of a success orientation under the title, Mastery Learning (1968). As often happens in the world of scholarship, other educators developed similar ideas independently. A retired psychology professor, Fred Keller, working at the University of Brasilia, developed a similar approach to university teaching, subsequently known as the Keller Plan, or Personalized System of Instruction. It was adopted in hundreds of universities around the world (Keller & Sherman, 1974). In Japan, Toru Kumon developed in the 1950s a similar approach to mathematics teaching that is now used in schools serving more than a million Japanese students (Finn, 1989).

We shall look later in this chapter at Mastery Learning in more detail. At this point we may merely note that Bloom's rallying cry, and the quantity of research it stimulated, changed the complexion of instructional thinking. In the course of two decades, so many studies showed that Bloom was correct in his assumption that under appropriate conditions almost all students could learn, that it was no longer the proponents of success who had to justify their claims; the onus of justification rested with scholars or teachers who believed that large numbers of students were incapable of learning.

STUDIES OF EFFECTIVE SCHOOLS

A few years after Bloom had first made the outrageous claim that almost all students can learn effectively (Bloom, 1968), a new approach to instructional research appeared that enabled scholars to begin to isolate the components of effectiveness. One of the main pioneers was Ron Edmonds, an educator who worked mainly with underprivileged pupils in such areas as Harlem, New York.

Edmonds, like others before him, had noticed a curious phenomenon about inner-city schools. Certain schools in underprivileged neighborhoods appeared to be at least as effective as most suburban schools. Teachers and administrators cooperated; absenteeism was low; the schools were attractive and happy places; and achievement of pupils was good. You could walk five blocks down the street and come to another school in which the teachers and the administration were at war; where the gates were locked during school hours to keep out the drug-pushers; where the hallways were patrolled by armed guards; where many students carried knives; where attendance by teachers and pupils was abysmal; and where little learning ever took place. As both schools shared the same socioeconomic environment, the differences between the schools could not be explained by theories about social class privilege or disadvantage.

Edmonds therefore devised a new mode of research. By the late 1960s standardized achievement tests were being used, at least in reading and mathematics, in most American school districts. Many of these tests were criterion-referenced and curriculum-embedded. While far from perfect, they were a long step ahead of the old norm-referenced tests of the 1950s. Suppose that a large urban school system has fifty elementary schools situated in decaying inner-city environments. If you have test results from all of the schools in a district, you can then rank the schools on the basis of average student achievement, from the school that produces the highest pupil achievement to the school with the lowest. It is not necessary to investigate all of the schools, only the "outliers." We send researchers into the ten most effective and the ten least effective schools. The researchers enter the schools with observation instruments, checklists, interview schedules, videocameras, and tape recorders. For weeks these investigators gather data in these schools. They sit in classrooms and systematically observe teachers and students. They interview principals, teachers, parents, and pupils. They observe patterns of behavior in hallways, cafeterias, school assemblies, and schoolyards. They count the amount of graffiti on the walls, the number of broken windows and water fountains, and how long they remain unrepaired. Then they feed all the information they have gathered into a computer, which searches the mass of data for systematic differences between the ten effective and the ten ineffective schools (Edmonds, 1979a).

It is easy to see why this research is so powerful. What we end up with is not theories or opinions, but the descriptive characteristics of effective schools. Suppose we find that in the ten effective schools much use is made of students' work. Student artwork decorates the hallways; recent work by students is found on classroom bulletin boards; teachers frequently read out or refer to exemplary student work in classes. (This, in fact, is one of the characteristics of effective schools [Guskey & Easton, 1983; Mortimore et al., 1988; Ramsay et al., 1983].) In the ineffective schools, on the other hand, we find little use of students' work. Then we can say that there is a relationship between effectiveness and display of student work. However, the oldest mistake in educational research is to assume that a correlation implies a cause-and-effect relationship. This can be proved only by further experimental research.

On the basis of the descriptive and experimental research conducted by 1979, a few years before his death, Ron Edmonds was able to say this:

> No notion about schooling is more widely held than the belief that the family is somehow the principal determinant of whether or not a child will do well in school. . . . Such a belief has the effect of absolving educators of their professional responsibility to be instructionally effective. . . . It seems to me, therefore, that what is left of this discussion are three declarative statements: (a) We can, whenever and wherever we choose, successfully teach all children whose schooling is of interest to us; (b) we already know more than we need to do that; and (c) whether or not we do it must finally depend on how we feel about the fact that we haven't so far.   (Edmonds, 1979a, pp. 21, 23)

The first studies of school effectiveness were conducted in elementary schools in the United States, generally in underprivileged areas and using as the criterion of effectiveness standardized test results in reading and mathematics. In the last fifteen years this perspective has widened considerably. Studies have been conducted in many different countries, across different social class levels and age groups, and using many criteria beyond reading and mathematics scores. Studies of effective teaching in universities and colleges have arrived at findings that are very similar to those for elementary and high schools (Chickering & Gamson, 1988; Guskey & Easton, 1983). Generalized conclusions have been illuminated by detailed case studies (Lightfoot, 1983; Teddlie, Kirby, & Stringfield, 1989; Wilson & Corcoran, 1988). The findings of the effective schools research apply not only longitudinally (Mandeville 1988; Mandeville & Anderson, 1987) and across different districts and states (Stringfield & Teddlie, 1988), but also across different nations and cultures (Joyce & Showers, 1985; Scheerens, Vermeulen, & Pelgrum, 1989). Likewise, the effectiveness studies are not the product of a single philosophical orientation. Research in schools in Auckland, New Zealand, was conducted by a group of researchers who

Effective schools in London, England

One of the most extensive studies of school effectiveness was conducted by Peter Mortimore and his colleagues in the Inner London Education Authority. This was a longitudinal study, following 2,000 pupils in 278 classes in 50 junior schools from age 7 to age 11. Criteria of effectiveness included mathematics and reading scores, practical mathematics skills, writing quality and ideas, oral language, attendance, behavior, attitude toward school, and self-concept. Some of the main findings were:

1. Schools that were effective for any type of pupil tended to be effective for all pupils regardless of sex, ethnic background, or social class.

2. Schools were not uniformly effective, however; some were effective in cognitive but less so in noncognitive areas, some in developing reading skills but less so in writing skills.

3. Children of manual workers in the most effective schools outperformed children of nonmanual workers in the least effective schools.

4. The most effective schools were small, that is, about 160 pupils.

5. In the most effective schools, the teachers kept individual records of students' work, including a folder of work that was passed on to the next teacher.

6. The principals of effective schools worked actively with teachers to develop and implement curriculum policies and plans.

7. "In schools where the headteachers indicated that they laid a particular emphasis upon a basic skills approach, the impact upon pupils' progress in reading and writing was negative" (p. 224).

8. An authoritarian style of leadership on the part of the principal was not related to effectiveness.

9. "Progress and development were promoted in those schools where the pupils tended to be happy and friendly—in schools where we found a 'fun factor'" (p. 225).

10. "Pupils made greater progress when teachers tended to organize lessons around one particular curriculum area" (p. 254).

Peter Mortimore et al., *School matters* (1988)

Maxims for educators

1. The first practical step in any reform is to take it.

2. In education, failures are more important than successes. There is nothing so dismal as a success story.

3. Teach on the verge of peril.

4. There are no more teachers. There is just a community of learners.

5. Do not design a philosophy of education for others. Design one for yourself. A few others may wish to share it with you.

6. For the 5-year-old, art is life and life is art. For the 6-year-old, life is life and art is art. This first school year is a watershed in the child's history: a trauma.

7. The old approach: teacher has information; student has empty head. Teacher's objective: to push information into student's empty head. Observations: at outset teacher is a fathead; at conclusion student is a fathead.

8. On the contrary, a class should be an hour of a thousand discoveries. For this to happen, the teacher and the student should first discover one another.

9. Why is it that the only people who never matriculate from their own courses are teachers?

10. Always teach provisionally; only God knows for sure.

Murray Schafer (composer) (*The Rhinoceros in the Classroom*, 1976, p. 2)

---

defined themselves as critical theorists (Ramsay et al., 1983). This is quite a different philosophical orientation from that of most American researchers, yet their findings fully confirmed those of their American colleagues.

META-ANALYSIS

The third breakthrough was statistical. Single studies are rarely a sufficient guide to educational practice. No matter how bizarre the practice, if you search the literature long enough, you will probably find a study that supports it. It is better to look at all the available studies before we commit ourselves to a conclusion. Until twenty years ago, the best that researchers could do was usually to count studies. But merely counting the number of studies showing that a practice has positive, negative, or neutral effects is a limited approach. It does not enable us to say how great the effect is. Nor can we readily take into account the fact that some experiments use much larger numbers of subjects or produce much more significant results. Meta-analysis allows us to take such factors into account and to produce a single statistic known as an "effect size."

The first step in meta-analysis is careful evaluation of the quality of the research studies on a particular topic and selection of those that meet predetermined criteria. Often this will reduce the sample of studies to less than 10 percent of the total. Only the studies that pass through this quality screen are used to produce an "effect size." The effect size is the proportion of a standard deviation by which the experimental groups differed from the control groups. (For the statistically minded, it is usually calculated by subtracting the mean of the control group from the mean of the treatment group, and dividing by the standard deviation of the control group [Glass, 1978b].) The Normal Curve shows the relationship between standard deviations and percentiles. If the experimental group outperformed the control group by one standard deviation, this would be equivalent to the difference between the control student achieving at the 50th percentile and the experimental students achieving at the 84th percentile.

Meta-analysis allows us not only to say with some precision what factors contribute to instructional effectiveness, but also how effective they are, and how they compare with other factors. For example, large-scale meta-analyses by Walberg (1984a) indicated that the average effect of social class (lower versus middle socioeconomic status) on school achievement was .24, while the average effect of regularly assigning and evaluating homework, at .79, was three times as much.

The debate on the techniques and assumptions of meta-analysis continues vigorously (Hedges, 1988; Hunter & Schmidt, 1990; Raudenbush, 1991a, Raudenbush, 1991b; Slavin, 1986). But there is general agreement that the development of meta-analysis has enhanced the value of synthesis of research results. We shall rely heavily on findings from meta-analysis in this chapter in reporting findings in the area of instruction.

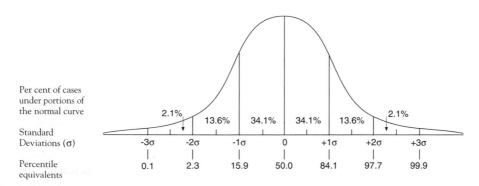

The Normal Curve: Percentiles and Standard Deviations

SPECIFYING INSTRUCTIONAL CONTENT ──────────

Most of this chapter deals with selection of instructional strategies. But first, a word about selecting and organizing subject matter or content. Here are a few basic principles:

1. Refer back frequently to the needs assessment, to ensure that the content reflects the real and perceived needs of students—in other words, that it is meaningful, significant, or relevant to them.

2. Ensure that each objective is matched by some appropriate curriculum content, and all of the content relates to one or more of the objectives. For example, if one of your objectives is that "students will develop skills of cooperative work," then ensure that there is appropriate instruction in cooperative skills—don't just put students in groups and expect them to be successful!

3. Identify those items of content that are of greatest importance.

4. Wherever there is a choice (there is always a choice), choose content that is of interest to the particular learners. Interest is often proportional to detail and specialization. A semester spent studying the events in Dallas, Texas, between November 22 and November 24, 1963, is likely to be very interesting. Survey courses on the history of western civilization from 400 B.C. to the present (lose your ballpoint and you miss a century) are often mind-numbing.

5. Always begin and end a course or unit with content of high interest.

6. The content should be sequenced in order of familiarity, difficulty, and logical progression. It makes more sense to *introduce* students to the study of drama, for example, by examining a popular television series than by means of Shakespeare, whose language and cultural environment are quite foreign to contemporary students. Shakespeare is a wonderful dinner, but a terrible breakfast. Similarly, teenage students who claim to dislike poetry all know by heart the lyrics of hundreds of pop songs. This provides an opening for all teachers other than those completely indoctrinated by elitist academic definitions of poetry.

When we define the curriculum, we are also defining the opportunities the young will have to experience different forms of consciousness. To have a musical consciousness, one must interact with music. To have a visual artistic consciousness, one must interact with visual art. To experience the poetics of language, poetry must be available.

Elliot Eisner (1979, p. 52)

Table 6-1   *Instructional Schedule for One Semester*

Program: Office Administration: Year 2:
Medical Course: Accounting 295

Week	Topic
1 & 2	**Starting a business** Fundamental accounting equations Transactions The balance sheet
3 & 4	**Profitability and the income statement** Revenue Expenses Net income Owner's equity Income statement Statement of owner's equity
5 & 6	**Debits, credits, and trial balance** "T" accounts Recording transactions Rules of debit and credit Chart of accounts Account sequence The trial balance
7	**Term test**
8 & 9	**General journal and general ledger** Recording transactions Posting Trial balance Correcting errors
10 & 11	**Adjustments and the worksheet** Matching principle Adjustments The 10-column worksheet The income statement The statement of owner's equity The balance sheet
12	**Term test**
13 & 14	**Correcting and closing entries** Correcting entries Closing entries The worksheet and the closing process The journal and ledger illustrated The post-closing trial balance
15	**Review for exams**

(Durham College, Business Division, 1990)

How detailed should the content section of a curriculum be? This is largely a matter of context and judgment. The risk of providing too little detail is that important material will be omitted by teachers. The risk of giving too much detail is that teachers will feel oppressed by absence of choice and excess of material to be covered. A typical schedule of instructional content for one semester is shown in Table 6-1. Table 6-2 shows a more detailed breakdown of a unit of instructional content. The amount of detail to be included in the schedule of instructional content is a matter of judgment, in which the needs of teachers should be the primary consideration.

Table 6-2 *Instructional Content for a Unit*

Program: Driver Education
Topic: Carbon Monoxide Poisoning*

1. **Causes** of carbon monoxide poisoning:
   —*leak in exhaust system* allowing CO to enter car
   —*running car engine in closed area* such as garage
   —pooling of CO under car; engine running in deep snow
   —heavy traffic in tunnels, etc., with inadequate air circulation

2. **Symptoms** of CO poisoning:
   —*drowsiness*, faintness, nausea, labored respiration, reddening of skin, increased pulse, pounding heartbeat, throbbing temples, *dizziness*, ringing in ears, failure of extremities, sweating, unconsciousness

3. **Effects** of CO poisoning:
   —*may be insidious*, produced by inhaling small amounts of CO over long period
   —*may be produced by very small concentrations* of CO in the air
   —*may be fatal*, or may leave permanent physical or mental impairment

4. **Means of avoiding** CO poisoning:
   —*never run car engine in enclosed space*
   —avoid staying in stationary car with engine running, especially in heavy snow or backed into snowbank
   —keep window open if there is risk of CO entering car from exhaust
   —close windows and vents in heavy traffic
   —have exhaust system checked if it is rusty, damaged, or sounds different

* Critical elements are in italics.

CURRICULUM INTEGRATION

Before leaving the issue of curriculum content, something should be said about curriculum integration. Many educators today are concerned that the knowledge students acquire in schools remains fragmented, isolated, and compartmentalized. The amount of curriculum integration in schools is partly determined by culture and tradition. In North American schools, social studies endeavors to integrate a number of disciplines which are kept distinct in British schools. Biology, chemistry, and physics are often taught as integrated science in Arab countries, but are usually taught separately in the Francophone world (UNESCO, 1986).

Almost everyone today is in favor of curriculum integration, without anyone being quite sure what it means. A 1988 survey of key educational leaders in the United States identified curriculum integration as the curriculum top priority (Jacobs, 1989). By 1991, at least three hundred titles had been published on the topic (Clark, 1991). But what is curriculum integration? Let us distinguish first between "vertical" and "horizontal" integration. If we try to consolidate the relationships between what a child learns in mathematics in Grade 6 and mathematics

Basically, everything is one. There is no way in which you draw a line between things. What we . . . do is to make these divisions, but they're not real. Our educational system is full of subdivisions that are artificial, that shouldn't be there. I think maybe poets . . . have some understanding of this.

Barbara McClintock (U.S.A.), Nobel Prize for Physiology, 1983. (Keller, 1983, p. 204).

in Grade 7, we are concerned with vertical integration. If we try to develop relationships between what the Grade 7 child learns in mathematics and what he or she learns in language arts, then we are working on horizontal integration (Tyler, 1958). Most discussion is primarily interested in horizontal integration. But even horizontal integration is not a single concept. Robin Fogarty (1991) distinguishes among ten different types of integration, including nested (within each subject area the teacher uses each element of content to develop multiple skills), shared (two or more teachers jointly plan instruction in an area of overlap), or webbed (a fertile theme is linked to content in different disciplines).

In thinking about the design of curriculum to achieve more integration, four points may be borne in mind.

1. **Curriculum integration is a matter of degree.** We will never achieve total integration of knowledge—not, at least, until we understand everything in the universe. On the other hand, our knowledge is never completely disintegrated. The links between all areas of knowledge are inextricable. There is a sense in which all teaching that aims at enhancing significant meaning is integrative.

2. **Each discipline represents an integration of knowledge.** Each discipline shares a common set of standards for evidence, a set of fundamental explanatory concepts, and established methodological procedures (Case, 1991; Pring, 1973). Disciplines evolve historically by establishing increasingly articulated networks of relationships among concepts within the discipline and with other disciplines. The study of physics, for example, will help students to integrate their understanding of light and electromagnetism, whether or not physics is integrated with other subjects. The second law of thermodynamics is a principle that integrates our knowledge of the physical world. To understand one thing very well is to understand many things. William Blake remarked on this when he aspired "to see the universe in a grain of sand." To enter fully into the world of biology is to understand much of life itself, and the same is true of music, or history, or system theory, or any other discipline.

3. **One of the best ways to integrate content is to integrate people.** We know that schools function more effectively when there is good communication among the people who work in them. The Grade 5 teacher needs to know about the work of both the Grade 4 and the Grade 6 teacher if vertical integration is to be enhanced. Grade 10 history teachers need to talk to Grade 10 English teachers, and even to Grade 10 math teachers. The first and best step toward curriculum integration is to establish a "collaborative culture" within the school (Hargreaves, 1989b). The kind of professional discussion among a school staff that leads to consensual formulation of meaningful mission statements or educational goals, and consideration of how each subject area can contribute to such goals, is one of the most promising ways of improving integration of content.

4. **To achieve integration, aim at it.** Not much that is worthwhile in schools is achieved either by accident or by rhetoric. If we want our students to integrate their learning in mathematics and music, then we need to plan courses in "Music and Mathematics" or "The Mathematics of Music," or to write aims or objectives that direct our efforts deliberately in that direction.

5. **The primary integration is of learning and life.** The problem of compartmentalization of learning is a subset of the bigger problem of learning not being meaningful to the learner. Whether or not students integrate their learning in biology with their learning in literature is a good question. Whether they integrate their learnings in these areas with their daily thought and action and view of the world is a much more crucial question. The focus of all our integrative efforts, therefore, must be the students themselves.

TWELVE PRINCIPLES OF EFFECTIVE INSTRUCTION

The research on effective schools, effective classrooms, effective teachers, and effective principals has yielded scores of factors that are related to instructional effectiveness. From this voluminous literature, twelve basic principles are summarized below. The evidence suggests that any one of these principles, systematically applied, will yield at least moderate effects—that is, effects greater than those normally resulting from differences in social class. Any two principles systematically applied in combination can be expected to yield strong effects.

1. Time on task

It appears self-evident that the amount of time devoted by learners to school work (and homework) will influence the amount of learning (Homes & Croll, 1989). This factor varies considerably from subject to subject, from school to school, and from nation to nation. When we calculate the length of school day and school year, amount of homework, and number of absences, we find that by the end of their secondary schooling, Japanese children have spent the equivalent of four more years on school work than American children. This may largely account for the fact that in math and science, after twelve years of schooling, Japanese students are approximately four years ahead of their American counterparts (Bishop, 1989a; Chen & Stevenson, 1989).

Although there have been some recent efforts in North America to lengthen the school day or the school year, this is expensive, politically difficult, and does not yield very significant results (Levin, Glass, & Meister, 1987). A more basic approach is to make better use of the time already available, and this is the rationale behind the research on time on task.

The term *time on task* began to interest several researchers in the 1970s. By 1980, Lorin Anderson, in a summary of the evidence, was able to report extremely consistent results from researchers coming from quite different theoretical orientations, a state of affairs "quite unique in the annals of educational research" (1980, p. 17).

In a typical study of 132 elementary school teachers, Rich and McNelis (1987) found that although the school day was nominally six hours, students were in class about four hours. During those four hours, such activities as distributing worksheets, collecting homework, calling the roll, making announcements, and clarifying classroom rules occupied an average of thirty-two minutes per day. Transitions from one subject or class to another, from class to recess or lunch, or from class to restroom, took twenty minutes per day, and interruptions occupied another five minutes. This left about three hours, and during that time the average child was on-task about 70 percent of the time. Altogether, the study found that elementary school students were on task about 32 percent of the total school day, or about *two hours daily*. This figure is close to that found by other researchers, at both elementary and secondary school levels (Croll & Moses, 1988; Frick, 1990; Karweit, 1985).

These, however, are average figures. Differences in average time on task have been found between schools as well as between pupils. A study of schools in Chicago showed that public schools where pupils had high achievement averaged about 75 percent of class time for actual instruction, whereas in schools where children achieved poorly an average of only 51 percent of class time was spent on instruction (Frederick, 1977). Both objective measurement and subjective observation of students show that time on task is one of the main discriminating factors between effective and ineffective schools (Louis & Miles, 1990; Teddlie et al., 1989).

Time on task research may provide a key to the problem of differences in learning speed. In a typical heterogeneous classroom, the fastest two or three learners may learn material three to seven times as fast as the slowest two or three learners (Anderson, 1976; Carroll, 1971). But this variation may not be the result simply of innate ability. It may be because, as Stallings (1980) found, low-achieving students were on task 40 percent of the time and high-achieving students 85 percent of the time. It seems reasonable to suggest that if we can increase students' time on task, we will increase their speed of learning.

Time on task and the principal: A case study

In a study of 116 teachers in 8 schools, Teddlie, Kirby, & Stringfield (1989) found that pupil time on task discriminated very significantly between the classrooms in the effective and the ineffective schools. The authors report a case study of two contrasting elementary schools, located a few blocks apart in the same middle- to lower-middle-class suburban neighborhood. Both schools had well-integrated student populations—about 50 percent white and 50 percent black.

The principal at School 1 (the effective school) was described by one observer as "having her finger on the pulse of the school." She was frequently seen in the hallways and the classrooms; she was observed in her not infrequent role of teaching a class. . . . She appeared knowledgeable regarding every significant innovation in every classroom and saw to it that teachers were exposed to new and creative ideas. . . . Academic time was maximized in School 1. One observer noted how smoothly the day progressed, with children responding quickly to bells and directions. "As the kids are coming in from recess, the teacher is telling them what book to get out and what page to turn to." Observers agreed that the most salient feature of School 1 was effective use of time.

The principal at School 2 (the ineffective school) had had a teaching career marked with honors. Although never observed in a classroom, she was visible in the hallways. She welcomed the visitors, conveying a "nothing-to-hide" attitude and expressing a sincere interest in the results of the study. She praised her school and staff, saying that everything there was "just great." "Everything was just great," noted one observer, "until we went into the classrooms." "The classrooms," continued another, "were total . . . disasters."

If the amount of time spent on academics was the most impressive feature of School 1, the lack thereof was the unifying characteristic of School 2. A week-long fundraising event was used as an excuse for the lack of class time spent on actual instruction. There was no attempt to tie the patriotic theme of the fundraiser into instructional activities. Collecting money in one class period took thirty-five minutes. The investigators were dismayed at the number of interruptions attributed to such nonacademic projects. One member of the research team returned to the school two weeks later. He was unsurprised to find the "one-week" fundraiser in its third week. Classes typically began fifteen minutes later than scheduled. Children returned from recess at their leisure. A fifteen-minute scheduled recess often lasted thirty minutes. A great deal of time was spent preparing for recess and lunch and return to class. Unfortunately, the relatively small amount of time spent in classrooms was often wasted.

The classes at the effective schools began on time, were characterized by proper instructional techniques, and had few interruptions. The classes at the ineffective school began late, did not consistently include defensible instructional techniques, and were constantly being interrupted. The ineffective principal was never observed to enter a classroom, was unaware of discipline problems throughout the school, and made no apparent attempt to decrease the constant interruptions. The ineffective principal seemed more concerned with schoolwide extracurricular and public relations activities than with academic instruction.

Teddlie et al. (1989, pp. 231-234)

We are hardly ever 100 percent on task. Even your attention, gentle reader, as you peruse these pages, is skipping backwards and forwards between the printed page and other thoughts quite unrelated to curriculum planning. Watching a really gripping movie, skiing a difficult slope, flying our first solo for a pilot's license, performing brain surgery, climbing a vertical rockface without ropes, making our first parachute jump: when in such situations, we may reach 99 percent time on task. Such activities are difficult to introduce into conventional lessons. We can, however, choose activities such as discussion, work in small cooperative groups, reading aloud, practice, direct interaction between teacher and learners, and supportive feedback that do tend to produce on-task behavior, while being cautious but not dogmatic about activities that have been shown to produce off-task behavior, such as time spent in classroom management, individual seatwork, and silent reading.

Students are most likely to be on-task when they are active and interactive rather than solitary or passive (Good, Reys, Grouws, & Mulryan, 1989; Stallings, 1980). Instructional research has found consistently that the more interaction the student has with the teacher, the greater the learning (Adams, 1990; Finn & Cox, 1992; Mason, Anderson, Omura, Uchida & Imai, 1989; Mortimore et al., 1988). This may be one reason why one-to-one professional tutoring is so effective (Bloom, 1984). A study of mildly mentally handicapped students showed that they were on-task 97 percent of the time during which they were the target of instruction of the teacher or an aide, and only 57 percent of the time during which there was no interaction (Frick, 1990). A recent British study found a direct linear relationship between the amount of time children were on-task and the amount of whole-class instruction used by the teacher (R = .65). In classrooms where teachers used whole-class instruction for 10–20 percent of the time, students were on task 45 percent of the time. In classes where teachers used whole-class instruction 40–50 percent of the time, students were on-task 65 percent of the time. The levels of on-task behavior were greater not only during whole-class teaching but also during the times when students were working on their own (Croll & Moses, 1988).

Researchers point out that if the work is too hard or too easy, not much learning will actually take place. If the child lacks critical prerequisites or is not at the appropriate level of intellectual readiness, no amount of time on task will produce significant learning. They therefore coined another term, *academic engaged time*, or academic learning time, to refer to the time during which students are actively working with instruction that is appropriate for them in such terms as level of difficulty. Academic engaged time will never be greater, and will usually be less than, time on task. One study of fifth graders reported that their academic engaged time ranged from only 49 to 105 minutes per day (Stallings, 1980).

What this discussion is leading to is this: *Almost all strategies for increasing instructional effectiveness seek to increase student time on task*. Clearly, strategies such as homework, having parents read to children, structuring lessons to avoid unrelated interruptions, using active rather than passive learning, engaging in dialogue rather than monologue, will all increase student time on task. But the difficulty is often one of attitude: It is simply more rewarding for the learner to think about tonight's

> Finally, this I account the worst of all, that when I have taken a great dele of paines, and have made my Schollers very ready in construing and parsing: yet come and examine them in those things a quarter of a yeere after, they will be many of them as though they had never learned them, and the best farre to seeke.
>
> John Brinsley, *Ludus Literarius or the Grammar Schoole*, 1627
> (Skilbeck, 1985, p. 20)

date or last night's basketball game than it is to concentrate on today's history or mathematics lesson. So we now need to turn to the question of motivation.

2. Motivation

From the earliest times, motivation has been recognized as essential to learning. Said Plato, 2,500 years ago: "Enforced exercise does no harm to the body, but enforced learning will not stay in the mind. So avoid compulsion, and let your children's lessons take the form of play" (1941, p. 252). Leonardo da Vinci made a similar statement two thousand years later: "Just as eating against one's will is injurious to health, so study without a liking for it spoils the memory, and it retains nothing it takes in." Educators have recognized for millennia that teaching anything to pupils who are not interested in it is the kiss of death; in the absence of motivation, instruction becomes a form of aversion therapy. On the other hand, pupils who enjoy what they are doing always seem to have the energy for it.

We need first to distinguish between two kinds of motivation: extrinsic and intrinsic. If a student is working hard in a program because she has been promised a new bicycle if she gets a good grade, or because she needs a high mark for university admission, or to please her parents or teacher, her motivation is primary extrinsic. But if the reason for devoting effort to learning is that what is being learned is interesting, significant, meaningful, or enjoyable, the incentive is intrinsic.

Grades and marks have become the primary incentive in schools, from the perspective of both students and teachers. This no doubt reflects the wider culture in which money is considered the most important medium of motivation. Dependence on marks as the only way to motivate learners is an admission of failure on the part of educators. It implies that we have been unable to develop curricula that are intrinsically motivating. Once again, we are forced back to the issues of learner need and the basic curriculum questions of meaningfulness and significance.

There is one important, indeed fatal, weakness in extrinsic incentives. *Once the reward has been received, the students will forget what has been learned.* This has been demonstrated in a number of experimental studies (Bates, 1979; Lepper, Greene, & Nisbett, 1973). In other words, if we are teaching subject matter that is not meaningful to students, or using strategies that do not interest them, we are wasting everyone's time. As I survey the glazed eyeballs and despairing postures of many students in the dozens of classrooms I visit every year, I am forced to ask certain harsh questions both about the selection and development of curriculum and about the selection and development of teachers.

A recent study of small-town high schools in twenty-one states by Schmuck and Schmuck (1990) paints a depressing picture. Classroom discussions were rare; three-quarters of class time was taken up by teacher talk, and three-quarters of that was lecturing. Few students were enthusiastic about schoolwork; most considered it boring.

> Students considered many of their teachers to be uninterested in them as individuals, lacking a sense of humor and teaching their subjects like robots, without involvement and enthusiasm. In contrast, students saw good teachers taking a personal interest in them, cracking jokes and appreciating their students' humor, and showing a genuine commitment to their subject.   (Schmuck & Schmuck, 1990, p. 15)

But sometimes we have to begin with extrinsic incentives. The teacher may be facing a class of Grade 10 students who are taking a course in history only because it is a requirement for graduation. All of them have previously been "turned off" history by incompetent teachers. There is not much point in preaching to them about the value of historical studies. We may have to start by promising a class trip to a popular current historical movie if achievement reaches a certain level. On the other hand, even in this case, appropriate intrinsic incentives might be found. An acquaintance of mine has been confronting this problem for years. Year after year he faces classes of students in Grade 9, most of whom enter his class with the belief that the study of history is irredeemably boring. So

---

A study of schooling

John Goodlad studied 1,016 classrooms in 38 elementary, junior high, and secondary schools. He found that about 43 minutes of every 57-minute class were used for instruction; 70 percent of that time was used for talk, with teachers out-talking students by a factor of 3:1.

"Students listened; they responded when called on to do so; they read short sections of textbooks; they wrote short responses to questions or chose from among alternative responses in quizzes. But they rarely planned or initiated anything, read or wrote anything of some length, or created their own products. And they scarcely ever speculated on meanings, discussed alternative interpretations, or engaged in projects calling for collaborative effort. Most of the time they listened or worked alone. The topics of the curriculum, it appears to me, were something to be acquired, not something to be explored, reckoned with, and converted into personal meaning and development."

John Goodlad (1983, p. 468)

the first, and most consistently successful, unit he teaches is "The Historian as Detective: Who Really Was Jack the Ripper?"

The first requirement for motivation is, Make it interesting! Choose material that interests and excites you and any other teachers who will work with the curriculum. If you are not enthusiastic about the curriculum content, why should students be? As one of my daughters, then in her senior university year, said in disgust one day, "If some of my professors had to listen to their own lectures, they'd drop their own courses!"

An example from New Zealand may illustrate this point. On a visit to that country in 1985, I was a guest at Flock House, which is an agricultural training center. In order to obtain a government loan to purchase a farm, young farmers in New Zealand were required to complete a three-month course at the center. Many of them had not completed secondary school, had low academic self-esteem, and felt that they had entered the course under duress. They were, in fact, classic reluctant learners. The program was heavily based on the curriculum principles of clear objectives, modular organization, and mastery learning. On entry to the program, each student was assigned to a group which was given responsibility for the care and growth of a number of sheep, pigs, cows, or rabbits on the college's six farms. Very quickly these young farmers developed great interest in their animals, working until midnight grooming pigs, designing breeding patterns for sheep, building pens for rabbits, or studying their way through the course modules in the college library.

While interest is the key factor in pupils' attitudes towards some subjects such as social studies (Klein, 1989), in other subjects such as mathematics, the learner's sense of competence is more important (Stodolsky, Salk, & Glaessner, 1991). In social studies pupils feel they can at least learn the material on their own. But in subjects like mathematics, where technical expertise is required, the student who has not mastered key skills is helpless, disempowered, and alienated.

A synthesis by Brophy (1987) of the research on motivating students to learn reads like a synopsis of the universal characteristics of good teaching. Brophy indicates the importance of preconditions such as a supportive environment, an appropriate level of difficulty, and meaningful objectives; planning for success; providing remediation, and offering rewards; adapting tasks to students' interests, using games, simulations, and novelty; allowing student choice; using active and cooperative learning; providing immediate feedback; projecting interest, appreciation, enthusiasm and intensity; making the abstract concrete and personal. We might add that humor, especially if it is related to the concepts taught, enlivens classes and aids long-term retention (Kaplan & Pascoe, 1977).

3. Mastery learning

Although the term "mastery" has a long pedigree in educational discourse (Broudy, 1961), it was in 1968 that Benjamin Bloom inaugurated a new era of educational thinking with the publication of an article entitled "Learning for Mastery." In that article Bloom (1968) argued that most teachers adopt a self-fulfilling prophecy that about one-third of their students will learn well, one-third will perform at a moderate level, and one-third will fail or just "get by."

> This set of expectations, which fixes the academic goals of teachers and students, is the most wasteful and destructive aspect of the present educational system. It reduces the aspirations of both teachers and students; it reduces motivation for learning in students; and it systematically destroys the ego and self-concept of a sizable group of students. (Bloom, 1968, p. 1)

In a later publication, Bloom summarized an alternative notion:

> What any person in the world can learn, almost all persons can learn if provided with appropriate prior and current conditions of learning. (Bloom, 1976, p. 7)

The key to achieving this, Bloom argued, was not student aptitude but effective instruction. Studies indicated that an average student, if classroom instruction is replaced by one-to-one professional tutoring, could rise to the ninety-eighth percentile—that is, could outperform 98 percent of his or her peers (Bloom, 1984). We should adopt the assumption, said Bloom, not that some students will never learn, but that all or almost all students can learn what we want to teach them. A generation earlier, Floyd Allport had noted that there were many learned behaviors that everyone seems to learn well (Allport, 1934). For example, almost everyone who tries to learn how to drive a car masters what is a highly complex, difficult, and dangerous task. The responsibility of educators is to establish the conditions that will allow similar success in school learning.

What are these "appropriate prior and current conditions" that are necessary for this to occur? Bloom identified six:

1. Clear, high, and realistic expectations.

2. Clear criteria of what constitutes success.

3. Rapid detection and remediation of underachievement.

4. Sufficient time for students to achieve mastery.

5. Appropriate cognitive and affective prerequisites.

6. Quality instruction. (Bloom, 1976)

Obviously, it is no small task to put all these factors in place in instructional situations. How to do so forms part of the subtext of the present book. The process has not been facilitated by oversimplification in some quarters of the ideas of mastery learning to the point of travesty. Many people still believe that Bloom advocated a universally fixed criterion of 80 percent for mastery, but there is no such assertion in any of Bloom's writing. A more contentious issue arose from the assumption that "sufficient time" would imply that what some students could learn in ten hours might require a thousand hours by other learners, making classroom operation an impossibility. In fact, Bloom believed that under mastery conditions, 80 percent of learners could achieve standards normally reached by the top 20 percent of learners by an addition of 10–20 percent of classroom time (1976). The most recent evidence suggests that the amount of instructional time required for mastery learning is approximately 4 percent greater than that for conventional instruction (Kulik, Kulik, & Bangert-Drowns, 1990).

In the generation since Bloom's 1968 article, many thousands of studies have been conducted into the ideas of mastery learning. Different interpreters of the research come to different conclusions about the effectiveness of mastery learning. Several syntheses of the research have been attempted, notably by Guskey and Gates (1986), Slavin (1987a), Block, Efthim, and Burns (1989), Kulik and Kulik (1989), and Kulik, Kulik, and Bangert-Drowns (1990). These studies ascribe an effect size to mastery learning of between .25 and 1.00, with the most recent and exacting study finding an effect size of .52 (Kulik et al., 1990). Effect sizes tend to be somewhat higher for elementary students than for secondary students (Guskey & Piggott, 1988). The research syntheses have also shown that mastery learning is most effective if programs are group-based rather than individualized, if high standards of achievement are expected, and if feedback to students is frequent. Mastery programs appear to benefit low-achieving students most, including the learning disabled (Kelly, Gerstein, & Carnine, 1990), but they do not have a "leveling down" effect on the learning of high achievers (Block et al., 1989). Pupils taught under mastery conditions begin to like the subject and the instruction more. Mastery learning is more effective if combined with other successful strategies such as cooperative learning (Guskey, 1990; Slavin & Karweit, 1984). Teachers who adopt mastery learning procedures begin to feel better about their teaching and to accept greater responsibility for student learning. They become less complacent about student failure and begin to view student learning more as the product of student and teacher effort and less as the result of unalterable personality factors (Guskey & Gates, 1986).

But perhaps as compelling as the research evidence is the face validity of Bloom's proposals. If we ensure that the necessary minimum background and interest are present prior to instruction, students are more likely to learn effectively. If we provide students with the experience of real success, their motivation will increase. If we provide prompt feedback and correction, failure and discouragement will be less likely to gain a foothold. And if we build student self-concept by repeated, significant success, we will provide students with the confidence and emotional security necessary to deal with the hardships, failures, and discouragements that are inevitable in life. None of these ideas were new. They have been used over the ages by parents teaching nursery rhymes to their children, by carpenters teaching apprentices, and by lions teaching their cubs to hunt. It was Bloom's contribution to bring these ancient principles to the attention of educators under a single evocative title. In so doing, he began to restore self-confidence in a generation of educators who had lost faith in their own ability to make a difference in the world.

4. *High expectations*

An essential feature of mastery learning, and one of the most consistent findings of the effective schools research, concerns expectations. In effective schools, administrators and teachers believe, and communicate this belief to pupils and parents, that every student can learn effectively. In their study of successful secondary schools, Wilson and Corcoran summarize their findings as follows:

> Good schools and school systems are populated by confident people who expect others to perform to their personal level of quality. Teachers expect students to achieve. Students know they are expected to achieve, and they expect, in turn, to have involved, competent teachers. Principals are surprised by teachers who fail. Teachers are surprised by administrators who ask little of themselves and others.   (Wilson & Corcoran, 1988, p. 121)

In ineffective schools, teachers tend to assert that limitations springing from students' backgrounds or abilities prevent them from learning. These teacher beliefs tend to be reflected in standards of pupil achievement (Ramsay et al., 1983; Teddlie et al., 1989). Teachers may also have differential expectations for particular students. Recent evidence shows that it is not merely the expectations, but the teacher actions that spring from them, that determine student attainment (Goldenberg, 1992). It has been found that students for whom teachers have low expectations tend to be seated farther away from the teacher, receive less direct instruction, are asked fewer and less thought-provoking questions, and are given less time to answer them (Blatchford, Burke, Farquhar, Plewis, & Tizard, 1989; Good, 1983). Different expectations for students from different social class backgrounds are so pervasive that many of the leaders in the school effectiveness movement refuse to label a school effective unless the achievement of poor children is virtually equal to that of middle-class children (Edmonds, 1979b; Lezotte, 1983; Sudlow, 1986). The Connecticut Department of Education defines an effective school as one "that brings children from low-income families to the minimum basic skills mastery level which now describes the minimally successful performance for middle-income children" (Gauthier, 1983, p. 2).

It should be no surprise that expectations are so influential. All of us respond to the expectations of others all of our lives. In the workplace, we respond to the expectations of superiors, colleagues, and clients. In our families, we respond to the expectations of family members. Indeed, some people carry the expectations of their parents like millstones around their necks for their entire lives, even when these expectations may be quite dysfunctional for them. As teaching and learning also involves human relationships, we can anticipate that expectations will also be influential in that context. This may help to explain why teacher expectations are among the factors most frequently related to student learning in different countries participating in international studies of achievement (Scheerens et al., 1989).

High expectations may be fostered in many ways. One is by setting and maintaining high standards of achievement and helping students successfully to meet those standards. A student at American High School in Miami, one of the successful schools studied by Wilson and Corcoran, says, "Teachers are on you all the time to do better. Even when you think you are working hard, they expect you to keep improving. They keep adjusting the goals upward" (1988, p. 104). Effective teachers model the behavior and values they advocate. Role models who are sensitive to pupils' gender and cultural background can also raise students' expectations. Adolescent girls can benefit from meeting women mathematicians, physicians, or scientists who have successfully combined career and family. An experiment exposing high-risk Puerto Rican adolescents to Puerto Rican hero/heroine models resulted in an increased ethnic identity and self-concept (Malgady, Rogler, & Costantino, 1990). But the primary vehicle for raising expectations will be the subtle and diverse day-to-day interaction of classroom teachers and their students.

Heroes

How can we live an exemplary existence? The measurement of that, the pattern for it, the guide for our own lives, comes from our heroes. How can we justify our dreams? How can we confirm our beliefs? How can we prove to ourselves that what we have been taught as children is true? How can we alleviate our doubts? How can we, in our own often naturally dormant lives, be inspired to action, sometimes even at the sacrifice of our own immediate well-being? We derive those inspirations from heroes.

Jimmy Carter (1990, p. 1)

---

5. Reading and study skills

Students with reading deficits face a disadvantage at every educational level. Before children enter school, they vary enormously in their amount of exposure to reading and their knowledge of text, and this single factor has a great impact on their learning in school (Adams, 1990; Holdaway, 1984; OERI, 1990). The literature on reading is too vast to summarize here. Let it simply be observed that one of the most effective ways of enhancing the performance of underachieving learners is to work directly on remediating their reading.

A related and rapidly developing area of investigation is *metacognition*, which refers to knowledge about one's own cognition—the awareness, monitoring, and regulating of one's own intellectual processes. Several metacognitive strategies have shown very promising results in the area of enhancing learning from text. They include teaching learners skills of self-questioning, summarizing, rereading, backward and forward search strategies, determining importance, drawing inferences, monitoring comprehension, contrasting textual information with prior knowledge, and comparing main ideas with each other and with details (Amigues, 1988; Dole, Duffy, Roehler, & Pearson, 1991; Haller, Child, & Walberg, 1988; Nist, Simpson, Olejnik, & Mealey, 1991). Not many scholars support

teaching thinking skills by a stand-alone approach. But there is controversy as to whether it is more effective to embed thinking skills in subject matter or to have them develop by immersing students in ideas and thought (Prawat, 1991).

Other kinds of metacognitive strategies include rules for cognitive operations and aids to memory. Jakow Trachtenberg was a brilliant engineer who spent most of World War II in Nazi concentration camps. Faced with appalling privation and the daily threat of death, Trachtenberg withdrew into his own mind and invented a system for mathematical calculation. After the war, he founded the Mathematical Institute in Zurich. Here, children and adults of all abilities learn to perform with lightning rapidity calculations such as the square roots of ten-digit numbers (Cutler & McShane, 1960). The system rests on remembering a number of simple rules. Mnenomics are a metacognitive strategy for use in those rare cases where a series of facts or names need to be committed to memory. Generations of children have remembered the notes on the treble stave lines (EGBDF) with the sentence, "Every good boy does fine." Medical students recalled the bones of the upper limb—scapula, clavicle, humerus, ulna, radius, carpals, metacarpals, and phalanges—by remembering "Some criminals have underestimated the Royal Canadian Mounted Police." The planets outward from the sun (Mercury, Venus, Earth, Mars, Jupiter, Saturn, Uranus, Neptune, and Pluto) correspond to "My very efficient memory just slipped under nervous pressure." The multipliers of metric units (tiera[10^{12}], giga, mega, kilo, milli, micro, nano, pico, femto, acto [10^{-18}]) can be recalled by: "To give me kicks my musicians now play for ages."

A great number of students at every educational level lack basic study skills. Few schools teach study skills in any systematic way, and most teachers appear to expect students to develop study skills by osmosis or maturation (Clift, Ghatala, Naus, & Poole, 1989). Underprivileged pupils are particularly vulnerable to lack of study skills, because their families may be unable to give them the support in this area available in middle-class homes. Underachievement might often be best approached not by further drill and practice in particular subject-matter, but by taking the time to teach some basic study skills, such as those in Table 6-3.

Learning styles research, while still controversial, suggests some insights that might help students find their most effective mode of studying. For example, most students in our culture believe that homework is necessarily an evening activity. But many of them would learn more and faster if they went to bed an hour earlier and spent an hour studying early in the morning. Teachers can encourage students to experiment in order to find out whether they work most effectively in silence or with background music; under bright or soft light; alone or with peers; in a cool or a warm environment; on soft or hard seating or on the floor (Dunn, Deckinger, Withers, & Katzenstein, 1990; Dunn & Dunn, 1987; Dunn, Gemake, Jalali, Zenjhausern, Quinn, & Spiridakis, 1990; Dunn, Sklar, Beaudry, & Bruno, 1990).

One of the students realized that her study environment, represented by a rocking chair, afghan, tea, and bright light, was *not effective for her*. After a conversation with her tutor, she became aware that she frequently dozed while studying. After some experimentation, she discovered that the best environment for her included sitting at a table near a window of a small spare room, earlier in the day than she had ever studied previously, and with a closed door. When she began studying this way, she experienced both consistently improved concentration *and* grades.

Dunn, Deckinger, Withers, & Katzenstein (1990, p. 105)

---

6. *Planned lessons*

At the heart of schooling and at the heart of its effectiveness lie the interactive experiences of students and teachers. The entire educational enterprise, and the primary energies of teachers, are directed toward the planning and provision of these experiences. The effectiveness studies point to the quality of lesson planning by teachers as a major factor in student learning. Lessons that best enhance student learning and attitudes are intellectually challenging, using more higher-order questions and encouraging creative imagination and problem solving.

Table 6-3   *Basic Study Skills*

Study orientation
developing confidence
planning and setting goals
keeping study records
monitoring own study processes
keeping up with homework

Classroom skills
reading ahead in the text
bringing required materials to class
listening effectively
self-questioning
asking questions
asking for help
taking and making notes
using notecards
participating in class
focusing on concepts
listing key terms
clarifying details and dates of
  assignments
discussing lesson with classmates
reviewing and highlighting class
  notes
following up teachers' feedback
initiating conferences with teachers
establishing a phone contact in each
  class
checking on missed assignments

Study organization
developing regular study habits
resolving problems (e.g., phone call
  before studying)
planning study time
allocating time for homework and
  review
finding optimal study methods
finding the ideal study environment
finding the best time of day to study
organizing materials for study
making notes—using headings, color
  coding, highlighting, marginal
  notes, underlining, numbering,
  editing, rewriting

copying key quotations with
  reference
organizing and filing notes and
  handouts
rereading teacher's comments on
  work
dealing with distractions
setting work limits
taking breaks
rewarding self
forming an effective study group

Studying text materials
getting an overview of the material
  using contents lists, indexes, headings, summaries
using a dictionary
reading for key points
self-questioning
underlining or highlighting text
identifying and using key words
speedreading, skimming, and
  rereading
outlining, summarizing, and paraphrasing
monitoring comprehension

Resource-based learning
using a library
locating books and periodicals
using encyclopedias and other reference tools
using audiovisual resources
using computer software
using human resources
keeping a list of sources

Writing skills
writing essays
reading old essays and friends' essays
using essay formats
using spellchecks or peer editing
using quotations
editing, revising, polishing
"Don't get it right—get it written"
  (James Thurber)

Table 6-3   *(Continued)*

Preparing for tests	Taking tests
organizing test preparation time	controlling test anxiety
memory, mnemonics, and concentration techniques	scanning a test
	reading questions carefully
review techniques	writing neatly and legibly
avoiding group hysteria	organizing time and priorities in tests
practicing with different kinds of questions	
	strategies for writing essay tests
obtaining clear test guidelines	strategies for selected-response questions
maintaining a test file	
preparing outlines of essay answers	rereading answers if possible
decreasing reliance on cramming	

Irving, 1985; King, 1992; NASSP, nd; Nist, Simpson, Olejnik, & Mealey, 1991; Russell, Caris, Harris, & Hendricson, 1983; Selmes, 1987; Van Nord, 1991; Weinstein, Goetz, & Alexander, 1988

Instructions to pupils are clear—an important point, in view of Goodlad's finding in his nationwide study that "over half of the upper elementary students reported that many students did not know what they were supposed to do in class" (Goodlad, 1984, p. 112). Pupils are actively engaged rather than passively listening and hence have high time on task. Topics are taught for mastery, not simply for exposure. The more closely lesson content and activities are aligned with the purposes of instruction, the more closely will student performance match those purposes (Ames & Archer, 1988; Elia, 1986; Mortimore et al., 1988; Porter, 1989; Pratton & Hales, 1986; Teddlie et al., 1989).

Professional teachers must always steer a middle path between underplanning, which is wasteful, and overplanning, which is suffocating. The key is modifiable plans:

> Instruction begins with a plan of teachers' intentions; however, as soon as a lesson begins, teachers modify the plan to accommodate students who, in the process of interpreting instructional information, create their own meanings. Effective teachers respond to students' restructured understandings by modifying their plans. This recursive process of reciprocal mediation by teachers and students continues throughout the lesson. Hence, planning remains a crucial component of effective instruction. It is not a script to follow but a blueprint from which teachers make adjustments in response to students' emerging understandings. (Dole, Duffy, Roehler, & Pearson, 1991, pp. 252-253)

In effective classrooms, pupils are "not given unlimited responsibility for planning their own daily programme of work, or for choosing work activities, but

[are] guided into areas of study or exploration and taught the skills necessary for independently managing that work" (Mortimore et al., 1988, p. 252). This reflects findings regarding the ineffectiveness of some efforts at individualizing student work: "Many students, particularly younger students in the elementary grades and those with lower entry-level skills, lack the sophistication and motivation to be effective self-managers of their own learning" (Guskey & Gates, 1986, p. 74).

However detailed a curriculum may be, at some point it must be translated into lessons for actual teachers to instruct actual learners. Although some curricula contain lesson outlines, it is difficult to plan lessons in the abstract. Only when we encounter our students in person can we determine the day-to-day content and teaching strategies that are most appropriate for them.

There is no universal lesson form. A conventional lesson plan will not apply very well to a classroom using ten different learning centers, or to a field trip to the recycling center. Tables 6-4 and 6-5 show a standard lesson plan that might be considered a "fall-back" position. It attempts to include all the main components that should be present in a well-designed lesson, based on what we know about effective formal teaching (Berliner, 1986; Joyce, 1987; Kallison, 1986).

Some explanatory notes are necessary. An *advance organizer* is "introductory material at a higher level of abstraction, generality, and inclusiveness than the learning passage itself" (Ausubel, 1978, p. 252). In other words, it is a summary of work that is to come. *Key questions* are intended to be thought-provoking or higher-order questions, the kinds of questions that we know are associated with more effective teaching (Redfield & Rousseau, 1981). It is well known that questions facilitate learning—questions before instruction, during instruction, and following instruction (Hamilton, 1985). It is easy enough to think of factual questions on the spur of the moment. Unfortunately, on the spur of the moment, one may not be able to think of anything else, and this may explain the overwhelming predominance (at least 99 percent) of low-level, factual questions in classrooms. (Mortimore et al., 1988). Hence the need to think of a few good, stimulating questions in advance. "What is the basis of our numeric system?" is a simple question. "How would our lives be different if we had twelve fingers?" is a more interesting question. "What is photosynthesis?" is easy. "What is the most basic biological difference between an elephant and a sunflower?" is more interesting. Note that when asking such questions, "wait time," that is, the time between completing the question and calling for an answer, should be from three to five seconds to stimulate student thought (Tobin, 1987).

A similar concern underlies the identification of *key students.* Without special care, teachers tend to concentrate their questions on a small number of students, particularly those sitting near the front of the room and those considered more able. To ensure that all students receive a minimum of attention, it is a useful plan to develop some kind of system for interaction with every student on a regular basis. A method as simple as picking three names each day in sequence from the class list will serve.

Table 6-4   *Standard Lesson Plan*

Class_____Date_____

Reminder_____

Topic_____

Objective: By the end of this lesson, the students will_____

_____

Materials and equipment_____

_____

Key students_____

Entry routine_____

Opening_____

Review: key questions_____

_____

_____

Overview of the lesson_____

_____

Content and strategies_____

_____

_____

Summary review: assess learning: key questions_____

_____

_____

Homework assignment_____

_____

_____

Advance organizer for next lesson_____

_____

Self-assessment: revisions for next time_____

_____

Table 6-5   *Illustration of Lesson Plan*

Class 8c Special.   **Date** 11 April 1993

Reminder Tomorrow is Hot Dog Day: collect money

Topic Math: Measurement

Objective: By the end of this lesson, the students will be able to use ml as a unit of measurement

Materials and equipment Recipe cards-4 muffin tins-4 measuring cups-2 big spoons-2 knives-flour, brown sugar, salt, bran, banana, baking soda, raisins, baking powder, 1 egg, margarine.

Key students Martha, Robert, Alicia

Entry routine Math review questions at door: wash hands at sink.

Opening Take 5 muffins out of microwave, butter and share-we're going to make some of these today

Review: key questions ...What makes liters and milliliters easy to use? How many ml in one l? Which is bigger, half a litre or 500 ml?

Overview of the Lesson Importance of measuring for cooking: go through recipe.

Content and strategies One group gets and mixes dry ingredients, the other wet. Mix wet and dry together. Each student pours 2 muffins into the tin. Cook muffins. Wash utensils and put away while cooking. Check progress with students. When muffins are cooled, eat up!

Summary review: assess learning: key questions Why was exact measurement important? What would have happened if you'd just guessed? If you'd added too much salt/milk/flour?

Homework assignment At home measure and record on the handout sheet exactly how much water each of these holds: a sandwich bag; a baseball hat; two hands; an eggshell; something else.

Advance organizer for next lesson At what temperature did we cook the muffins? Why was exact temperature important? Tomorrow: measuring temperature.

Self-assessment: revisions for next time Supervise while students grease tin or muffins will stick!

As a footnote to lesson planning, a note should be made about homework. Only 10 percent of twelfth-graders spend more than two hours a day doing homework (National Assessment of Educational Progress, 1990). Higher-achieving students and students in high-achieving schools spend more time on homework (Keith, 1982; MacKenzie, 1983; Walberg, 1985; Wilson & Corcoran, 1988). A British study shows that working-class students who spend slightly more than the average amount of time on homework outperform middle-class students who do slightly less than average (Holmes & Croll, 1989). The same applies to differences in ability. "When low-ability students do just 1 to 3 hours of homework a week, their grades are usually as high as those of average ability students who do not do homework. Similarly, when average-ability students do 3 to 5 hours of homework a week, their grades usually equal those of high-ability students who do no homework" (U.S. Department of Education, p. 51).

Mere quantity of homework assigned is probably not the important factor; students report doing less than half of the hours of homework that teachers say they assign (Keith, 1982). What matters is that the homework be relevant and integral to the instruction, seen as useful and interesting by students, and followed up by the teacher in class (Walberg, 1985). Homework that is assigned loses two-thirds of its effectiveness if it is not subsequently reviewed by the teacher (Walberg, 1984a). Time spent by teachers planning homework activities that are interesting and challenging is likely to earn dividends in student learning. Here, for example, is a mathematics problem for Grades 7–9:

> There are 1,000 lockers in a school hallway. The first student to leave the school assembly closes every open locker door. The second opens every second door; the third changes the (open/closed) state of every third door; the fourth changes every fourth door; and so on, until the 1,000th student leaves. How many locker doors are closed and which are they? To solve this problem, students may make a diagram, chart or graph; try a small problem of 20 lockers; experiment in the hallway; set up a concrete manipulative model, etc. (The answer is based on a series of 3, 5, 7, 9 . . . ; the lockers closed will be numbers 1, 4, 9, 16, 25, 36, 49, etc.) (Alberta Education, 1985, pp. 11–12)

Even if interesting, homework should not be excessive. Many students work part-time or full-time after school, others have family responsibilities, and all of them need some time to live, not just to do homework!

7. An orderly environment

A safe, orderly environment is a prerequisite for instructional effectiveness (Sudlow, 1986; Teddlie et al., 1989). To a great extent, this factor depends on the ethos and leadership in the school as a whole. We shall discuss school ethos later in this chapter, and leadership by principals is discussed in Chapter 10. At this point, we may observe merely that effective principals support their teachers by helping to protect instruction from interruptions and disruptions (Lightfoot, 1983; Louis & Miles, 1990; Short & Spencer, 1990; Wilson & Corcoran, 1988). Ineffective principals undermine their teachers' instructional efforts by focusing on noninstructional goals such as athletics or community relations, and even by interrupting lessons with trivial announcements from the office. Inside the classroom, however, much depends on the individual teacher. Much classroom management is contextual: decisions must be made depending on the specific situation rather than by reference to general principles. Nevertheless, there are some axioms that seem to apply to most situations. Experienced teachers often remark that most problems of discipline arise as a result of poor planning. As Bloom puts it, "If the management of learning is effective, it is likely that the teacher will need to give relatively little attention to the management of the learners" (Bloom, 1976, p. 114).

When students are busy, happy, and learning successfully, classrooms tend to be quiet and orderly. Conversely, when there are insufficient activities or students are frustrated by work that is too difficult, classrooms tend to become noisy and unruly (Jorgenson, 1977). There are also some principles drawn from basic ethics that are important in classrooms, such as treating every individual with respect and insisting that students treat one another respectfully. The following points indicate some steps teachers can take to plan classroom structures and instruction to minimize disruption and some possible directions when and if confrontation does occur. More detail on approaches to classroom management can be found in the literature (Coloroso, 1987; Emmer, Evertson, Sanford, Clements & Worsham, 1984; Evertson, Emmer, Clements, Sanford, & Worsham, 1984; Ginnott, 1972; Gordon, 1974; Seeman, 1988).

Structures.   Develop and negotiate rules and routines. Set clear expectations for behavior and attendance. Establish a regular opening routine for lessons.

Identify difficult and hyperactive students, separate them, and place them in key locations. Coopt leaders and give them responsibilities. Respond to students' moods and feelings. Give students "Help!" cards. Distribute "Leave Me Alone" cards that students can place on their desks on bad days.

Get to know all your students and their names. Acknowledge, read out, or display good work. Participate in extracurricular activities. Interact systematically with all students. Call absentees. Get to know parents and phone them at least once each semester.

Place teacher's desk strategically. Avoid congestion in high traffic areas. Have materials and supplies readily accessible. Make the classroom comfortable and attractive. Create appealing, welcoming bulletin board displays. Ensure that all students can see and hear and that you can see all the students. "Manage by walking around." During work periods, with agreement of students, play a radio tuned to students' favorite station, linked to an acoustical switch that cuts power when classroom noise rises above a preset level.

Allow breaks. Get students out of the classroom occasionally. If students are coming to class late or hungry, introduce a breakfast program.

Instruction.   Ensure the curriculum is meaningful to students. Make instruction interesting, challenging, and varied. Provide success experiences. Provide intrinsically valuable and significant experiences. Don't distrust having fun. Be well prepared and organized. Let students know the plan. Have a backup plan. Use active learning and keep students busy. Allow some class time for homework. Change activity at least every twenty minutes. "If it can be taught, it can be taught with a game."

Audiotape or videotape and review your classes periodically. Plan cooperative, team, and dyad activities. Institute peer tutoring. Learn and utilize students' interests and backgrounds. Teach at an appropriate difficulty level. Plan strategies for faster and slower learners.

Confrontation.   If you implement all of the above strategies, confrontation will rarely occur. But it may. A student may come to school raging from a home situation you cannot control. If confrontation occurs, try to model interpersonal respect. Acknowledge and invite expression of feelings. ("You sound angry, Joseph; are you?") Try to establish the underlying cause of the student's reaction. Avoid "why" questions. Don't argue with students. Learn positive listening. Avoid win/lose situations. Avoid making heroes. Do not touch the student. Don't put students down in public (or in private). Allow students to save face. Stay calm. Allow time out. Interact one to one. Use the student's name and use eye contact. Set up a three-way meeting with a counselor. If the whole class is resistant, examine your teaching and try to diagnose the cause of the problem.

Do not condone abuse of yourself or anyone else—ever.

8. *Instructional variety*

In the science of cybernetics, there is a principle known as Ashby's Law, named for its inventor, the psychiatrist and cybernetician Ross Ashby. Ashby's Law states that only variety can absorb variety (Ashby, 1956). What this means is that a system can achieve stability only by an array of strategies sufficiently varied to deal with the variety of input into the system. Let us put this in practical classroom terms. A typical classroom of thirty students represents enormous variety in terms of student motivation, interests, attitudes, self-concept, preferred learning style, and background. A teacher who uses one predominant teaching style will disadvantage all the students who do not share the same learning style. The solution is to use as wide a variety of learning styles as is feasible. Furthermore, everyone likes variety, and students are no exception.

In most of our schools, we probably have too much variety of content, and too little variety of method. We might be more successful if we concentrated on teaching only the most important content, but teaching it more effectively. This is what Alfred North Whitehead recommended in 1929: "Let the main ideas which are introduced into a child's education be few and important and let them be thrown into every combination possible" (Whitehead, 1967, p. 14).

Recently, some interesting observational studies have been conducted in classrooms in Asia. Observers have noted that Japanese and Chinese teachers deal with

---

Assignments to stimulate writing

Write about what has just happened or is about to happen in a photograph.

Write captions for a cartoon from which they have been removed.

List all the things you would like to do by the age of 40.

Write a note to put in a bottle to throw into the sea.

List 10 items you would put in a time capsule.

What 10 things would you like to invent?

Write about your experiences on a life raft as the sole survivor of a shipwreck.

Write to a pen pal in another school or country.

Instead of a book review, make a poster for a book.

Write a story in which you are ten feet tall, or a shoe, or a bird.

Ronald L. Cramer (1981)

---

far fewer mathematics problems and reading passages per class-hour than their American colleagues, but that these problems and passages are dealt with in much greater depth (Mason et al., 1989; Resnick, 1989). Japanese children tend to be more persistent at learning tasks than their American counterparts. Repetition is used extensively in Japanese classrooms; Japanese teachers will often cite proverbs such as, "Read it one hundred times, and understanding will follow spontaneously" (Hess & Azuma, 1991, p. 6). At the same time, a great variety of teaching strategies is used by Japanese teachers. A majority of the following activities were observed in *every* reading lesson witnessed by an American/Japanese team visiting Japanese classrooms: Teacher reads aloud; class reads aloud in unison; individual students read aloud; teacher evaluates quality of oral reading; class evaluates quality of individual oral reading by applause; class reads silently; teacher writes on board; class copies from board; class takes dictation; teacher asks questions; class writes answers to teacher questions; class responds in unison to teacher questions; teacher evaluates individual responses to questions; whole-class discussion; small-group discussion; individual students act out scenes from story; class sings (Mason et al., 1989).

American classrooms tend to be dominated by a small number of teaching styles. Teacher talk, teacher questions, and individual student seat-work account for the overwhelming bulk of lesson time in most classrooms (Goodlad, 1983; Schmuck & Schmuck, 1990). The checklist of 221 instructional strategies and resources shown in Table 6-6 is intended to provide teachers with a wider range of alternatives. You can use it like this: When planning a lesson, unit, or course, work systematically through the list, considering each strategy or resource briefly but imaginatively. Check each item that has possibilities. You will probably end with at least a hundred. Then go through your short-list and select only the ten or so items that promise to be most interesting or effective. You will almost certainly end up with a more interesting selection of teaching strategies than if you attempted to use unaided imagination.

Different strategies may be used concurrently as well as consecutively. For example, a teacher managing an environmental studies unit on "garbage" could set up a number of different learning stations in the classroom. Students working at a video station could view videos on garbage, take a video camera to the local dump, film student generation of garbage in the cafeteria, or make a commercial on the issue. At the art station, students could make posters for a garbage reduction campaign or make collages using garbage as art materials. A statistics station could suggest data that students could collect on garbage nationally, locally, and within the school, plotting seasonal trends and the different components of garbage. Students at an oral history station could interview parents and grandparents, garbage operators, and municipal officials about garbage policies and practices in the past

Table 6-6   *Instructional Strategies and Resources*

advertisement	choral reading	diary
album	cloze technique	display
anecdote	club	drama
anthology	collage	drawing
aquarium	collection	drill
artifact	coloring book	electric map
audio record	comedy	essay
autobiography	comic book	exercise
balloons	community	exhibit
bibliography	competition	experience
bingo	computer	experiment
book	cooking	facsimile
book review	cooperation	fantasy
brainstorming	correspondence	feelbag
bulletin board	costumes	feltboard
calculator	crafts	field research
campaign	cutout	field trip
card game	dance	filmstrip
cartoon	data sheet	flags
case study	debate	flashcards
celebration	demonstration	flip book
chalkboard	design	flowchart
charade	diagram	food
chart	dialogue	*(Continued)*

Table 6-6   (Continued)

game	newspaper	sandtable
globe	notebook	scrapbook
grab bag	novel	sculpture
graph	obituary	seminar
group project	oral history	senior citizens
guessing	oral report	silence
guest	outdoors	silkscreen
hall of fame	overhead	simulation
holograph	painting	sketch
homework	pamphlet	skit
imitation	panel	slides
improvisation	pantomime	song
interview	parents	source material
invention	peer tutoring	sports
jigsaw	pegboard	stamps
jigsaw group	pets	sticker book
job performance aid	photography	story
laboratory	picture book	suggestion box
lecture	play	survey
letter to editor	poem	tachistoscope
letter to expert	portfolio	task cards
library	poster	teacher
learning center	printing press	teacher aide
lyric	problem	team teaching
machine	programmed instruction	telephone
magazine	project	telephone directory
magic	psychodrama	telescope
magnetic board	puppets	television
map	puzzle	terrarium
meditation	questionnaire	test
microfilm	questions	textbook
microscope	quiz	time-lapse photography
mnemonic	quotation	tools
mobile	radio	toy
mock trial	recipe	treasure hunt
model	relaxation exercise	tutorial
modelling	replica	typewriter
montage	reports	videotape
movie	research paper	visualization
museum	riddle	volunteers
mural	ritual	word game
music	role playing	work book
myth		

and the changes that have taken place over time. A drama station might involve students in creating skits or collaborating with the video station on creating a commercial. An invention station asks students to invent devices for reducing or eliminating garbage. The creative writing station invites students to write a poem, a short story, an essay, or a parody on the topic of garbage. The instructional possibilities are limited only by the energy, time, and imagination of the teacher (Cory Laverty, personal communication, October 1, 1990).

Many of the resources listed are extremely versatile. There are hundreds of uses, for example, for newspapers in the classroom. In mathematics, you can have students plot the prices of used cars by year and calculate average depreciation by make. In composition, students write their own newspaper obituary. In art, they roll newspapers into tubes, paint them, and build abstract sculptures. In driver education, they collate statistics on the time of day of accidents and the age and sex of drivers and develop a plan for reducing accidents (Berryman, 1973). Cooking does not immediately strike one as a standard pedagogical strategy, but it holds the promise of memorable experience because it involves senses in addition to hearing and vision. Thus, in the language class we can try our hand at French or Spanish cuisine; in history, recreate a Roman or a seventeenth-century New England meal; in mathematics, practice liquid and solid measurement and conversion; in physics, experiment with and observe the changes in food produced by different kinds of heat; in health, practice cooking that preserves nutrients; in art, work with color in presentation and sculpting sugar icing; with imagination, you can come up with applications even in welding and auto mechanics.

9. Cooperative learning

Cooperative learning is one of the success stories of contemporary education. Four basic structures are available for classroom learning: (1) *individualistic* learning, where the teacher may teach to the whole class but each learner does his or her own work independently; (2) *competitive* learning, similar to individualistic learning, except that students are ranked by comparison with one another, and evaluation is norm-referenced; (3) *team competition*, in which learners cooperate to learn in groups, but groups compete against one another; (4) *cooperative* learning in which students learn in groups and groups do not compete with each other. These structures may be illustrated by examples from sports. Recreational skiing is an example of an individualistic sport; the 100-meter dash an example of a competitive sport; basketball an example of team competition; and mountaineering an example of a cooperative sport.

There is much competition in our society, and this leads some people to urge that schools train students in competition in preparation for a competitive world. Others contend that as the world already teaches competition, schools should concentrate on developing cooperation. Douglas Anderson comments that "By and large, American public education, like America itself, ignores losers. And the category losers includes, by and large, all but the winner" (Anderson, 1974, p. 41). In this debate, five factors might be borne in mind: (1) Competition appears to be highly effective in such arenas as sports, business, and warfare. However, people who choose a career in sports or business are *electing* a competitive environment, and it is a different situation when a teacher *requires* students to work competitively. (2) Increasingly, the world of employment is seeking people who can cooperate—who have highly developed skills in team leadership and membership, human relations, and communication. (3) Competition is most congenial to white, middle-class, male students (although not to all of them). Caution must be used in applying competition to different groups from these, particularly to such ethnic groups as native Americans, for whom competition is often culturally alien (Soldier, 1989). (4) The empirical evidence provides no basis for the belief that faster learners suffer when their learning involves cooperation with less able peers. (5) However, to condemn all competition out of hand would be to condemn everyone who ever enjoyed a game of bridge, tennis, football, or bingo, or aspired to become a star athlete, or to enter the *Guiness Book of World Records,* or to own the world's best collection of Mongolian postage stamps. The implication of this discussion is that we need to respond sensitively to student differences by using a variety of structures in the classroom.

> Two are better than one, for if they fall, the one will lift up his fellow; but woe to him that is alone when he falleth, for he hath not another to help him up.
>
> Ecclesiastes 4:10

The effects of competitive and cooperative structures are illustrated in a study of physical education by Marsh (1988):

> High school girls were randomly assigned to competitive, cooperative, or control groups. In the competitive groups, the exercises were done individually and feedback emphasized comparison with whoever performed best on each exercise. In the cooperative group, the exercises required the cooperation of at least two girls and feedfack stressed progress rather than comparison with others. Both competitive and cooperative interventions significantly enhanced physical fitness, but the competitive intervention lowered physical self-concept whereas the cooperative intervention increased physical self-concept.   (Marsh, 1991, p. 472)

Bringing about cooperative structures in the classroom involves more than simply asking learners to work in groups. Schools tend to socialize their students into individualized and competitive patterns, and they need to be taught skills of cooperation. Some of these leadership and membership skills are summarized by David Johnson and his colleagues: contributing ideas, asking questions, expressing feelings, actively listening, expressing support and acceptance toward ideas, expressing liking of other group members, encouraging, summarizing, checking for understanding, and relieving tension by humor (Johnson, Johnson, Holubec,

& Roy, 1984). One of the key factors in any cooperative learning situation is the manner in which rewards are distributed. Experiments by Robert Slavin suggest that assigning goals to a group without individual accountability for achievement is not very effective. Nor is it effective to require individual accountability without group goals. The most effective pattern entails both group goals and individual accountability (Slavin, 1988a). In this pattern, students study together and may collaborate in testing situations; but each student submits an individual assignment or test response for individual evaluation. Bonus marks may be added based on the total achievement of the group.

There is a widespread myth among teachers that cooperative learning means simply telling students to work together in groups. This may do more harm than good if no group skills are developed. Groups may degenerate into socializing or bickering; more conscientious learners may begin to view less motivated learners as parasitic. There are several conditions that need to be in place if cooperative learning is to achieve its potential.

One necessity in establishing cooperative learning groups is to pay attention to student subcultures. Bullough, Knowles, and Crow (1989) report the complexity

---

Cooperation in college

Uri Treisman, when a graduate student at the University of California at Berkeley, observed that in the first-year honors calculus course he was teaching, black and Hispanic students performed below the class average, and many were in danger of failure, while Asian students performed better than average. Treisman rejected the idea that these differences were due to aptitude and resolved to shadow individual students to observe how they studied and prepared for class. He found that the disadvantaged students actually spent more hours studying than the Asian Americans, but they typically studied alone, and spent most of their study time reading the assigned textbook and studying class notes, and less time attempting the homework problems. When they got stuck on a problem, their strategy was to keep trying one method of solution. These students were reluctant to go to the math center for help. They had been good students in high school and thought that only poor students went for remedial help. The Asian-American students, on the other hand, spent only a small proportion of their time reading. They met regularly as a group to review the homework problems, and spent more of their time in the group discussing and helping one another with the most difficult problems. If they could not solve a problem, someone would consult the instructor. Treisman set up an honors workshop for the black and Hispanic students where he coached them to follow the same group problem-solving process he had observed among the Asian-American students. Before long, the minority students in the honors workshop were performing as well as the rest of the class.

Treisman (1983)

teachers experience in attempting to achieve cooperation among the rockers, wavers, jocks, stoners, normies, and preppies in their classes. Students, particularly early adolescents for whom friendship bonds are strong, like to have some control over membership of their learning groups. Johnson et al. (1984) suggest a compromise, inviting students to list other students with whom they would like to work, then placing them in a learning group with one person they choose and others selected by the teacher. Three or four members is the number usually preferred. To achieve maximum benefit, groups should contain varied abilities. Daniel Fader recommends groups of three, each group containing one student from the upper third of the class, one from the middle third, and one from the lower third (1969).

A list of practical steps to establish cooperative learning structures is provided by Johnson, Johnson, and Holubec (undated):

Specify the academic and/or collaborative skills you want students to learn, starting with something easy.

Assign students to groups, starting with groups of two or three, mixing abilities, sexes, and cultural backgrounds.

Arrange furniture so students are eye to eye and knee to knee.

Assign a role to each group member, for example, reader, recorder, calculator, checker, reporter, materials hander, encourager, checker for understanding.

Explain and ensure students understand the task and the criteria for success; teach necessary prerequisite material.

Specify the expected behaviors, such as helping, listening, encouraging, asking for help or clarification, taking turns, speaking quietly, and so on.

Teach collaborative skills one at a time, giving definitions, rationales, and examples.

Circulate; monitor student behavior; give immediate feedback, reinforcement, and praise.

Provide task assistance as needed; intervene as necessary to teach collaborative skills.

Structure positive interdependence by establishing mutual goals or joint rewards such as bonus points if all members achieve above a certain score.

Structure individual accountability by frequent assessment of written work or oral or written quizzes of groups of randomly selected members.

Structure intergroup cooperation by having groups check with and help other groups.

Assess student learning and give feedback.

Process group functioning with individuals, groups, or the whole class.

Provide closure; students may summarize major points.

Several researchers have summarized the effects of cooperative learning. As compared with students taught in individual or competitive structures, students of all ability levels who learn cooperatively tend to like each other, the teacher, and the subject more. They become more accepting of ethnic, class, gender, and ability differences. They demonstrate more on-task and less disruptive behavior. They engage in more critical thinking and achieve better integration and retention of subject content. They develop higher levels of self-esteem and achieve at a higher level. More friendships develop in cooperative classrooms, particularly between handicapped and nonhandicapped students (Guskey, 1990; Johnson & Johnson, 1989; Johnson & Johnson, 1990; Leming & Hollifield, 1985; Newmann & Thompson, 1987; Salend & Sonnenschein, 1989; Sharan et al., 1984; Slavin, 1989a). While researchers agree that cooperative learning raises achievement significantly, they disagree as to how much. Johnson and Johnson (1990) claim the effect size is between .67 and .88 when students taught under cooperative conditions are compared with those taught under competitive or individual conditions; Slavin claims that the effect is closer to .30 or .40 (Slavin, 1987a, 1988a, 1991). What is now clear is that cooperative learning is more effective than either individualized instruction or competition. A number of experiments have shown that mastery learning, with its emphasis on developing high achievement in all students by reference to criteria rather than to interstudent comparisons, lends itself to cooperative instruction (Guskey, 1990; Slavin & Karweit, 1984). A recent thought-provoking finding is that as the quality of instructional leadership by school principals rises, competition between students for grades diminishes (Short & Spencer, 1990).

The group could be asked to get into line on a low beam or log. Once everyone is on the log, they could be asked to get into alphabetical order by first name without getting off the log. Once completed by cooperation, another task could be for the group to get in order of birth date from oldest to youngest without talking and without falling off the log or beam. If a student falls off the log, they return to their place on the log and try again. Do not eliminate people for falling. Talking while trying to complete the last variation will not be a cause for elimination, but the student will be reminded that the idea is to communicate in other ways than talking, just for the fun of it. Early, nonthreatening, successful group cooperative exercises such as the above are to build cohesion, cooperation, fun, and trust in the group. The exercises break down previously established groups and allow all the students to participate, since it is up to the whole group to aid each other.

Bill Ghent, *A Ropes Course Curriculum* (1990, p. 16)

Cooperation applies to teachers as well as to students. Robert Houston reports that when preparing a paper on collaboration in teacher education, he looked up "collaboration" in his university library card catalog. The card he found said, "Collaboration—see treason" (Houston, 1986, p. ii). Many teachers live lonely lives. Surrounded by children all day, some teachers interact very little with other adults (Sarason, 1971). This pattern is less common in effective schools. A study of secondary schools in London, England, showed that the most effective schools were those that had a strong departmental organization in which a senior teacher took responsibility for leadership, and to whom junior teachers felt accountable and to whom they looked for advice (Rutter, Maughan, Mortimore, Ouston, & Smith, 1979). Many studies of effective schools in the United States and Canada have identified collegiality as a key factor in effectiveness (Barth, 1990b; Coleman, Mikkelson, & LaRocque, 1991; Little, 1982; Murphy, Weil, Hallinger, & Mitman, 1982). Little (1981) found that collegiality in schools had its most effective expression in teachers and administrators talking about professional practice, observing one another teaching, working together on curriculum, and teaching one another; principals modeled, rewarded, promoted, and protected collegiality among their teachers. Collegiality, however, as Hargreaves (1989b) points out, must evolve authentically; it is not effective to attempt to coerce teachers into contrived collegiality.

10. Computer-assisted instruction

"If human beings are lucky," a scientist at M.I.T. is supposed to have said, "fifth-generation computers will keep them as pets." Few educators need to be told about the potential of computer-assisted instruction (CAI). One of the strengths of CAI is that it can incorporate many of the other factors of instructional effectiveness. Interesting and well-designed programs can be motivational and ensure high student time on task. Assessment, diagnosis, and remediation can be built into programs to produce mastery learning. High expectations can be set. Reading skills can be assessed and reinforced. When a hundred or even a thousand hours of planning are dedicated to production of one hour of software, instruction can be designed with a sensibility and a variety of strategies impossible for an individual teacher. Programs can be designed that require students to work in pairs or groups in order to reap the benefits of cooperative learning. Students with such physical handicaps as cerebral palsy can use specially modified computers to write and communicate with a facility that would otherwise be impossible (Tougas, 1987). It is important that computer resources be equitably distributed, because it has been found that poor, minority, and female students tend to have less access to computers both at home and at school (Sutton, 1991).

The computer has the potential to adapt every learning sequence to the particular responses made by students. It can provide personalized pretesting, tuition, practice, simulations, diagnosis, feedback, assessment, remediation, and encouragement twenty-four hours a day. The word processing capability of computers allows students to compose rapidly, produce professional-looking text that is relatively easy for the teacher to read and assess, and produce revised drafts without having to rewrite an entire document. Collaborative writing and coaching is facilitated, and students who use word processors tend to have positive attitudes toward writing (Cochran-Smith, 1991).

When linked to interactive videodisk technology, CAI programs can integrate high-quality film material. At the same time as they are improving their academic learning, students working with CAI are enhancing their computer skills, which are now prerequisite to an increasingly wide range of occupations. Teachers can use the computer for recordkeeping, for individualizing instruction, for testing, for inventory control, and for generation of instructional materials.

Reviews of the research on CAI with elementary and secondary students show significant and fairly uniform effects. The reported effectiveness of CAI (typically 10–15 minutes per day) in thirteen meta-analyses published since 1980 ranged from .12 to .57, with a mean of .34 (Anderson, 1983; Bangert-Drowns, Kulik & Kulik, 1985; Bangert-Drowns, Kulik & Kulik in Kulik & Kulik, 1989; Burns, 1981; Fletcher, Hawley, & Piele, 1990; Kulik & Kulik, 1989; Kulik, Kulik, & Bangert-Drowns, 1985; Levin, Meister, & Glass, 1987; Niemiec, 1985; Niemiec, Blackwell, & Walberg, 1986; Niemiec & Walberg, 1985; Schmidt, Weinstein, Niemiec, & Walberg, 1985; Slavin, 1987b). This is a sizeable effect for a small investment of student time. Although there does not appear to be a historical trend in these statistics, it is reasonable to predict that in the course of time better and better instructional programs will be written, while it is certain that the cost of computer equipment will continue to fall, making computer-assisted instruction increasingly cost effective.

In other areas, results of CAI have been more modest. While CAI has a positive effect on students' attitudes toward computers and toward the courses they are studying, it has not been shown to have much effect on student attitudes toward the subject being taught (Kulik, 1983). Researchers are not agreed whether the claims of Papert (1980) and others, that CAI would lead to major breakthroughs in children's cognitive development, are supported by the research evidence (Carmichael, Burnett, Higginson, Moore, & Pollard, 1985; Pea & Sheingold, 1987). This may be because effective use of computers in the classroom requires changes in the traditional mode of teaching. Olson calls the computer a "Trojan horse," because it "offers teachers ways to enhance what and how they teach, but at the same time threatens those very practices by calling them into question" (1992, p. 77).

11. School ethos

Effective schools are marked by a pervasive atmosphere that Michael Rutter and his colleagues (1979) labelled "school ethos." This ethos is the product of philosophical agreement about purpose that is shared by teachers and administration. Sara Lightfoot summarizes the ethos of effective high schools succinctly: "Good schools are places where students are seen as people worthy of respect" (1983, p. 350). She lists seven contributing factors. Good schools, she says:

1) reveal a sustained and visible ideology;

2) give teachers the opportunity for autonomous expression;

3) exhibit coherent and sturdy authority structures which support and legitimize the individual disciplinary acts of teachers;

4) are preoccupied with the rationale, coherence, and integrity of their academic curriculum;

5) exercise collegial leadership;

6) treat students with fearless and empathetic attention;

7) make students feel visible and accountable.   (Lightfoot, 1983, pp. 25–26)

When principals of effective schools are asked about their major goals, their answers have to do with the intellectual, personal, or social development of learners (Mortimore et al., 1988). In ineffective schools, the answers may have to do with winning the basketball finals, developing the best gospel choir in the district, or developing good community relations. In effective schools, school philosophy is often spelled out in a mission statement or overall curriculum policy developed collaboratively by principal and teachers. This document is kept in the staff room or on teachers' desks, not as a token, but as a well-thumbed and consistently followed guide to day-to-day practice (Ramsay, 1983). Such a policy statement articulates

a sense of shared purpose among faculty, students, parents, and community. In most cases, these schools' written goal statements are the same as in most schools, but they are taken seriously and translated into actions in day to day activities. Policymakers and administrators are committed to following up and assessing progress toward goals. By articulating goals, schools are forced to set priorities, which help give them a clear identity and strengthen bonds of loyalty in the school community.   (Corcoran & Wilson, 1987, pp. 22–23)

Experienced observers often state that the qualities of an effective school are readily visible: "Two things stand out for a visitor. First, the students look active and happy; they seem to lack that quality of sullen passivity one often sees in urban high schools. Second, the school is unusually orderly and quiet" (Louis & Miles, 1990, p. 56). There is less litter and graffiti. Teachers arrive earlier and leave later than in ineffective schools (Ramsay et al., 1983; Sudlow, 1986; Teddlie et al., 1989). Rewards outnumber punishments. There is a climate of mutual respect among teachers, students, and administration. The culture of minority students is the object of genuine respect and interest on the part of teachers (Ramsay et al., 1983). Achievement is expected and recognized, and pupils tend to be happy and friendly (Mortimore et al., 1988, p. 225).

A small retailer . . . got all of her people together, some seventy-five, on about five occasions. She had them submit their best stories, orally or in written form, about when they were most proud of the way they had presented themselves to their customers and fellow employees. Those stories, edited down, formed a thirty-page booklet of "examples of how we do things." They are the heart of the company's training program and constitute both its philosophy and its book of rules. Moreover, the document is a living one: people are proud to add to it, to get their examples into it, and so they constantly offer up new material.

Tom Peters & Nancy Austin (1985, p. 315)

12. *Parent involvement*

Parents represent a readily available, effective, motivated, and generally underacknowledged resource for the school. In the past decade, many studies have shown the significant benefits of involving parents in the education of their children. The benefits are particularly significant for, but are not limited to, elementary school children, underprivileged children, and beginning readers (Carlson, 1991).

Parents have at least nominal supervision of their children for 87 percent of the child's life up to the age of 18, as compared with the school's 13 percent (Wallace & Walberg, 1991). There is plenty of scope for educators who want to help parents enhance the learning climate of the home. For example, on average, American mothers spend less than 30 minutes a day talking to their children, and fathers less than 15 minutes (Walberg, 1984b). Typical fifth graders spend only 7 or 8 minutes a day reading in school, and only 4 minutes at home. But they spend 130 minutes a day watching television (Anderson, Hierbert, Scott, & Wilkinson, 1984).

Most parents—at least 80 percent according to Epstein (1986)—are eager to help their children succeed in school. Most teachers express interest in working collaboratively with parents, but few of them actually take advantage of this resource, despite the fact that parent involvement in their children's education is mandated in legislation such as P.L. 94-142, the Education for All Handicapped Children Act, and advocated in a number of government reports such as the Plowden (1967) and Bullock (1975) reports in Britain (Becker, 1981; Dauber & Epstein, 1989; Epstein, 1986; D. Johnson, 1990).

The two main ways in which schools can develop partnerships with parents are by teaching them to help their children with their learning at home and by recruiting them as volunteers to work in the school.

The first step is to make contact with parents. Parents can be invited to visit their child's classroom, to attend story times, or to spend time in the school's reading center. Newsletters giving suggestions to parents as to how to help their children, and including children's writing or artwork, can be sent home, and articles can be published in local newspapers. Schools with declining enrollment can sometimes set

"No, Timmy, not 'I sawed the chair'. It's 'I saw the chair' or 'I have seen the chair'."

a room aside as a parent resource room, equipped with reading resource materials and coffee. Teachers can be given release time to meet with parents during the school day. Schools should be welcoming places for parents. The school office and the hallway leading to it can be decorated with children's work and with symbols that indicate what the school stands for (Anderson & Pavan, 1992).

At a more formal level, parents may be invited to (or even requested to attend) a meeting or workshop at the school, and home visits may be used to follow up parents who do not respond. Meetings should be scheduled at times that are convenient for parents or held more than once at different times. It may be desirable to provide transportation and to telephone a reminder before the meeting. Meetings may be held in locations other than the school, such as a neighborhood center or a church. Coffee and babysitting may be provided. Sometimes potluck suppers are successful. Parents are more likely to attend a meeting if it is followed by a performance, such as songs or skits, or a fashion show, by their own children (Olmstead, 1991).

Such meetings provide an opportunity to tell parents about some of the ways in which they can be helpful to their children's learning:

Regularly reading to their children and hearing their children read.

Talking to their children.

Knowing how to identify and find suitable books.

Knowing about local library hours and services.

Engaging in learning activities with their children that are fun and are different from those at school, rather than more of the same (booklets of interesting activities can be prepared).

Working with teachers on collaborative homework projects.

Incorporating learning into normal family routines such as shopping, cooking, or washing the car.

Focusing on processes such as telling a story rather than on right or wrong answers.

Asking their children questions that stimulate thought.

Providing a quiet, well-lit place for study.

Keeping informed about their child's progress and providing encouragement.

(Criscuolo, 1982; Epstein, 1990; Olmstead, 1991; Wallace & Walberg, 1991)

The effects of such activities on children's learning, especially on that of underprivileged children, is well documented (Fehrman, Keith, & Reimers, 1987; Johnson, Brookover, & Farrell, 1989; Lueder, 1989; Walberg, 1984; for a dissenting view on the effects of parent involvement in early intervention programs, see White, Taylor, & Moss, 1992). School principals are more likely to enlist parent help in middle-class than in lower-class neighborhoods (Hallinger & Murphy, 1986). But even parents with low levels of schooling can be effective in helping their children learn (Goldenberg, 1987; Goldenberg, 1989). In an experiment in a small city, parents of disadvantaged first-grade children were trained to tutor their children in reading for fifteen minutes, three times a week for nine months. The impact on the reading achievement of children whose parents participated at the planned levels was an impressive .96 effect size (Mehran & White, 1988).

Some parents and other members of the community, such as senior citizens, are willing to be extensively involved in the school program. They can be involved in special school events, in the music program, in athletics, in the lunchroom, schoolyard, office, and library. All such activities enhance school climate (Haynes, Comer, & Hamilton-Lee, 1989).

Barry Vail, a school principal, outlines procedures for developing a *parent volunteer program* in a school:

1. Determine the needs and expectations of teachers and parents; ask teachers the days, times, and areas in which they could use parent help.

2. Send out a request for parent volunteers with an application form, an explanation of the volunteer role, and an invitation to orientation sessions.

3.   Conduct orientation sessions for volunteers and teachers. Make them relaxed and informal. Include a tour of school facilities that volunteers might want to use, such as storage and work areas. Have a senior district official come to transmit the support of the school board, and assure parents of the same liability insurance as all employees. In teacher sessions, discuss how to deal with breakdown in volunteer-teacher relationship.

4.   Match parent volunteers and teachers and arrange meetings between them.

5.   Help maintain the relationship by providing feedback, praise, and constructive criticism.

6.   Appoint a program coordinator, such as the principal or her/his delegate; as the program develops, an experienced parent volunteer should assume this role.

7.   Practice good public relations. If you ensure the program is meeting parents' needs, they will recruit other parents.

8.   Give recognition to volunteers—for example, a special tea prepared by students, and/or a certificate of appreciation.

9.   Provide for further training for more specialized volunteer functions, such as work with the gifted, remedial, problem children, and early childhood programs.

10.   Conduct a formal evaluation of the volunteer program at the end of each year.   (Vail, 1980)

A study involving parents with their children's education was conducted in four primary schools in London, England. The parents came from a wide variety of ethnic and social backgrounds. They met with the teachers each week and received suggestions about activities they, their adult friends, and their children could enjoy together out of school and at home. A random, pretest–post-test, matched-control-group experimental design showed that the children experiencing the parental involvement program made significant gains on 22 of 44 areas tested, while the control group made gains in only 3 areas. Among the areas of most significant gain were mathematical skills, thinking, and concepts; and language development, reading, writing, observing, conversation, and social skills.

Janet S. Dye (1989)

It seems that in general teachers underestimate the commitment of parents to their children, and parents underestimate the commitment of teachers to their students. This deprives both groups of the motivation to use all the resources available for education of the young. But, more importantly, it is an example of one of the more serious errors that people can make on this earth, the error of under-estimating the power of human love.

RAISING THE HORIZON

Benjamin Bloom speculated a few years ago that, as we already had a fairly good idea of what instructional strategies were effective, implementing any two or more of them should raise student achievement by two standard deviations: the equivalent of raising an average child's attainment to the 98th percentile (1984). This was, perhaps, a little optimistic. However, it is worth pointing out that it is strategies such as those described in this chapter that are used by commercial tutoring enterprises. The Sylvan Learning Center® (undated) has taught over one million students by such means and guarantees that students will gain one grade-level-equivalent in reading or mathematics in thirty-six hours of instruction. What this author would be prepared to predict is this: Introduce any two of the twelve strategies described above and implement them systematically for one year. The increase in the attainment of your students will be greater than the average difference (about one-third of a standard deviation) that has historically been observed between the achievement of lower-class and middle-class students.

It may well be remarked that few of the ideas confirmed by the last two decades of educational research are new. Most of them have been practiced by good teachers across the ages—all the more reason to emphasize them in the planning of instruction. Daniel Benor was an agriculturalist with the World Bank. He used to teach farmers in developing countries how to double their yields without use of new seed types, fertilizer, machinery, or irrigation, but rather by simple practices like good spacing of plants. "There are almost no new ideas," he said, "merely well-known principles applied systematically" (Rowen, 1978, p. 16).

▪ SELF – ASSESSMENT

1. Mortimore found that some London schools were more effective with working-class pupils than some other schools were with middle-class pupils (Mortimore & Sammons, 1987). What notion does this finding disprove?

2. What common belief about expectations in school did Benjamin Bloom want to change in his proposals for mastery learning?

3. What social strategy do some researchers suggest can be used to enhance the effects of mastery learning?

4. Suppose we found that the ten schools in a district that are most effective in raising student achievement all have excellent libraries; the ten least effective schools have weak libraries. This does not prove that excellent libraries raise student achievement. How would one try to prove that?

5. An instructor who teaches real estate investment to adults says, "The school effectiveness research is not relevant to me because it was conducted with working-class, elementary-age children in reading and mathematics." How would you respond?

6. The parents of a Grade 2 child whose reading is slightly below average ask you what they can do to help their child's reading. What would you suggest?

7. One of the simplest and cheapest ways of raising achievement is by raising expectations. Why does this work, and what are its limitations?

8. Name three important "study skills" that schools could and should teach systematically.

9. What are some of the problems of extrinsic motivation—for example, when students work mainly to "get good grades"?

10. A colleague tells you she does not believe in cooperative learning because schools should prepare people for life in a competitive world. What points might you make in reply?

For feedback, see Appendix F.
If you were able to make responses that you considered satisfactory to eight or more questions, you understand most of the material in the chapter.
If you were doubtful about three or more questions, reread the appropriate parts of the chapter.

CHAPTER 7

Planning for Individual Differences

*We are all
special cases.*

Albert Camus

Summary

Individuals are highly diverse, and the organization of schools on the basis of age does little to reduce this diversity. Some important ways in which students differ from one another are in aptitudes, learning styles, culture, experience, and language skills. Schools often respond to learner differences by selection and deselection strategies, including tracking, grade retention, and acceleration. But individual teachers can respond directly to learner differences in ways that will help to maintain achievement. Some strategies for doing so include preassessment, formative assessment, remediation, enrichment, and peer tutoring.

219

SIGNIFICANT DIFFERENCES

As human beings we share one common feature: we are all different. With the possible exception of identical twins, every one of the six billion people on earth is different. And the complexity of the human genome would ensure that we were all different even if the earth was home to a million times as many people. Educators have long been interested in the implications of human diversity. In 1925 the twenty-fourth yearbook of the National Society for the Study of Education was entitled *Adapting the Schools to Individual Differences* (Whipple, 1925). It looked for answers to the problems of learner diversity. Three generations later, we are still looking. As educators, we do not have to be concerned with every kind of human difference. Differences in height, eye color, or blood type are rarely of concern in the classroom. The kinds of difference that are of interest in the classroom are differences in such characteristics as aptitude, motivation, and learning style. This chapter explores ways in which teachers and planners can design curriculum that is adaptive to the variety of learner characteristics that presents itself in every classroom.

Before any other steps in the liberation process, a human being must become aware that he or she is a person.

Adolfo Peréz Esquival (Argentine), Nobel Prize for Peace, 1980. (Peréz Esquival, 1985, p. 26)

INTELLIGENCE AND APTITUDE

Many teachers consider one of the major constraints on their teaching to be differences among students in terms of intelligence. The belief that there is such a thing as general intelligence appears to be held more strongly by school people than by researchers. Educators who believe (1) that there is a single factor of intelligence that determines people's ability to learn, (2) that it can be accurately measured, (3) that it is fixed at or soon after birth, and (4) that it is relatively unchangeable by school experiences, hold these beliefs contrary to the accumulated research evidence. More importantly, they undercut their own motivation and that of their students, producing on both sides a sense of fatalism and helplessness (Snow, 1989).

While few researchers today support the concept of a unitary intelligence, they tend to disagree about how many factors of intelligence there are, about whether or not different kinds of intelligence are hierarchically organized, and indeed, about the utility of the concept of intelligence itself. These disagreements are acute enough that in the 1979 California case of *Larry P. vs. Riles,* in which the labeling of a student as educationally mentally retarded (EMR) was challenged, social scientists of equal repute were found testifying for each side (Reschly, 1988).

J. P. Guilford spent much of his 90-year life studying human intelligence. Working in the U.S. Army Air Corps in World War II, he identified 25 ability factors, the use of which in pilot selection resulted in a reduction of the failure rate in pilot training by two-thirds. The final version of his theory, published after his death, represented intelligence as consisting of 180 distinct abilities (Guilford, 1967; Comrey, Michael, & Fruchter, 1988). More recently, Howard Gardner has proposed that there are seven main types of intelligence: logical-mathematical, linguistic, musical, spatial, bodily-kinesthetic, interpersonal, and intrapersonal (Hatch & Gardner, 1990).

Current scholarship suggests that it is more productive to talk about specific aptitudes than about general intelligence. Everyone recognizes that an individual who is gifted in music or cooking is not necessarily also brilliant in physics or in wilderness survival. Indeed, brilliant individuals such as Darwin, Einstein, and Freud were incompetent in certain easy skills (Howe, 1989). Some abilities, such as color blindness, are fixed at birth (Snow, 1989). But increasingly evidence points to the effect of motivation and experiences on human aptitude (Cahan & Cohen, 1989). Michael Howe (1989) points out that quite ordinary people can master extraordinary skills; for example, individuals who have little mathematics background but who master the intricate and rapid mathematical problem-solving involved in betting on horses.

None of the foregoing is intended to imply that aptitudes do not vary. Every teacher is aware of this variability. Aptitude is manifested mainly in speed of learning, and in a typical classroom some students may learn a skill or concept five or six times as fast as other students. If teachers teach to the average student, they will frustrate learners at each end of the continuum. Curriculum planning

"Your feelings of insecurity seem to have started when Mary Lou Gurnblatt said, 'Maybe I don't have a learning disability – maybe you have a teaching disability.' "

must offer more creative responses than this. In this chapter, we recognize that human aptitudes vary. But they vary within as well as between individuals; they vary from one field of endeavor to another, and even from subfield to subfield; and they are alterable by the experiences that education can provide.

GIFTEDNESS

Many jurisdictions endeavor to identify gifted learners and provide special programs for them. Both the identification and the programming are problematic. Identification is frequently by IQ tests and teacher nomination. Neither these measures, nor the programs developed, have yet been properly validated. Robert Hoge writes that

> serious inadequacies usually exist in the way in which the giftedness construct is developed in applied settings. Frequently, neither the official nor the operational definition is fully developed; there is often a discrepancy between official definition and operational definition; and the definitions generally fail to take account of the uses made of the construct or of its broader value connotations. (Hoge, 1988, p. 13)

One of the problems in this area may be the search for global descriptions of ability. As with defining "slow" learners, so with defining the "gifted": We may legitimately speak of a gifted pianist, but can we talk of a gifted person? The only person in history who appears to have been gifted in every area was Leonardo da

---

Leonardo

Leonardo da Vinci . . . displayed infinite grace in everything he did. . . . He possessed great strength and dexterity; he was a man of regal spirit and tremendous breadth of mind. . . . He made designs for mills, fulling machines, and engines that could be driven by water-power. . . . His writings conveyed his ideas so precisely, that his arguments and reasonings confounded the most formidable critics. . . . Often when he was walking past the places where birds were sold he would pay the price asked, take them from their cages, and let them fly off into the air, giving them back their lost freedom. . . . Leonardo was also the most talented improviser in verse of his time. Moreover, he was a sparkling conversationalist. . . . [He wrote] a reference book . . . on the anatomy of horses. Leonardo then applied himself . . . to the study of human anatomy . . . and . . . composed a book annotated in pen and ink in which he did meticulous drawings in red chalk of bodies he had dissected himself. . . . In appearance he was striking and handsome, and his magnificent presence brought comfort to the most troubled soul. . . . He was physically so strong that he could withstand any violence; with his right hand he would bend the iron ring of a doorbell or a horseshoe as if they were lead. He was so generous that he sheltered and fed all his friends, rich or poor.

Georgio Vasari (1511–1574) *Lives of the Artists*
(Vasari, 1965, pp. 255–270)

Vinci. For the rest of us mortals, our gifts in certain domains tend to be offset by limitations in others.

A cost of labeling certain students as "gifted" is that we implicitly label all other students as "not gifted." Personally, I have never met anyone who was not gifted. The tragedy is that we fail to discover, reveal, and develop the gifts of all learners. These criticisms refer to the practice of global description. We are left with the practical issue of how best to develop the talents of pupils who appear to learn, in specific areas, much faster or better than other learners. Some light is thrown on this issue by a study by Benjamin Bloom of 120 highly successful people. All of these people had, by the age of 35, demonstrated the highest international levels of accomplishment in piano, sculpture, swimming, tennis, mathematics, or research neurology. Lengthy interviews showed that in most cases the role of parents was crucial; parents had a strong interest in the area of accomplishment and gave early support and encouragement. In adolescence, these individuals gave as much time to their area of interest as to all of their other school work. To develop and perfect their skills, they willingly followed a disciplined and often lonely regimen. Their interest determined their companions and their use of free time (Bloom, 1981). Clearly, when special gifts are nurtured early, enormous reserves of energy and motivation are available for their development.

> I hate the impudence of a claim that in fifty minutes you can judge and classify a human being's predestined fitness in life. I hate the pretentiousness of that claim. I hate the abuse of scientific method which it involves. I hate the sense of superiority which it creates, and the sense of inferiority which it imposes.
>
> Walter Lippmann (1923, pp. 145–146)

The first step is accurate identification. The exceptional abilities of some pupils can pass unnoticed by classroom teachers. Perhaps we simply recognize more easily those who have less ability than our own than those whose ability is greater. In their work at Johns Hopkins University, Richard Stanley and his colleagues have for many years used specifically designed mathematics tests to identify children in the state of Maryland who have exceptional ability in mathematics. They have found that many such students, even those whose abilities place them in the top one-tenth of 1 percent, are not recognized by teachers as exceptional (Stanley, 1976). Often these students docilely work through assignments. Sometimes they become bored and disruptive.

—— **The cost of success** ——

The Smeltzer family of Pennsylvania withdrew their child from school in 1984 in order to teach her at home. She was doing poorly; the superintendent classified her as learning disabled and gave the family no problems. In 1987, however, he denied them permission to continue home education, claiming that, because of the daughter's high achievement test scores, she is now gifted and talented, and needs a better education than she could get at home.

Parent Educator and Family Report (Jan/Feb 1987)

LEARNING STYLE

Important work has been conducted over the past two decades into differences in preferred learning style. As mentioned in an earlier chapter, it has been found that highly anxious learners, for example, prefer a highly-structured learning environment in which they can absorb and repeat factual information. Low-anxiety learners like to control their own learning and prefer discussion to memorization. Many psychological differences—assertiveness versus submissiveness, introversion versus extraversion, field dependence versus field independence, open-mindedness versus closed-mindedness—have been shown to influence learning preferences. Dorothy Dunn and her colleagues and students have studied differences in learning style intensively for two decades. Their findings suggest that learning can be enhanced when instructional mode and environment are matched to learners' preferred style. Some students, for example, prefer to learn with music in the background, some in silence. Some students learn best in a noisy environment. Some prefer bright illumination, some dim illumination. Some people learn best early in the day, some in the afternoon or evening, and underachievement can sometimes be remedied simply by switching the time of day of a class in which the student is underachieving. Some people require a cool environment for concentration, some a warm environment. Some students prefer to sit still while learning, some to move around, some to eat popcorn or chew on raw vegetables. Some work better in groups, some individually (Dunn, Gemake, Jalali, Zenjhausern, Quinn, & Spiridakis, 1990; Dunn, Deckinger, Withers, & Katzenstein, 1990; Dunn, Sklar, Beaudry, & Bruno, 1990). Some students learn best by reading, some by listening. Least well served by schools, and often mislabeled as slow learners, are those students who learn best by touching, handling, and performing. Dunn & Dunn (1987) suggest that, rather than setting all students the same assignment, one might give students a choice of tasks. For any given topic—for example, in economics, the relationship between demand and price—students could choose to develop their understanding of the principle by writing a poem, or by drawing a flowchart, or by listening to a recorded lecture, or by performing a skit. Marie Carbo has applied learning styles research to the specific area of reading. Considerable advances in reading achievement are claimed when reading activities are planned in accordance with children's environmental, emotional, sociological, physical, and psychological preferences (1990).

Various tests are available which can help identify students' learning styles (Dunn, Dunn, & Price, 1989; NAASP, 1988; NRSI, 1988), and which enable teachers and learners to identify their learning styles and adjust their study habits accordingly. Dunn suggests that, as minimal measures, classrooms provide varied levels of illumination and seating, students be encouraged to wear clothing that provides individual thermal comfort and to bring nutritious snacks to class if they wish, and that teachers use a variety of teaching styles (Dunn, Deckinger, Withers, & Katzenstein, 1990; Dunn, Gemake, Jalali, Zenjhausern, Quinn, & Spiridakis, 1990; Dunn, Sklar, Beaudry, & Bruno, 1990).

It should be noted that the learning styles research remains controversial, with critics questioning the findings of advocates (Adams, 1990; O'Neil, 1990). Cohen, Hyman, Ashcroft, and Loveless (1989) claim that the results of learning styles experiments are due not to adaptation of instruction to students' learning styles, but simply to good alignment of instruction with objectives. Nevertheless, it makes intuitive sense to recognize that human beings are diverse and that learning will be enhanced if the classroom environment acknowledges and attempts to respond to that diversity.

CULTURE

James Crawford (1989) reports that a few decades ago one of the first words that some native American children learned in English-speaking schools was *soap*, because having their mouths washed out with soap was a common penalty for using

I know they can learn because I've taught them

My first sight of Junior High School 22 in New York City, to which I had just been assigned that day in 1975, was not reassuring. The building was covered with graffiti. And although it was 10:00 on an October morning, the sidewalks and schoolgrounds were swarming with 12- to 16-year olds dressed in their "colors." . . . Some were fighting, some smoking pot.

I was to teach 180 boys remedial reading in an old electricity shop. When I asked the superintendent if he cared what teaching methods I used, he said, "I'll be grateful if you can get them out of the corridors and into your classroom." I had taught such students before, but I wondered if this time I had taken on too much.

The next morning I went out to the courtyard and into the corridors and invited my students to learn about aerodynamics. "What's that, a new dance?" they asked. No, I told them, it was how airplanes fly. I brought a model airplane (no books), and we started. Soon more and more students were coming to my shop (sometimes when they were supposed to be in other classes). And they began learning basic skills, always in connection with learning about flight. For example, they designed and built rockets, which required reading about how to make them, figuring dimensions, and so on. When they were ready, we took the rockets outside and fired them, calculating trajectories and carefully measuring the distances they flew.

Although my students were sometimes quite agitated when they came from elsewhere in the school, they did not misbehave in my classes. In the spring they won first prize in a city-wide model airplane construction contest sponsored by the New York Bureau of Industrial Arts and the Aviation Development Council.

The next year I was given permission to start an alternative school several blocks away for 20 of the most "incorrigible" students of Junior High School 22. We spent the first three weeks cleaning and painting a rented basement, throwing out garbage and dead rats. Soon Madison Prep, as we called our school, had become a place of learning for these "delinquent nonachievers."

For 14 years I taught such students successfully in every ghetto of New York City. I found that they can and will learn, but not from the analytical, lecture-and-recitation type of teaching found in most classrooms. Millions of young people are "at risk" because, to be full-fledged participants in our society, they desperately need an education. It is simply not true that we don't know what to do about it. We do. We must teach them in accord with the way they learn.

Helené Hodges (1987, p. 3)

their native language. Approaches to cultural differences in the classroom have in the past often been punitive at worst and patronizing at best. Such orientations violate the ideals of a multicultural society and fail to recognize that cultural diversity is a resource, not a constraint.

A study of effective schools in Auckland, New Zealand, showed that in those schools that were most effective in helping Maori and Pacific Island children learn, the teachers took a serious and committed interest in Maori and Pacific Island culture. They were also prepared to ignore officially prescribed curriculum and textbooks in favor of content and materials more appropriate to cultural minorities.

> The cultures of the various groups were treated as being alive and changing, and while the treatment was sympathetic the position adopted was never relativistic. Indeed, what we observed was a lively treatment of cultural interaction and process in a contemporary situation in which culture contact was seen as being reciprocal, with each group continuously influencing the others.   (Ramsay, Sneddon, Grenfell, & Ford, 1983, p. 283)

Writers on multicultural education describe some of the strategies that are effective in working with culturally diverse groups of students.

> *Teachers* can learn about the cultures of their students, including their religious faith, customs, traditions, holidays, festivals, art, and literature; they can learn a few words in the students' native languages; learn students' names and their correct pronunciation; become acquainted with their families and maintain contact with them. It is worth noting that respect for minority learners' background does not mean neglecting their need for mastery of the dominant form of language. As Paulo Freire points out, the standard language in a society is the language of power, and subordinate groups must either master it or remain powerless (Freire & Macedo, 1987).

> The *classroom* can be decorated with art, photographs, artifacts, and bulletin board displays that reflect the learners' culture; students can be involved in planning special classroom events and the celebration of culturally significant festivals; successful minority members can be brought into the classroom as role models, to serve as guest lecturers, volunteers, aides, and tutors.

> *Materials* and activities can be used that feature characters from different cultural groups in nonstereotyped ways; that provide both same-age models and eminent adult models; that teach about the great nonwhite civilizations, such as the Mayan, the Aztec, the Malian, and the Chinese; that highlight the contributions and achievements of various cultures in local, national, and world history; that avoid facile, specious, patronizing, or sentimental attitudes in favor of recognition of the complexity of

cultural issues; that provide a wide choice of learning activities; and that challenge the students academically.

Instruction can integrate a multicultural orientation in daily learning activities and across the curriculum; it can help students understand that everyone has a culture, not just minorities, and build a sense of commonality by emphasizing family and everyday life of various cultures, rather than stressing the different and the exotic; and it can develop with learners the concepts of stereotyping, prejudice, and ethnocentrism, and provide opportunities for them to examine their harmful effects and to learn ways to combat them in their daily lives (Asante, 1991; Grugeon & Woods, 1990; Kehoe, 1984; Kendall, 1983; Lee, 1985; Lynch, 1983, 1987; New York City Public Schools, 1991; Wright, 1991).

PRIOR EXPERIENCE AND MOTIVATION

More than anything else, it is students' prior experiences that make them different from one another. Some come from homes filled with love and affection; some from a background of physical and emotional abuse. Some have experienced support and encouragement at each step of their lives; some have experienced only disparagement and pain. Such experiences deeply affect the level of motivation that students bring to any learning experience. It is important to ascertain the learners' level of motivation early in any program. Those whose motivation is high are likely to embark willingly on instructional tasks. Those whose motivation is low expect that their previous failures will be repeated and will be reluctant to engage in learning. For these students, experiences must be provided early in the program that allow them to experience interest and success.

We are all malformed

We are all malformed! It is not because I have black hair and you have red or brown hair that one of us is malformed and the other not. I am malformed when I cannot hear you cry for help. I am malformed when I seek personal glory over wisdom. I am malformed if I do not relish every moment with the hope that it will last forever. . . . I am malformed when I cannot tell you that you have a beautiful thought; I am malformed when I hear you only for how I will respond; I am malformed when I separate scholarship from friendship; I am malformed when I hear only words and not our meanings; I am malformed when I organize a course and forget what I have organized it for; I am *malformed*. We are all malformed, but . . . we can do something about some of that deformity. And something begins *now* and *here!* Give us the courage to do so.

John Arnold (1985, p. 15)

Let us repeat what has been said earlier. If learners are not interested in the curriculum, we need to ask why. If they are not interested in this material, then what are they interested in? In other words, issues of motivation take us directly back to needs assessment. If there are universal laws of education, one must be that *it is pointless to teach anything to a learner unless or until that learner can be motivated to learn.*

I talked once with a language arts teacher who had experienced this problem with a Grade 9 class. All of his students, he told me, could be classified as reluctant learners. They were streamed into a vocational track; they had experienced consistent failure in school; they did not want to be there; they did not want to cooperate; they did not want to learn. After two initial weeks of zero progress, he began to ask, if these students are not interested in what I want to teach, what are they interested in? He discovered that without exception, they were interested in rock videos. The following week he told the class that they were going to make rock videos. The students greeted this suggestion with skepticism. They couldn't sing; they couldn't play instruments; they didn't know how to use cameras; they didn't know anything about making films. He persevered. He borrowed the district's mobile sound studio. He showed the students how to lip-sync to rock music. He persuaded them to experiment with stage makeup. Their interest began to flicker, then to burn, then to blaze. They learned how to organize lighting, set design, and filming. Within two weeks, the class had all become involved in making several creditable videos. The class members, who earlier were regarded with scorn in the school, became stars. At the end of two weeks, the rock video project was completed and the class returned to the language arts curriculum. From that point on, there were no further problems with motivation.

LITERACY

Of all the differences among students present in a typical classroom, one of the most significant is differences in levels of literacy and experiences with written language. When children enter school, they vary in the amount of exposure they have received since birth to stories and written materials, from less than a hundred hours to more than a thousand hours. Some children entering school have been read to almost every day of their lives. Others enter school having never looked at a newspaper, a magazine, or a book (O'Neil, 1991). There is a mass of evidence showing that the amount of exposure to print and to stories in infancy is a powerful predictor of reading success in school, which in turn is a powerful predictor of academic success throughout schooling (Adams, 1990; Holdaway, 1984). The U.S. Office of Educational Research and Improvement (OERI, 1990b) reported that understanding the speech sounds that correspond to letters was the most powerful predictor of reading success, and that it was closely linked to the amount of exposure of children to reading in the home. For children who have been starved of this exposure, schools need to provide rich reading programs as early as possible.

This is the principle behind the "reading recovery" programs, pioneered in New Zealand by Marie Clay (1987) and now being successfully implemented in the United States and Canada (Boehnlein, 1987; Scarborough Board of Education, 1990). Reading recovery is an early-intervention program that provides identified first-graders with thirty minutes of daily intensive one-to-one instruction in reading and writing. The instructional situation is individualized, based on ongoing analysis of the child's progress, and simulates in many ways the early parent-child reading situation experienced by more fortunate children (Clay, 1987; Jongsma, 1990). About fifteen to twenty weeks of such work with specially trained teachers has proved sufficient to bring at least 80 percent of students in the bottom 20 percent of their class up to at least average standing. Longitudinal studies, notably in Ohio, show that these gains are permanent (Pinnell, Fried, & Estice, 1990).

Reading recovery is a remedial-accelerative program. It is interesting to reflect on the implications of the proverb that an ounce of prevention is worth a pound of cure. As educators, we might reduce very considerably the amount of school failure if we began to work seriously and collaboratively with maternity departments in hospitals. New mothers typically take home with them from the hospital a package containing such items as baby powder and diapers, along with instructions from the nursing staff on breastfeeding, etc. I suggest that we include in these packages two or three children's books—books that can be read by parents and listened to by children with pleasure not once but a hundred times—and that we include in the training of obstetrical and pediatric nurses some basic advice regarding the importance of reading and telling stories, as well as conversation, play, and other forms of stimulation to young children.

AT-RISK LEARNERS

Vilfredo Pareto was an Italian economist and sociologist who died in 1923. He gave his name to what is known as the Pareto principle. The Pareto principle claims that 80 percent of resources will always be consumed by 20 percent of the population. Thus, for example, the richest 20 percent of a population may control 80 percent of a nation's wealth. Twenty percent of drivers will cause 80 percent of accidents. Twenty percent of staff members will do 80 percent of the talking at staff meetings. Many practicing educators will agree that this principle applies in schools: 20 percent of the learners will consume 80 percent of the teacher's or administrator's time and energy. Some of those learners will be those currently known as "at risk." A cluster of related characteristics appears to be typical of these learners. Some of these characteristics are:

children born to teenage and/or single mothers

children of families afflicted by poverty

children whose parents did not complete high school

children malnourished in the first year of life and/or born to mothers malnourished during pregnancy. (Furstenberg, Brooks-Gunn, & Chase-Lansdale, 1989; Lozoff, 1989; Offord, Boyle, & Racine, 1990; Pallas, Natriello, & McDill, 1989)

Some of the difficulties "at-risk" learners have in school are poor academic performance; poor reading skills; poor problem solving skills; gross and fine motor problems; perceptual problems; low motivation; poor memory; short attention span; distractibility; impulsivity and recklessness; hyperactivity or hypoactivity; test anxiety; low self-esteem; a sense of helplessness; behavior difficulties; difficulties in social relations; truancy; and psychiatric disorders (Bergan, Sladeczik, Schwarz, & Smith, 1991; Kirby & Williams, 1991).

Much attention has been paid in recent years to the needs of these students. But a word of caution is in order. Because at-risk learners are disproportionately the children of single or teenaged mothers, this does *not* mean that all such children are at risk. Oakland and Stern (1989) have shown in a longitudinal study that low school achievement, and its relation with social class, ethnicity, and family characteristics, is "neither chronic nor persistent" (p. 127). Marsh (1990) found little difference in achievement among high school students related to family configuration. Weisner and Garnier (1992) conducted a 12-year longitudinal study of 146 nonconventional families and a comparison group of 43 stable, two-parent, conventional families. They found that their sample of children from nonconventional families performed as well or better in school than children in the conventional group. Key factors were the stability of families and their commitment to the values underlying their chosen life-style. There are major dangers in stereotyping certain types of students and allowing such stereotypes to produce low expectations, which in turn become self-fulfilling prophecies. It is more productive to think of all students as potentially effective learners and to find the most appropriate ways to help them become effective. The important thing is to identify and remedy learning deficits before the pattern of academic failure, negative feedback, self-doubt, lowered effort, negative beliefs, and loss of motivation result in a fixed sense of learned helplessness (Elliott, Sheridan, & Gresham, 1989; Kelly, Gerstein, & Carnine, 1990; Kirby & Williams, 1991).

How do we do this? Space does not permit detailed description of the available techniques for dealing with different kinds of learning difficulty, but an example may be given. Kirby and Williams recommend the following blend of cognitive and behavior therapy for helping hyperactive-distractible children: (1) Choose an easy task like a puzzle made from the cut-up photograph of a sports star. (2) An adult model demonstrates the task by performing it while talking out loud to himself/herself about how he/she is doing it and how well. (3) The child then performs the task under the direction of the adult's instructions. (4) The child performs the task while instructing himself/herself out loud. (5) The adult performs the task whispering. (6) The child whispers instructions as he/she proceeds through the task. (7) The child performs the task while guiding his/her performance via private speech (Kirby & Williams, 1991).

Classroom in the sky

In the late 1960s, a classical experiment was conducted in a downtown San Francisco school. Supported by a generous grant, researchers selected a class of 25 thirteen-year-old boys for a two-year experiment. The school was drab and uninviting, located in a decayed neighborhood. The boys in the selected class were mostly from disadvantaged backgrounds; their reading ability ranged from average to nonreader; they had all been in trouble with school authorities or the law; their self-concept was low, and their future looked unpromising. An equivalent class was selected as a control group.

For the experimental class, the official school curriculum was suspended. They began a flight training program, taught by two instructors in their twenties, one a graduate student and the other a flight instructor, both skilled in dealing with teenagers.

The first obstacle to overcome was that the boys considered they had been singled out as inferior learners and began to act out to the extent that the entire class (for the first time in district history) had to be suspended. But, partly because the project had previously obtained the support of parents, this difficulty was overcome, and the students began to take more interest in the course, especially once they began going out to the airport where the single-engine dual-control Cessna, leased for the program, was located.

As the students worked on the issues of navigation, fueling, and instrumentation, they were, without realizing it, learning a great deal of language, geography, mathematics, and other subjects. Before long they were in the air. Within two years, every member of the class had learned how to fly.

Comparisons between the experimental and the control group were made before, during, and for five years after the program. At the beginning of the program, both groups would agree with such statements as, "What happens to me is outside of my control." By the end of the program, that view had changed radically for the flight-training group, but not for the controls.

Five years after completion of the program, in the experimental group one graduate was between jobs. More than half of the others were enrolled in post-secondary education, some of them in aerospace engineering at the University of California. The others were all employed either in the aerospace industry or in the Air Force. Only two of the control group had reached post-secondary education, and several were unemployed.

Lee Conway (1976)

At risk of repetition of points made elsewhere, some more general principles for working with at-risk learners may be mentioned:

communicate to learners high, rather than low expectations;

identify the critical learnings and ensure that students master them;

give learners frequent and meaningful success experiences;

make use of mixed-ability cooperative learning groups;

provide peer and adult tutoring;

provide learning tasks that different students can perform at different levels of sophistication;

ensure that terminology is understood;

use strategies to increase learner time on task;

provide systematic practice of small steps;

provide practice in discriminating steps and separating confusing elements;

ensure that the curriculum addresses learners' real needs and interests;

avoid tracking and grade repetition;

recruit parents to assist their children's learning;

minimize test anxiety by using informal and formative assessment rather than formal and summative assessment;

identify and remediate learning skill deficits;

make provision for learners who learn best by tactual and kinesthetic modes.

OTHER SPECIAL NEEDS

A general reaction against discrimination and segregation of individuals who differ from prevailing norms has resulted in extensive mainstreaming of students with special needs. Visually impaired, hearing impaired, and wheelchair-bound students have been integrated into regular classes, often with considerable success. Students with Down's syndrome, cerebral palsy, and other conditions are often found in normal classrooms, sometimes with an assigned teacher's aide.

This means that curricula can no longer be designed solely for hypothetically "normal" pupils. The designer needs to indicate in the curriculum the specific adaptations that will be made for any special-needs students who may be members of a class. The Physical Education Curriculum Guide produced by the Kelso Public

_____ **There are no hopeless children** _____

There is no "method" in reaching the unreachable. It is an all-out effort, opportunistic, using the entire arsenal of human communication: touch, feel,
song, sounds, drawing, music, psychology, games, words, objects, illustrations,
allegories, fairy-tales, action, acting, projects, hobbies, sports, physical and
mental exercises, jokes, humor, nature, animals, affection, love, hero-worship,
father-figure, identification, suggestion, auto-suggestion, hypnosis, rewards,
dreams, science, history, logic, semantics. Whatever works is the method.

Kaare Bolgen, *There Are No Hopeless Children* (1970, p. 16)

Schools (1990), for example, provides specific instructions to teachers regarding
adaptation of the curriculum for students who are diabetic, hearing impaired,
obese, asthmatic, visually impaired, or suffering from cardiac or other conditions.
The presence in the classroom of students with special needs should not be viewed
narrowly as a constraint. The designer must ask not only, How can these learnings
be made accessible to these students? but also, How can the presence of these students enhance the social learning of the other students in the classroom?

Perhaps what all students can learn from mainstreaming is what I learned a few
years ago. I was in hospital following an accident and struggling with my first attempts to walk with crutches. One day, I encountered in the hallway a one-legged
man who moved around with amazing speed using only one crutch. "We are all
handicapped," he said. "Only with some of us it is more visible than with others."

PROGRAMMATIC APPROACHES TO DIFFERENCES _____

Student learning is affected both by teacher's instructional strategies and by
structural or programmatic factors. The ways in which learners are grouped and
the ways in which they advance through their schooling can have significant effects on their learning. We shall look first at the effects of organizational factors
on different kinds of learners, and then at the impact of instructional factors.

The selection of instructional groups

Most formal education takes place in groups. The necessity of working with
twenty or thirty different individuals in a group setting is perhaps the major constraint facing teachers. A key question in the design of learning environments is,
On what basis are individuals selected into the instructional group?

For most schools in the Western world, the answer is: on the basis of age.
This is an innovation of the last 150 years. It was introduced as an administrative
measure with the intention of standardizing schools and classrooms and simplify-
ing their operation. In the rural one-room school prior to about 1840, children

typically entered at various ages and proceeded more or less at their own pace. No previous society had ever segregated preadolescents by age. Instead, the mixed-age playgroup, ranging from the toddler to the adolescent, was, for millions of years, the normal social environment of the young (Pratt, 1986b).

Underlying the continued use of age as a criterion for the structure of learning groups is an implicit belief that age provides for uniformity in learning and instruction. But this is a fallacy. Children learn and develop at very different rates, only weakly related to age. The single school-entry point, and the subsequent age-grouping of learners, have a number of consequences:

1. "Late-born" children consistently underperform in schools and have higher rates of failure and anxiety (Mortimore, 1988; Shepard & Smith, 1986; Uphoff & Gilmore, 1985; but for a contrary view, see Jones & Southern, 1988).

2. By removing the possibility of cross-age play and interaction, we deprive children of modeling, teaching, and nurturance by older children, and of the opportunity for older children to teach and take responsibility for younger ones.

3. Faster learners who might move ahead of their peers are constrained by either being held back with their age group or becoming the exception in an older class.

4. Slower learners are either left behind or made conspicuous failures by being demoted to a younger class.

5. We create classes uniform in age but diverse in those aspects relevant to instruction (Anderson & Pavan, 1992; Goodlad & Anderson, 1987; Hartup, 1989; Mounts & Roopnarine, 1987; Pratt, 1986b).

Consider, by way of contrast, a ski school. Often there is some age segregation—there may be separate children's and adult classes—but this, it often seems, is mainly to spare the adults the embarrassment of falling on their faces in front of children. Individuals are placed in an instructional group based on their initial performance and moved up into the next group as soon as their performance warrants it. The grouping is not by age, but by *readiness*.

There are three main aspects of learning readiness: background, motivation, and intellectual development. Provided that a group of learners all have (1) the minimum cognitive prerequisites in terms of prior learnings, (2) a minimum level of interest in the subject, or at least "motivatability," and (3) the necessary level of intellectual development (e.g., level of formal operations if the subject matter is abstract), then the group is homogeneous for instructional purposes.

Over the past two decades, partly as a result of Goodlad and Anderson's 1982 book, *The Nongraded School,* a few schools have begun to depart from strict grade segregation, especially in the early grades. In a masterful summary of the theoretical and research evidence, Anderson & Pavan (1992) found that in 57 empirical studies of pupil achievement and mental health in nongraded versus graded schools, only 9 out of 94 comparisons favored the graded school. These results were similar to those Pratt (1986b) discovered in an earlier review of 51 quantitative studies. Anderson and Pavan (1992) provide detailed and practical recommendations for schools that want to move in the direction of nongradedness.

If the day ever dawns when schools are structured on the basis of what is good for learners and for learning, rather than what is administratively convenient, then readiness will become the criterion for selection into learning groups. This chapter assumes that we have not yet arrived at that point and that teachers must grapple with a high degree of diversity in their classrooms. We shall consider four programmatic responses by schools and students to diversity: tracking, grade retention, dropout, and acceleration.

Tracking

Many trees have died to produce the volumes written on tracking. Despite this, a definitive judgment on the practice remains elusive. This may be because the issue of tracking is not a single question. Tracking individuals into separate streams for all subjects is a quite different practice from tracking subject by subject. Making special provision for the fastest and slowest 5 percent of learners is quite different from dividing an age cohort into two groups at the 50th percentile. Grouping learners into separate classes is not the same as forming separate groups within a classroom. Parallel classes where student progress is dictated by the calendar are not the same as tracked classes in which student progress is self-paced.

On a few general points, however, a consensus appears to be emerging:

1.   Grouping students separately for all subjects is not an effective strategy. The stereotyping of learners that it produces is not faithful to the evidence on differential ability in different subjects. Tracked classes often separate students by behavior, ethnicity, or social class rather than ability. The practice impoverishes the intellectual environment of low-ability students and is particularly damaging to the language development of children for whom English is not their first language. The Carnegie Foundation for the Advancement of Teaching made this observation:

> To call some students "academic" and others "nonacademic" has a devastating impact on how teachers think about students and how students think about themselves. The message to some is *you are the intellectual leaders, you will go on to further education*. To others it is *you are not academics, you are not smart enough to do this work*. Students are thus divided between those who think and those who work, when in fact, life for all of us is a blend of both.   (Carnegie Foundation for the Advancement of Teaching, 1988, their italics)

Misclassification, even with the best instruments, will often occur (Dar & Resh, 1986; Oakes, 1985; Oakes, Gamoran, & Page, 1992; Tye, 1984). In syntheses of the research on grouping, Slavin found that the median effect of comprehensive ability grouping was exactly zero in both elementary and secondary settings (1987c, 1990). Students achieve much more in heterogeneous classrooms using cooperative instruction than in tracked classes using conventional instruction (1991).

2. Tracking reinforces initial differences in achievement, especially in mathematics (Kerkhoff, 1986). It also reinforces differences between achievement of students from different social classes and ethnic groups (Willms & Chen, 1989). But, say Gamoran and Mare (1989), on the basis of a large-scale study, when background factors are taken into account, tracking increases the probability of graduation by females, blacks, and Hispanics.

3. Teachers, especially those who work in tracked systems, express a preference for tracking; but they also prefer to teach the upper-stream rather than the lower-stream classes, and those who teach lower-stream classes tend to be less experienced and specialized and to lack knowledge about the most appropriate pedagogy for such groups (Findley & Bryan, 1970; Murphy & Hallinger, 1989).

4. Instruction in lower-track classes tends to be less focused, less interactive, less task oriented; there is less time on task, less exposure to complex meaningful learning, less interstudent cooperation, less clear standards, and lower expectations. Students in lower-track classes form less cohesive groups and are less likely to feel connected to the school. It is much easier and more likely for a student to move downward into a lower track than to become upwardly mobile into a higher track. Tracking is least effective when no instructional adjustment is made for the particular needs of each specific ability group (Kulik, 1991; Means & Knapp, 1991; Murphy & Hallinger, 1989; Oakes, 1985).

5. Grouping students separately by subject is best done for only one or two subjects, and it is most effective for mathematics, perhaps because of the sequential nature of its prerequisites (Braddock, 1990; Braddock & McPartland, 1990; Slavin, 1987c).

6. Within-class grouping is likewise more likely to be effective in mathematics than in other subjects and is of most benefit to more able students (Kulik & Kulik, 1987). But within-class grouping also carries dangers of establishing classroom elitism and underprivilege if it becomes too rigid or pervasive; classrooms should also contain mixed-ability groups.

7. Tracking into separate classes has a small but significant benefit for more able learners. But this is due almost entirely to the accelerative effect, because in separate classes the more able students can proceed

through work at a faster pace (Kulik, 1991; Kulik & Kulik, 1987; Kulik & Kulik, 1989; Murphy & Hallinger, 1989; Slavin, 1990).

8.   Mildly and moderately handicapped students, including Down's syndrome individuals, can benefit by being placed in regular classes, which reduces the labeling effect of placement in special classes (Casey, Jones, Kugler, & Watkins, 1988).

9.   Placement of low-ability students in separate vocational schools is most likely to be effective if facilities and resources are available to provide a wide range of work-related programs; if the curriculum is not a "watered down" academic curriculum, but is designed to meet the specific needs of the students; if students feel they are being given useful job preparation skills; and if students have ample opportunity to participate in student leadership and extracurricular programs (King, 1986; King & Peart, 1990).

Simply mixing students together will not solve the problems of tracking. Far more revolutionary changes are needed. . . . The knowledge to be offered to children must be important, challenging, complex, and, most of all, rich with meaning. Indeed, it must stretch the sense-making of all children. But providing all children access to such knowledge will require dramatic alterations in instructional practice. . . . Teachers must function more like orchestra conductors than lecturers: getting things started and keeping them moving along, providing information and pointing to resources, coordinating a diverse but harmonious buzz of activity.

Goodlad & Oakes (1988, p. 19)

Slavin (1987c, 1988b) made the following recommendations:

1.   Students' primary identification should be with a heterogeneous class; they should be regrouped by ability only in subjects such as reading and math in which reducing heterogeneity is particularly important.

2.   Grouping plans should reduce heterogeneity in the specific skill being taught, not just in IQ or overall achievement.

3.   Programs should frequently reassess placements and should allow for easy reassignment.

4.   Teachers should vary the level and pace of instruction to correspond with students' levels of readiness in differentially grouped classes.

5.   The number of groups within a classroom should be kept small to allow for adequate direct instruction by the teacher to each group.

Grade retention

Requiring children to repeat a grade in which they have been unsuccessful, notably in the early grades, is a common practice, and one apparently supported by the majority of teachers (Tomchin & Impara, 1992). Its advocates argue that it is not in children's interest to advance them to a level for which they lack critical prerequisites. Most retention takes place in Kindergarten or Grade 1 (Schultz, 1989). By the eighth grade, 18 percent of students have repeated at least one grade and 2 percent more than one grade (OERI, 1990d). One effect of this is to increase the average age of the students at each grade level, and this, a recent report suggests, is the hidden agenda of retention (NAEYC & NAECS/ SDE, 1991). Within the last ten years, we have acquired considerable knowledge about the effects of this practice. The effects are almost wholly negative and in most cases catastrophic.

There appears to be only one small group of children who may sometimes benefit from grade repetition. These are children who are behaviorally immature and are more comfortable with a younger age group. If they are placed with an understanding and skillful teacher, who works on remediation rather than mere repetition, they may benefit from the experience (Ames, Gillespie, & Streff, 1972). For other pupils, the result is, on average, to reduce overall academic achievement. In a meta-analysis of 63 studies, C. T. Holmes (1989) found an average difference between the progress of retained and promoted pupils of .31 of a standard deviation in academic achievement. Of the 63 studies examined, 54 showed negative effects. In studies that show an apparent advantage to retained pupils, the benefit disappeared over time (Holmes, 1989; Mantzicopoulos & Morrison, 1992; Peterson, DeGracie, & Ayabe, 1987). The decline in achievement is particularly marked in language arts and mathematics. But there are similar declines in social and emotional adjustment, and in self-concept and attitude toward school (Holmes & Matthews, 1984). The negative effects appear to continue throughout the individual's schooling, and many school dropouts are people who have been required to repeat a grade. In fact, dropouts are five times as likely to have repeated a grade than are graduates (Shepard & Smith, 1989). Students who repeat two grades have almost a 100 percent probability of dropping out (Shepard & Smith, 1990). As the extra years of schooling required by grade repetition cost North America many billions of dollars every year, this is a high price to pay for a strategy that does not work.

It is easy, with hindsight, to see why grade repetition is an unsuccessful strategy. Children are taken out of the friendship group in which they have grown up; they are placed with a younger group who may reject them, as they are older and publicly labeled a failure; and they may also be rejected by their former peers. In a study by Yamamoto (1980, cited in Shepard & Smith, 1990), children rated repeating a grade as more shameful than "wetting in class" or being caught stealing; only going blind or losing a parent were rated as more stressful. Few teachers and programs can counteract a blow to a child's self-concept of this magnitude.

In light of what has been said earlier about critical learnings and prerequisites, what should be done about pupils who fail to master the critical learnings at a given grade level? The first answer is to prevent this from happening. Design and develop programs that are effective in instilling the critical learnings. But what if, despite all our efforts, failure still occurs?

Suppose a child has been unsuccessful in Grade 4. One strategy is to place the child the following year in a split Grade 4/5 class, with a teacher who is willing to help the child master the critical content of the Grade 4 and of the Grade 5 program. Another possibility is summer school. Many districts operate highly successful summer programs in which pupils can receive skilled remediation by teachers who work on pupils' self-concept as well as their academic learning. The per-pupil financial cost of summer school is less than a third of that of repeating a full year (Shepard & Smith, 1990). If none of these remedies are available, it is better to advance the pupil anyway. Unsatisfactory as this is, it is less damaging than grade retention.

Dropouts

Much attention has been paid in recent years to the issue of students failing to complete their secondary education. Care must be taken with dropout statistics, which Willett and Singer describe as often being politically motivated and "among the most misleading educational statistics published today" (Willett & Singer, 1991, p. 429). One-third of those students who drop out of high school "drop back in" within four years and earn a diploma. By 1990, only 12 percent of 16–26-year-olds were not enrolled in and had not completed high school (National Center for Educational Statistics, 1992). The history of the last fifty years is one of significant progress. In 1890, less than 7 percent of Americans aged 14–17 were in school (Kleibard, 1986). In other words, the "dropout rate" in 1890 was over 90 percent! In 1940, over 60 percent of Americans aged 25–29 had not completed high school. By 1989 this figure was down to 14.5 percent (OERI 1992). This compares with a dropout rate of 68 percent in England (Simmons & Wade, 1988). Over the last twenty years, the dropout rate in Grades 10–12 has been quite stable in the United States at between 4.8 and 6.6 percent per year (Frase, 1989).

The effects of dropping out of high school, however, are considerable. The unemployment rate among dropouts is almost twice as high as that of graduates. Earnings average 12–18 percent less, which amounts to a lifetime difference in total earnings of perhaps $250,000. It is estimated that every $1.00 invested in dropout prevention would generate $6.00 in national income and $2.00 in taxes (Rumberger, 1987).

Why do students drop out of school? Pregnancy is a significant factor among females. The main overall reason, cited by 29 percent of dropouts, is that they dislike school. Absenteeism is the best early predictor of dropout. In a sense, students do not drop out all at once, but a bit at a time. The isolation and nonparticipation of many students in large high schools appears to be a factor. Students are more likely to drop out of tracked than untracked high schools. Schools plagued by, or preoccupied with, absenteeism, violence, and substance abuse have high dropout rates. Dropouts tend to be characterized quite early by difficulty with reading and arithmetic and by high aggression and low academic performance; they tend to associate with other students at risk; they tend to have repeated one or more grades; their parents are not much involved in their education and are more likely to be single, poor, and less well educated than parents of graduates. Of all minority groups, aboriginal peoples tend to be most vulnerable to dropout. Dropouts tend to cite teachers they disliked and subjects with a high verbal content that were considered irrelevant to their life goals. Many dropouts subsequently regret their decision (Borgrink, 1987; Bryk & Thum, 1989; Cairns, Cairns, & Neckerman, 1989; Cashion & MacIver, 1988; OERI, 1992b; Pittman & Haughwout, 1987; Rumberger, 1987; Rumberger, Ghatak, Pouos, Ritter, & Dornbusch, 1990; Simner & Barnes, 1991; Weber, 1987).

Successful dropout prevention programs begin early; develop a sense of identification of the student with the school; provide timely identification and counseling; inform and involve parents; have a strong vocational component; provide extensive career exploration experiences; advise students early and clearly about their career and postsecondary education options; use sensitive, committed, and responsive staff; use a variety of integrated strategies; and provide more individualized instruction than conventional programs (Finn, 1989; King & Peart, 1990; Rumberger, 1987; Weber, 1987). Like most successful special programs, their features are those that characterize all good education.

Acceleration

"I skipped Grade 4 and I still can't multiply" is a typical comment about acceleration. Strictly speaking, however, this comment applies to "skipping," which is not quite the same as acceleration. A child who, after a successful year in Grade 4, is placed in a split Grade 5/6, masters the work of both grade levels, and the following year is placed in Grade 7—that child is experiencing acceleration in the true sense of the word.

The reservations many parents and educators have about acceleration often concern the social effects (Southern, Jones, & Fiscus, 1989). How will it be for an 8-year-old in a class of 10-year-olds? Or how will an adolescent of 16 years fit in with a group who are all 18-year-olds? Those who have themselves experienced acceleration tend to mention this as the principal difficulty. It is worth noting that this problem arises only because classes are structured primarily on the criterion of age; in classes selected on the basis of readiness, neither the 6-year-old nor the 66-year-old would feel out of place. Despite these difficulties, in informal surveys I have conducted over the years with teachers, about two-thirds of those who were accelerated (including those who were "skipped") say that it was a good decision. The research evidence suggests that the more personal experience people have with acceleration, the more favorably disposed they are toward it (Southern, Jones, & Fiscus, 1989). This may reflect the recognition that the alternative to acceleration may be considerable boredom and frustration as a fast learner is forced to work at the speed of the average.

The mean effect of accelerating a student by one year is to increase the student's achievement by one grade level. In other words, the accelerated student catches up with his or her new group of older peers (Feldhusen, 1989; Kulik & Kulik, 1984a, 1984b, 1989). At Johns Hopkins University, several hundred students with precocious ability in mathematics have over the years been moved from Grades 7, 8, and 9 into first-year university programs in mathematics, physics, and computer science. Very careful selection procedures have been used, with lengthy consultation with the students and their parents. The students have been uniformly successful, not only in their academic achievement, but also in their social adjustment (Benbow & Stanley, 1983; Brody & Benbow, 1987; Richardson & Benbow, 1990). A ten-year, longitudinal study showed no significant differences in social or emotional adjustment between accelerants and nonaccelerants; only 6 percent of accelerants reported negative social or emotional effects at age 18, and only 3 percent at age 23 (Richardson & Benbow, 1990). In another experiment at Johns Hopkins, a group of highly able adolescents was offered separate Saturday morning classes. In one year, they mastered the entire high school mathematics curriculum. Clearly it would not have been to the advantage of these students to trudge through the curriculum at the same pace as the average high school student (Stanley, 1976).

David Elkind points out that acceleration is not "hurrying" learners, but, rather, is allowing them to progress at their own pace—refusing to "decelerate" them, in fact (1988). There appears to be no basis in fact for the popular belief that faster learners are socially incompetent (Schneider, Clegg, Byrne, Ledingham, & Crombie, 1989). Accelerated classes containing age spans of up to five years have reported excellent social and academic interaction (George & Denham, 1976). Finally, an astonishing finding was reported by Peterson, Wilkinson, and Hallinan in 1984. A group of remedial math students placed in an accelerated program made more progress in areas of problem solving, math concepts, and computational skills than peers placed in a remedial class. Clearly, acceleration works not only for gifted learners!

INSTRUCTIONAL APPROACHES TO DIFFERENCES

Of the four approaches described above, only acceleration appears to have consistently positive effects in adapting school programs to learner diversity. Although acceleration is a strategy for dealing with superior aptitudes, the underlying principle of allowing students as much as possible to proceed at their own pace is generally sound in dealing with learner diversity.

Programmatic responses to diversity usually require consensus among those who work in schools. We will now look at instructional responses: strategies teachers can adopt within their own classrooms. But first, a short diversion into theory.

The cybernetics of instruction

All living systems grow and maintain themselves by means of processes of self-regulation. Mechanical systems can also be constructed to maintain equilibrium in similar ways. The study of these processes is known as cybernetics.

Let us take, by way of example, the regulation of heat in the human body. Despite enormous variations in exterior temperature, as human beings we maintain the internal temperature of our bodies, and especially of our brains, at an almost unvarying 37°C. We do this in five main ways: (1) We reduce the extremes of heat and cold affecting our bodies by constructing buildings which may be heated and cooled, by wearing clothes, by moving out of the sun or the wind, and by taking winter vacations in the Caribbean. (2) We constantly monitor the temperature state of our bodies. Sensors for heat and cold are located in the skin, the body core, and the brain. (3) We have an optimal internal temperature setting. In cybernetic terms, this is known as the "set point," and in human thermoregulation it is set at about 37°C. (4) A structure in the brain, the posterior hypothalamus, constantly compares information about the temperature of the body with the set point. (5) Physiological processes act to restore temperature to equilibrium. Heat is dealt with principally by means of sweating and dilation of external blood vessels to transmit heat to the body surface and hence to the environment. Cold is dealt with by shivering, "gooseflesh"—the erection of body hair—and constriction of external blood vessels to shunt blood to the body core. The whole process is similar to thermoregulation in a house, but more elegant, more precise, more continuous, and more stable.

All cybernetic systems operate by means of these same five processes: a boundary that protects the system; sensors that pick up information about the state of the system; a set point that establishes the optimum state of the system; a director that monitors the system for departure from the set point; and effectors that intervene to restore the system to equilibrium. The same five processes can be observed in instructional environments. Admissions criteria and prerequisites form the boundary; formative assessment collects information about student learning; objectives and performance criteria constitute the set point; the teacher monitors the class for discrepancies between objectives and performance; remediation intervenes to restore equilibrium.

The kind of stability needed in an instructional system is not a narrow band of achievement, but an achievement "floor" through which none or very few of the learners sink. Learners arrive in classrooms with great diversity on many dimensions, including aptitude and motivation. The instructional system must manage this diversity in such a way as to produce stable minimum output—achievement by all learners of the critical learnings.

In instructional terms, the implications are as follows:

1. The more relevant and exacting the prerequisites, the more homogeneous the learners, the less time and energy will need to be spent on remediation, and the easier it will be to maintain high achievement.

2.   Understanding and acceptance by all parties of objectives, priorities, and performance standards will facilitate their attainment.

3.   Formative assessment that is sensitive and frequent will identify minor learning problems before they escalate into major difficulties.

4.   Formative assessment is of limited usefulness unless the data it provides are used as the basis for prompt correction.

5.   Remedial strategies need to be developed that will effectively correct the learning problems identified.   (Pratt, 1982, 1990, 1991b)

These principles underlie earlier discussions in this book regarding learning intentions. In the discussion that follows, we will examine additional ways in which teachers can manage instruction so as to produce more stable learning output.

Preassessment

The benefits of pretesting have been mentioned earlier (Chapter 5). Students are sometimes mislabeled as slow learners because they have missed certain critical prior learnings. A child who is still having trouble with basic multiplication facts is going to appear slow in solving complex multiplication problems. There are considerable benefits in identifying and repairing such omissions early in a course or prior to its beginning. Pretests may also give us useful information about children's problem solving abilities and their attitudes, interests, and learning styles. This information can be used to plan appropriate instructional experiences.

Formative assessment

One of the keys to dealing with problems of underachievement is to *detect and correct minor error before it becomes major failure*. This entails collecting information about students' learning on a frequent or continuous basis. Such information is not intended to generate marks and grades, but to identify learning difficulties so that we can intervene promptly. Experienced teachers do this by monitoring seatwork and homework, by asking questions and initiating discussions in class, by observing learners working individually or in groups, by reading students' body language, by talking with parents, and by the use of noncredit tests and quizzes. Effective formative evaluation seeks information on the learning of every student. With oral questioning, it is easy to consistently overlook certain students. This tendency can be offset by using a class list to select a random group of students daily, each of whom will be given special attention; or you could put the pupils' names on cards, shuffle the deck and draw four or five names each lesson.

I once observed a beginning teacher making use of a simple piece of instructional technology for formative evaluation in a Grade 1 class. He had given each child a card about the size of a postcard. On one side, in large letters, was the word YES. On the other side, NO. For each lesson, he prepared several questions that were "Yes/No" questions. The learners held up the card they considered

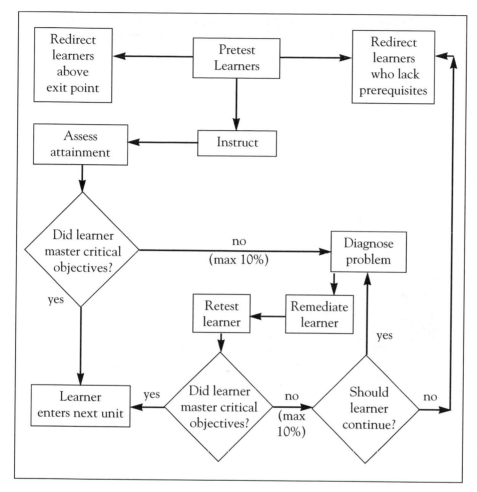

Cybernetics of Instruction

appropriate. By this means, the teacher could monitor the responses of every student to every question. If one learner persistently showed the wrong card, that child needed additional help. If the whole class held up the wrong card, that concept needed more time. The problem with questioning in normal whole-class teaching is that one can ask only one student a question at a time. By a simple piece of instructional technology, this teacher had greatly increased the effectiveness of his classroom questioning.

It will be recalled from Chapter 4 that as the purpose of formative evaluation is to discover how students are learning; permanent marks should not be awarded for achievement on formative measures. A question sometimes asked is: In that case, how can we persuade students to take such measures seriously? Completing a test without being rewarded with marks is seen, in the mark-based economy of schools, as working without pay. An idealistic answer is to ensure that the learning is sufficiently meaningful and significant to the learners that such extrinsic incentives as marks are unimportant. For a less than perfect world, other possibilities may be suggested.

Let us take a conventional situation. Halfway through a two-week unit on fractions, Jocasta takes a quiz. She has some problems with the concept of the lowest common denominator, and scores 5 out of 10. This mark is recorded. She overcomes her difficulty, and at the end of the unit, she takes the summative test and scores 10 out of 10. These marks are combined to give her a total of 15 out of 20. Yet this mark does not represent her ultimate mastery, which was complete. We expect students to make errors while learning: making and correcting errors is a basic method of learning. To penalize such errors in the final marking scheme is a questionable practice, even though it is an almost universal one.

Here is an alternative scenario. The students are informed that their mark on a quiz will not be recorded until it reaches at least 8 out of 10. There is an incentive to do well on the first quiz, but the only "penalty" for not doing well is to receive additional help and then try the quiz again, or to take another equivalent quiz. Any quiz on which students score less than 8 out of 10 is formative; any other score makes the test summative.

A second approach which seems to work quite well is to allow group work on formative assessment. This seems to be particularly effective if (1) there are three students in each group; (2) one of these students is from the top third of the class, one from the middle, and one from the lower third; (3) the students discuss the exercise, or each question, together, but each student submits a separate piece of work or answer sheet; (4) ample time is allowed, typically about twice as much as if the task were completed individually. This approach capitalizes on the known benefits of cooperative learning, while insisting on individual accountability. It also removes much of the anxiety from testing situations, provides a high level of student engagement, and tends to produce much informal and spontaneous peer tutoring.

A third alternative is not to award marks for formative assignments, but to make satisfactory completion of such assessments a prerequisite to summative assessment. Formative evaluation is particularly important for underperforming students. Such students are often highly anxious about summative tests, and this affects their test performance. They also underperform in situations where tests appear to be used to control their behavior, where the level of difficulty is too high for them, and where the comparison is between their performance and that of other students, because such comparisons are usually to their disadvantage. In these situations, the motivation of slower learners is undermined; they tend to give up and develop "learned helplessness." This disempowering condition, familiar to every teacher, is defined by the American Psychological Association as "the learned expectation that one's responses are independent of rewards, and hence do not predict or control the occurrence of the rewards" (American Psychological

Association, 1988, p. 108). On the other hand, these students perform better when tests are used primarily to give them helpful feedback and information about their progress. They also find it very helpful when formative tests allow them to practice the same kind of performance that will be required on summative tests (Crooks, 1988).

Both pretests and formative tests should be diagnostic rather than merely evaluative. It is not enough to know that a learner is making a mediocre score on a test on fractions. We need to know the nature of his or her difficulty. Is it a prior deficiency in basic number facts? Or does the difficulty lie in addition, subtraction, or multiplication of fractions? If in one of these, at what stage in the calculation is the difficulty found? We also need to check some apparently simple factors, such as whether students can read the blackboard and hear the teacher. Or are they having difficulty because their first language is not English? or because they are having problems at home? or because they have not learned how to listen, or how to learn, or how to study?

Remediation

In an effective classroom, formative evaluation and remediation are almost continuous. Ideally, when a teacher is asking questions in a classroom, about 8 out of every 10 student responses should be correct (Earl, 1987). A higher figure might indicate redundancy, a much lower figure would point to a risk of discouragement and practicing errors. The 2 out of 10 questions that are wrongly answered should result in immediate informal review, discussion, explanation, elaboration, and correction.

We should endeavor to design and try out our instruction so that even formative assessments do not produce a "failure" rate in excess of 20 percent of students. Preferably, the figure would be under 10 percent. In the following discussion of remediation, it is assumed that we are normally remediating only a few students at a time.

Inviting underachieving students to come in after school for extra help is not going to meet the requirements for effective remediation. While it is commendable for teachers to offer their time, some students will view this arrangement as a punishment, some will choose not to come, and some will be unable to. The arrangement is also onerous for teachers. To be effective, remediation must be as simple, fast, and painless as possible.

At this point, instructional technology can come to our aid. There are many computer programs that allow students to reinforce and practice knowledge and skills. Alternatively, you might prepare a fifteen-minute audiotape summarizing, in as interesting a way as possible, the critical points covered in the previous week or two. Lend students the tape, with a short list of questions, over a weekend, with instructions to listen to it several times. A teacher of woodworking tells me he has students film all his machine safety lessons. If a new student arrives, or if he sees a student using a machine unsafely, that student can view the videotape without interrupting the work of the rest of the class. A key to effective remediation is that it is prompt. Long-distance runners know that there is a psychological turning point when the gap between you and the runner ahead widens to a distance at which you "lose contact": at that point you abandon hope of catching up. It is important that this does not happen to slower learners. A quiz on Friday, an interesting self-administered remedial exercise over the weekend, and a successful retest before school begins on Monday is an ideal pattern.

There is evidence that many children are reluctant to seek help with schoolwork voluntarily for fear of being considered "dumb" by classmates or adults (Newman & Goldin, 1990). This is an additional reason why teachers need to be proactive in the identification of underachievement and in offering remediation.

Because underachievement is almost invariably linked with motivation, remedial strategies should be as interesting and enjoyable as possible. If three of your Grade 5 pupils neither understand, nor are interested in, the classification of mammalian species, perhaps the best remediation is a trip to the local zoo. A group of minority students find your unit on the Civil War irrelevant and uninteresting: invite them, or the whole class, to view the movie *Glory*, about a black battalion in the war. Take the underachieving students in your French class to dinner at a nightspot where a French folk singer is performing. A teacher of sign language once told me that on one occasion the achievement and motivation of some of the hearing students he was instructing was inadequate. He took them one evening to a disco so noisy that the only means of communication was sign language. On the principle that prevention is better than cure, the more high-interest strategies are used in instruction, the less remediation will be needed.

Homework helpline

A strategy that has been introduced into a number of school districts is the "Homework Helpline." Typically, the line is staffed by volunteers such as retired teachers or senior high school students. Posters are put up in schools advertising hours of operation. Help is given when and as needed. A student calls the Helpline number, a coordinator answers . . .

Coordinator: Homework Helpline. Can I help you?

Student: Hi, this is Karen Amodeo. I'm in Grade 12 Physical Geography at Hilltop High, and I don't understand this water cycle stuff.

Coordinator: OK, Karen. We do have a geography specialist on the line. His name's Mr. Jones. Hold on while I call him. . . .

Mr. Jones: Hi Karen, this is Art Jones. What is it you don't understand about the water cycle? . . .

Enrichment

Faster learners generate "marginal time" by mastering skills or concepts faster than their peers. This time needs to be used in productive ways. "Busy work," "free time," "going to the school library," and "more of the same" are not appropriate responses, because they fail the basic test of being enriching. Allowing a student who is ahead in mathematics to work on the history assignment on which she is behind or to practice the violin may be enriching.

Providing the mathematically able student with projects producing a broader and deeper understanding of mathematics is also enriching, but will increase the distance between this student and the rest of the class. This means that sooner or later acceleration will need to be considered. As Julian Stanley writes: "The more relevant and excellent the enrichment, the more it calls for acceleration of subject-matter or grade placement later. Otherwise it just puts off the boredom a while and virtually guarantees that eventually it will be more severe" (Stanley, 1976, p. 235).

Peer and volunteer tutoring

It has long been clear that one-to-one instruction is highly effective. Even in large classes, the amount of one-to-one contact between teacher and child is an important factor in student achievement (Mortimore, 1988). Bloom claims that one-to-one tutoring by a professional can raise a learner's achievement by two standard deviations—the equivalent of moving a pupil from the 50th to the 98th percentile (Bloom, 1984). Other researchers have confirmed that one-to-one professional tutoring is the most effective form of instruction known (Slavin, Karweit, & Madden, 1989). Slavin's analysis of four preventive tutoring programs, in which at-risk students were tutored for 15–30 minutes a day by paraprofessionals or teachers, showed effect sizes averaging just under one standard deviation (Slavin, 1987b). Such programs are relatively expensive, and in this discussion we shall focus on the much less expensive, but also effective, practice of peer tutoring.

The effects of peer tutoring on student achievement are modest. But they are so consistent, so economical, and effective in so many different ways that one authority has termed peer tutoring an "educational conjuring trick" (Bond, 1982). Japanese elementary schools take systematic advantage of peer tutoring. Marsha Fortner reports, "Ability grouping in Japan is never allowed. Rather, teachers form mixed ability groups and depend on the fast learners of a group to coach the slower members" (1989, p. 17).

Peer tutoring was common in the mixed-age, one-room schools of the eighteenth and early nineteenth centuries. It became less common with the increasing age segregation of larger schools and professionalization of teachers in the twentieth century. But it survived wherever teachers had students work together in pairs, and whenever students monopolized telephone lines in the evenings in collaborative wrestling with homework problems. Formal studies of peer tutoring have provided a measure of exactness in predicting its effects.

A meta-analysis of the effects of peer tutoring in fifty-two studies was conducted by Cohen, Kulik, and Kulik in 1982. They reported an average effect size of .40 on achievement, .29 on student attitudes, and .42 on student self-concept. The inexpensive character of peer tutoring makes it especially cost-effective (Levin et al., 1986). Peer tutoring seems to be effective whether the subject matter taught is academic content, study skills, or social behavior (House & Wohlt, 1991; Trapani & Gettinger, 1990).

Peer tutoring also has positive effects on the learning of tutors. Typically, their achievement rises 10 to 12 percentile points as a result of the experience. In addition, peer tutoring has long-term beneficial effects on the self-concept and attitudes of tutors. In a study conducted in England, secondary school students who were persistent truants were asked to tutor younger children from a local elementary school. An immediate effect was that the truancy stopped immediately and completely. Remarkable changes were also apparent in the tutors' attitudes toward school, education, and themselves (Bond, 1982).

Almost everyone can become an effective tutor. When young people are involved, the ideal appears to be an age gap of three to four years, which happens to be the normal space between siblings in preindustrial societies. Children have great

respect for other children and adolescents older than themselves. They respect and imitate children of the same age whom they have been told are older; they do not tend to imitate children they judge younger or less competent. A gap of only two years is not consistently more effective than same-age tutoring (DePaul, Tang, Webb, Hoover, Marsh, & Litowitz, 1989; Konner, 1975; Schunk, 1987).

Some schools establish a buddy system, whereby every child upon entry to school is assigned a buddy three or four years older. The buddy is not only a friend, model, and mentor, but also a storyteller, writer, and reader; a listener, playmate, and tutor. This relationship can be maintained until the buddy graduates from the school. One common finding is that, for obvious reasons, schoolyard bullying disappears and general school climate improves (Cameron, Politano, & Morris, 1989).

Buddies

The most important thing about speaking in a buddy program is being the focus of someone's attention. . . . The most important thing about listening in a buddy program is the feeling that someone cares enough to listen. . . . The most important thing about buddies reading to each other is the shared experience. . . . The most important thing about writing in a buddy program is the opportunity for meaningful practice. . . . The most important thing about sharing in a buddy program is the bond that develops. . . . The most important thing about presenting in a buddy program is accepting and valuing all efforts. . . . The most important thing about observing in a buddy program is the learning opportunity it provides.

Cameron, Politano, and Morris (1989, pp. 17–40)

It is not necessary to restrict the opportunity to tutor to the more able pupils. The best person to teach a learning disabled child how to use a knife and fork is another disabled child who has just learned to do so. Handicapped children can readily be trained to tutor one another (Maheady, Harper, & Sacca, 1988). The self-image of a class of low-achieving students can be improved by teaching them something, for example, how to use a word processing program, and then having them teach these skills to academically successful pupils. One of the best things you could do for a Grade 5 child who is having difficulty in language arts is to assign him or her to listen to and help a Grade 2 child reading for ten minutes every day.

The social effects of peer tutoring, as of cooperative learning in general, are probably as important as its academic effects. We know that children without siblings are less socially responsive (Vandell & Mueller, 1980). With the shrinking size of the average household, fewer children have siblings. When members of a family gather, it is often to watch television without much interaction among themselves. In terms of social development, values, and behavioral choices, as in so many other ways, the school has become obliged to assume a role once held by the family. Studies of successful anti-smoking, substance abuse, and AIDS education programs show that peers are much more effective than professional teachers in bringing about behavioral change (Botvin, 1986; Flay, 1985; Sabatier, 1989).

Peer tutoring seems to work well under almost any circumstances. The reasons for this are both evolutionary and psychological. As mentioned earlier, peer learning in the mixed-age playgroup was the primary mode of socialization and education for millions of years before the invention of schooling. And, at least in the view of Jean Piaget, interaction between individuals at different levels of cognitive functioning is the most basic requirement for learning, because it forces learners to reconsider their suppositions and ways of thinking about a problem, which leads to disequilibrium, equilibration, and growth (Piaget, 1976).

For peer tutoring to be most effective, a number of points need to be kept in mind:

1. Tutors should be volunteers. Not everyone makes an effective tutor. Not everyone wants to be a tutor.

2. Tutors should be trained and supervised. Training needs neither to be formal nor lengthy. A few simple principles may be sufficient: give frequent feedback and reinforcement, don't use blame or sarcasm, model desired responses, and so on. A supervisor needs to be available for advice, troubleshooting, and reinforcement.

3. Tutoring should be organized. Not many programs work well if unorganized or disorganized. The ideal is to free part of the timetable of one teacher or administrator to organize and supervise the program.

4. The program should be approved by administration and parents. Skeptical parents can be advised of the evidence of improved learning by tutors.

5. The work of tutors should be recognized. Some schools give academic credit for involvement in tutoring. It is not usually necessary to pay tutors. For secondary students, a letter of reference to future employers constitutes important recognition.

In addition to fellow students, there are many other potential tutors in most communities. Parents, even if they have little formal education themselves, can become highly effective tutors for their children (Goldenberg, 1989). Senior citizens often make excellent tutors and value the opportunity to interact with young people. Sometimes they can play a role that is missing in children's lives. Many single parents, and some married parents, simply have difficulty finding the time to interact with, and read to, their children. The average American mother spends less than thirty minutes a day talking or reading with her children; the average father, less than fifteen minutes (Walberg, 1984b). Grandparents, who in an earlier era often performed a crucial backup role to parents, today often live far away. There are boat people and other immigrant children who will never again see their grandparents. For such children, seniors can become honorary grandparents. For older students, cross-generational writing projects, in which they interview and write biographies of senior citizens, are personally and educationally enriching experiences.

Morris, Shaw, and Perney (1990) report on a tutoring program that has been operating successfully for more than a decade in an inner-city school on the north side of Chicago. The program serves twenty children a year, selected from underachieving students in Grades 2 and 3. Volunteers include students in local universities, suburban mothers whose children are away in college, and retirees; after the first few years tutors were readily recruited by word of mouth. The program operates four days a week from October to May. Two groups each of ten children are tutored two days a week. At 2:30, the supervisor takes them to a storefront building near the school, where they are served milk and cookies and listen to a story or play a game. The supervisor is crucial and must have a good background, experience, and confidence in teaching reading, as well as the ability to work with and train tutors. The tutors arrive by 3:00; each works with one child from 3:00 to 4:00. The lessons are planned and supervised by the supervisor and are work-filled with very few interruptions. Tutoring focuses on reading and writing, using good stories in natural language. Training of tutors is largely on the job. At 4:00 P.M., the children and tutors leave for home. Results show that all of the tutored children make significant progress in reading. About one-third make gains greater than their nontutored but more able peers; one-third make a year's progress during the year; and one-third progress in reading but at a slower rate than their peers.

Effective instruction

Generally, strategies for increasing the effectiveness of instruction have disproportionately high effects on underachieving students. This may be illustrated by the example of time on task. Suppose the highest-achieving fifth of your class are on-task on average 80 percent of the time, and your lowest-achieving fifth are on-task 20 percent of the time. You use several of the strategies described in Chapter 6 to increase time on task. You might be able to triple the time on task of the low achievers, from 20 percent to 60 percent. But you will probably not increase that of the high achievers above about 90 percent, as they are already close to their time on task "ceiling." The result will be that your fast learners are now learning 50 percent faster, rather than 400 percent faster, than your slower learners.

The same is true of such strategies as curriculum alignment. It will be recalled that curriculum alignment consists of deciding exactly what to teach and then teaching and assessing exactly that. Koczor (1984) found that the effect of increasing the alignment of instruction was .30 for intellectually gifted students, but over 1.00 for average students. It is particularly important for at-risk students, therefore, that the strategies linked to effective instruction (Chapter 6) and assessment (Chapter 4) of low achievers be systematically employed with these learners.

THE ROLE OF THE CURRICULUM PLANNER ⸺⸺⸺⸺⸺

Official curricula are often written as though individual differences in learning did not exist. This is one of the ways by which the credibility of official curricula tends to self-destruct. Of one hundred curricula examined by Pratt (1989), only eleven mentioned the special needs of slower learners, only three discussed the special needs of faster learners, and none discussed any other kinds of learner differences. Similar findings were reported a decade earlier by Klein (1979).

Curriculum planners need to include in the document they prepare practical and sound advice on treatment of individual differences. Without appropriate guidance, teachers may try to teach in ways that are uniform and hence effective only for a few students. Curricula need to remind teachers of the different ways that human beings learn and how they can respond to those differences. It is diversity that makes the world an interesting place, and curricula that are interesting acknowledge, respond to, and celebrate human diversity.

■ SELF - ASSESSMENT

1. What is the main criterion by which students are selected into instructional groups in most schools?

   A   age
   B   aptitude
   C   social class
   D   achievement

2. What is the term used to describe the capacity to engage in certain mental or physical activities by reason of motivation, maturation, or prior experience?

   A   interest
   B   readiness
   C   intelligence
   D   developmental level

3. Which proverb reflects an effective approach to the remediation of underachievement?

   A   a stitch in time saves nine (English)
   B   never lift a stone to drop it on your own toe (Chinese)
   C   a fool loves to teach, but a wise man loves to learn (Russian)
   D   in much wisdom is much grief, and he that increaseth knowledge increaseth sorrow (Hebrew)

4. What is the greatest risk that slow learners run?

   A   that they will give up
   B   that they will develop unrealistic expectations
   C   that they will demand too much of the instructor's time
   D   that they will spend too much time working in their areas of weakness

5. What principle should guide the design of formative evaluation and remediation?

   A   students should repeat units that they fail
   B   formative evaluation should be norm-referenced
   C   formative evaluation and remediation should be frequent
   D   if some students fail, the whole class should receive remediation

6. Which of the following is a feature of peer tutoring?

   A   peer tutoring is more effective if the tutor is older than the tutee
   B   peer tutoring is more effective if the tutor is younger than the tutee
   C   peer tutoring is more effective if the tutor is the same age as the tutee
   D   the effectiveness of peer tutoring is unaffected by the relative ages of tutor and tutee

7. What belief is maintained by educators who support tracking or streaming?

   A   that it will be fairer to minority students
   B   that it will reduce the variance in aptitude in each classroom
   C   that it will help to compensate for differences in home background
   D   that it will facilitate interaction between more and less able students

8. What is the usual effect on children of repeating a grade?

   A   their self-concept improves
   B   they perform better in most areas
   C   they perform worse in almost all areas
   D   they perform at about the same level in most areas

9. On what basis do schools typically identify some learners as "gifted"?

   A   by selecting the most creative students
   B   by generalizing from a few specific areas of ability
   C   by taking into account a wide variety of areas of endeavor
   D   by identifying students who possess the unique trait of giftedness

10. A student succeeds so well in Grade 3 that the following year she is placed in Grade 5. What term best describes this procedure?

   A   skipping
   B   enrichment
   C   acceleration
   D   ability grouping

For answers, see Appendix F.
If you answered nine or ten questions correctly, you understand most of the material in this chapter.
If you answered seven or eight questions correctly, reread the appropriate parts of the chapter.
If you answered fewer than seven questions correctly, reread the chapter carefully.

CHAPTER 8

Specifying Learning Resources

Civilization gets its basic energy not from its resources, but from its hopes.

Norman Cousins (Muller, 1978, p. 12)

Summary

A crucial step in curriculum planning is the specification and provision of the human and material resources necessary for the delivery of instruction. The consumables and communication materials, including textbooks, audiovisual materials, and computer software, needed to support the curriculum should be identified. Instructional equipment must be listed. Consideration needs to be given to the layout, decor, lighting, temperature, and noise of instructional facilities, to the size of instructional groups, and to use of space outside the classroom. The qualities and responsibilities of teachers and other people involved with the curriculum should be specified. The total expected time consumption and costs of the curriculum should be calculated.

HEROISM VERSUS PLANNING

In 1910 two teams of explorers set out for the South Pole, one of the last points on the earth until then never reached by human beings. A British team was led by Captain Robert Falcon Scott, and a Norwegian expedition was led by Captain Roald Amundsen. The five-man Norwegian team arrived at the Pole first and returned safely to their base. The British team, also of five men, reached the Pole six weeks after the Norwegians and perished on the return journey.

Both teams were experienced in polar exploration. Both consisted of brave and intelligent men. The overall strategy of both teams was similar: leaving the base camp as soon as weather permitted, dropping off food dumps every 100 km on the way south for the return journey. The fundamental difference between the teams was their attention to, and attitude toward, the logistics of the expedition.

Amundsen set off with four sleds pulled by fifty-two dogs. His men were expert skiers, dog drivers, and navigators. Following field tests the previous fall, his team had spent the winter planing the sleds down to a third of their original weight. They had broken down and rebuilt their boots until they had essentially invented the modern ski boot—warm and insulated but firm on the ski. Amundsen dressed his men from head to foot in Inuit fur clothing made from caribou hides. They lived on a diet containing large amounts of fresh meat, which contains enough vitamin C to keep scurvy at bay. They took two tons of food more than the minimum required. On the expedition they skied all day; if a man got tired, he could ride on a sled for a while and let the dogs pull him.

Scott's party set out with motor sledges, ponies, and one dog team. The motors broke down a week into the expedition and had to be abandoned. The last of the ponies had to be shot before they were half-way to the pole, and the dog party, with insufficient food to take it to the Pole, was sent home. From there on, the men pulled the sleds themselves on a journey that included climbing the 3,000 m glacier up to the polar plateau. Their diet contained no vitamin C. The work was sufficiently exhausting that they had to stop for two hours in the middle of each day to rest and eat lunch. Their poorly insulated fur moccasins broke down, resulting in frozen feet. Their gabardine parkas and wool sweaters did not allow moisture to escape and their clothes froze. They could travel only at two-thirds of the speed of the Norwegians. Rations and fuel were insufficient. Scurvy and frostbite incapacitated them. The last three survivors died 200 km from their base camp (Huntford, 1980).

The British explorers, five men selected from some 10,000 applicants, were tough, experienced, and courageous. No one could question the quality of their courage and comradeship. They merit their place in the pantheon of British heroes. Their failure was a failure of logistical planning. It was a failure to pay meticulous attention to apparently insignificant details, like properly sealing fuel cans against evaporation. They relied excessively on courage and good luck. Courage they did not lack. With better luck, they might have completed the expedition successfully.

But in his book, *My Life as an Explorer*, Amundsen comments on planning and luck:

> The greatest factor in the success of an exploring expedition is the way in which every difficulty is foreseen and precautions taken for meeting or avoiding it. Victory awaits him who has everything in order—luck, people call it. Defeat is certain for him who has neglected to take the necessary precautions in time—this is called bad luck.   (Amundsen, 1927, p. 258)

PLANNING CURRICULUM RESOURCES

In planning a curriculum, resources need to be considered in six main areas: materials, equipment, facilities, personnel, time, and cost. Most official curricula provide a list of textbooks, but official documents tend to be silent about the other resources required (Pratt, 1989). When it comes to implementing a curriculum, clear specification of required resources can make a difference between success and failure.

MATERIALS

One of the major factors in successful implementation of curriculum innovations is whether or not the curriculum is accompanied by useful, high-quality instructional materials. A curriculum is unlikely to succeed if it is expected that teachers will spend large amounts of time acquiring or creating new materials. Providing teachers with materials that help them teach effectively and arouse student interest greatly increases the probability of successful implementation of a new curriculum. Sometimes instructional materials are included in the curriculum document or provided in an accompanying teacher handbook.

Ideally, materials should be available that enable students to use several different sensory channels for learning. Materials, both two-dimensional and three-dimensional, need to be available that invite exploration and manipulation. The ideal, in any classroom, but perhaps particularly in the early grades, is an environment that is rich in a variety of materials that invite exploration. As Jim Greenman says:

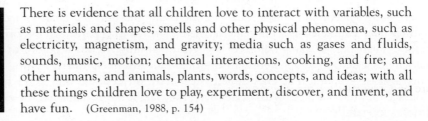

> There is evidence that all children love to interact with variables, such as materials and shapes; smells and other physical phenomena, such as electricity, magnetism, and gravity; media such as gases and fluids, sounds, music, motion; chemical interactions, cooking, and fire; and other humans, and animals, plants, words, concepts, and ideas; with all these things children love to play, experiment, discover, and invent, and have fun.   (Greenman, 1988, p. 154)

Materials for distribution to students or for classroom projection need to be of professional quality. Permission should be obtained for reproduction of copyrighted materials. Some general criteria for the selection of commercially produced materials are shown in Table 8-1.

We may divide curriculum materials into two classes: consumables and communication materials.

Table 8-1   *Criteria for Selection of Instructional Materials*

General Criteria for Evaluating Instructional Materials

Producer claims
Are the materials described clearly and realistically?
Are claims for effectiveness substantiated?
Are details provided concerning development and field testing?
Is data provided on user satisfaction?
Are author credentials explicit and convincing?

Cost
Is the total price and the per-student cost specified?
What supplemental materials are required?
Are the materials compatible with other materials?
How much time do the materials require of students and teachers?
What teacher qualities or in-service training are required to use the materials?
Is support or troubleshooting available from the producer?

Content
Is the material appropriate to the program and the learners?
Is the material accurate, interesting, and up-to-date?
Is the material free of ethnic, gender, and other forms of bias?

Instructional implications
Are the objectives clear?
Is the audience defined?
Do the materials challenge students at different aptitude levels?
Is the role of the teacher defined?
Do materials use diverse modes of presentation?
Can the materials be used for self-instruction?
Do the materials actively involve the students?
Are opportunities for practice provided?
Are self-testing and feedback included?

■ **Consumables** ■

Consumables are items that are used up in instruction and have to be replaced. They include articles that different curricula may consume, such as paper, paint, crayons, chalk, chemicals, biological specimens, batteries, electricity, food, soap, and motor oil. Planners need to think through the requirements for consumables, provide an adequate margin for overconsumption, and ensure that users are advised what is needed and how to obtain it. Table 8-2 shows part of the consumables section from a Grade K-3 Science Curriculum.

John Olson (1979) reports his experience as a teacher field testing one of the new Nuffield Biology Curricula when they were first introduced in Britain. The

Table 8-2   *Science Materials for K–3*

aluminum foil	hammer	rocks, samples
apples	hand lenses	rubber bands
aquarium	ice	rulers
bags, lunch	index cards	salt
bags, plastic	jars	sand
balloons	knives, plastic	sandpaper
balls	lamps	scale, bathroom
bean seeds	leaves	scale, kitchen
cans, coffee	magazines	scissors
cans, empty	magnets	seeds
chalk, white	marbles	shoe boxes
clay	marking pens	sponge
cloth	matches	spoons
coins	microscope	stopwatch
cotton balls	mirrors	straws
crayons	nails	string
cups, measuring	napkins	sugar
cups, plastic	needles	tape, masking
detergent	newspapers	tape, plastic
egg cartons	paint	thermometer
eye-droppers	paper	thumb tacks
fish from store	paper clips	toothpicks
fish food	paper plates	vinegar
flashlight	paper towels	washers
flowers	paste	waxed paper
food coloring	pencils	wire
foods	pie pans	wooden blocks
globe	plants	yardsticks
glue	record player	yarn

(California State Department of Education: Science Curriculum, 1987, p. 121)

first unit was about locusts and called for a dozen pairs of locusts to be obtained and bred. The locusts, however, didn't come with the curriculum—you had to find your own locusts. Eventually, he found a tropical pet store in London that sold locusts and bought a dozen pairs. Now, to breed locusts and have the eggs hatch, you have to establish an environment similar to that of their natural habitat, the Empty Quarter of the Arabian desert—that is, very hot in the day and very cold at night. So he built a cage and by means of a heater and a cooler kept the temperature balanced. Soon the locusts were mating all over the classroom, although the eggs never hatched. The next unit called for the breeding of African toads, and at that point this teacher abandoned the Nuffield Biology Program and returned to the old curriculum. The lesson is obvious. If a curriculum is going to require exotic materials, it must either provide them with the curriculum or advise teachers where they can be easily obtained.

▪ Communication Materials ▪

Communication materials include such items as textbooks, workbooks, reference books, films, tapes, worksheets, and computer software.

It is ideal if high-quality instructional materials can be included in the curriculum itself or published in a companion document. This applies particularly to such items as print material that can be photocopied; worksheets; self-tests; maps, graphs, diagrams, and other graphic materials; masters for overhead transparencies; and so on. Bear in mind that U.S. copyright law allows a teacher to make only one copy for each student of articles or chapters or illustrations from books, or up to 10 percent of a prose work up to 1,000 words, or up to 250 words of a poem. Copyright law in many countries such as Canada is even more restrictive.

The business community is increasingly interested in providing instructional materials to schools. Educators need to ensure that such materials present the issues with which they deal in a way that is balanced and truthful. The orientation and interests of business are not necessarily the same as those of the schools and may, in fact, conflict with them, as for example in areas of health and nutrition or material values. Business tends to view students as present and future consumers; educators should view students as people and learners (ASCD Task Force, 1989; Molnar, 1990).

Teaching materials are everywhere. Books, cartoons, drawings, flashcards, graphs, magazines, movies, poems, slides, stamps, and videos are all full of instructional potential. A teacher's (or a student's) attic or basement will often yield forgotten heirlooms, artifacts, gadgets, photographs, newspapers, and relics that can make lessons come alive and give them a personal touch.

Textbooks

Most states in the United States allow schools to select textbooks from an authorized list. Most provinces in Canada insist that the textbooks used in schools be written and published in Canada. New Zealand, by contrast, encourages schools and teachers to search worldwide for the best texts and reading material for their curricula, while conducting national competitions for excellent, locally developed materials (Mabbett, 1990).

> It sometimes seems to me that a pestilence has struck the human race in its most distinctive faculty—that is, the use of words. It is a plague affecting language, revealing itself as a loss of cognition and immediacy, an automatism that tends to level out all expression into the most generic, anonymous, and abstract formulas, to dilute meanings, to blunt the edge of expressiveness, extinguishing the spark that shoots out from the collision of words and new circumstances.
>
> At this point, I don't wish to dwell on the possible sources of this epidemic, whether they are to be sought in politics, ideology, bureaucratic uniformity, the monotony of the mass media, or the way the schools dispense the culture of the mediocre. What interests me are the possibilities of health. Literature, and perhaps literature alone, can create the antibodies to fight this plague in language.
>
> Italo Calvino (1988, p. 56)

In recommending texts and other reading material, planners need to pay attention to a number of factors. Many of these are listed in Table 8-3. One criterion that deserves special attention is readability. If the texts are written at too high a reading-grade level, pupil frustration will result. Typically, a Grade 8 classroom will contain a range of eight grades in reading level, that is, Grade 4 to Grade 12; a Grade 4 class will range from Grade 2 to Grade 6, and so on. The "smog readability formula" is a simple formula for estimating the readability of a work. This is how to use it: (1) Take 10 consecutive sentences from near the beginning, 10 from near the middle, and 10 from near the end of the work. (2) Count the number of words in these 30 sentences that contain 3 or more syllables. (3) Calculate the square root of this number. (4) Add 3. This statistic is an estimate of the reading grade level (McLaughlin, 1969).

Readability, however, is not just a matter of length of words and sentences. Familiarity with content radically enhances readability. A Grade 4 student who is a baseball fanatic may be able to read text about baseball written at the Grade 12 level. Readability is also enhanced by careful use of text layout, subheadings, bold print, and good illustrations with clear labels and captions (Hartley, 1978). The instructional value of a text also depends on the author's ability to help the reader connect new ideas with those previously learned; to insert thought-provoking questions at appropriate points; and to use structural devices such as introductions, conclusions, and topic sentences (Armbruster & Anderson, 1991).

More than three hundred years ago, the great Czech educator Johannes Comenius noted that "Children (even from their infancy almost) are delighted

Table 8-3   *Some Criteria for Selection of Textbooks*

Production criteria

Are the paper, cover, and binding of good quality?

Are the print and layout readable and attractive?

Is the price reasonable?

Organization

Is there effective use of helpful subheadings?

Does each chapter or section have an overview or summary?

Does each chapter have prequestions or postquestions?

Are there useful end-of-chapter exercises?

Are there sufficient illustrations, tables, figures, and diagrams?

Are they helpful and conveniently located in the text?

Are the table of contents and index adequate?

Are references and bibliography adequate?

Could the text be used for self-instruction?

Style and content

Is the writing style clear, unpretentious, and free of unnecessary jargon?

Are new or unfamiliar terms defined? Is there a glossary?

Does the content match the program objectives?

Are the style and content interesting?

Are there plenty of examples?

Is the content logically sequenced?

Is the content accurate, comprehensive, current, and scholarly?

Is the content acceptable in terms of community values?

Is the content accurate, unbiased, and balanced in its treatment of women, minorities, and ideological and value issues?

with pictures" (Heinick, Molenda, & Russel, 1989, p. 75). Illustrations and diagrams are particularly helpful for poor readers and those with little prior knowledge (Kozma, 1991). Too much or too little realism in illustrations may affect achievement adversely. A good line drawing may often be more effective than a photograph (Heinich, Molenda, & Russel, 1989). Color does not seem to be important in textbooks (Van Houte Walters, Kerstjens, & Verhagen, 1990), but overall interest value is (Garner, Alexander, Gillingham, Kulikowich, & Brown, 1991).

Another important criterion for instructional materials is absence of bias. Textbooks have been frequently and justly criticized as major repositories of racial, ethnic, religious, political, and gender bias (McDiarmid & Pratt, 1971). Sometimes this bias is overt, by use, for example of epithets such as "savage" to describe

> The failure to present the meaning of mathematics is analogous to teaching students how to read musical notation without allowing them to play the music. . . . The traditional curriculum has been reproduced in thousands of textbooks. The strongest reaction induced by the traditional texts is that they are insufferably dull. Most textbook writers seem to believe that scientific writing must be cold, spiritless, mechanical and dry. . . . Textbook writers also seem to take inordinate pride in brevity, which can often be interpreted as incomprehensibility. . . . Brevity in mathematical exposition is the soul of witlessness and obscurity.
>
> Morris Kline (1974, p. 15)

North American Indians. Sometimes it is more subtle, when, for example, whites "kill" Indians, but Indians "murder" whites. A simple and often quite revealing method known as ECO Analysis (Pratt, 1971, 1983a) for assessing this kind of bias can be performed as follows: (1) Choose the subject of interest, for example, people of color, women, the elderly. (2) Note all of the evaluative terms that are used to describe this group (typically adjectives like "wise" and "barbarous" and nouns like "expert" and "extremist"). (3) Count the total number of terms that are positive and negative. (4) Calculate the percentage of the evaluative terms that are positive. This provides a rough index of evaluation, 50 being neutral or balanced, a lower score being negative, and a higher score positive.

Sometimes bias is expressed by omission, as when the contributions of black soldiers in the Revolutionary War are ignored, or when historical instances of persecution of minorities are omitted. Sometimes it is bias by lack of balance, as when illustrations in medical settings show all the nurses as female and all the doctors as male. And sometimes the bias is extremely subtle and ideological, as when textbooks present the study of science as a linear, objective, product-oriented search for truth. We do not know exactly how much influence textbooks have on student attitudes. There is not much evidence on this point. But advertisers believe that words affect the attitudes of consumers, and corporations are willing to back that belief with millions of dollars. The point is, however, that, regardless of whether biased textbooks affect pupils' attitudes or not, bias in textbooks is offensive in itself. It is repugnant per se. It is reprehensible in any materials or media intended for educational purposes to put down, belittle, discount, diminish, disparage, ignore, or patronize any group of human beings.

Some teachers undoubtedly rely excessively on textbooks to structure their curriculum, although this is not as widespread as is commonly thought (Freeman & Porter, 1989). Despite their known faults, good textbooks are invaluable learning tools. They are relatively cheap, portable, lightweight, can store enormous amounts of information, do not require electricity, and can be used at the student's own pace.

Literature used most widely in Grades 7–12

1963	1988
Macbeth	Romeo and Juliet
Julius Caesar	Macbeth
Silas Marner	Huckleberry Finn
Our Town	To Kill a Mockingbird
Great Expectations	The Pearl
Hamlet	The Scarlet Letter
A Tale of Two Cities	Of Mice and Men
The Scarlet Letter	Lord of the Flies

Literature survey (1989)

It is worth spending time in careful review and selection of texts. Table 8-3 shows some main criteria for evaluating textbooks. Many of these criteria will also apply to other kinds of print material.

Audiovisual materials

The quantity of audiovisual material available to teachers today is staggering. It includes pictures, overhead transparencies, slides, film, videotape, and audiotape. The latest videodisk technology allows the storage of 30,000 frames on a single disk. State-of-the-art video projectors can take input from a videotape or videodisk player or a computer and project it into a crisp image the size of a classroom wall, even in partial darkness.

Despite the quantity of materials available, they are not generally very widely used by teachers. A study of 545 teachers in Fort Worth showed that the medium teachers used most frequently was overhead transparencies, which the average teacher in the study claimed to use "a few times a month." Least used were 35 mm slides, for which the average response was midway between "a few times a year or less" and "never" (Seidman, 1986).

The research evidence on the effectiveness of media-based instruction is less encouraging than that for many other instructional innovations. A meta-analysis by Cohen, Ebeling, and Kulik (1981) of 64 studies of media-based instruction in college courses found a mean effect of .15, a small but positive effect. Willett, Yamashita, and Anderson (1983) found the mean effect on student achievement of 75 studies of media-based instruction in elementary and secondary schools was −.03, a trivial but negative effect.

Table 8-4   *Checklist for Evaluation of Film*

Title _____

☐ Film _____ ☐ Video_____ ☐ Videodisc_____

Producer _____

Supplier_____

Price: Rental_____Purchase_____

Running time_____

Film content_____

Relevance to course or program_____

Appropriateness for audience_____

Accuracy and currency of content_____

Interest_____

Production quality_____

Color, tone, light, and contrast_____

Sound, narration and background music_____

Freedom from bias_____

Teacher's guide, if provided _____

Overall judgment_____

Recommended action_____

Date Viewed _____

Evaluator_____

(Kemp & Smellie, 1989; Heinich, Molenda, & Russel, 1989)

It is beyond the resources of most teachers and curriculum planners to review all of the audiovisual material available for any given curriculum. This is not a reason to neglect film resources. If films are used as entertainment, students will develop, at best, shallow representations of the information presented; but if they watch film with a purpose, more detailed processing of the information will occur (Kozma, 1991). Fortunately, there are many sources of information on and reviews of instructional films. Some of these are listed in Appendix C. One particularly valuable evaluation source is the EPIE Institute (Educational Projects Information Exchange, P.O. Box 839, Water Mill, NY 11976), a nonprofit agency that evaluates instructional materials, equipment, and systems. It publishes two monthly newsletters, *EPIEgram: Materials* and *EPIEgram: Equipment*. It also reviews educational software and instructional equipment and conducts in-service workshops on materials selection.

Instructional software

There are few curriculum areas for which no computer software exists. The quality of instructional software varies at least as much as that of textbooks. Table 8-5 shows some criteria for evaluating instructional software. Some sources of software reviews are listed in Appendix C.

Teacher-made and student-made materials

It is often difficult to find commercially produced materials that exactly match instructional needs. Although the production of educational materials is labor-intensive, many teachers do produce large amounts of such material, in the form of worksheets, handouts, overhead transparencies, bulletin board displays, and so on. Kemp and Smellie's text, *Planning, Producing, and Using Instructional Media* (1989) is an extremely practical and detailed guide to the creation of teaching materials. A widely overlooked source of excellent learning materials is students themselves. Having a group of students collaborate to produce a video, a set of color slides, a brief computer program, an anthology of poems on a particular theme, or a cutaway display model, will not only provide materials for future use, but can also be a highly effective learning experience.

EQUIPMENT

Instructional and classroom equipment ranges from pencils to pianos, from microscopes to tachistoscopes, from bulletin boards to Bunsen burners. It includes stationary equipment like parallel bars and pottery kilns, and movable equipment like violins and nerf balls. There are far fewer sources of evaluative information on instructional equipment than on instructional materials. Perhaps for this reason, much classroom equipment is badly designed, poorly manufactured, and overpriced. For example, Seymour (1937) showed more than fifty years ago that the easiest writing to read is dark letters on a light surface, but schools continue to install chalkboards that are black.

The range of equipment used varies greatly by school subject. Such areas as art, science, and physical education make heavy equipment demands. California's handbook for physical education lists more than sixty kinds of equipment for physical education, from air pumps and balance beams to volleyballs and whistles (California State Department of Education, 1986). In such fields as

Table 8-5   *Criteria for Instructional Computer Software*

Title _____

Version_____

Disc size_____

Source_____

Length (completion time) Range _____Average_____

Subject_____

Grade/ability level_____

Required hardware_____

Required memory_____

Required software_____

Field test data_____

Instructional techniques_____

Objectives _____

Prerequisites: Reading ability, knowledge, vocabulary_____

_____

Content _____

_____

Is content accurate?_____

Is content unbiased?_____

Are implicit values acceptable?_____

Is purpose of program clear? _____

Is program relevant to the curriculum?_____

Is program appropriate for the students?_____

Does program achieve its purpose?_____

Is presentation clear?_____

Is level of difficulty appropriate?_____

Are graphics, color, and sound appropriate?_____

Is material interesting? _____

Table 8-5 *(Continued)*

Are students creatively engaged?_____

Can students control the program?_____

Is feedback to students used effectively?_____

Is learning generalizable?_____

Is program self-paced?_____

Can student enter at appropriate point?_____

Are program and manual user-friendly? _____

Is organization of content logical and pedagogically sound?_____

Are user support materials adequate?_____

Is software teacher-friendly?_____

Is it easily integrated into the curriculum?_____

Can it be used with small and large groups and individuals?_____

Does program store information about student performance?_____

Is the program reliable?_____

How much student and teacher time does the program consume?_____

(A fuller version of these criteria can be found in International Council for Computers in Education [1982] and Owston [1987].)

technical education, maintenance of equipment can be a major expense; but keep in mind that students can share responsibility for sharpening, storing, and cleaning tools. Areas such as language arts and mathematics have traditionally been more paper- and print-oriented, but this is changing in the hands of teachers who recognize the importance of a variety of stimuli in teaching all subjects.

Attention also needs to be paid to classroom furniture. Precise ergonomic criteria have been developed for office furniture. A properly designed office chair, for instance, has a backrest that supports the lower back; the seat curves downwards at the front edge; the fabric of the seat is breathable; the height of the seat allows the legs to cross under the desk; seat height can be adjusted so that the highest point is just below the kneecap of the user when standing; when sitting, the feet rest flat on the floor or on a footrest (Stones, 1989). By contrast, the typical pupil's desk forces the child's trunk into an acute angle with the thighs, putting pressure on the intestines and the lower back (Scriven, B., 1975), while 75 percent of the total body weight is borne by the tissue over a 10 cm^2 area of bone (Dunn, 1987). The edge of the seat cuts into the lower thigh; desks are all of standard size, despite the wide variation in pupil size at a given age;

Table 8-6   *Criteria for Evaluation of Instructional Equipment*

Physical characteristics
Size, weight, portability
Power consumption
Stability, fragility, noisiness
Safety features and hazards

Operating criteria
Clear and complete instructions
Ease and convenience of use
Operator prerequisites or training
Usability by students without supervision?
Usability by several students simultaneously?
Time to assemble, disassemble
Compatibility with other equipment and materials
Expandability

Costs
Price and per-student cost
Additional equipment or materials needed
Facility requirements
Operational life and obsolescence
Durability, maintenance required
Anticipated cost of repair and parts replacement
Warranty
Risk of theft

and their design often overlooks the fact that children at a given age are increasing in height by about 1 cm per decade (Helmuth, 1982).

Table 8-6 shows some criteria that may be used in evaluating and selecting instructional equipment.

FACILITIES

The principal teaching facility is the classroom, but it is not the only one. The school library and resource center are other teaching spaces. So are the gymnasium, the basketball court, the schoolyard, the outdoor studies center, and the local museum. If a physical education program is planned that involves public displays, it may be necessary to set specifications for the sound system, spectator accommodation, fire regulations, balconies, stages, instructors' offices, storage

─── **Facility requirements for a photography program** ───

1. **Darkrooms.** Six individual rooms each approx. four feet by six feet, leading into a common processing room. Darkrooms require two double-outlet 110V electrical outlets, and one white room light on a switch.

2. **Processing room** of twelve feet by twelve feet requires four double-outlet 110V electrical outlets, sink with hot and cold running water, a work bench, tempered water, a white room light, a (number 13) safelight, and an exhaust fan.

3. **A work area** and classroom of 20 feet by 40 feet equipped with ten lab benches and twenty stools, and ten 110V–15A outlets and one 220V–30A outlet.

John Perrins (1991, p. 15)

areas, changing rooms, drying rooms, washrooms, shower rooms, traffic flow, fire exits, and community access. In the discussion that follows, we shall focus primarily on the classroom.

As human beings, we are profoundly affected by the environments in which we live. "We shape our buildings," Winston Churchill once said, "and afterwards our buildings shape us." Environmental effects are the more significant for being largely unconscious. It is one of the roles of the curriculum planner to bring unconscious factors to consciousness in the minds of teachers. It is rarely possible to change architectural features, once built, to suit a particular curriculum, but certain aspects of the environment can be altered. Some aspects discussed in this section are layout, noise, lighting, temperature, and decor.

Classroom layout

Classrooms are crowded places. The most spacious schools allow up to 200 square feet of floor space per pupil, the most crowded as little as 70 square feet. In a typical classroom, the child has an average of from 20 to 50 square feet of floor space, more than in a crowded train, but much less than in an office or home.

The most effective use of space is often found in primary-level classrooms. There are areas where children can work independently, at a table, in an armchair, at a workstation, at a sandtable, at a water center, and so on. There are groups of seats and tables where small groups can work collaboratively, and there is a large carpeted area where the whole class can gather. Traffic patterns are taken into account, so that the art area is near the sink, and traffic to and from doors is minimally distracting. Primary teachers also tend to use the outdoors, weather permitting, as an extension of the teaching space.

The ideal environment for young children appears to be one that is physically stimulating. This is particularly important for high-risk children. Maria Montessori designed an environment for her underprivileged Italian children that contained much large-scale equipment such as ladders, stairs, platforms, and movable furniture (Montessori, 1964). Many children today spend much of their preschool years in front of a television set. The presence or absence of a stimulating environment in the early years appears to have been a major factor in the finding by Ramey and Smith (1976) and Ramey and Campbell (1979) that high-risk children reared at home for their first three years lost ground in their cognitive development relative to matched children in daycare.

> I used to go to nursery school but now I go to day care 'cause my mom works. Everything's the same 'cept I get to eat and go to the bathroom a lot more now and we don't line up any more. And the hamster had babies.
>
> Julie, age 4 (Greenman, 1988, p. 37)

Unfortunately, the flexible use of space in the early years is not maintained. The pattern of rows of seats becomes more entrenched with each grade level. In universities the seats are typically bolted to the floor. In fact, throughout history and throughout the world, this is the dominant pattern of classroom layout. It is neat and orderly, almost military in appearance. It is a pattern of authority in which one person, who is superior, speaks to a group of people who are subordinate. The arrangement encourages eye contact only between pupils and teacher; it provides maximum physical and social separation between pupils. The layout reflects a world view that is sharply focused and task-oriented, a world in which people work individualistically and as subordinate to authority. Teachers need to ask themselves whether this is the world they want their students to develop or to live in. A further point worth mentioning is that this model of focus, task orientation, authority, and individuation is a highly masculine model. It is not a model that reflects such characteristics of a feminine phenomenology as caring, collaboration, diffusion of focus, and concern with process (Noddings, 1984).

> Some few years ago I was looking about the school supply stores in the city, trying to find desks and chairs which seemed thoroughly suitable from all points of view—artistic, hygienic, and educational—to the needs of the children. We had a great deal of difficulty in finding what we needed, and finally one dealer, more intelligent than the rest, made this remark: "I am afraid we have not what you want. You want something at which the children may work; these are all for listening." That tells the story of the traditional education.
>
> John Dewey (1902, p. 31)

Classroom layout needs to be driven by the curriculum. A curriculum that uses a variety of instructional modes and strategies will require a flexible teaching space. Classroom discussion requires maximum eye contact among participants; film requires that everyone can see the screen; writing requires a firm, nonglare surface in front of the student; groupwork requires furniture that can be easily moved.

Size of instructional group

Size of group is an important factor in the planning of instructional facilities, so this is an appropriate point to mention the issue of class and school size. The effects of class size have been examined in many studies over the past twenty years. In the first major synthesis of the available research, Glass and Smith (1978) found a difference of only 6 percentile points in the mean achievement of students in classes of 20 versus those in classes of 40. Other studies have found similarly small effects (Dennis, 1987; Jarvis, Whitehurst, Gampert, & Schulman, 1987; Levin et al., 1987; Robinson, 1990; Slavin, 1986, 1989b).

But these early studies have been rendered somewhat outdated by a large-scale, experimental study conducted in 76 elementary schools in Tennessee. This is a longitudinal, 4-year study, following 6,500 pupils from kindergarten to the end of Grade 3. It compares the achievement of pupils in classes averaging 15 with those in classes averaging 22. The results for the first two years of the study were reported in 1990 (Finn & Achilles, 1990; Finn, Achilles, Bain, Folger, Johnston, Lintz, & Word, 1990). The differences in achievement between large and small classes were statistically significant. Children in smaller classes gained the equivalent of 1.5 months in reading and 2.5 months in mathematics more than their peers in larger classes. The differences were twice as great for minority pupils than for whites. For suburban white students, size of class made little or no difference. Class size did not appear to make any difference in motivation or self-concept. While these differences are important, it is worth noting that reducing class size is an extremely expensive way of improving achievement. The results reported above are lower than those that have been obtained by the introduction of peer tutoring, computer-assisted instruction, or mastery learning, all of which are considerably less expensive (Kulik & Kulik, 1989).

One finding on which the research is unanimous, however, is that teachers prefer smaller classes. The amount of marking, the attention needed for organization and administration, and the level of stress increase with the size of the instructional group. The mental health and job satisfaction of teachers are important considerations, and for these reasons the issue of class size cannot be debated solely in terms of student achievement.

School size is also a subject of some importance. As Husén points out (1985), school size has tended to increase throughout the industrialized world. Studies conducted thirty years ago by Barker and Gump (1954) and by Smith (1961) suggested that the most appropriate size for a secondary school was about 700 students, and that there were few gains to be realized in per-pupil costs and significant educational disadvantages in raising school size above 800. Unfortunately, Barker and Gump were less influential than James Conant, the famous president of Harvard University, who in his book *The American High School Today*, recommended closure of all high schools graduating fewer than 100 students a year (Conant, 1959). It was at this time that construction began on the mega-schools that still exist today. In 1965 E. P. Willems summarized the research on size of employment settings. The evidence indicated that in smaller settings, people quit their jobs less often, are more punctual, take more responsibility, demonstrate more leadership, take more interest in the organization, interact more with one another, have greater group cohesiveness, and obtain more satisfaction. Many studies since that time have found in favor of smaller schools. In large schools dropout rates are higher and extracurricular participation is lower (Schoggen & Schoggen, 1988). In his massive study of schools, John Goodlad concluded, "It is not impossible to have a good large school; it simply is more difficult" (Goodlad, 1984, p. 309). Barker argues that many currently popular strategies for instructional effectiveness, such as peer tutoring and cross-age grouping, have been pioneered in small rural schools, despite the efforts of urban bureaucracies to close them down (Barker, 1986).

The younger the pupils, the smaller the school needs to be. Mortimore (1988) found that the most effective junior schools in London had about 160 pupils. In a study of childcare centers, Moore (1987) found that the maximum desirable size was 60–75 children. In centers of more than 60 children, there tended to be excessive emphasis on rules and routines; play areas were low on organization, variety and number of activities; children tended to be overwhelmed by the numbers of staff and children and the size of the space, and were less often observed to be enthusiastically interested or involved. Larger centers, however, could be effective if they were subdivided on a village or campus plan.

Decor

In one of his books on educational architecture, Robert Sommer (1974) says that he had taught for twenty years in universities and never once found himself in a classroom that contained a single picture. He found that reactions of students and colleagues were uniformly positive to introducing artwork into the classroom (so much so that most of the works were purloined within a few weeks).

Many teachers do spend considerable time and energy decorating their classrooms. Posters and other display materials that support instruction are readily available from suppliers. Bulletin board displays can reinforce and add interest to classroom instruction. They are time-consuming to construct, but this work can be assigned to groups of students as a project. It has also been noted in the research that the most effective teachers tend to display students' work—a good way of providing models and acknowledging success (Teddlie et al., 1989). If this is done, it is important that all students be recognized occasionally, so that display does not become the perquisite of a small elite.

The "affective decor" of a classroom is also important. Santrock (1976) found that first- and second-grade children persisted longer at tasks in classrooms that were decorated with happy pictures and in which they were told happy stories and encouraged to verbalize happy thoughts.

Lighting, temperature, and air quality

Lighting consultants have long known that if bars are brightly lit and noisy, there will be a quick turnover of customers; if they are sound-absorbing and dark, customers will stay longer and couples will sit closer, making more efficient use of space (Sommer, 1969). Light, however, has more than social significance; it is a critical variable in the biological environment. During this century, people in the Western world have been conducting a biological experiment on themselves. They have stopped living in the sunlight under which they evolved for millions of years and instead live under artificial light. One effect of this is to reduce the intake of ultraviolet light.

Too much ultraviolet can result in skin cancer, but too little results in potential vitamin D deficiency. Sunlight is a much more important source of vitamin D than is food. Deprivation of ultraviolet light leads within three months to impairment of the ability of the intestinal mucosa to absorb calcium (Wurtman, 1975a, b). Rickets, tooth decay, and osteoporosis are among the conditions resulting from inadequate calcium absorption. People living in northern climates are particularly susceptible to the effects of lack of sunlight during winter months. The amount of sunlight in northern parts of the United States is one-third of the national average, and the level in December is one-fifteenth the level in the month of June.

In a national survey of nutritional levels of Canadians, it was found that potential vitamin D deficiency was one of the major areas of malnutrition among the young. By their teens, 33 percent of those studied had inadequate levels of potential vitamin D, and another 46 percent were found to have less than adequate levels (Nutrition Canada, 1973). Whether or not a classroom has windows is not relevant, because ultraviolet light is blocked by window glass. In northern parts of the Soviet Union, children are given weekly doses of ultraviolet light. The same practice was followed in Britain during World War II with workers who lived under ground for long periods of time.

A two-year study in Alberta showed that Grade 4 and 6 children in schools illuminated by ultraviolet-enhanced, full-spectrum fluorescent light, as compared with those in schools lit by cool-white fluorescent light or high-pressure sodium vapor lights, had significantly lower rates of tooth decay and classroom noise, and significantly higher rates of attendance, language, mathematics, and overall

> To live in an environment that has to be endured or ignored rather than enjoyed is to be diminished as a human being.
>
> Sinclair Gauldie (1969, p. 182)

achievement, and height and weight gains (Hathaway, Hargreaves, Thompson, & Novitsky, 1992). Differences in absenteeism as high as 6.9 versus 16.4 days per year were observed between some of the experimental and control groups, and differences of 0.17 versus 1.53 in decayed tooth surfaces were observed over two years. Annual savings resulting from better lighting were estimated at $203 per pupil in reduced absenteeism and $118 in reduced dental costs. At its most conservative, this study suggests that if lighting cannot be changed, teachers need to try to ensure that on sunny winter days students get outside for at least fifteen minutes.

The illumination level, or brightness (that is, the stimulation of the photoreceptors in the retina), in most artificially lighted rooms is typically between 50 and 100 foot-candles. Brighter levels of illumination are required for reading fine print, and for such activities as sewing and drafting. Insufficient illumination, glare, reflection, shadows, low contrast, and flickering can all affect human performance (Knirk, 1987). Glare is produced by gloss paints, reflective floor surfaces, polished wood or plastic furniture, bright colors, high contrast between light and dark surfaces, excessively bright lighting, and sunlight in rooms with windows facing south. Glare forces the eyes to keep readjusting, distracts the learners, makes it difficult for the teacher to see the students, makes gymnasium activities hazardous, and accelerates fatigue (Smith, 1974).

Color of paint is one of the most cheaply controlled elements in the classroom environment. Yet many schools appear to be painted in the dingiest possible colors. There is some evidence that people concentrate and learn best in rooms painted in pleasing pastels—yellow, rose, blue, and green (McGuffey, 1982; Sharpe, 1974). The nature of the curriculum, not the cost of paint, should determine colors in learning spaces. Blue-green is preferred for operating rooms because it is the complementary color to blood and facilitates vision into surgical wounds (Granville, 1962). Black laboratory benches make it easier to read instruments and check the cleanliness of glassware.

Temperature also affects human performance. Preferred temperature varies with both age and activity. For sedentary activities, adults prefer a temperature of about 73°F whereas preadolescents, who have a higher metabolic rate, prefer about 66°F (McIntyre, 1973). Fifty-five degrees Fahrenheit is more comfortable for strenuous activity. People's perception of temperature is influenced by humidity, air movement, and clothing. Humidity levels of 40–60 percent are ideal; levels above this make cold air feel colder and warm air warmer. The humidity level in the Sahara Desert averages about 15 percent. Levels lower than this are sometimes found in schools during the winter months.

The fuel crises of the 1970s resulted in enhanced methods of sealing buildings. In the process, fresh air was sealed out. Sealed in, and in the case of organisms, breeding in the uncleaned screens and condensation trays of ventilation and heating or cooling systems, were fungi, algae, bacteria, viruses, glass fiber particles, tobacco smoke, dust, numerous allergens, carcinogenic and otherwise dangerous chemicals, carbon monoxide, nitrogen dioxide, formaldehyde, and other gases. The result: sick building syndrome (Brief & Bernath, 1988; Environmental Protection Agency, 1988). Another feature of sealed buildings, especially those with metal ductwork and large quantities of plastic or metal furniture and office equipment, is that the proportion of negative ions in the air tends to become depleted. Negative ions are a stimulant—they are found in large quantities in such environments as waterfalls, beaches, and fountains. Although the research is not yet definitive, there is evidence that low levels of negative ions in an environment are associated with headache, nausea, and a general feeling of malaise. Environments rich in negative ions, on the other hand, produce feelings of physical and psychological well-being (Hawkins, 1981; Lips, Salawu, Kamber, & Probert, 1987; Testone, 1986; Yates, Gray, Misiaszek, & Wolman, 1986).

Noise

In the urban environment in which most of the world's population lives, noise is almost never absent. We are rarely in an environment of total silence, and the ambient noise level seldom drops as low as 10 decibels, about the level of a quiet night in the country. The sounds of the typical home, with heating, cooling, ventilation fans, refrigerator and freezer compressors, and exterior traffic noise, produce an ambient noise level of about 40 decibels. But silence is in any case not an

"They can do wonders with sound-proofing nowadays."

optimal working environment: a background noise level of about 35 decibels produces maximum alertness (Knirk, 1987).

It is generally believed that as the level of distracting noise rises, productive work deteriorates. However, there is some evidence that people differ in their preferred background noise level. Pizzo (1982) found that some sixth graders performed better in a quiet classroom (40–45 decibels) and some in a noisy classroom (75–80 decibels). In a controlled experiment, Slater (1968) found no difference in reading performance of seventh graders in quiet, average, or noisy classrooms. Prolonged exposure to high noise levels, however, does appear to damage the cognitive level, speed of performance, persistence, and auditory discrimination of young children, and to increase their distractibility and learned helplessness (Moore, 1987). In one study of children growing up in thirty-two story apartment buildings adjacent to busy freeways, researchers found the lower the floor, the lower the reading scores (Cohen, Glass, & Singer, 1973). Apart from the long-term effects on children, there is some loss of instructional time in classrooms subject to high external noise, as teachers stop teaching while planes go overhead or trains go by (Weinstein, 1979).

Architects in England have described the ideal educational environment:

> The aim is to produce a building where, for example, discussion in class can be held in a normal conversational voice, where music can be enjoyed pianissimo or fortissimo, where one can use an electric drill or a vaulting horse without spoiling another's efforts to practice on the violin, to hear French verbs on a tape recorder or just to concentrate on a book. In short, the aim is to be able to hear clearly what one needs to hear, and not be distracted by other noises.   (UK, Department of Education and Science, 1975, p. 1)

In practice, this means that learning environments need to be designed with sound-absorbing characteristics such as carpets and upholstered furniture, rather than designing sound-reflecting surfaces and then needing to design remedies to shut out or control unwanted noise. As one authority puts it, "Carpeting is the first line of defense in a school against potentially distracting sounds" (Knirk, 1987, p. 35).

Background music is an environmental factor widely overlooked by educators. Industry discovered in the 1920s that "music while you work" increased productivity. Forty years ago, Hall found that music was of greatest benefit at eighth- and ninth-grade levels, at the beginning of morning and afternoon sessions, and with underachieving students (Hall, 1952). These findings were similar to those of industrial psychologists, who found that music enabled people to achieve more consistently at their potential level. Background music also appears to improve the behavior of hyperactive children (Knirk, 1987). Another use of background music is to control classroom noise. Wilson and Hopkins (1973) conducted an experiment in a number of classrooms, in which a radio tuned to the students' favorite music station played while they were engaged in seat-work and learning tasks. A

Medical school facilities, 1909

California Medical College, Eclectic . . . Laboratory facilities: the school occupies a few neglected rooms on the second floor of a 50-foot building. Its so-called equipment is dirty and disorderly beyond description. Its outfit in anatomy consists of a small box of bones and the dried-up, filthy fragments of a single cadaver. A few bottles of reagents constitute the chemical laboratory. A cold and rusty incubator, a single microscope, and a few unlabeled wet specimens, etc., form the so-called equipment for pathology and bacteriology. Clinical facilities: there is no dispensary and no access to the County Hospital. The school is a disgrace to the state whose laws permit its existence.

From a site evaluation by Abraham Flexner (Flexner, 1910)

---

microphone was hung 8 feet above the floor, leading to a voice-operated relay that was set to turn the radio off whenever the noise level in the classroom exceeded 70 decibels. Within a short period, the noise levels in the classrooms had reduced to a level consistently below 70 decibels.

Safety

Safety is an important consideration in the design and maintenance of educational environments. Classroom and playground furniture and equipment should have rounded edges. There should be no loose or exposed bolts, nuts, screws, nails, hooks, wire ends, or other hardware. Crush and pinch points should be covered. Wooden surfaces should have no splinters, cracks, rotting, or sharp ends. Metal structures should have no sharp edges, holes, gaps, or open tubing ends. Gaps should be smaller than three inches to prevent a child's head from entering and larger than ten inches so that the whole body can go through. Slides and climbers should have appropriate railings. Play areas should be bounded by fences or barriers and kept free of litter, glass, sharp objects, or animal feces (Greenman, 1988; Weinstein & David, 1987). Surfaces should be as soft as possible: a 12-inch fall on concrete or asphalt can produce an impact force of 50G, sufficient to give a child a concussion; it would take a fall of 48 inches to produce the same impact force on standard rubber tile (Mason, 1982).

Facilities outside the classroom

I know a school situated 200 yards from a swamp. Only once in twenty years has a biology class visited the swamp, and that was when they were taken there by a guest speaker. Many teachers will be reassured by Peter Mortimore's (1988) finding that the most successful schools in London, England, were more likely to make use of frequent field trips.

It happens that there is a useful handbook of out-of-school facilities that is readily available to every teacher. It is called the *Yellow Pages*. The facilities available are, in fact, far more than we need. For example, if you were teaching a unit on plane geometry, there could be considerable benefit in taking the students to a construction site, a cemetery, a lumber yard, a printing plant, a race track, a vacant lot, a graphic arts studio, an architect's office, an airport control tower . . . the list is almost endless.

Role of library resource center in a history program

The library resource center plays a fundamental role in history and contemporary studies. Indeed, most of the activities recommended in the guideline are related to the use of resources. Students must develop the learning and research skills necessary to use materials effectively, if resource-based strategies are to succeed. Focusing on the appropriate cognitive-skills objectives included in this guideline, the teacher of history and contemporary studies, in partnership with the teacher-librarian, should develop a sequential program for teaching these skills. Teachers should ensure that the skills are learned not in isolation but within the context of meaningful activities derived from the history and contemporary studies program. Students should be given opportunities to develop resource-related skills, not only with traditional print and audio-visual materials, but also with those of the new technologies.

Ontario Ministry of Education,
Curriculum Guideline, History and Contemporary Studies (1986, p. 31)

In addition, there are resources within the school that are logistically much easier to access, and the neglect of which is thus even more surprising. Most educational jurisdictions publish documents on the use of the school library–resource center. But these injunctions are rarely referred to in curricula. It is not enough to assume that curriculum users will automatically use such resources. Curriculum documents need to remind teachers frequently that school librarians can provide important services to teachers and students. One such service is advice on curriculum planning and resource utilization. Some of the ideas in a rich array of suggestions for school librarians by Margrabe (1981) include awarding ice cream prizes for the best mobile, model, poster, and so on; student-of-the-week awards; treasure hunts; ongoing board games; displays of summer souvenirs; a comic book exchange; story time for young children; and slide-tape presentations.

HUMAN RESOURCES

Education is a process in which the interaction among human beings is of paramount importance. The designers of a complete curriculum therefore take the trouble to reflect on the attributes and responsibilities of the people who will be involved in the implementation and delivery of a curriculum.

My country is a country of teachers. It is therefore a country of peace. We discuss our successes and failures in complete freedom. Because our country is a country of teachers, we closed the army camps and our children go with books under their arms, not with rifles on their shoulders. We believe in dialogue, in agreement, in reaching a consensus. We reject violence. Because my country is a country of teachers, we believe in convincing our opponents, not defeating them. We prefer raising the fallen to crushing them, because we believe that no one possesses the absolute truth.

Oscar Arias Sanchez (Costa Rica), Nobel Prize for Peace, 1987. (Arias Sanchez, 1988, p. 260)

Defining teacher qualities

When the National Science Foundation asked a number of "breakthrough" scientists to identify the critical factor in their education, they almost uniformly answered, "Intimate association with a great, inspiring teacher" (Fuller, 1970, p. 82B). From case studies, we know that an outstanding teacher in the early grades can have an impact that can be clearly identified thirty years later (Pedersen, Faucher, & Eaton, 1978). A good teacher will transcend a mediocre curriculum, while a mediocre teacher will undermine the best-designed curriculum. Curriculum planners have little control over who will ultimately teach the curricula they plan. The planners need therefore to think about and specify the qualities needed by those who will teach or otherwise be involved with the curriculum. The responsibilities of teachers and implementers should also be specified.

Recent studies of teaching have shown that a sophisticated knowledge of subject matter is often crucial for teachers at every educational level. Karen Karp (1988) examined the differences in classroom behavior and effects on students of

Table 8-7   *Average Salaries of Public School Teachers, 1990 (in US dollars)*

Canada	42,075
France	33,574
Sweden	32,525
United States	26,230
Japan	19,410
Britain	16,525
Italy	15,738

(OERI, 1990a; Bishop, 1989b; Statistics Canada, 1987)

elementary school teachers who possessed and who lacked confidence and competence in mathematics. The expert teachers tended to give more elaborate, re-
sourceful, and flexible lessons that included varied examples, careful directions,
frequent evaluations, and clear focus on the content. They were able to guide students to creative and divergent problem solving and independent thinking. The
teachers with negative attitudes to mathematics tended to exhibit novice teaching
behavior regardless of their actual years of experience; they concentrated on the
ability to produce "one right answer"; their instruction was based on rules and
memorization and made heavy use of worksheets; they tended to encourage passivity, dependence, and learned helplessness. In both cases, the teachers passed on
their own attitudes toward mathematics to their students. In another study of elementary mathematics teaching, Stein, Baxter, and Leinhardt (1990) pointed to
"the unique problems that arise when an unprepared teacher communicates ill-
understood concepts to elementary students" (p. 639). Inadequate background in
mathematics led to a narrowing of instruction in three ways: "the lack of provision of groundwork for future learning in this area, overemphasis of limited truths,
and missed opportunities for fostering meaningful connections between key
concepts and representations" (p. 660). We could say that both mathphilia and
mathphobia are infectious conditions and are contracted by students from teachers. This is a somewhat sobering thought when one considers the significance of
competence in mathematics in the contemporary world and the low level of mathematics achievement normally required of elementary school teachers.

In the late 1980s some American states, facing a shortage of teachers and
high costs of teacher education, began to authorize the employment of teachers
without professional qualifications. How important is teacher education? There
is a vast critical literature on the shortcomings of teacher education. However,
in a study of outstanding teachers in the Chicago community college system,
researchers found that of the twenty-five instructors named by colleagues, superiors, and students as outstanding, twenty-four had received formal teacher education (Guskey, 1983). Pamela Grossman has recently published case studies of

academically well-qualified teachers who were teaching without having received any pedagogical education. She found that, lacking other models, they based their teaching on their own experiences in school and university, even when working with students whose backgrounds were radically different from their own. Not knowing how to plan, or even believing in the value of planning, they felt that their own expertise and interest in literature would be sufficient to teach effectively. The results were a shock to them. "I can't believe they can't get this," said one. "They hated it," said another. "It was horrible. I was really scared" (Grossman, 1989, pp. 195, 198). Here again, however, it is worth remembering that it is not the paper qualifications that are important, but the relevant skills and qualities possessed by teachers that are significant.

Teacher responsibilities

One sure way of helping a curriculum self-destruct is to tell teachers that the new curriculum requires no more work than the old one; then, when teachers embark on the new curriculum, they find that they have acquired a host of new tasks and responsibilities. For this reason, all the significant responsibilities of the teacher should be clearly and candidly described in the curriculum. An example is shown on page 284.

The role of administrators

The literature on curriculum implementation is full of references to the critical role of administrators in successful implementation of curriculum innovations. Despite this, their role is rarely discussed in curriculum documents. Ignoring administrators in curriculum documents is not a promising way to recruit their support! A rare example of attention to this area is provided by the Manitoba *English Language Curriculum Guide* (Education Manitoba, 1981), in a section entitled "Implications of the Program for Administrators." The guide reminds administrators of the importance of supporting classroom teachers by becoming knowledgeable about language teaching and language development; by encouraging creative and activity-based learning; by supporting professional development and cooperative planning by teachers; and by recognizing the importance of suitable teaching space, library resources, and resource personnel.

Other human resources

The curriculum document provides an opportunity for the planners to remind teachers of all the human resources that are available to assist in the delivery of programs. **Students** themselves are such a resource, and the attention of teachers can be drawn to the benefits of using students as peer tutors, buddies, and experts. **Parents** are an important resource, and every effort should be made to include them in the work of the school. The use of parent volunteers in classrooms has been shown to be related to gains in achievement levels of students (Cussons &

The role of the teacher in the English program

The effective teacher of English accepts certain responsibilities:

— assesses the stage of development of each child and on the basis of this assessment determines the forms of instruction appropriate for him;

— plans language experiences carefully (taking into account the students' development, interests, and needs, both personal and academic), establishes priorities, considers materials, activities, time, and facilities, as well as grouping possibilities;

— stimulates the students' interest in language;

— generates intellectual involvement and enthusiasm for excellence;

— listens, observes, and creates a climate in which students can best develop their skills, take calculated risks, and practice all forms of orderly communication;

— participates actively in students' language experiences, supporting positive attempts, clarifying, pointing up alternatives, etc.;

— is one of the authorities on English to whom students can turn for information;

— uses precise and effective English, and is seen by students to appreciate language, while refraining from imposing personal value systems and tastes;

— assumes all of these roles, growing with experience and making increasingly effective use of support personnel, professional reading, courses, and association with other teachers.

Ontario Ministry of Education, English Intermediate Division (1977)

Hedges, 1978). So has the training of parents to help their children learn to read (Walberg, 1984; Whitehurst et al., 1990). The fully professional childhood educator educates parents as well as their sons and daughters. Workshops can be organized for parents, and requests, rather than merely invitations, issued for their attendance. It is a good idea for each teacher, at the beginning of every year or semester to send to every parent a letter that describes the curriculum, its subject-matter and intentions, the teacher's expectations regarding such matters as attendance and homework, availability of the teacher for consultation by students and parents, and ways in which parents can help their children with their school work. It is also good practice to call each parent once each semester to report on progress, affirm good work by the student, and indicate any ways in which parents can be involved. Parents are often surprised to receive a phone call from the school which is not a message of doom; this is a bias that needs to be redressed. The caring teacher gives parents his or her home phone number; experience shows that this is appreciated by parents; it is rarely used, and still more rarely abused.

> No one becomes a prophet who was not first a shepherd.
>
> Mohammed

Senior citizens are a rich and widely neglected resource. They make excellent tutors, and they often have great expertise in such areas as local history, crafts, and fields in which they spent their working lives. They can provide the experience of interaction with a generation that is unfamiliar to many young people living in nuclear families far away from grandparents. The interaction that school programs can provide is equally enriching to the seniors and helps to mitigate the isolation and marginalization imposed on them in our society. All such programs fuel public involvement in and support for the school. Twin Peaks Middle School in Poway, California, runs a Grandpeople Program for people, most retired, who

are not parents of school children. They help with programs in art, science, reading, and technology. They serve as consultants and confidants to pupils. "The school reports that the elderly participants find their lives revitalized. The teachers observe their students being more courteous and caring. The students express their appreciation for the additional personal attention and help they receive" (Wilson & Corcoran, 1988, p. 112). In some jurisdictions, social service agencies will provide funds to support programs involving senior citizens in the schools, as they recognize the therapeutic value of such activities.

The range of human resources available to schools is amazing—and underutilized. Members of the U.S. Marine Corps serve as volunteer tutors in an elementary school in Arlington, Virginia ("Skeptical third-grader," 1991). Every community has numerous experts, and programs can often benefit significantly by making use of their expertise. It is a minor tragedy when a unit is taught on nuclear physics without inviting a nuclear engineer into the classroom, or a course on poetry to which no practicing poet is invited, or a program on banking which neglects to ask a local banker to speak. It is particularly important that exemplary role models be introduced to students. Some schools, for instance, invite successful women scientists to speak about careers in science for women (in such cases, it is important that they also be effective speakers and that they have a family life outside their career; otherwise students may conclude that there is an exclusive choice between career and family). It is vital in a course for adolescents aimed at responsible parenthood to invite into the class such experts as teenage single mothers for frank and authentic discussion of the consequences of choices regarding pregnancy and parenthood. As mentioned previously, successful programs in such areas as smoking addiction and AIDS education are beginning to show that peers are the most effective kinds of teachers in problematic, value-laden areas. If we are to make any kind of breakthrough in preventing adolescents from addicting themselves to smoking (which, if they begin at 18, by age 30 will provide them with an expectation of life 18 years less than that of non-smokers), then it will probably be by having the instruction conducted by other adolescents (Flay, 1985).

One time something incredible happened. A man from up that way, from Alaska—a mail carrier—did actually give a lesson in geography to a room full of children. And in order to do it properly, what did he have to have— maps and books? Dear Lord, no! He had twelve or so Eskimo dogs, and he had one dog in particular that he wanted particularly to talk about, a dog that was really a great gray wolf. That dog understood the geography of Alaska even better than his master did; and that dog and his master together so impressed the geography of Alaska on those children that their souls and bodies trembled and shook with the power of that experience; and thereafter, to their dying day, that lesson in geography was at least one perfectly real and ecstatic piece of life.

Edward Yeomans (1921, pp. 15–16)

In high school I once took the opposing side in a debate on capital punishment that took my team-mate and me through a local debating contest, then a county competition, and finally a state contest. Clarence Darrow, a Chicago lawyer, had just become quite prominent by successfully defending Loeb and Leopold. . . . In preparation for the debate, I wrote out my basic presentation and sent it to Mr. Darrow for "comments" (never doubting that he would reply!). My rashness paid dividends in the form of a three-page, single-spaced letter, obviously pecked out on a typewriter by Mr. Darrow himself. This "ammunition" wiped out the competition and assured our team of success. (Would that I had had enough vision to have saved that letter!)

Hugh Wood (1990, p. 1)

Organizations that can be of assistance to teachers and students can be listed in the curriculum document, with addresses and telephone numbers. These might include such organizations as the National Clearinghouse for Drug Abuse Information in a health curriculum; the local historical society in a social studies curriculum; the National Council on the Teaching of Mathematics in a math curriculum; the Smithsonian Institution in a science curriculum; and the United Nations Information Office in a curriculum on international relations. The Grade 1 social studies curriculum for the Fort Worth Independent School District (1989) lists thirty-four "Community Resources for Physical and Psychological Safety," including hospitals, social agencies, youth organizations, family services agencies, police departments, and rape crisis centers, together with contact persons and phone numbers.

At some point a curriculum needs to outline legal requirements. For example, if there are physical risks involved, students and their parents should be informed of these risks and told about safety precautions. Instructions should be provided in the curriculum about provision of adequate insurance coverage. Relevant federal and state laws should be accessed and reported. United States law requires that all handicapped children will have the same opportunities as other students in all curriculum areas.

Required permissions can be outlined at this point. A good deal of teacher time can be saved if the curriculum includes sample forms. An example is shown below.

TIME

Time is our most precious resource. It is the only resource that is totally finite. And it is the resource above all others that education consumes. This is the basic rationale for efficient and responsible curriculum planning.

The first draft of a curriculum should show estimates for the allocation and consumption of time. These can be corrected when the curriculum is piloted and field-tested. All of the time used by all of the participants should be calculated.

—————— **Example for parent permission** ——————

Dear Parents:

During the next two months, the grade six class will be involved in a "Growth and Development Unit" as part of the health curriculum. I have previewed a series of videos produced for an audience of nine to twelve-year-olds.

The **Growing Up Series** is designed to help young viewers develop the survival skills they will need to cope with the pressures of puberty and adolescence. **Head Full of Questions, Changes,** and **Especially You** are based on the assumption that sex education involves the whole child and his or her self-concept and body image.

As educators, we believe that the well-informed child with a positive self-concept and a sense of respect for others is in a good position to withstand the uncertainties of adolescence.

During parent-teacher day, on March 8th, the **Growing Up Series** will be available in the science room for parent viewing.

Sincerely,

Cecelia Hill

Please return the section below to the school.

- ❑ I give my permission for _____ to view the **Growing Up Series.**

- ❑ I do not give my permission for _____ to view the **Growing Up Series.**

- ❑ We would be interested in viewing the videos on March 8th.

Signature _____

Hill (1990, p. 11)

For students, this will include time for field trips and homework, as well as in-class time. For teachers, estimates need to be made of time required for preparation, administration, remediation, and marking. The time required of administrators, guest lecturers, tutors, or janitors should also be included. Most official curricula, if they pay attention to this factor at all, indicate only the allocated time. But this is just the tip of the iceberg. The job of the planner is to calculate the size of the whole iceberg!

It is worth noting that the time required for successful learning depends not only on the total time available, but also on how the time is distributed. These factors appear to operate differently depending on what is being learned. In learning to speak a foreign language, for example, it was noted during World War II

Table 8-8 *Time Consumption Summary*

People	Activity	Hours
Students	Instruction	10
	Homework	5
	Field trip	4
	TOTAL	19
Teacher	Instruction	10
	Field trip	4
	Preparation	4
	Administration	2
	Remediation	2
	Marking	1
	TOTAL	23
Volunteer	Field trip	4
	TOTAL	4
Guest lecturer	Lecture	1
	Travel	1
	Preparation	3
	TOTAL	5
Principal	Discussion	1
Janitor	Extra clean-up	1

that high-aptitude learners, if provided with at least six hours of instruction and practice a day, could become fluent in a simple language like Spanish or French in about nine months. However, if the time were reduced by 50 percent, to three hours a day, they never reached fluency (Cleveland, Mangone, & Adams, 1960). This finding has been confirmed by many studies of "core" versus "immersion" foreign language teaching, which suggest that fluency in a foreign language is more likely to result from brief total immersion programs than from prolonged exposure for 20–80 minutes a day (Day & Shapson, 1988; Safty, 1988; Swain & Lapkin, 1983). James Powell (in Robinson, 1992) reports that despite the large funds expended on native American language instruction in recent years, there is no evidence of anyone raised in English recovering fluency in a native language through formal school programs.

On the other hand, there is considerable research supporting the "spacing effect" on learning, particularly on long-term retention (Dempster, 1988). As early as 1913, W. H. Pyle ran an experiment that showed that third-graders drilled in addition once a day for ten days outperformed peers drilled twice a day for five days (Pyle, 1913). Although all the classroom implications of this research are not yet clear, there is evidently a case to be made for periodic and distributed practice and review of important learnings.

At a broader level, it is time that schools reexamined the time structure of the school year, which has remained frozen from the agricultural society of the late nineteenth century. The school year still observed by most jurisdictions produces massive underutilization of plant, excessive competition for part-time work by students during the summer, and alternating overcrowding and underutilization of recreational areas. It severely limits the periods during which families can take vacations together, forcing up prices during school breaks and obliging many workplaces to adjust their production quotas during school vacations.

A different pattern has been adopted in several jurisdictions. For example, in Denver, Colorado, the school year is divided into six terms of forty-two days. Students attend for two terms, and are then on vacation for one term. At any one time, two-thirds of the students are in school and one-third on vacation. In a number of California districts, the "45-15" plan has been adopted, whereby all students, on a staggered basis, are in school for nine weeks and out for three weeks. The schools operate continuously, except for a brief shut-down at Christmas and a two-week period in the summer for maintenance. Achievement and attendance appear to be unaffected by these plans. Student dropout rates, as well as costs for buildings and transportation, decline (Parker, 1986).

COST

Costs loom large in the thinking of most people and organizations. The total cost of elementary and secondary schooling in the United States for the school year 1990–1991 was estimated as $231 billion (OERI, 1990c). As U.S. Senator Everett Dirkson is reported to have said, "Take a billion here, and a billion there, and pretty soon you're talking real money." Costs are the last logistical item to be

Table 8-9   *Official Length of School Year in Different Countries*

Country	Days
Japan	220
Germany	210
USSR (former)	205
England	200
Canada (Ontario)	185
United States (average)	180

(Hlebowitsh, 1988; Rury, 1988)

calculated because every other item carries cost implications. As with time, all of the incurred costs should be shown.

Budgets normally indicate only "add-on" costs, such as equipment and materials, that will have to be especially purchased for the program. It is helpful to separate the "start-up," or capital costs, such as computer hardware, from the operating costs, such as paper, that will be repeated each time the course is offered. Thoughtful curriculum planners will also be conscious of other kinds of cost. "Shadow costs" are those hidden costs such as the contribution by parents toward the costs of field trips. "Spillover costs" are those incurred by another budget, as for example when the maintenance budget pays the costs of broken windows incurred by the indoor softball program. And "opportunity costs" are the costs of forgoing one option by choosing another. If the program allows us to choose only one foreign language, then one of the costs of choosing Spanish is not being able to learn German.

The belief that capital investment and teacher salaries are related to pupil achievement is held by many educators with an almost religious conviction. Nevertheless, large-scale studies in the United States (Hanuschek, 1986; Walberg & Fowler, 1987) and Canada (Coleman, 1986) have been unable to find a linear relationship between financial expenditures and student achievement. Hanuschek summarized the results of 187 studies in this area as follows: "Two decades of research into educational production functions have produced startlingly consistent results: variations in school expenditures are not systematically related to variations in student performance" (Hanuschek, 1990, p. 45). In developing countries, on the other hand, where an additional investment of five dollars per pupil may make the difference between having and not having a textbook, quite small investments can make a major difference (Fuller, 1987). In both cases, we may

Table 8-10 *Budget for Orienteering Course*

Item	Startup Costs	Operating Costs*
30 compasses	$ 300	$ 30
30 whistles	150	15
Maps	50	20
Film purchase	350	100
Film rental	80	80
Slide film	30	30
Graph paper	20	20
Display cardboard	30	30
Orienteering Association dues	30	30
Bus to competition	100	100
	$1,140	$455

* adjusted for inflation

conclude that it is not the number of dollars that count, but whether they are spent on items that are directly related to the effectiveness of instruction.

Cost-effectiveness and cost-benefit analyses can sometimes be conducted. Cost-effectiveness compares the costs, relative to the effects, of different programs. Cost-benefit compares the value of the benefits with the value of the costs. If curriculum policy-makers paid more attention to cost-benefit analysis, we would probably cancel many of our existing programs, the benefits of which are often obscure, and emphasize much more heavily curricula that save people from inappropriate vocational choices, poverty, unmanageable debt, predictably unhappy marriages, criminal activity, addictions, mental illness, malnutrition, unwanted pregnancy, behaviorally induced diseases, and early death, the costs of all of which, to the individual and to society, are astronomical.

LOGISTICS

In military science the acquisition and deployment of resources in warfare is known as logistics. In 1977 Martin Van Creveld, a professor of military history at the Hebrew University of Jerusalem, defined logistics as "the practical art of moving armies and keeping them supplied" (1977, p. 1). Sixty years earlier, an obscure officer of the U.S. Marine Corps, George Cyrus Thorpe, published a book called *Pure Logistics.* He argued that the whole sphere of war-making fell naturally into three subdivisions: strategy, tactics, and logistics (Thorpe, 1917). This corresponds to the three main areas of curriculum planning: purposes, methods, and resources. Caution must be exercised in applying to education, which is concerned with human growth, development, and freedom, examples from such fields as the military, which is concerned with the achievement of political goals by force, violence, and destruction. Nevertheless, some of the parallels are telling. Logistical errors by military commanders result in loss of life. Logistical errors by educators can result in waste of time (which is also loss of life), as well as diminishment of such life-enhancing qualities as competence and self-concept.

Van Creveld describes the ways in which logistical failures accounted for the defeat of Operation Barbarossa, the Nazi invasion of the Soviet Union with three million troops, in 1941–1944, as "the largest single military operation of all time" (p. 175). The campaign opened in June, before many of the German generals felt fully prepared, but already having lost two months of good weather. The invasion proceeded ahead of schedule for the first four months. But problems of supply dogged the campaign from the start. Most of the few roads running eastward into Russia were unpaved, resulting in increased fuel consumption and engine wear on the German vehicles. Any invading army expects to some degree to be able to live off the land, but the Russians destroyed everything they could as they withdrew. This meant that food and fuel had to be trucked in from Germany, but there were insufficient numbers of German trucks. Civilian vehicles, impressed in France and Czechoslovakia, were used. More than a million different spare parts were

Table 8-11 *Budget for a One-Room School in Pine Lake, Alberta, Canada, 1907*

Item	Cost (in Canadian dollars)
1 desk	$ 16.00
1 teacher's chair	6.00
1 map case	50.00
1 globe of the world	25.00
1 blackboard 4' × 10'	8.00
1 clock	6.50
1 Webster's dictionary	12.00
1 thermometer	1.00
1 wastepaper basket	.75
1 pointer	.25
1 punishing strap	.25
1 mirror	1.00
2 bells	1.60
2 visitors' chairs	7.50
20 seats with desks	65.00
crayons and dusters	1.40
pail, basin, cup and roller	2.80
coal scuttle, etc.	1.75
hand numeral	.75
	$208.05

(Jean Cochrane, 1981, p. 28)

needed to keep this miscellaneous fleet of vehicles moving. When Russian gasoline was captured, its octane level was too low for the Western vehicles.

As for the trains, what lines had been left undamaged by the Luftwaffe and the retreating Russians were of a different gauge than those in Germany. (This precaution had been taken by the Russians decades before precisely for the purpose of frustrating any future German invasion.) The railway engineers, an elite corps in the Wehrmacht, moved hundreds of miles of rail. But the German trains would not run on Russian coal; the water stations were too far apart and often destroyed, and when the cold weather came, the pipes on the German locomotives froze and burst. Transfer points became gigantic bottlenecks.

As Rommel put it in his papers, "The battle is fought and decided by the quartermasters before the shooting begins" (Van Creveld, 1977, p. 200). In this case, the chief enemy of the German logisticians was "General Winter." Making exactly the same mistake as Napoleon 130 years earlier (Nicolson, 1986), Hitler had expected rapid victory followed by a Russian surrender and had failed to provide his troops with supplies for a long winter campaign. The vehicles lacked heaters, snow tires, or antifreeze. The men lacked warm footwear, clothing, and mittens. Their dark uniforms made them easy targets against the snow. On sentry duty, men would freeze to death. Amputations of fingers and feet from gangrenous frostbite became commonplace (Sajer, 1971).

As the German army penetrated farther into Russia, its communications and supply lines became increasingly vulnerable and its army diminished. The Soviet armies increased almost daily, reinforced by troops used to cold weather and equipped with warm clothing. The winter of 1942–1943, in which the Germans were defeated at Stalingrad and lost 500,000 men, spelled ultimate loss of the war. The early successes of Operation Barbarossa were due primarily to the morale and determination of the German forces; in its defeat, logistical failures were a major factor.

"The first prerequisite for any regular logistic system is, of course, an exact definition of requirements" (Van Creveld, 1977, p. 18). In the case of curriculum logistics, this principle applies exactly.

> Amateurs talk strategy while professionals talk logistics.
>
> Michael Clarke, Director, Center for Defense Studies, London (1991, p. 8)

■ SELF – ASSESSMENT

Fill in the blanks.

Curriculum **logistics** involve the specification and provision of the resources for the delivery of (1) _____. This entails specifying requirements for materials, equipment, facilities, (2) _____, time, and cost. The two main kinds of **materials** are (3) _____ and communication materials. One of the first educators to realize the importance for young children of large-scale, stimulating **play equipment** was Maria (4) _____. It appears that children's auditory discrimination can be damaged by long-term exposure to high levels of (5) _____. In **school design**, the (6) _____ the children, the smaller the school needs to be. Description of personnel should include qualities and (7) _____. The role of **administrators** is too often (8) _____ in curriculum documents. The amount of **time** per day spent in instruction and practice is a critical factor in successful learning of (9) _____ _____. Curriculum **budgets** should show both capital and (10) _____ costs.

For answers, see Appendix F.
If you answered nine or ten correctly, you understand the material presented in this chapter.
If you answered seven or eight correctly, reread the relevant parts of the chapter.
If you answered six or less correctly, reread the chapter carefully.

CHAPTER 9

Evaluating Curricula

There is no such thing as professionalism without a commitment to evaluation.

Michael Scriven (1983, p. 238)

Summary

Once a curriculum is designed, it may be evaluated by internal evaluation, expert appraisal, and confidential review. The next step is small-scale pilot testing, followed by typical-use field testing. Testing and implementation of a curriculum should be accompanied by program evaluation. Program evaluation may be preordinate, aiming to compare effects with intentions; or nonpreordinate, interested in all of the effects of the program. Program evaluations should draw on as wide an array of information sources and measures as possible.

We can do no great things—only small things with great love.
Mother Teresa (Yugoslavia/India), Nobel Prize for Peace, 1979. (Mother Teresa, 1983, p. 45)

THE NEED FOR CONTINUITY

Completing the design of a curriculum ends one phase of the curriculum process and begins another. Some would argue that the most difficult stage now begins. We have so far only drawn the blueprints, now we must evaluate them and then submit them to the test of reality by constructing the building itself.

It is important that, if possible, the team that planned the curriculum continue to oversee its evaluation and installation. The designers are the people with the most intimate knowledge of the curriculum and the greatest commitment to it. They are best placed to see that its integrity is maintained.

CURRICULUM EVALUATION

Before the curriculum is ready even to be tested, it needs to be "debugged." This is the purpose of curriculum evaluation. Evaluation, writes B. R. Worthen, "can be defined most simply as the determination of the worth of a thing" (1990, p. 42). Curriculum evaluation involves determining the worth of a *document,* as compared with program evaluation, which involves evaluating the *activities* that occur when a curriculum is implemented in classrooms.

The first step might be called *internal evaluation.* Allow an interval to elapse, perhaps two or three weeks, after the curriculum document is completed. Then return to it and reread it carefully. Almost inevitably, you will want to make corrections, deletions, and additions. It is the same principle as not mailing an important letter the same day you write it. Out of this process comes a revised draft.

The revised draft can now be submitted for *expert appraisal*. You need to get the opinion of one or more people who are experts in curriculum development, and one or more who are experts on the subject of the curriculum. In rare instances, these competences may be combined in one person. Each evaluator will bring different criteria to bear on the curriculum being judged. The authors of a curriculum are obviously committed to their document; so as far as possible the expert should be independent of them. As Michael Scriven comments, "Crude measurements are not as good as refined measurement, but they beat the hell out of judgments of those with vested interests" (1983, p. 253). Some of the most basic criteria that may be used to evaluate a curriculum are presented below in the form of a checklist. This checklist essentially recapitulates the key points of design discussed in the book.

Curriculum Evaluation Guide

1. Needs Assessment
- ❑ Was a needs assessment conducted?
- ❑ Are the methodology and results described?
- ❑ Are the results used appropriately in the design of the curriculum?

2 Aim
- ❑ Is the aim of the curriculum stated?
- ❑ Does it express the overall intent of the curriculum?
- ❑ Does it match the objectives and the curriculum content?
- ❑ Is it clear and concise?
- ❑ Is it worthwhile?
- ❑ Would it be meaningful and significant to the learners?

3. Rationale
- ❑ Is the justification for the program given?
- ❑ Are all the important arguments for the program included?
- ❑ Does the rationale document current evidence on which the curriculum is based?
- ❑ Are the arguments valid and rigorous?
- ❑ Is the rationale eloquently written and convincing?
- ❑ Are the main objections anticipated and dealt with?
- ❑ Does the rationale deal appropriately with the social and personal significance of the curriculum?

4. Objectives
- ❑ Are all the main intentions of the curriculum identified?
- ❑ Do the objectives reflect student needs?
- ❑ Do the objectives go beyond the cognitive?

❐ Are social and personal objectives included?
❐ Are priorities, particularly the critical objectives identified?
❐ Are the objectives written in a clear and consistent style?
❐ Are the objectives relevant to the aim?
❐ Do the objectives collectively exhaust the meaning of the aim?
❐ If all the objectives were achieved, would the aim be realized?

5. Assessment
❐ Are appropriate means suggested to assess attainment of each objective?
❐ Are measures valid, reliable, and efficient?
❐ Are measures low in anxiety for less able learners?
❐ Are assessment measures intrinsic to the curriculum, rather than formal or artificial?
❐ Is there adequate diagnostic formative assessment?
❐ Where appropriate, are standards of mastery clearly indicated?
❐ Do mastery standards set high expectations?
❐ Could students make valid judgments about their own proficiency?
❐ Is the grading system clearly described?
❐ Is the grading system aligned with the objectives?
❐ Does the grading system ensure that critical objectives are mastered?

6. Context
❐ Are the social, community, and institutional contexts described?
❐ Is it clear how this curriculum fits with other programs?
❐ Is linkage clear with preceding and following courses or units?
❐ Is the relationship of the curriculum to state or district guidelines shown?

7. Entry characteristics
❐ Are the learners adequately described?
❐ Is the cultural background of students acknowledged and respected?
❐ Is the selection process clear?
❐ Are the necessary prerequisites identified?
❐ Is provision made for students who lack prerequisites?
❐ Is provision made for students who have already mastered the objectives?
❐ Is there guidance for design and use of preassessment?

8. Instruction
❐ Does the instruction match student needs?
❐ Does the instruction match the curriculum objectives?
❐ In instructional content appropriate and interesting?
❐ Does the instruction ensure early significant success?
❐ Is the sequence and pacing of instruction appropriate?
❐ Are teaching strategies varied, interesting and challenging?
❐ Are there appropriate strategies for students with different learning styles?
❐ Do strategies involve active and cooperative learning?
❐ Is there provision for regular, interesting, and monitored homework?

9. Individual differences
❏ Is there provision for identifying individual difference in aptitude and motivation?
❏ Are there plans for effective remediation?
❏ Is there appropriate use of tutoring and peer tutoring?
❏ Is there adequate provision for faster and more motivated learners?
❏ Is there provision for cultural differences?
❏ Is there provision for students with special needs?

10. Resources
❏ Are consumables and communication materials described?
❏ Are High-Quality materials included in the curriculum or readily available to teachers?
❏ Is relevant instructional software listed?
❏ Is the required equipment described?
❏ Are there recommendations for classroom layout?
❏ Are uses of facilities outside the classroom suggested?
❏ Are instructor qualities and responsibilities defined?
❏ Are the roles of parents, guests, administrators, indicated?
❏ Is total time consumption calculated?
❏ Is the budget complete?

11. Tryout
❏ Is there provision for pilot and field testing?
❏ Are the results of pilot and field tests described?

12. Program evaluation
❏ Are criteria suggested for evaluation of all aspects of the program?
❏ Are multiple measures and data sources suggested?
❏ Is there provision for feedback on the curriculum from users?
❏ Is there provision for ongoing revision of the curriculum?

13. Implementation
❏ Were significant groups involved throughout development of the curriculum?
❏ Are the names and affiliations of the curriculum planners shown?
❏ Are they credible?
❏ Do they include people other than educators?
❏ Is there a realistic adoption and implementation plan?
❏ Is there sufficient provision for in-service training?

14. Production qualities
❏ Is the curriculum professional in appearance?
❏ Is it printed and illustrated?
❏ Are the binding and cover attractive?
❏ Is it well written and easy to follow and read?
❏ Is it free of jargon, vagueness, and pretentiousness?

Table 9-1   *Percent of State and District Curricula Including Specific Components*

Component	State	District
Objectives	83	61
Evaluation	59	44
Content	89	84
Methods	77	66
Individual differences	24	27
Materials	59	71
Time	23	37
Facilities	17	7

(Klein, 1980)

Any curriculum that met all of the outlined criteria would be fairly complete. Certainly it would be more complete than most state and district curricula. Table 9-1 summarizes data from an analysis of curricula reported by Frances Klein in 1980, which showed that many state and district curricula at that time omitted important elements. There is reason to believe that this situation has not greatly improved in the last ten years (Pratt, 1989).

CONFIDENTIAL REVIEW

Once the curriculum document has been evaluated by the planning team and by experts, and revised accordingly, it is ready for confidential review. This stage involves informal submission of the curriculum to some of the gatekeepers, that is, to some of the people who are in a position to influence or to block its implementation. Such people may include teachers, administrators, government officials, members of the board of education, community leaders, or representatives of teachers' associations.

Gatekeepers, it will be recalled, are one of the groups that should be included in the needs assessment that preceded development of the curriculum. Some gatekeepers may have been involved on the curriculum planning committee, and in any event there should have been ongoing contact with them during development of the curriculum. If these earlier steps have been taken, there is less likelihood of difficulty at the implementation stage.

Spivak (1974) describes a classical innovation failure. A group of play leaders and children spent weeks planning and collecting materials and creating an adventure playground. Two days after it was completed, the playground was bulldozed, blacktopped, and replaced by conventional metal playground structures.

"The following is a test from the Emergency Broadcasting System: What is 197 divided by 18? What is the capital of Nebraska? Who was the ninth President of the United States?"

The community had not been consulted and objected to a playground that looked untidy and unconventional.

The kinds of objections raised by gatekeepers will fall into one of three main categories: (1) constructive suggestions that can be used to improve the curriculum; (2) criticisms that can be accommodated by some reasonable compromise; and (3) criticisms or recommendations for change that the planners are not prepared to accept.

In the last case, the rationale for the curriculum can be strengthened and rebuttals prepared for objections that can now be anticipated. The standard we are seeking in the entire curriculum development process is excellence, not perfection.

TRYOUT

The cost of unsuccessful programs is usually passed downwards—in hospitals to patients, in prisons to inmates, in schools to students. Minimizing these costs is an important task of curriculum planners, and one way to do so is by trying a curriculum out on a small scale before a full-scale implementation. Here we shall consider two kinds of tryout: pilot testing and field testing.

Pilot testing

Testing of a new aircraft does not begin when the test pilot flies it for the first time. Long before that point, the engine has run for hundreds of hours on a test stand, components and the plane itself have been tested in real and computer-simulated wind tunnels, and numerous taxiing trials have been conducted without the plane leaving the ground (Stewart, 1989). Without such preliminary testing, chances are high that the plane would crash on its test flight. So might your new curriculum.

───────────── **Pilot testing** ─────────────

An experimental test pilot is not a popular person in a design department. Most of the designers are highly optimistic about their own design and it is not a pleasant task after a flight to explain or to prove that optimism is not justified. See, I don't believe a designer can be objective enough to assess his own work. Quite often the reaction of a designer is to say that everything is excellent, that the pilots are simply too fussy, or that they want to have their own way, or that they have the prima donna complex. It's unpleasant to tell a designer that his plane is not good. . . . In a production department the experimental pilot again is not a popular person. Nearly every production manager would like to set up his assembly line, set up a schedule, and run the production smoothly without any interruption. He is furious when every week five or more modifications have to be incorporated somewhere on the assembly line.

Janusz Zurakowski, Air Force Ace and Chief Test Pilot,
AVRO Aircraft Co. (Stewart, 1988, p. 227)

Pilot testing is small-scale testing. It may be conducted either under highly controlled conditions, sometimes termed "laboratory tryout" (Lewy, 1991b), or under field conditions sometimes termed "prototype evaluation" (Alkin, 1991). Both types of pilot testing are conducted with small numbers of learners. The designers of "programmed instruction" units in the 1970s used to find that a "jury of eight" learners was usually sufficient to identify most design defects (Earl, 1987, p. 73).

Pilot testing may be conducted on parts of the curriculum rather than on the whole. It may be conducted with individual students or small groups rather than with whole classes. Rather than typical students, pilot testing is often better conducted with students of above-average and below-average aptitude. The faster learners may be more articulate about shortcomings of the curriculum; the slower learners will make more errors, which will point to areas of weakness in the curriculum. Pilot testing should be accompanied by a great deal of discussion, interviewing, and debriefing with students. We want, if possible, to get inside the mind of the student to find out about the kinds of cognitive activity, change, and problem solving; the levels of motivation and time on task; the difficulties, redundancy, and the boredom; and insights, illuminations, and excitement that the curriculum induces.

If a new curriculum is interesting (as all new curricula should be), it should not be difficult to recruit learners to try it out. Let us suppose that we want to introduce a unit on biofeedback into the health curriculum. (Training in biofeedback enables people to obtain some control over aspects of their bodies often considered involuntary. For example, if an individual is given a sensitive temperature probe to hold, he or she can use the feedback it provides to learn how to increase or decrease the temperature in the hand by directing more blood to the hand. This is apparently helpful for people who suffer from the kind of headaches that can be ameliorated by decreasing the flow of blood to the brain [Green, Green, & Walters, 1971]). The unit, or parts of it, could be tested by using it as enrichment for faster learners; as an extracurricular offering; as an elective evening course for adults; as a workshop at a teachers' in-service; or by inserting portions of it into the program of a health class. Ideally, the budget for curriculum development would set aside some funds for pilot testing. A few hundred dollars would go a long way in hiring students to pilot test key parts of a new curriculum.

Tom Peters urges corporate leaders to "encourage pilots of everything" (1988, p. 220). His practical advice is readily applicable to school situations:

> Ensure through every form of recognition you can dream up, that the organization's haves are those who are piloting, not merely speculating. Formally (and informally) . . . ask at each staff meeting, on each visit, in each performance appraisal: What are you testing? Where are the pilots? Always be on the lookout for pilots and tests. . . . Commend them on the spot, including any interesting failures. . . . Test bits and pieces unobtrusively. Can you segment or "chunk" the project? . . . Stuff some of the partially developed new material into an ongoing program, perhaps as an extra half day. . . . By now, pilots of chunks should be popping up in various places, and word should be leaking out. After some months of this, it is finally time to float the proposal more formally. . . . There is a slow, low-level, virtually invisible start, followed by a wildly efficient takeoff as word of mouth, led by the field, rather than by headquarters, starts to do the selling for you.   (Peters, 1988, pp. 226, 272)

Many teachers pilot test new instructional components or strategies on an informal and continuous basis. For instance, they take their own children to the science center before they take their class. The model for pilot testing a curriculum is test—analyze results—modify—retest. This cycle is repeated until the curriculum is as good as we think we can make it. Then we are ready for field testing.

Field testing

Unlike pilot testing, field testing tries out a new curriculum under conditions of typical use. The whole curriculum is tried with a whole class or with a number of classes. Both the students and the teachers should be representative of those for whom the curriculum is intended. Field testing teachers should not be drawn from the design team—obviously, the designers are more knowledgeable about and committed to the curriculum than the typical teacher.

Almost invariably, field testing will point to unexpected problems in the curriculum, most of which can usually be dealt with by elaborating the curriculum. For example, a public health nurse told me about a course she planned and taught for expectant parents who were anticipating delivery by cesarean section. The first time she taught the course, it became apparent that the clients had strong feelings of guilt and anger resulting from the upset of their original expectations of a normal delivery. They needed an opportunity to express these emotions, and this was built into future offerings of the program.

Field testing serves two purposes: It "test flies" the curriculum, and it builds support for it. By this stage, the curriculum should be highly effective—if it is not, it is not ready for field testing. Field tests begin to build a reputation for the innovation. Teachers who find that the new curriculum inspires an enthusiastic response on the part of students are its best advertisers and advocates. Official curricula often overlook this source of support. In one study of one hundred curricula examined, only four referred to pilot or field tests (Pratt, 1989).

Good records should be kept during field testing, particularly of anecdotal comments by teachers and students and of interesting and significant incidents. It is ideal if teachers, and if possible also students, keep daily journals. Videotaped classroom episodes will be particularly useful for later in-service sessions.

Program evaluation

"Curriculum evaluation" and "program evaluation" are often confused. As indicated earlier, we shall use the term "curriculum evaluation" to refer to the evaluation of a curriculum document. Program evaluation occurs after the curriculum has been adopted and implemented, either for tryout or full-scale implementation, as a program. Whether a program is evaluated by the developers or by others, it makes sense to recommend in the curriculum document some criteria and procedures for evaluation of the program.

Program evaluation is not new. When a Roman military architect built a new bridge, he was required to stand underneath it as the first troops, elephants, and heavy equipment rolled across (McGaghie, 1991). But the first modern program evaluation in education is usually considered to be Joseph Rice's evaluation of spelling programs in schools, conducted between 1887 and 1898. He compared schools that taught spelling for up to 200 minutes a week with those that spent 10 minutes a week and found no differences in student learning (Madaus, Stufflebeam, & Scriven, 1983). Today, program evaluation is a rapidly developing field in which significant advances have been made in the last decade. Several new books appear on the topic each year, and many significant articles appear every month. As in other educational fields, the theory is advancing far ahead of practice. By 1981 the field had reached the stage at which a formal set of standards had been developed for program evaluation, and these standards are included in Appendix B.

Lee and Sampson of the New South Wales Department of School Education recommend that program evaluators direct their attention to ten basic questions:

1. What is the program to be evaluated?

2. Why is the program being evaluated?

3. How are people to be prepared for the evaluation?

4. What are the major issues and questions with which the evaluation is to deal?

5. Who will do what?

6. What are the resources for the evaluation?

7. What data need to be collected?

8. How will the data be analyzed?

9. What will be the reporting procedure?

10. How will the report be implemented?   (Lee & Sampson, 1990, p. 158)

Who should conduct a program evaluation? If it is conducted by the original developers, they may be too biased in favor of the program to render an objective judgment. If it is conducted by outside professionals, both the developers and the teachers may be unduly threatened. There are some advantages in having teachers develop their own program evaluations. The processes of deciding what aspects of a program are to be evaluated, and what criteria and levels of performance are to be used, is an opportunity for professional development, as well as for peer and self-evaluation.

An advance of recent years is the development of "nonpreordinate" designs for program evaluation. The classical model "preordains" certain outcomes of instruction, then tests students to find out to what extent those outcomes have been achieved. Nonpreordinate evaluation is interested in everything significant that has happened during and as a result of the program, whether or not it was intended. Cronbach comments on this distinction:

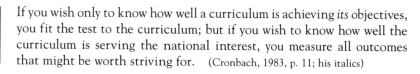
If you wish only to know how well a curriculum is achieving *its* objectives, you fit the test to the curriculum; but if you wish to know how well the curriculum is serving the national interest, you measure all outcomes that might be worth striving for.   (Cronbach, 1983, p. 11; his italics)

Preordinate evaluation

As an example of classical or "scientific" program evaluation, consider the testing of a new drug. Let us suppose a drug has been found for curing the common cold. We select a sufficiently large number of subjects for the clinical trials and then randomly assign them to the experimental group or the control group, checking that we have equivalent groups in terms of age, sex, occupation, medical history, state of health, and so on. As subjects develop colds, the new drug is administered to the experimental group and a placebo is given to the control group. The study is "double-blind," so that neither subjects nor attending physicians know which are the experimental and which the control subjects. In a "crossover study," halfway through the trials the two groups are switched, so that now the experimental group receives the placebo, and vice versa. At the end of the testing period, we examine the duration of colds and other outcomes to determine whether there are statistically significant differences between the two groups.

This kind of experimental study aims at standards of objectivity that are normally unattainable in educational settings. The chief difficulty is that it is usually impossible to conceal from either students or teachers the fact that the program in which they are taking part is an innovation or experiment. Typically, the effect of the introduction of any innovation is temporarily to improve results—what is known as the "Hawthorne effect." A decision to adopt a change based on a "one-shot" evaluation study may be followed by a gradual regression of results to their previous level. This was apparently the case in an evaluation by Slavin of federally funded "Chapter 1" programs.

▎In our search for effective Chapter 1 programs, we wrote to every one of 116 Chapter 1 programs identified as "exemplary" by the U.S. Department of Education. All the programs that sent us multi-year data showed significant gains in percentile ranks for fall-to-spring testing, but by the following fall these gains had disappeared in almost every case.   (Slavin, 1987b, p. 111)

The misleading potential of one-shot studies is the strongest argument for the longitudinal, or *time-series*, study. This is an important kind of study to assess the impact of changes over the long term. For example, the adolescent birthrate varies only slightly from year to year. But long-term studies show that the birthrate to adolescent mothers declined by 45 percent in the United States between 1957 and 1980, a period that also saw the introduction of (but cannot be attributed solely to) improved sex education programs in schools (Putnam-Scholes, 1983).

Unfortunately, the demand for quick information and results often leads to the neglect of time-series studies. Suppose we introduce a new urban geography program in 1993. As shown in Table 9-2, we find that scores in 1993 were 5 percent better than in 1992. Expansion of the time frame might show that scores in 1992, before the new program was introduced, were 5 percent better than 1991. In other words, scores were already rising and that trend was unaltered by the new curriculum.

Disaggregation is an important step in program evaluation, whether preordinate or nonpreordiante. Table 9-3 shows results for a new program. If we look at the average effect alone, we might conclude that the new program is highly successful. But if we disaggregate by social class and sex, we would realize this is misleading. The program is, on average, an improvement, but this effect is due to the achievement of high Social Economic Status (SES) and female students. The performance of low SES students is unaffected by the new program, and the performance of male students is worse.

Table 9-2   *Time-Series Study*

Year	Program	Mean Score
1990	old program	66.0
1991	old program	69.3
1992	old program	72.8
1993	new program	76.4
1994	new program	80.2
1995	new program	84.2

(Using data from only 1992 and 1993 could be misleading.)

Table 9-3   *Effects of a New Program on Mean Student Achievement*

Students	Old Program	New Program
All students	67	75
High SES students	74	90
Low SES students	60	60
Male students	70	65
Female students	64	85

Many researchers in the field of school effectiveness now make it a criterion of effectiveness that, to be regarded as effective, programs must achieve comparable results with lower and higher SES students (Sudlow, 1986). It is often appropriate also to disaggregate data by sex, age, cultural background, and other factors of interest.

Criteria for evaluation

In all program evaluations, the criteria need to be determined with care. Typically, student learning is a major criterion—often, unfortunately, the sole criterion. Windham and Chapman (1990) make a distinction between attainment and achievement. "Attainment refers to performance at one point in time. Achievement refers to the change in performance over time, the change in attainment from one point to another" (Windham & Chapman, 1990, p. 195). These authors recommend that attainment be used as the criterion, rather than achievement, on account of the unreliability of gain scores unless adjusted in quite complex ways (Stake, 1971).

While attainment may be the major focus of interest, it is important that an effort be made to collect data on other program effects. These may include "objective" information about costs, transfers, awards won by students and graduates, and number of parental complaints or compliments. Or the data may include more "subjective" information about levels of student, teacher, parent, and employer satisfaction, and quality of teaching and learning. The basic principle is that, providing we do not suffer from information overload, the more measures of program effects that we use, the better informed we will be. We should also be prepared to evaluate wholistically and impressionistically. Michael Scriven states, "Holistic evaluation is sometimes considerably more valid—as well as far more economical—than syntheses of micro-evaluations" (1983, p. 247).

Cost analysis

Various kinds of cost analyses are used in program evaluation. *Cost-benefit analysis* compares the value of program results to the costs of investment. (A federal government commission to reduce the number of government forms was once reported to have saved 350 times the cost of the commission [Posovac & Carey, 1989]). *Cost-efficiency analysis* compares the results of different kinds of programs relative to their consumption of resources; an example is shown in Table 9-4. *Least-cost analysis* seeks to identify the least costly way of producing a given result. *Cost-utility analysis* attempts to weigh multiple costs and returns, public and private, personal and political, objective and subjective, in making policy decisions.

Nonpreordinate evaluation

Preordinate evaluation designs have developed out of scientific fields such as chemistry and biology, and applied sciences such as medicine and agriculture. Nonpreordinate evaluation has grown primarily out of work in such fields as anthropology and ethnography. Classic preordinate models have been heavily quantitative in nature, resting on the great strides made in the physical and biological sciences in the nineteenth century. The late twentieth century saw an increasing realization that quantitative science was insufficient to address every paradox faced by human beings. This is acknowledged by scientists themselves. Barbara McClintock, a Nobel prize recipient in physiology, remarked that "Things are much more marvelous than the scientific method allows us to conceive" (Keller, 1983, p. 203). Werner Heisenberg, Nobel prize recipient in physics, gave his name to the "Heisenberg Uncertainty Principle" through his work on atomic physics:

> What we establish mathematically is only to a small extent an "objective fact," and in large part a survey of possibilities. Thus the statement "Here is a hydrogen atom in its normal state" no longer contains a precise statement about the path of the electron but tells us instead that if we observe this path with a suitable instrument, the electron will be encountered at point x with a certain probability $p(x)$.   (Heisenberg, 1974, p. 42)

Curriculum workers need to build models of curriculum that are generous and inclusive rather than exclusive and partisan. This suggests that curriculum

Table 9-4   *Relative Returns to Different Innovations per $100 per Student*

Innovation	Effect Size
Increasing instructional time 30 minutes per day	.05
Computer-assisted instruction 10 minutes daily	.10
Reducing class size from 35 to 30	.14
Cross-age peer tutoring 30 minutes per day	.46

(Levin, Glass, & Meister, 1987)

research might well utilize both quantitative and experimental designs from classical science, and qualitative and descriptive models that draw from such fields as anthropology, literacy criticism, psychotherapy, and autobiography.

One of the limitations of classical evaluation models in education is that they have been designed essentially to answer a single question: Did the program work? But this is only one of the questions that an educational program evaluation needs to answer. Like evaluation of student achievement, program evaluations may be formative (aimed at improvement) or summative (aimed at a final judgment). Stufflebeam and Webster define an education evaluation study as "one that is designed and conducted to assist some audience to judge and improve the worth of some educational object" (1983, p. 24). In order to improve a program, we need much more varied and richer data than is provided simply by, for example, a display of test results.

Accordingly, increasing emphasis is being placed today on evaluation that is qualitative rather than quantitative, and naturalistic rather than experimental. The purpose is not so much to pinpoint exact outcomes as to get inside the experience of the people involved and describe it in detail. While the scientific evaluator enters the evaluation with a tightly designed plan, the naturalistic evaluator is prepared to develop and modify the evaluation as the inquiry proceeds.

Interviews are widely used for nonpreordinate evaluation. Interviews may be held with students, teachers, graduates, dropouts, parents, employers, and administrators. They may be individual or group interviews, face-to-face or by telephone, and they may include such variations as public hearings and debates. The quality of interview data will depend to some extent on the skill and training of interviewers and the careful structuring of interviews. However, informal interviews also have a place. A principal in a high-performing school district reports that he organizes

> every Thursday morning from 9:00 to 10:00 well-advertised coffee meetings. We invite particular parents—we just go through the student filing system and call. . . . If they don't say anything, I'll start asking them questions: Is your child getting homework? Is your child happy in his classes? (Coleman & LaRocque, 1990, p. 5)

The importance of **feedback from students** needs to be emphasized. Evaluations of human services all too frequently ignore the clients. Hospital evaluations may fail to interview patients; reviews of train services may ignore passengers. It is ironic that a twenty-minute classroom visit by a principal will usually carry more weight in teacher evaluation than the views of thirty human beings who are the teacher's students for a semester or a year. But who is better placed than the students to comment on the program in which they have participated day in and day out as the focus of instruction? Whether interviewed individually or in groups or asked to respond to a questionnaire, students can provide rich and detailed data (Rogers, 1989).

Written course evaluations may also be used. Even in the earliest grades, children can provide useful feedback. For example, a form might be developed listing such statements as "I am enjoying reading this year." The statements are printed and are also read out loud by the teacher, and children respond by circling a "happy face" or a "sad face." In some language schools in Japan, foreign language teachers are rated every month by their students by means of a questionnaire ("I am satisfied with this course"; "I would like to study with this teacher again"; "The teacher instills enthusiasm," and so on). On this basis, teachers are rated from A to C; an A produces a salary bonus, while a C may lead to termination (Rosemary Pratt, personal communication, December, 1991).

The end-of-course evaluation form is a standard feature of most university courses, but is less commonly used in secondary and elementary schools. Extensive studies suggest that student satisfaction expressed on such forms does correlate with student achievement (Abraami, d'Appollonia, & Cohen, 1990). The course characteristics that seem to be most important to students are good organization, creative and interesting teaching, and student participation in discussion (Cranton & Smith, 1990). Formative course evaluations are even more useful, conducted at mid-term and combined with group interviews and instructor reaction (Abbot, Wulff, Nyquist, Ropp, & Hess, 1990). It is particularly important to assess student reaction to a new course at the field testing stage, because the enthusiasm of students is one of the best predictors that other teachers will adopt the new program.

Whether we are using course evaluations, interviews, or analysis of student achievement, it is necessary to ensure an adequate sample of responses. Suppose 500 students took a new course. If you took a 30 percent sample (150 students), but were able to contact only half of them (75 students), it would be unsafe to generalize to the whole population. You would be better off with a 10 percent sample (50 students), of whom you contacted 75 percent (38 students) (Posovac & Carey, 1989).

Observation is a central technique in the field of anthropology, which also pioneered the technique of "participant observation," in which the observer does not stay at a distance, but becomes actively involved in the events being observed. There is prolonged engagement at the site, rather than a single quick visit to collect data. Observational reports tend to include much anecdotal detail and direct quotation. "Thick description" is often employed, "by which is meant providing enough information about a context, first, to impart a vicarious experience of it and second, to facilitate judgments about the extent to which working hypotheses from the context might be transferable to a second and similar context" (Guba & Lincoln, 1983, p. 328). A variety of records may be collected, including documents, photographs, film, and audiotape. Site visits have advantages over paper evaluations, providing the possibility for EBWA—evaluation by walking around. Suggestion boxes and telephone answering machines can be used to solicit anonymous comments on the program.

Unobtrusive measures may also be collected. In school contexts, absenteeism and dropout rates may provide information about the acceptability of curricula. Discipline problems, graffiti, and damage to facilities or equipment may also indicate student attitudes toward programs. Absenteeism and illness of teachers, teacher resignations, transfers, and requests to teach or not to teach certain programs are also important evidence in program evaluations.

Course evaluations, samples of work, and student journals may be examined. The evaluation may also be interactive. Evaluators can check with subjects to see whether their interpretations match the perceptions of the participants. The many different data sources and types of evidence can be cross-checked to provide triangulation of evidence and confirmation of conclusions.

Naturalistic designs are interested primarily in the meanings with which people endow actions and events. What values, social roles, and relationships are involved in the setting? What are the criteria by which people choose courses of action? What do people mean by what they are saying and doing? (Dorr-Bremme, 1991).

It is principally the nonpreordinate evaluators who have reminded the field of the importance of producing information that is of immediate value to those responsible for program maintenance. What Malcolm Partlett and others have termed "illuminative evaluation" is a model in this regard:

> The basic emphasis of illuminative evaluation applied to education is on investigating and interpreting a variety of educational practices, participants' experiences, institutional procedures, and management problems, in ways that are recognizable and useful to those for whom the study is made. . . . If this is to be more than a pious wish, it means paying special attention to the audiences of each study—their requirements for information, their interests, questions, and needs. It means designing the study in ways that do not affront their common sense, with reports being written lucidly, with minimal resort to jargon, and with attention paid to presentation and brevity.   (Parlett, 1991, p. 420)

Controversies between proponents of qualitative and quantitative, or preordinate and nonpreordinate, designs have tended to present sharply contrasted dichotomies. Program evaluation, however, needs to employ all of the tools at its disposal; it is appropriate to use whatever methods are useful, and this will usually mean using both preordinate and naturalistic methods.

Some of the aspects, questions, and data sources for program evaluation will be discussed later.

The evaluation report

A program evaluation normally leads to a report containing recommendations. Hendricks (1990) makes some practical suggestions for evaluation recommendations, including the following:

1. Allocate sufficient time and resources to developing the recommendations.

2. Consider all aspects of the issue "fair game."

3. Draw possible recommendations from a wide variety of sources.

4. Work closely with agency personnel throughout the process.

5. Consider the larger context within which the recommendations must fit.

6. Generally offer only realistic recommendations.

7. Decide whether to be as general or as specific as possible.

8. Think twice before recommending fundamental changes.

9. Show the future implications of recommendations.

10. Make the recommendations easy to understand.

11. Stay involved after recommendations have been accepted.

12. If a recommendation is not accepted, look for other opportunities to recommend it again.

Program Evaluation

ASPECTS AND QUESTIONS	DATA SOURCES
NEEDS Is the need that the program was designed to meet still significant? Is a school program still necessary to meet the need? Is the need recognized by the learners? Is it recognized by teachers and gatekeepers? Is the program based on the ascertained needs? What other significant need could the program meet?	Review of needs assessment data; rerun of all or part of needs assessment; interviews, questionnaires, card-sorts with students, parents, teachers, and others; analysis of program results.
INTENTIONS Are the curriculum intentions clear to and adopted by teachers and students? Were students involved in goal selection? What other intentions are apparently being pursued? Are teachers and students recognizing and giving priority to critical objectives? What changes need to be made in the aim and objectives? What additional objectives should be included?	Classroom observation; analysis of students' work, projects, folders, test and examination responses; analysis of lesson plans, teaching materials, tests, and examinations; interviews with students, teachers, parents.
ASSESSMENT Is achievement of the significant objectives being assessed? Are the measures used consistent with the curriculum? Are	Analysis of graded student work, tests, examinations; discussion with teachers and parents; interviews with students,

they valid, reliable, efficient, and fair? Are they intrinsic rather than artificial? How do students feel about the evaluation? Do tests stimulate excessive anxiety, particularly among slow learners? Is there adequate formative evaluation? Is the emphasis on useful feedback to learners rather than judgment and social comparison? Do the teachers model self-assessment?

especially dropouts and low achievers; classroom observation.

ENTRY CHARACTERISTICS

Do the students actually in the program correspond to those expected? Does the student description give teachers sufficient advance information about students? Are prerequisites and pretests used as intended? Are students who lack prerequisites receiving remediation? Is student difficulty indicating a need for additional prerequisites? Are any prerequisites proving redundant? Are pretests being used to provide teachers with all the critical information they need about the students?

Student complaints of difficulty, easiness, or inappropriateness of program; gender and ethnic rations; age distribution; student failure, transfer, absenteeism, and dropout rates; analysis of pretest data; classroom observation; interviews with teachers.

INSTRUCTION

Is the planned content being presented? What changes or additions to content need to be made? How well are various teaching strategies being used? Do the instructional strategies engage and interest students? Do they engage the different senses? Are different kinds of learners sufficiently involved? Is there high time on task? Can students make input into the instructional plan? Is there opportunity for social learning? Are students encouraged to use their imagination and to take risks? Is instruction free of gender, ethnic, or other kinds of bias? Do students treat one another with respect? How do students and teachers feel about the instruction? What new strategies and/or content

Class room observation; analysis of students' work and test results; student and teacher survey; interviews with students and teachers; student absenteeism and dropout rates; student time on task; classroom video's, photographs, and audio record; suggestion box and telephone answering machine for student suggestions; student and teacher journals recording interesting or important classroom events; card-sort of topics by students and teachers in order of importance and quality of teaching: list topics and have students say which they enjoy most, think most important, difficult, or interesting.

should be suggested in the next edition of the curriculum?

INDIVIDUAL DIFFERENCES

Are learning problems promptly identified and remediated? Are faster learners recognized and treated appropriately? Are aptitude, cultural, and class difference respected by teachers? Are there opportunities to learn about and value the variety of human experience? Are learners' different ways of learning recognized and honored? Is the program accessible to students with special needs? Is the classroom a friendly place for all kinds of students?

Disaggregation of achievement data; classroom observation; interviews with students, teachers, parents.

RESOURCES

Are the materials, equipment, and facilities specified being used? Are they effective? Are students enjoying interacting with the materials? What defects are apparent? Are better materials or equipment now available? Are facilities comfortable, attractive, and appropriate for the instruction? Are sites outside the school used? Are teachers competent? Do they feel comfortable with the program? Do students like the teachers? Are the teachers good role models for students? Is there an attitude of mutual respect? What additional qualities and responsibilities need to be recognized? Are other personnel identified in the curriculum involved? Are parents involved? Are there additional people in the school or community who could assist with the program? Is the program given enough time? Are all students completing the curriculum on time? Is the time of any students wasted? Are costs in line with projectionsl?

Site visits and observation; discussion with teachers, students, administrators; examination of materials; have students read a passage from the instructional materials and retell it in their own words; teacher job satisfaction; equipment availability and utilization; teacher complaints of difficulty or lack of time; teacher time allocation; requests for in-service training; teacher qualifications; student/teacher ratios; analysis of expenditures; per-student costs; cost overruns.

IMPLEMENTATION

Was implementation completed smoothly and on time? Were approvals received?

Observation and records of implementation process; analysis of school board and

Was there support from colleagues, administrators, elected officials, parents, and community? Were the media supportive? Were teachers willing or enthusiastic? Was in-service training sufficient and well received?

committee discussions; letters and articles in newspapers; telephone calls to administrators and officials; evaluations of in-service sessions.

RESULTS

What was the average level of student achievement? What were the disaggregated levels? Did any a specific groups of learners underachieve? Did all students achieve the critical objectives? What other effects did the program have on students, teachers, and other people? How much did students and teachers enjoy and appreciated the program? How did it change them intellectually, socially, and personally? Do students now use vocabulary and concepts taught in the program? What were the greatest strengths and weaknesses of the program? What was the effect of the program on the image of the school? How did administrator, parents, and others respond? Did the results justify the expenditures of money, time, and energy? How did the program compare with previous or alternative programs?

Analysis of test results; time-series analysis; student attainment and achievement; progression rates; interviews with students, teachers, parents, administrators, employers, and others; earnings analysis of graduates; observation; participant observation; analysis of written work by students and teachers; photographs, audio and videotape of events and discourse; thick description; anecdotes and quotations; review of suggestion box, course evaluations, and student or teacher journals; analysis of enrollment, dropout rates, absenteeism, disciplinary incidents, damage, and graffiti; long-term follow-up of students; graduate employment, earnings, and admission to further study; graduate social attitudes, involvement, and consumer behavior.

THE TENTATIVENESS OF CURRICULUM ─────────

A curriculum document is always a draft. To treat any curriculum as permanent is to violate our understanding of the evolution of knowledge. In any nontotalitarian system, teachers need to know that they can adapt, question, improve, or challenge official curricula. A genuine request in the curriculum document for input from users regarding additions, deletions, successful teaching strategies, new resources, and other amendments, is evidence of open-mindedness and a desire for the kind of improvement that school systems should exemplify.

■ SELF – ASSESSMENT

1. Ideally, how long should a curriculum design team continue to function?

   A   until the curriculum is adopted
   B   until the curriculum is implemented
   C   until the curriculum has been field tested
   D   until the curriculum document has been written

2. What is evaluated in a curriculum evaluation?

   A   a program
   B   instructional activities
   C   the quality of teaching
   D   a curriculum document

3. Somerset Maugham, the writer, once said, "People ask you for criticism, but they only want praise." What does this imply with respect to expert appraisal of curriculum?

   A   the appraisal should be based on pilot test results
   B   the appraiser should be a member of the curriculum planning team
   C   the appraiser should be independent of the curriculum developers
   D   the appraiser should be an administrator rather than a teacher

4. To whom is it most important to submit a curriculum for confidential review?

   A   clients
   B   gatekeepers
   C   experts
   D   members of the curriculum planning team

5. Which of these procedures for validating a curriculum is conducted *last?*

   A   field testing
   B   pilot testing
   C   internal evaluation
   D   confidential review

6. What kind of teachers should field test a curriculum?

   A   teachers typical of those who will implement the curriculum
   B   teachers who are members of the design team
   C   teachers who are generally hostile to innovations
   D   teachers who are wildly enthusiastic about the new curriculum

7. A team of curriculum developers plans a preordinate program evaluation designed to tell them whether or not students are meeting the program objectives. What question is this evaluation limited to?

A   how effective is the program?
B   how worthwhile are the objectives?
C   how efficient is the program?
D   what unintended consequences did the program have?

8. You develop and implement a curriculum on auto repair. You want to determine whether the savings by graduates on auto repair costs are greater than the cost of running the program. Which kind of analysis will you use?

A   cost-efficiency analysis
B   least-cost analysis
C   cost-benefit analysis
D   cost-plus analysis

9. What is the major purpose of disaggregation of program evaluation results?

A   to ascertain the reliability of test items
B   to make program evaluation less preordinate
C   to ascertain the average effect of a program on all students
D   to find out how the program affected particular subgroups of people

10. Which of the following kinds of data is most "naturalistic"?

A   student achievement scores
B   attitude questionnaire results
C   dropout rates
D   conversations with learners

For answers, see Appendix F.
If you answered nine or ten correctly, you understand the material in this chapter.
If you answered seven or eight correctly, reread the relevant sections in the chapter.
If you answered less then seven correctly, reread the chapter carefully.

CHAPTER 10

Implementing Curriculum Change

If it is true that all really great undertakings are carried out in poverty and in faith, we appeared destined to accomplish great things.

Gilbert Renault-Roulier (1948, p. 24)

Summary

Implementation of a new curriculum entails social action that builds a climate of acceptance for the change. It may be facilitated by establishing a climate of trust, ensuring the change meets recognized needs, consulting widely, establishing clear goals, developing support systems, using personal contact, providing in-service training and needed resources, and maintaining a focus on institutional growth. Curricula should not be regarded as permanent installations, but as subject to continual improvement and renewal.

To oppression, plundering and abandonment, we respond with life. Neither floods nor plagues, nor famines nor cataclysms, nor even the eternal wars of century upon century have been able to subdue the persistent advantage of life over death.

Gabriel García Marquez (Colombia/Mexico), Nobel Prize for Literature, 1982.

(García Marquez, 1983, p. E-17)

THE GREAT BARRIER REEF

Implementation has been referred to as "the Great Barrier Reef" (Pratt, 1980), the point at which many a good curriculum sinks without trace. Why is this so? At its simplest, perhaps it is because when we enter the field of implementation we leave the green pastures of educational planning and enter the harsh arena of politics—the field that political scientist Harold Lasswell (1958) once summarized as "who gets what, when, how."

William van Til said once (I cannot now determine where), "Changing the curriculum is like moving a cemetery." A classic case is described by Oonagh Wilms (1986). A new art curriculum was written specifically for aboriginal students on a reserve in southern Ontario. Native teachers and artists were involved in developing the curriculum, which included a large section on native arts and artists. The guidelines were sent out to the schools in 1975. Eight years later, none of the teachers to whom the researcher had talked had heard of them. Some of the principals thought the name sounded familiar and checked their shelves; the curriculum guidelines were still sitting there unused and unopened (Wilms, 1986).

Such cases might be considered the rule rather than the exception. The high casualty rate among new curricula has been one of the factors stimulating the study of implementation. Unfortunately, one aspect of the specialized study of curriculum implementation has been the development of a "first design curriculum, then implement it" approach. This book has attempted to describe a different approach: "design implementable curricula." One part of this approach is the needs assessment that is conducted before curriculum planning begins, so that the existence of significant local needs is established and the potential political support and opposition identified. The inclusion of significant individuals and groups in discussions of the change helps to ensure smooth implementation. Failure to consult from the beginning with key players, such as parents or academics in the discipline, can doom a curriculum before it even reaches the implementation stage. (Fowler, 1989; Kenney & Orr, 1984). Let us look more closely at three of the key players in curriculum innovation: superintendents, principals, and teachers.

Superintendents

Superintendents and other district office personnel provide the framework within which schools operate. Individual schools can excel even in a mediocre district; but success is much more likely if the district and the schools share and implement a common philosophy. Phillip Schlechty comments that "Superintendents who do not use their office to lead will create a school system incapable of leadership in the community" (1990, p. 128).

But the time of superintendents is typically spread very thin. In a study of eight superintendents in Alberta, Canada, Duignan (1979) found that they averaged 26 discussion sessions a day; they spent only 7 percent of their time with teachers, and less than 1 percent with students. Schmuck and Schmuck (1990) report on the state of the superintendency in small-town America: "We saw superintendents not only developing budgets, working on curriculum, and meeting with the board, but also driving a bus, attending out-of-town sports events, and directing traffic" (p. 18). Of the 25 superintendents they interviewed, only 3 had a collaborative vision of leadership, and no more than 2 had heard of organizational development.

In contrast, Murphy and Hallinger (1988) and Coleman and LaRocque (1991) have examined the characteristics of leadership in effective school districts. They found that such districts were marked by labor peace and support by the school board and the community for school policies and programs. The ethos of such districts was one of rationality without bureaucracy. Superintendents had a people orientation and a problem-solving approach; they exercised strong leadership with an active administrative team. Curriculum improvement was a priority. The system was driven and coordinated by goals, and the goals emphasized curriculum and instruction. These goals determined district initiatives and the distribution of resources. Superintendents led and monitored curriculum and instruction throughout the district, and they selected principals for their expertise in curriculum and instruction. They invited input from principals and gave them considerable autonomy.

Coleman and Larocque found that perceptions of principals and superintendents were quite different in high- and low-performing districts. Low-performing districts were marked by a sense of powerlessness both in the central office and the schools. Principals were unable to state district goals: "I don't think they have ever been stated, unless they were in the Superintendent's message in September"; "We are not a collegial district at any level. . . . Nobody trusts anybody else, and it goes all the way from bottom to top." In high-performing districts, on the other hand, principals and superintendents worked together and respected one another's work. Principals would say of superintendents, "We see a lot of them in spite of the distance. I appreciate their presence, they are on top of things. They do get around and their follow-up is good." A superintendent commented, "We allow the principals a lot of autonomy, at the same time trying to give them as much support as possible" (Coleman & LaRocque, 1991, p. 164). This is the kind of environment in which people feel sufficiently supported and safe to take risks and try out innovations.

Principals

Principals are key figures in curriculum innovation. In practice, principals have the power of veto over any significant curriculum innovation in their schools. The support of the principal is almost invariably essential for successful innovation to take place.

How do principals exercise leadership in curriculum improvement? Apparently, the most effective principals have a clear vision that focuses primarily on the learning and well-being of students and that transcends implementation of specific innovations. They work continuously to establish a professional and collaborative ethos in their schools. They facilitate professional development, visits, and interaction in a responsible rather than merely permissive way, and they attend in-service sessions with teachers. They set high expectations for student academic achievement and monitor achievement throughout the school. They work to prevent interruptions and disruptions in instruction. They provide feedback to teachers on their classroom performance. They take a proactive role in the placement of teachers. And they mobilize community resources and central office administration in support of school programs, ensuring teachers have the resources they need (Corcoran and Wilson, 1987; Fullan, 1985; Hallinger, Bickman, & Davis, 1989; Hall & Hord, 1987; Hargreaves, 1989a; Hord & Hall, 1987; Louis & Miles, 1990; Mortimore, 1986; Pellicer, Anderson, Keefe, Kelley, & McCleary, 1990; Smith & Andrews, 1989; Webster & Olson, 1988; Wilson & Corcoran, 1988).

If the principal does not take charge . . . mediocrity will prevail over excellence. The overwhelmed principal yields to dependency. The focussed principal insists on consistency with purpose. . . . Successful schools were characterized by principals who supported and stimulated initiative-taking by others. . . . An increase in selective acts of fearlessness in reference to major school goals would be a good thing. . . . Effective principals . . . are men and women who take independent stances on matters of importance, and in most cases are all the more respected for it.

Michael Fullan (1988, pp. 28–30)

All of these things are done in a manner that is authoritative but not authoritarian. Sara Lightfoot comments that the leadership style of principals in good high schools diverges from traditional masculine stereotypes. "Part of the goodness of these schools has to do with the redefinition of leadership [which] includes softer images . . . based on relationships and affiliations as central dimensions of the exercise of power" (1983, p. 333). It is worth noting in this regard that women constitute about 70 percent of the school teaching force but only about 25 percent of principals and vice-principals (Fullan, 1991a). Women principals (and superintendents) tend to be better qualified and to have spent more years in the classroom than their male counterparts (Fullan, Park, Williams, Allison, Walker, & Watson, 1987; Shakeshaft, 1987). There is evidence that women administrators engage in more cooperative planning, leave the school less frequently, visit classrooms and interact with teachers, parents, and students more frequently. Claudine Baudoux (1987) found that women vice-principals in Quebec spent five times as much time interacting with parents and seven times as much time interacting with teachers as did men vice-principals. Women administrators are more likely than men adminis-trators to be concerned about the effectiveness of the curriculum and the academic and social development of students. They value supervision more than men, but ad-ministration less. They make fewer decisions unilaterally, and more by democratic and participative means of consensus and coalition (Eagly & Johnson, 1990). Charol Shakeshaft (1987) suggests that women's patterns of communication, which tend to be gentle, friendly, and enthusiastic, are more appropriate in the ad-ministration of schools than male patterns, which are more likely to be forceful, fac-tual, and authoritarian. These studies suggest that school administrators, whether male or female, might enhance their effectiveness by modifying traditional, hierar-chical, and authority-based models of leadership, and adopting patterns that more fully reflect interpersonal values and collegial relationships.

Cross-national comparisons show that in Western countries, principals view themselves as responsible for curriculum implementation, but not for curriculum planning (Farrell, 1989). Principals who are successful in bringing about program improvement build and support curriculum planning and steering teams in their schools. These teams may contain administrators, parents, and students as well as teachers. Principals provide time and resources to these groups, and maintain ac-tive involvement and liaison with them. While principals cannot be experts on every subject, effective principals do endeavor to develop expertise in curriculum planning, through reading, in-service work, and graduate study (Fullan, 1991b). The principals most committed to curriculum development are most likely to have taken graduate coursework in curriculum (Vann, 1979). Principals who have taken graduate work in educational administration express the wish that their programs had included more curriculum coursework (Pratt & Common, 1986).

Research such as this has generated the slogan, "the principal as instructional leader." This may be quite appropriate in small elementary schools. But in a large high school of many departments, the principal's role is more likely, as Carl Glick-man points out, to be that of a leader of instructional leaders:

> The arrogance by which the education community has embraced the con-cept of "principal as instructional leader" is mind-boggling. The principal of successful schools is not the instructional leader but the educational leader who mobilizes the expertise, talent, and care of others. He or she is the person who symbolizes, supports, distributes, and coordinates the work of teachers as instructional leaders.   (Glickman, 1990, pp. 7–8)

As Roland Barth succinctly puts it, the best principals are not heroes, but hero-makers (1990b).

Teachers

Whatever the talents of superintendents and principals, curriculum improve-ment will stand or fall by the actions of individual teachers in their classrooms. Implementation strategies that attempt to change or manipulate teachers against their will almost inevitably fail. If a curriculum innovation is not actually initiated by teachers, then it must at least be understood, supported, and internalized by them. The idea of "school-based curriculum development" is a recognition that change is more likely if implementation is conducted by the teachers who are most involved in, and affected by, the innovation (Holt, 1987; Walker, 1988).

Teachers have also been asked about the reasons for not implementing curriculum changes. The main reasons given by two hundred teachers surveyed by Dow, Whitehead, and Wright (1984) were: the curriculum contained an unrealistic amount of material to be covered, had too few suggestions for student assessment, and came with insufficient support materials; teachers had been given too little opportunity to make input into the guideline, study it, or discuss it with other teachers prior to implementation; they had not been allowed sufficient time as individuals or teams to plan the implementation; there was little support or communication from the central office; and principals were not knowledgeable, supportive, or clear about their role in implementation.

It is beginning to become clear that in order to succeed, implementation must be a process not of command, but of negotiation.

GUIDELINES FOR CURRICULUM IMPLEMENTATION

Enough information has been collected from studies of successful and unsuccessful implementation, that we can begin to build a set of guidelines.

■ 1. Establish a Climate of Trust ■

Teaching is a very public activity. There are few occupations in which every blunder is reported that evening in dozens of homes. This is one reason why many teachers are reluctant to take the risks involved in adopting changes. Another is their recognition that "if the change works, the individual teacher gets little of the credit; if it doesn't, the teacher gets most of the blame" (Fullan, 1991a, p. 127). As principals and others farther up the educational hierarchy are even more exposed, they also are often reluctant to be the first to try out unproved innovations.

Demands by the central office that curriculum be implemented exactly as stipulated indicate a lack of trust in the professionalism of local schools and teachers. Centrally designed curriculum may be effective, say Louis and Miles, provided that "the local school people who will implement it are empowered to make significant choices about the details of design and action, and get central office support as they proceed" (1990, p. 27). Educational change has to be viewed as evolutionary: "there is a general destination, but many twists and turns as unexpected events occur along the way" (1990, p. 77).

Glickman points out an additional peril faced by innovators: the peril of success. As he puts it: "The more an empowered school is recognized for its success, the more non-empowered schools criticize it" (1990, p. 71). Excellence and success are

bitter reminders to the mediocre of their own mediocrity and will sometimes result in jealousy, resentment, and efforts to sabotage successful innovations.

To overcome these conservative tendencies within and outside the innovating institution, a climate needs to be established in which risk-taking is actively encouraged and rewarded. This means that it will be rewarded even if it fails. If we penalize students every time they make a mistake, they will never try to learn, and the same applies to teachers. Tom Peters urges managers to "support fast failures":

— support failure by actively and publicly rewarding mistakes—failed efforts that were well thought out, executed with alacrity, quickly adjusted, and thoroughly learned from;

— actively and publicly reward defiance of our own often inhibiting regulations;

— personally seek out and directly batter down irritating obstacles . . . that cumulatively cause debilitating delay.   (Peters, 1988, p. 258)

How to change professors

There are two ways to get faculty members in higher education to attend to the quality of their teaching. The first is to handle them the way Peter the Great handled his nobles: Order them to line up, and stand there with a scissors ready to snip off their beards as they walk by. The second method is the way you teach a cat to like mustard: You put a little on the cat's tail. At first, the cat doesn't like the taste, but, being naturally a fastidious animal, it realizes that licking the mustard off will ultimately be in its best interest. After a while, the cat will come to not mind the taste, and in fact will eat mustard quite readily.

M. K. Poltev, Head, Directorate of Qualification Raising of the Ministry of Higher and Specialized Secondary Education, USSR (Kerr, 1982, p. 106)

At the same time, educational leaders need to build a record of credible innovation. If your last three innovations have been fiascos, don't expect many teachers to volunteer to try out the next one. If the conditions for success—such as acceptable student behavior—are not in place, innovation is likely to fail, and its failure will affect the chances of future initiatives. Just as mastery learning builds on student successes, school improvement begins with small successes and builds upon them (Louis & Miles, 1990).

▪ 2. Implement Changes that Meet Recognized Needs ▪

Appeals to national or international needs do not seem to be very effective in building support for change. There must be people within the community and the school who perceive the change as meeting local needs. Middle-class communities will typically support changes seen as beneficial to university-bound students. But working-class communities cannot necessarily be counted on to support changes considered to benefit their children. In both kinds of communities, parents are more likely to become involved to oppose, rather than to support, curriculum innovations. And when the community unites to oppose a curriculum change proposed by the school, it almost always prevails (Fullan, 1982).

When changes are adopted not on the basis of local need but on account of the availability of outside funds (this is known as opportunistic change), what usually happens is "surface innovation." Enough changes are made to capture the funds, but "when the soft money goes away, so will the program" (Louis & Miles, 1990, p. 27).

The fact that the need for a new curriculum is supported by academic or pedagogical experts does not carry much conviction with teachers. In fact, Charles Silberman ascribes the failures of much of the curriculum reform movement of the 1960s to "the fact that its prime movers were distinguished university scholars" (Silberman, 1970, p. 179). Besides their lack of credibility to teachers, "well-intentioned, intelligent university authorities and 'experts' on education can be dead wrong," comments Michael Fullan (1991a, p. 22).

In a perfect world, it would be enough if the change met the needs of learners. The evidence is that changes are adopted only if they also meet a recognized need of teachers. This means that educational leaders must be close to teachers and understand how they view their work. In particular, it is necessary to understand the rewards that are important to teachers. Two Australian educators, Waugh and Punch, write that "These rewards need not be in the form of salary increases, fringe benefits or professional status. Far more significant for most teachers is assurance of improved student progress and more stimulating learning conditions" (Waugh & Punch, 1987, p. 74). The most gratifying moments are when a class comes alive, when an epiphany of new understanding occurs, when a student rises to a new level of achievement, when a graduate returns years later to thank a teacher. Farmers will adopt new agricultural techniques when they are convinced that they will result in significantly improved yields. Teachers will adopt new curricula when they believe that these curricula will enable them to become more effective in producing student excitement, interest, and learning (Guskey, 1986; Leithwood & MacDonald, 1981).

The relationship between student and teacher interest is symbiotic. This suggests that it would be wise to consult students frequently during the curriculum development process. Generally speaking, students do not feel that teachers or administrators understand or listen to them (Fullan, 1982). If they did, they might find curriculum content and instructional methods that would be more interesting for everyone.

The belief that the involvement of a few teachers in designing innovations would make implementation more likely, a belief that flourished twenty years ago, was always naive, and was ultimately shown to be mistaken. "As far as most teachers were concerned, when the change was produced by fellow teachers it was just as much *externally experienced* as if it had come from the university or the government" (Fullan, 1991a, p. 127, his italics). It is important to consult teachers widely and open-mindedly. Louis and Miles warn that curriculum change designed by small teams of teachers runs the risk of creating "an in-group of believers and

---

A lesson from the cake-makers

Some years ago a new instant cake mix failed in the marketplace. Since taste tests had shown the product to be superior and homemakers were known to prefer mixes that were easy, what went wrong? After some head-scratching, the manufacturer discovered the mix was so "instant" the cake-makers felt left out of the process and, consequently, rejected the mix. When the manufacturer modified the formula to require the cake-maker to add one egg before baking, there was a turnaround in sales.

Jerry L. Brown (1981, p. 109)

an out-group of resisters" (1990, p. 28). It is also important that teachers know that they are invited to make input to curriculum development if they wish. But the basic task of educational leaders is not to show a few teachers why they will benefit from being involved in designing the change, but to show all teachers how they will benefit from implementing it.

■ 3. Consult Widely ■

It is implicit in the foregoing, but worth repeating, that the key players in curriculum must be regularly consulted throughout the development and implementation phases. The findings in sex education by Kenney and Orr (1984), showing that 79 percent of parents supported sex education programs when their consent was sought, while only 34 percent gave that support when they were not consulted about the program, also apply to teachers. Consultation with all of those involved in educational change—parents, teachers, students, members of the community—is not only judicious political practice. It is also a requirement of democracy. It is not an effective strategy for leaders unilaterally to announce firm curriculum decisions. School goals, mission statements, curriculum policies are most effectively developed in collaboration. As Fullan puts it, "Taking charge does not mean that one eschews interdependencies. . . . Effective empowerment and interdependency go hand in hand" (1988, p. vi).

Broad-based consultation can also counteract another enemy of innovation: the special-interest group. As long ago as 1926, curriculum thinkers recognized that "the propaganda and interference" of such groups "constitutes one of the greatest menaces in modern education" (Rugg et al., 1926, p. 16). Such groups often claim to speak for the community as a whole. Many school systems are facing charges, for example, that programs aimed to foster such attributes as critical thinking are guilty of Eastern, New Age, or Secular Humanist religious indoctrination ("South Carolina," 1991, p. 5). At worst, special interest groups can sabotage innovations and distort school programs. At best, they consume inordinate amounts of time. School leaders are in a position of strength to rebut the claims of such groups only if they have trustworthy data on the opinions of the community at large.

Team work

We have established a little republic on board Gjøa. . . . I decided, as far as possible to use a system of freedom on board—let everybody have the feeling of being independent within his own sphere. In that way, there arises—amongst sensible people—a spontaneous and voluntary discipline, which is worth far more than compulsion. Every man thereby has the consciousness of being a human being; he is treated as a rational being, not as a machine. . . . The will to do work is many times greater—and thereby the work itself. We were all working towards a common goal and gladly shared all work.

Roald Amundsen (1912)

■ 4. Establish Clear Goals and Limited Scope ■

Programs with vague and uncertain goals will be implemented, if at all, vaguely and uncertainly. Clear goals imply and require a degree of candor and "up-frontness" on everyone's part. They make it possible to gauge progress and feed evidence of success back to teachers.

But the goals for curriculum innovations are often far from clear. Sometimes they are not clear to people at the top of the organization, and when they are, this clarity has sometimes been replaced by uncertainty about the change, or even ignorance of it, on the part of teachers (Aoki et al., 1977; Gross, Giacquinta, & Bernstein, 1971).

> Can teachers be guided to be better by the institutions in which they work—by bureaucracy? I don't think so. I don't think people can be made to be good by bureaucracies. Bureaucracies have a poor record in this regard. Teachers will have to do it themselves. The most honest, courageous, and just amongst them will have to lead the way. Those who have these virtues will have to reaffirm the values of their work and shake their peers out of their torpor. They will not get much help from the bureaucracies which run their institutions—although there will be voices there to join with teachers in re-affirming the educational values teachers strive to achieve. When these values prevail sustained by virtuous practitioners, new, more congenial institutions will follow.
>
> John Olson (1990, p. 5)

Educational change is incremental, not revolutionary. There is nothing so satisfying as revolutionary slogans. They salve our social consciences while rarely posing a serious threat to the status quo. The bigger the projected change, and the less focused it is, the less likely it is to be implemented. As Fullan says, "Large plans and vague ideas make a lethal combination" (1982, p. 102). The bumper-sticker version of this principle is, "Don't start vast projects with half-vast ideas." This is not an argument for trivial change. Proposals for trivial change may obtain people's consent, but hardly their commitment. It does suggest that complex changes need to be broken down into their component parts for serial implementation. By the same token, teachers cannot be expected to make several major changes concurrently; each additional requirement reduces the probability of any change occurring.

■ 5. Develop an Ethos of Collegiality ■

Roland Barth (1990b) observes that collegiality is difficult to spell, hard to pronounce, and harder still to define. Judith Little (1981, 1982) suggests that collegiality is recognizable by four behaviors: the adults in schools talk about their professional practice, observe each other teaching, develop curriculum cooperatively, and teach each other. She found collegiality to be most common when principals expected, modeled, rewarded, and protected it. Hargreaves (1989b) cautions that collegiality cannot be legislated: "contrived collegiality" produces few benefits.

Clearly one role of educational leaders is to bring about an environment in which teacher cooperation and collaboration will flourish. In effective school systems, superintendents and principals support one another. Sara Lightfoot observes that "What is often perceived as solitary leadership . . . is fueled by partnerships and alliances with intimate, trusted associates" (1983, p. 26). Typical comments from effective systems are "they know they won't be judged badly if they call for help"; "we support one another's efforts; we share a lot"; "you are encouraged to try things, and if an idea works, others will take it up" (Coleman & LaRocque, 1991, p. 164). Norms of collegiality appear to pervade innovative institutions. In schools where principals and teachers collaborate, students are also more likely to do so (Short & Spencer, 1990).

Teachers need both support and consultation from their principals; these factors are related to their motivation, involvement, morale, and their willingness to consult with one another (Blase, 1987; Erb, 1987; Goodlad, 1984). For innovations to flourish at the local level, a group of supportive teachers is needed at each site. These are teachers who are trained in the program and committed to it, who model it in their own classrooms, and who provide guidance and leadership to their colleagues. It is an occupational hazard for nurturing professionals, including teachers, to invest in the support of others and to ignore their own needs for nurturance. Consequently, teaching is a profession often marked by considerable personal isolation and loneliness (Sarason, 1971). Curriculum improvement is most likely to come about in an institution that has developed an ethos of collegial support.

The support of central administrators will not be sufficient to ensure implementation; but without it, failure is almost certain. Nor is lip-service enough. There are a hundred ways in which administrators can damn an innovation by faint praise, and teachers are perceptive enough to recognize when their superiors are serious about a curriculum change.

How much support should be given to teachers who adopt, but then radically modify, the curriculum? Michael Fullan suggests that if teachers are to be committed to a change and take ownership of it, they must feel free to adapt it to their own needs and to that of their students. On this point, he is explicit: "The more committed an individual is to the specific form of change, the less effective he or she will be in getting others to implement it" (1991a, p. 9). Huberman and Miles (1984), however, argue from the basis of a series of case studies that if fidelity to the original plan is not insisted on, teachers will water down the change until it is trivialized out of existence:

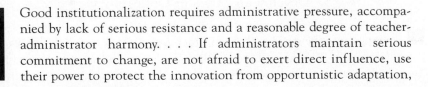

Good institutionalization requires administrative pressure, accompanied by lack of serious resistance and a reasonable degree of teacher-administrator harmony. . . . If administrators maintain serious commitment to change, are not afraid to exert direct influence, use their power to protect the innovation from opportunistic adaptation, and above all, supply a steady flow of support, success is likely. . . . Enforcing fidelity for substantial, good-quality innovations really paid off—if it was accompanied by effective assistance. When adaptation went too far because of administrative latitude, what often occurred was blunting or downsizing, trivialization, and weak student impact. . . . We found that enforcement scenarios could be quite effective if the muscle was accompanied by tutoring and tenderness. (Huberman & Miles, 1984, pp. 221, 270, 279)

Louis and Miles, on the basis of more recent studies of schools, suggest a middle position: "School improvement efforts are most likely to succeed where there is a combination of internal commitment to and incentives for change, and external pressure and support" (1990, p. 42).

▪ 6. Use Personal Contact ▪

The late 1960s and early 1970s were a period of much curriculum-making. Many dollars were spent in developing new curricula. More dollars were spent printing them. They were then distributed by courier van to the schools, where they disappeared without trace.

The way to convince another is to state your case moderately and accurately. Then scratch your head, or shake it a little, and say that is the way it seems to you, but that of course, you may be mistaken about it; which causes your listener to receive what you have to say, and as like as not, turn about and try to convince you of it, since you are in doubt. But if you go at him in a tone of positiveness and arrogance you make an opponent of him.

Benjamin Franklin

There are few circumstances in which people change on command. In everyday life, we tend to be influenced most by word of mouth of our friends. Tom Peters reminds corporations that "Purchasers buy the new based principally upon the perceptions of respected peers who have already purchased or tried the product" (1988, p. 238). We buy a car, call a plumber, choose a lawyer, see a movie, or try a recipe based on the recommendation of our friends. Face-to-face contact, not memoranda, is essential between the advocates and the users of new programs. Ernest House puts it this way:

As the flow of blood is essential to human life, so direct personal contact is essential to the propagation of innovation. . . . Direct personal contacts are the medium through which innovations must flow. Innovation diffusion is directly proportional to the number, frequency, depth, and duration of such contacts. (House, 1974, pp. 8, 11)

The skills needed by change agents are not the skills of political rhetoric or bureaucratic manipulation; these will produce, at best, short-term and surface changes. Rather, as Michael Fullan writes, "The abilities to communicate, listen, motivate, gain trust, and the like are all critical interpersonal skills necessary for effective leadership for change" (1982, p. 93). The chances of success are even greater if the advocates are people whom the users know and trust. Miles, Saxl, and Lieberman (1988) conducted a study with seventeen change agents working in three New York City improvement programs, to determine what were the skills such change agents needed. They reported:

> Twelve specific skills appeared, in four areas. In the "personal" area the skill of initiative-taking was crucial. In the "socio-emotional process" area, the skills were rapport-building, support, conflict mediation, collaboration, and confrontation. In the "task" area, the skills were individual diagnosis, organizational diagnosis, and managing/controlling. Finally, in the area of "educational content" the key skills were resource-bringing and demonstration.   (p. 157)

▪ 7. Provide Systematic In-Service Training ▪

It is standard practice to blame teacher education for the shortcomings of schools. The following is a typical critique:

> It seems as if accusing pedagogical institutes of training teachers poorly has become chronic. Schools directors complain about the practical helplessness of young specialists; directors of studies are despondent over young teachers' lack of methodological abilities, while yesterday's graduates of higher educational institutions suffer from their inability to deal with the children.

This statement is by V. Men'shikov, writing in a publication of the (former) Soviet Ministry of Education (Men'shikov, 1991, p. 37). The catalog of inadequacies of initial teacher education is lengthy. Likewise, the inadequacies of in-service teacher education are frequently blamed for the failure of an innovation, whether the innovation is open classrooms or instructional systems development in the armed forces (Anderson, 1986). We will refrain from itemizing these complaints. As John F. Kennedy used to say, we are here not to curse the darkness, but to light a candle.

The large amount of attention to in-service teacher education in recent years has produced some new insights and orientations. Most important is a shift away from the attitude that teachers have deficits that need to be fixed, and toward the belief that teachers are human beings who need and want to grow personally and professionally. Growth is best facilitated not by hit-and-run visits by charismatic experts or one-time orientation sessions, but by a school climate that provides social support, shared experiences, and collaborative staff development (Barth, 1990b; Fullan, 1991; Joyce & Showers, 1982; Little, 1981). As in many other fields, such as

AIDS education or addictions education, there is growing evidence that the greatest influence on people's behavior are the words and actions of their peers (Flay, 1985; Rugg, O'Reilly, & Galavotti, 1990; Sabatier, 1989).

Collegial visitation, classroom observation, videotaping and reviewing lessons, and professional discussion in small groups are all valuable strategies (Robinson, 1992; Shymansky & Kyle, 1988). Teachers and administrators need to be given the opportunity to share and discuss their anxieties, reservations, and doubts about curriculum innovations. George Beauchamp (1983) points out that "engagement in and discussion of curriculum planning is one of the key ways in which we foster the professional development of teachers." We are beginning to realize that effective in-service education (like effective education in general) is an interaction, not a monologue. Where a high level of trust exists between colleagues, they can be of enormous help to one another by observing each other's classes, talking with one another's students, and listening, supporting, and counseling one another (Tiberius & Silins, 1980). Ideally, the relationship among teachers and between teachers and principals becomes one of mentoring, the dimensions of which, according to William Schubert (1988), include inspiring a vision, promoting liberation, giving genuine attention, being morally committed, exercising humility, integrating the personal, and living on in the other person.

Principals also need appropriate in-service training. They need to be persuaded of the merit of an innovation before they can be expected authentically to advocate it to teachers. They need the opportunity to meet with principals in whose schools the innovation is working effectively, to be able to question administrative details, talk about their concerns, share their anxieties, and be assured of a network of support while supervising change. Teachers take notice of whether or not their principal attends in-service sessions associated with a curriculum innovation.

Local teachers who have field tested a new curriculum are more credible advocates than distant experts (Fullan, Anderson, & Newton, 1986). They should be invited to talk through the fine details of implementing the innovation, and to respond to the doubts of teachers who are considering adopting the innovation (Sparks, 1983). Talking with them, visiting their classrooms, or viewing videotapes of the new program in action will be more effective than listening to lectures on the merits of the innovation.

■ 8. Provide Time and Resources ■

Like everyone else, teachers never have enough time. In fact, shortage of time is "the single most frequently cited barrier to implementation" (Fullan, 1982, p. 293). Teachers are busy people, and classrooms intensely busy places. One study found that in elementary classrooms, teachers began a new activity every thirty-seven seconds (McDaniel-Hine & Willower, 1988). Principals can earn the gratitude of teachers by giving them a number of "time coupons" that can be redeemed by asking the principal to take over their class for a period while they are involved in in-service training, development of teaching materials, or some other professional activity.

Development of materials is one of the most time-consuming tasks for teachers. Curricula with heavy requirements for teacher generation of new materials do not stand a good chance of implementation. Curricula that are accompanied by high-quality, practical, field-tested materials that stimulate student enthusiasm and learning are much more likely to be successful.

It may take a teacher two hours of steady work to produce a detailed map, diagram, illustration, or graph for a handout or overhead transparency. A folder of masters of such visual material, suitable for printing or making overheads, and with clear permission to make multiple copies, will greatly facilitate implementation. Similarly, it should not be necessary for teachers to search all available videos or software to find appropriate programs. Preselection should be done by the curriculum planning committee. The curriculum should list the titles of recommended programs, and these should be obtainable from the school or the central office with a minimum of paperwork.

Very frequently, a curriculum is introduced in September and its success measured in June. When this procedure shows no change in student learning, or perhaps a decrease, the innovation may be abandoned. The fact is that a new curriculum is rarely completely implemented in the first year. (Reinhold Neibuhr, who as a theologian took the long view, declared that "Nothing worth doing can be accomplished in a single lifetime" [Keen, 1992, p. 185]). Typically, teachers try out parts of the new program, while relying heavily on materials, content, and methods that they know to be effective from previous years. Short-term studies of program effectiveness (often stimulated by the requirements of funding or doctoral theses) are a plague in education and have probably resulted in the premature rejection of many potentially beneficial programs. Five cycles of implementation (e.g., five years or semesters) may be necessary before an innovation is completely in place.

Shortage of money is chronic in schools, but in curriculum innovation, it is probably the provision of time, rather than merely money, that is critical. There is, in fact, not much evidence that more money makes for better education. A number of large-scale studies, both in North America and in developing countries, have come to the surprising conclusion that the average correlation between expenditure and student achievement is approximately zero (Coleman, 1986; Fuller, 1987; Walberg & Rasher, 1979).

▪ 9. Do Not Try to Change Everyone ▪

To wait to introduce change until we have unanimity is usually to wait forever. Using an enthusiastic majority to steamroll a reluctant minority is an abuse of democracy. But consensus decision making can also be abused if it gives power of veto to every individual. Max Planck, who won the Nobel Prize for Physics in 1918, is reported to have said, "The only way to overcome opposition to a new theory is to wait for the opponents to die out." Every institution contains its opponents of change. There are the fainthearts, who fear change. There is the old regime, who have benefited from the old model and stand to lose by the new. There are the bureaucrats, for whom any change means more paperwork. There are the nostalgics, who look back misty-eyed to a nonexistent past. There are the hard-core romantics, to whom any kind of planning is anathema. And, my personal favorite, there are the futilitarians. Futilitarians, often "experts," believe that almost all change is futile. They respond to any proposed innovation with the declaration that it won't work. When it works elsewhere, they say it won't work here. There is probably no innovation that has benefited humankind that was not originally condemned by experts as impractical, impossible, or immoral. This was certainly the case with proposals for university education of women, decolonization, lyric poetry, postage stamps, the telephone, the Xerox copier, and the exploration of space.

Dr. Dionysius Lardner, a nineteenth-century mathematician, clergyman, Fellow of the Royal Society, and Professor of Natural Philosophy at London University, was one of history's great Futilitarians. He devoted his life to condemning the steam engine, the steam locomotive, and the steam ship. Shortly before the advent of railway passenger travel, he argued that the speed and acceleration of railway trains would cause all the passengers to suffocate. Two years before the *Great Western* crossed the Atlantic, he declared that no large steamship would ever be able to cross the ocean, as it would require more coal than it could carry. Eventually, he eloped to Paris with the wife of a Director of the London and Brighton Railway, crossing the English Channel by steamship.

Coleman (1976, p. 20)

Vanity is a great obstacle to innovation. Some people are opposed to innovations simply because they didn't think of them first. It has often been said that you can accomplish anything if you don't care who gets the credit. Field Marshal Bernard Montgomery's generals learned how to turn his vanity to advantage in the North African campaign in 1942:

> One of them would go to his caravan in the evening, and put their case. Monty would shake his head and say:
> "Can't do that, can't do that."
> Then in the morning he might say: "I've been thinking, and had an idea . . ." He would then explain the idea which would be the one put to him the night before.   (Barnett, 1982, p. 294)

■ 10. Do Not Despair ■

The world is full of the prophets of doom. The economy is in collapse, schools are declining, test scores are a disgrace, the end of the world is at hand. An unrealistic optimism can be almost equally depressing. We might counter with the idea that life is seasonal: human beings and human institutions live through cycles of summer, fall, winter, and spring; through light and dark; through inspiration and expiration; through the yin and the yang. Such a belief lends credence to the injunction of

Winston Churchill, speaking in the dark days of 1941 to the boys at his old school: "Never give in, never give in, *never, never, never, never*—in nothing, great or small, large or petty—never give in except to convictions of honor and good sense" (Churchill, 1974, p. 6499, his italics).

A Swedish psychologist, Claes Janssen, has developed a model of change that integrates personal and institutional psychology. Individuals and institutions, Janssen suggests, experience four main phases that tend to follow one another in sequence. The phases are inspiration, contentment, denial, and confusion (Claes Janssen, personal communication, September 1992).

Let us see how Janssen's model applies to a historical example. The British Empire was probably at its highest point in the years 1815–1854, a period of unchallenged ascendancy on land and sea, of domestic reform and economic growth, of colonial consolidation and expansion, and of literary and artistic greatness. But in British minds, the high point was probably Queen Victoria's Diamond Jubilee in 1897, when bejeweled maharajahs rode elephants in procession through the streets of London and Edward Elgar was beginning to write the music to *Land of Hope and Glory*. In fact, by this point, Britain was already in decline, as shown by the catastrophes of the Indian Mutiny, the Crimean War, and the South African War. Following World War I, with the loss of over a million young men and of colossal economic resources, Britain's belief in its hegemony could be maintained only by a process of denial—a process that continued in some quarters even after World War II. Dean Acheson pointed to Britain's confusion in his famous comment that "Britain has lost an empire and has not yet found a role."

We can see how this cycle of inspiration, contentment, denial, and confusion is played out also in a very small institution such as a marriage. There is a

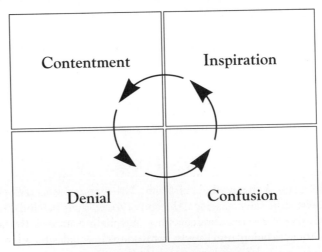

The Janssen Change Model

courtship and honeymoon stage, followed by a period of comfort and contentment that may gradually shade into predictability and boredom. If the relationship declines, the first impulse of one or both partners is typically denial. Denial continues until the partners are prepared actively to rebuild the relationship or to separate, and a period of confusion will ensue until one or both partners achieves renewed inspiration alone or in the previous or a new relationship.

Everyone can think of schools that follow this pattern. Successful schools are the product of the hard work and inspiration of many people. But once they begin to believe in their own reputation, complacency often sets in. Any suggestion that reform is needed is almost always met by denial. Often such institutions have to hit bottom—for example, be threatened with closure—before their members will face up to their own denial and be willing to find their way through confusion to renewed institutional health.

While Janssen maintains that the four phases normally follow a fixed sequence, there is no limit to the amount of time an individual or an institution can spend in any one phase. Some institutions appear to be stuck in permanent confusion. Janssen points out that universities "can take much more confusion than the ordinary organization; they even, perhaps, *should* take more of it, for it reflects the multitude of conflicting ideas, which must be permitted to flourish in a place of learning" (Claes Janssen, personal communication, September 1992; his emphasis). The role of the educational leader is to accept an institution where it is, guide it through the phases to inspiration, and keep it in inspiration as long as possible. If an institution does slip into contentment, the leader needs to confront the institution with its status (which will result in denial), help it to face up to its denial (which will result in confusion), and guide it back to inspiration and renewal.

Any experienced teacher can attest to the speed at which a school can deteriorate, and the somewhat slower speed at which it can recover. School systems do periodically implement successful innovations. More frequently, individual schools institute new policies or programs that make a difference to the lives of students. Still more often, individual teachers find new ways of motivating, encouraging, and teaching their pupils. Pessimism and passivity are symptoms of denial. We may not yet know how to transform schools and curricula. But we certainly know enough to improve them.

CURRICULUM RENEWAL

A curriculum should never be considered a final draft. Rather, it is an interim document awaiting further improvement.

The task of curriculum and program evaluation, therefore, does not end when a curriculum is implemented. Rather, a dialogue should continue between users of the curriculum—both teachers and students—and the sponsors of the curriculum. A New York City prekindergarten guide, for example, includes an addressed tear-out sheet, asking users of the curriculum to return it with specific suggestions for additions, deletions, and revisions for the next edition (New York City Board of Education, 1986). This is evidence of a real commitment to feedback and renewal.

People go on teaching, go on learning, go on hoping, toiling, troubling, and trying. Beaten down by racism, sexism, class exploitation, by the great White whale and the great White myth and the great White cultural emptiness, and also by fear of dying, fear of being different, fear of being impolite, still people rise. We rise because we perceive an alternative, we begin to identify the unacceptable. We find free voices that say "No!" and free minds that dare to dream of something different. We find then that our bodies move in new ways, that new freedoms demand new actions and together we reclaim our lives and begin to build our futures. . . . We can perhaps contribute as builders of a new world, a world where people can care more, love more fully and more widely, touch each other more, think more clearly, solve more problems, laugh and cry more. This is worth our trouble.

William Ayers (1989, p. 527)

THE FUTURE OF CURRICULUM PLANNING

"Everyone knows that the world is full of mischief," writes Welles Foshay. "So is the curriculum field" (1990, p. 273). Part of our task as curriculum planners is to make mischief: to challenge teachers and students to think about curriculum in new ways, to question old assumptions, to break out of the cocoon of inertia and tradition.

The task of teachers and of schools is in many ways harder than it was a generation ago. Public expectations of the variety of roles that schools should perform have risen. Schools have become more inclusive, and as a result the variety of students in schools is greater. The proportion of pupils with learning disabilities, physical handicaps, or behavioral difficulties, is greater than it was in the 1960s, and will be greater still thirty years from now (Pallas, Natriello, & McDill, 1989). But we also know how to be effective with a much wider range of pupils than we did in the past.

The last twenty years have provided us with an enormous amount of information—more than can be readily assimilated—about "what works" in terms of curriculum and instructional effectiveness. The systematic application of that knowledge would enable us to accomplish most of the traditional cognitive goals of schooling with most of our students. The days in which young people left school without good reading skills, mathematical competence, fluency in a foreign language, and ability to participate in many of the arts should be long gone.

The first task of professional educators is the application of what we already know. That alone should be sufficient to design learning environments that produce cognitive competence in the overwhelming majority of our students. But the next priority is a greater challenge: to discover ways to become effective in bringing about the more subtle and difficult changes involved in noncognitive areas. No less important than cognitions are those personal qualities such as a strong self-concept, a sense of control over one's destiny, social competence, responsibility, altruism, empathy, and a sense of meaning and identity. For the future happiness and well-being of our students and our society, it is the development of qualities such as these that will be crucial. To discover ways to bring such qualities into being is the next frontier of curriculum research. The combined application of research in this area, of what we already know about teaching and learning, and of the commitment of dedicated teachers could in the next century produce educational systems of which at present few people even dream.

▪ SELF–ASSESSMENT

1. In what ways can needs assessment facilitate implementation of a curriculum innovation?

2. In the relationship between superintendents and principals, neither an authoritarian nor a laissez-faire approach seems very effective. What kind of approach is preferable?

3. What kinds of activity are likely to occupy most of the time of effective principals?

4. What are some ways in which school systems tend to alienate teachers from proposed curriculum changes?

5. Why does "opportunistic implementation" normally make little long-term difference?

6. Who are the best people, and what are the best means, to advocate curriculum change to teachers?

7. What problems can result when teachers are required to implement a new curriculum without being allowed to modify it?

8. Why may evaluation results at the end of the first run-through of a new program be misleading?

9. Pick an institution you know well and see how accurately the Janssen change model applies to it.

10. What is your most optimistic scenario for schools in the year 2020?

For feedback, see Appendix F.
If you were able to give satisfactory responses to nine or ten questions, you understand the material in this chapter.
If you were able to give satisfactory responses to seven or eight questions, reread the relevant parts of the chapter.
If you were able to respond satisfactorily to six or less questions, reread the chapter carefully.

A Glossary of Curriculum Terms

Academic Engaged Time   The time that a learner spends learning material that is personally appropriate and educationally relevant.

Acceleration   Progress through certain phases of schooling at a faster rate than normal.

Achievement   Growth of a learner from one stage of learning to another.

Advance Organizer   Instructional activity that focuses the learner on the essence of what is about to be taught.

Aim   A general instructional intention.

Aptitude   Capacity for learning (*Webster's New Collegiate Dictionary*, 1973, p. 57).

Assessment   A process of judgment about people, and in particular about student learning.

At-Risk Learner   A learner experiencing serious academic, intellectual, behavioral, emotional, social, or psychological difficulty.

Attainment   Accomplishment by a learner of a specified level of learning.

Authentic Assessment   Assessment that asks students to display the actual qualities they are intended to learn under the "real world" conditions for which the curriculum is intended to prepare them.

Behavioral Objective   An educational objective stated in terms of an overt and specific action to be performed by the learner.

Cognitive   Related to knowledge or intellectual activity.

Collegiality   Professional practice marked by peer interaction and collaboration.

Conscientization   A dialectical and shared process between teachers and learners intended to make people aware of the political, cultural, historical, and social assumptions of their society.

Constructed-Response Test   A test in which examinees have considerable freedom of choice in response; for example, to write an essay in their own words.

Consumables   Resources such as paper and electricity that are used up in instruction and have to be replaced.

Content   Subject matter to be taught in a curriculum.

Context   The environment of a curriculum, including the program of which it is part, and the institutional, community, and social setting.

Criterion-Referenced Assessment   Assessment based on comparing of learner attainment against fixed criteria.

Critical   Directly related to the success or failure of a system or to the achievement of the aim or central purpose of a curriculum.

Curriculum   A plan or blueprint for instruction.

Cybernetics   The study of communication, control, and self-regulation in systems.

Difficulty Index   An estimate of the percentage of examinees answering a question correctly.

Disaggregation   Separation of data in order to examine values for specific populations.

Discrimination Index   An estimate of the difference between scores on a test item of more and less proficient examinees.

Effectiveness   Production of, or capacity to produce, a result.

Efficiency   Production of output relative to input of energy and other resources.

Empowerment   Process by which people assume greater control over their lives.

Enrichment   An increase in the depth or variety of subject matter or activities in a student's program.

Entry Characteristics   Knowledge, skills, and other qualities possessed by a learner at the point of entry to a program.

Ethos   The distinguishing character, sentiment, moral nature, or guiding beliefs of a person, group, or institution (*Webster's New Collegiate Dictionary*, 1973, p. 393).

Evaluation   The determination of worth, especially of instruction, curricula, policies, and programs.

Experiential Objective   An objective stated in terms of an intrinsically significant experience.

Extrinsic Motivation   Motivation that arises from some factor unrelated to the learning itself.

Feasibility   The capacity to be successfully realized in the real world.

Field Test   A tryout of a program under conditions of typical use.

Formative Assessment   Assessment conducted during the course of instruction, primarily to diagnose, monitor, and provide feedback on student learning and/or the instruction.

Gatekeeper   Person who has power or authority to influence a program.

Giftedness   Superior aptitude in one or more areas of endeavor.

Grade Retention   Requiring a student to repeat a grade or year.

Grading   The process of classifying students on the basis of data from assessment.

Implementation   Realization of an intended change.

Instruction   Planned or deliberate effort to teach something to someone.

Intelligence   A general ability to learn, reason, or deal with new situations.

Intrinsic Motivation   Motivation arising from the conscious interest, value, meaning, or significance of the learning to the learner.

Item Analysis   A technique for the evaluation of individual test items by examination of the pattern of responses.

Learning Style   Tendency of an individual to learn more efficiently or effectively under a particular set of environmental conditions.

Logistics   The detailed planning of the human and material resources required for the conduct of an organized activity.

Mastery Learning   An approach to instruction utilizing feedback and correction, aiming at the development of a high degree of proficiency in almost all learners.

Mean   The average of a set of scores.

Measurement   The assignment of numbers to objects or events according to rules (Stevens, 1951, p. 22).

Median   The middle score of a set of scores.

Medium   A mode of communication.

Meta-Analysis   A technique for combining the results of many different experimental studies to produce a single statistic indicating the effect of a treatment.

Metacognition   Awareness, monitoring, and regulating of one's own intellectual processes.

Methodology   The means, processes, and activities used for instruction.

Mode   The most frequent score in a set of scores.

Naturalistic   An approach to inquiry or evaluation that emphasizes the perspective of participants, views events as embedded in a network of interdependent relationships, and uses the researcher as the primary instrument of data collection and analysis (Dorr-Bremme, 1990).

Need   A discrepancy between a present and a preferred state.

Needs Assessment   An empirical and judgmental process for identifying human needs and establishing priorities among them.

Nonpreordinate   An approach to analysis, evaluation, or assessment that is not limited by attention to specific anticipated outcomes.

Norm-Referenced Assessment   Assessment based on comparison of a person's attainment with that of other people.

Objective   A specific instructional intention.

Peak Learning Experience   An educational experience marked by a high level of significance, meaning, interest, or engagement on the part of the learner.

Peer Tutoring   Instruction of a student by another student.

Percentile   A value on a scale of one hundred that represents the percentage of a set of scores that is equal to or below it.

Performance Criterion   A prescribed action on the part of a learner or learners that represents attainment or degree of attainment of an objective.

Pilot Test   A preliminary small-scale tryout of all or part of a program prototype under conditions that produce detailed evaluative data.

Portfolio   A collection of work, typically written or graphic, by a student.

Preordinate   An approach to analysis, evaluation, or assessment that gives primary attention to the attainment of specific anticipated outcomes.

Prerequisite   A characteristic or experience stipulated as a necessary antecedent to another experience.

Process Objective   An objective stated in terms of a learning activity.

Program   A structured organization of educational activities.

Rationale   A reasoned argument in justification of a curriculum.

Readiness   The capacity to engage in certain mental or physical activities by reason of maturation, motivation, or prior experience.

Reliability   The consistency of a test score when factors other than quality of student response are altered.

Remediation   Process by which the attainment of students who, following instruction, perform below a criterion, is raised to the criterion level.

Retention in Grade   See GRADE RETENTION.

Selected-Response Test   A test in which the examinee chooses an answer to each question from a given list of alternatives.

Skill Ability to perform an activity that has requirements (e.g., of speed or accuracy) that can be met only as a result of practice or training.

Snapshot Assessment Judgment based on a single sample of behavior.

Social Indicator Data on the status or behavior of individuals that when aggregated and analyzed throw light on social conditions or trends.

Somatic Objective An objective involving a physiological change in the learner.

Standard Deviation A measure of the dispersion of a frequency distribution.

Strategy The method, process, procedure, or technique used in instruction.

Streaming See TRACKING.

Summative Assessment Assessment at the end of an instructional sequence, intended to judge student attainment and provide a mark or grade.

System A complex of interacting and interdependent processes serving a common purpose and constituting a unified whole.

Table of Specifications A detailed plan for the content of a test indicating the proportions of a test devoted to each main topic or objective.

Task Analysis The examination of an activity by decomposition into and description of its component elements and their interrelationships.

Test-Wiseness Skill in test-taking that allows the student to magnify test score independent of actual attainment.

Time-On-Task The time a learner spends actually engaged in learning.

Time Series Analysis Observation or assessment of a phenomenon at regular intervals over a period of time.

Tracking (or STREAMING) An organizational pattern in which students are segregated on the basis of assumed aptitude into parallel but separate streams or tracks that lead to different academic and occupational outcomes.

Training A deliberate process of developing in a person new or changed mental or physical capacity.

Transfer The carry-over or generalization of learned responses from one type of situation to another (*Webster's New Collegiate Dictionary*, 1973, p. 1240).

Tryout Test-running of an innovation prior to full-scale implementation.

Unobtrusive Observation A method of studying typical or voluntary behavior by observing the actions of people who are unaware that they are being observed.

Validity The extent to which a measure enables an observer to draw correct, meaningful, and useful inferences about a learner (adapted from Messick, 1989).

Well-Being A subjective and objective state of health and happiness.

Appendix A

Code of Fair Testing Practices in Education

The Code of Fair Testing Practices in Education states the major obligations to test takers of professionals who develop or use educational tests. The Code is meant to apply broadly to the use of tests in education (admissions, educational assessment, educational diagnosis, and student placement). The Code is not designed to cover employment testing, licensure or certification testing, or other types of testing. Although the Code has relevance to many types of educational tests, it is directed primarily at professionally developed tests such as those sold by commercial test publishers or used in formally administered testing programs. The Code is not intended to cover tests made by individual teachers for use in their own classrooms.

The Code addresses the roles of test developers and test users separately. Test users are people who select tests, commission test development services, or make decisions on the basis of test scores. Test developers are people who actually construct tests as well as those who set policies for particular testing programs. The roles may, of course, overlap—as when a state education agency commissions test development services, sets policies that control the test development process, and makes decisions on the basis of the test scores.

The Code presents standards for educational test developers and users in four areas:

A. Developing/Selecting Tests

B. Interpreting Scores

C. Striving for Fairness

D. Informing Test Takers

Organizations, institutions, and individual professionals who endorse the Code commit themselves to safeguarding the rights of test takers by following the principles listed. The Code is intended to be consistent with the relevant parts of the *Standards for Educational and Psychological Testing* (AERA, APA, NCME, 1985). However, the Code differs from the Standards in both audience and purpose. The Code is meant to be understood by the general public; it is limited to educational tests; and the primary focus is on those issues that affect the proper use of tests. The Code is not meant to add new principles over and above those in the Standards or to change the meaning of the Standards. The goal is rather to represent the spirit of a selected portion of the Standards in a way that is meaningful to test takers and/or their parents or guardians. It is the hope of the Joint Committee that the Code will also be judged to be consistent with existing codes of conduct and standards of other professional groups who use educational tests.

▪ A. Developing/Selecting Appropriate Tests* ▪

| Test developers should provide the information that test users need to select appropriate tests. | Test users should select tests that meet the purpose for which they are to be used and that are appropriate for the intended test-taking populations. |

Test developers should:

1. Define what each test measures and what the test should be used for. Describe the population(s) for which the test is appropriate.

2. Accurately represent the characteristics, usefulness, and limitations of tests for their intended purposes.

3. Explain relevant measurement concepts as necessary for clarity at the level of detail that is appropriate for the intended audience(s).

4. Describe the process of test development. Explain how the content and skills to be tested were selected.

5. Provide evidence that the test meets its intended purpose(s).

Test users should:

1. First define the purpose for testing and the population to be tested. Then, select a test for that purpose and that population based on a thorough review of the available information.

2. Investigate potentially useful sources of information, in addition to test scores, to corroborate the information provided by tests.

3. Read the materials provided by test developers and avoid using tests for which unclear or incomplete information is provided.

4. Become familiar with how and when the test was developed and tried out.

5. Read independent evaluations of a test and of possible alternative measures. Look for evidence required to support the claims of test developers.

* Many of the statements in the Code refer to the selection of existing tests. However, in customized testing programs test developers are engaged to construct new tests. In those situations, the test development process should be designed to help ensure that the completed tests will be in compliance with the Code.

6. Provide either representative samples or complete copies of test questions, directions, answer sheets, manuals, and score reports to qualified users.

7. Indicate the nature of the evidence obtained concerning the appropriateness of each test for groups of different racial, ethnic, or linguistic backgrounds who are likely to be tested.

8. Identify and publish any specialized skills needed to administer each test and to interpret scores correctly.

6. Examine specimen sets, disclosed tests or samples of questions, directions, answer sheets, manuals, and score reports before selecting a test.

7. Ascertain whether the test content and norms group(s) or comparison group(s) are appropriate for the intended test takers.

8. Select and use only those tests for which the skills needed to administer the test and interpret scores correctly are available.

■ B. Interpreting Scores ■

> Test developers should help users interpret scores correctly.

> Test users should interpret scores correctly.

Test developers should:

9. Provide timely and easily understood score reports that describe test performance clearly and accurately. Also explain the meaning and limitations of reported scores.

10. Describe the population(s) represented by any norms or comparison group(s), the dates the data were gathered, and the process used to select the samples of test takers.

11. Warn users to avoid specific, reasonably anticipated misuses of test scores.

Test users should:

9. Obtain information about the scale used for reporting scores, the characteristics of any norms or comparison group(s), and the limitations of the scores.

10. Interpret scores taking into account any major differences between the norms or comparison groups and the actual test takers. Also take into account any differences in test administration practices or familiarity with the specific questions in the test.

11. Avoid using tests for purposes not specifically recommended by the test developer unless evidence is obtained to support the intended use.

12. Provide information that will help users follow reasonable procedures for setting passing scores when it is appropriate to use such scores with the test.

13. Provide information that will help users gather evidence to show that the test is meeting its intended purpose(s).

12. Explain how any passing scores were set and gather evidence to support the appropriateness of the scores.

13. Obtain evidence to help show that the test is meeting its intended purpose(s).

▪ C. Striving for Fairness ▪

Test developers should strive to make tests that are as fair as possible for test takers of different races, gender, ethnic backgrounds, or handicapping conditions.

Test users should select tests that have been developed in ways that attempt to make them as fair as possible for test takers of different races, gender, ethnic backgrounds, or handicapping conditions.

Test developers should:

14. Review and revise test questions and related materials to avoid potentially insensitive content or language.

15. Investigate the performance of test takers of different races, gender, and ethnic backgrounds when samples of sufficient size are available. Enact procedures that help to ensure that differences in performance are related primarily to the skills under assessment rather than to irrelevant factors.

16. When feasible, make appropriately modified forms of tests or administration procedures available for test takers with handicapping conditions. Warn test users of potential problems in using standard norms with modified tests or administration procedures that result in non-comparable scores.

Test users should:

14. Evaluate the procedures used by test developers to avoid potentially insensitive content or language.

15. Review the performance of test takers of different races, gender, and ethnic backgrounds when samples of sufficient size are available. Evaluate the extent to which performance differences may have been caused by inappropriate characteristics of the test.

16. When necessary and feasible, use appropriately modified forms of tests or administration procedures for test takers with handicapping conditions. Interpret standard norms with care in light of the modifications that were made.

▪ D. Informing Test Takers ▪

> Under some circumstances, test developers have direct communication with test takers. Under other circumstances, test users communicate directly with test takers. Whichever group communicates directly with test takers should provide the information described below.

Test developers or test users should:

17. When a test is optional, provide test takers or their parents/guardians with information to help them judge whether the test should be taken or if an available alternative to the test should be used.

18. Provide test takers the information they need to be familiar with the coverage of the test, the types of question formats, the directions, and appropriate test-taking strategies. Strive to make such information equally available to all test takers.

> Under some circumstances, test developers have direct control of tests and test scores. Under other circumstances, test users have such control. Whichever group has direct control of tests and test scores should take the steps described below.

Test developers or test users should:

19. Provide test takers or their parents/guardians with information about rights test takers may have to obtain copies of tests and completed answer sheets, retake tests, have tests rescored, or cancel scores.

20. Tell test takers or their parents/guardians how long scores will be kept on file and indicate to whom and under what circumstances test scores will or will not be released.

21. Describe the procedures that test takers or their parents/guardians may use to register complaints and have problems resolved.

The Code has been developed by the Joint Committee on Testing Practices, a cooperative effort of several professional organizations, that has as its aim the advancement, in the public interest, of the quality of testing practices. The Joint Committee was initiated by the American Educational Research Association, the American Psychological Association, and the National Council on Measurement in Education. In addition to these three groups, the American Association for

Counseling and Development/Association for Measurement and Evaluation in Counseling and Development, and the American Speech-Language-Hearing Association are now also sponsors of the Joint Committee.

This is not copyrighted material. Reproduction and dissemination are encouraged. Please cite this document as follows:

Code of Fair Testing Practices in Education. (1988). Washington, DC: Joint Committee on Testing Practices.

Mailing Address: Joint Committee on Testing Practices, American Psychological Association, 1200 17th Street NW, Washington, DC 20036.

Note: The membership of the Working Group that developed the Code of Fair Testing Practices in Education and of the Joint Committee on Testing Practices that guided the Working Group was as follows:

Theodore P. Bartell	John J. Fremer	Kevin L. Moreland
John R. Bergan	(Co-Chair, JCTP and Chair, Code Working Group)	Jo-Ellen V. Perez
Esther E. Diamond		Robert J. Solomon
Richard P. Duran	Edmund W. Gordon	John T. Stewart
Lorraine D. Eyde	Jo-Ida C. Hansen	Carol Kehr Tittle (Co-Chair, JCTP)
Raymond D. Fowler	James B. Lingwall	
	George F. Madaus (Co-Chair, JCTP)	Nicholas A. Vacc
		Michael J. Zieky

Debra Boltas and Wayne Camara of the American Psychological Association served as staff liaisons.

Additional copies of the Code may be obtained from the National Council on Measurement in Education, 1230 17th Street NW, Washington, DC 20036. Single copies are free.

(Prepared by the Joint Committee on Testing Practices)

Appendix B

Standards for Evaluation of Educational Programs, Projects, and Materials

UTILITY STANDARDS _____

The utility standards are intended to ensure that an evaluation will serve the practical information needs of given audiences. These standards are:

Audience identification

Audiences involved in or affected by the evaluation should be identified, so that their needs can be addressed.

Evaluator credibility

The person conducting the evaluation should be both trustworthy and competent to perform the evaluation, so that their findings achieve maximum credibility and acceptance.

Information scope and selection

Information collected should be of such scope and selected in such ways as to address pertinent questions about the object of the evaluation and be responsive to the needs and interests of specified audiences.

Valuational interpretation

The perspectives, procedures, and rationale used to interpret the findings should be carefully described, so that the bases for value judgments are clear.

Report clarity

The evaluation report should describe the object being evaluated and its context, and the purposes, procedures, and findings of the evaluation, so that the audiences will readily understand what was done, why it was done, what information was obtained, what conclusions were drawn, and what recommendations were made.

Report dissemination

Evaluation findings should be disseminated to clients and other right-to-know audiences, so that they can assess and use the findings.

Report timeliness

Release of reports should be timely, so that audiences can best use the reported information.

Evaluation impact

Evaluations should be planned and conducted in ways that encourage follow-through by members of the audiences.

FEASIBILITY STANDARDS

The feasibility standards are intended to ensure that an evaluation will be realistic, prudent, diplomatic, and frugal. They are:

Practical procedures

The evaluation procedures should be practical, so that disruption is kept to a minimum and needed information can be obtained.

Political viability

The evaluation should be planned and conducted with anticipation of the different positions of various interest groups, so that their cooperation may be obtained and so that possible attempts by any of these groups to curtail evaluation operations or to bias or misapply the results can be averted or counteracted.

Cost effectiveness

The evaluation should produce information of sufficient value to justify the resources extended.

PROPRIETY STANDARDS

The propriety standards are intended to ensure that an evaluation will be conducted legally, ethically, and with due regard for the welfare of those involved in the evaluation, as well as those affected by its results. These standards are:

Formal obligation

Obligations of the formal parties to an evaluation (what is to be done, how, by whom, when) should be agreed to in writing, so that these parties are obligated to adhere to all conditions of the agreement or are obligated formally to renegotiate it.

Conflict of interest

Conflict of interest, frequently unavoidable, should be dealt with openly and honestly, so that it does not compromise the evaluation processes and results.

Full and frank disclosure

Oral and written evaluation reports should be open, direct, and honest in their disclosure of pertinent findings, including the limitations of the evaluation.

Public's right to know

The formal parties to an evaluation should respect and assure the public's right to know, within the limits of other related principles and statutes, such as those dealing with public safety and the right to privacy.

Rights of human subjects

Evaluations should be designed and conducted so that the rights and welfare of the human subjects are respected and protected.

Human interactions

Evaluators should respect human dignity and worth in their interactions with other persons associated with an evaluation.

Balanced reporting

The evaluation should be complete and fair in its presentation of strengths and weaknesses of the object under investigation, so that strengths can be built upon and problem areas addressed.

Fiscal responsibility

The evaluator's allocation and expenditure of resources should reflect sound accountability procedures and otherwise be prudent and ethically responsible.

ACCURACY STANDARDS

The accuracy standards are intended to ensure that an evaluation will reveal and convey technically adequate information about the features of the object being studied that determine its worth or merit. These standards are:

Object identification

The object of the evaluation (program, project, material) should be sufficiently examined, so that the form(s) of the object being considered in the evaluation can be clearly identified.

Context analysis

The context in which the program, project, or material exists should be examined in enough detail so that its likely influences on the object can be identified.

Described purposes and procedures

The purposes and procedures of the evaluation should be monitored and described in enough detail so that they can be identified and assessed.

Defensible information sources

The sources of information should be described in enough detail so that the adequacy of the information can be assessed.

Valid measurement

The information-gathering instruments and procedures should be chosen or developed and then implemented in a way that will assure that the interpretation arrived at is valid for the given use.

Reliable measurement

The information-gathering instruments and procedures should be chosen or developed and then implemented in ways that will assure that the information obtained is sufficiently reliable for the intended use.

Systematic data control

The data collected, processed, and reported in an evaluation should be reviewed and corrected, so that the results of the evaluation will not be flawed.

Analysis of quantitative information

Quantitative information in an evaluation should be appropriately and systematically analyzed to ensure supportable interpretations.

Analysis of qualitative information

Qualitative information in an evaluation should be appropriately and systematically analyzed to ensure supportable interpretations.

Justified conclusions

The conclusions reached in an evaluation should be explicitly justified, so that the audiences can assess them.

Objective reporting

The evaluation procedure should provide safeguards to protect the evaluation findings and reports against distortion by the personal feelings and biases of any party to the evaluation.

(Joint Committee on Standards for Educational Evaluation, 1981)

Appendix C

Sources of Instructional Materials and Reviews

CATALOGS AND INDEXES OF AUDIOVISUAL MATERIALS ⎯⎯

American Association for the Advancement of Science. Journal, *Science Books and Films*.

American folklore films and videotapes: A catalog (2nd ed.). (1982). New York: Bowker.

Boyle, D. (1986). *Video classics: A guide to video art and documentary tapes*. Phoenix AZ: Oryx Press.

Business and technology videolog. New York: W. W. Norton.

Catalog of audiovisual materials: A guide to government sources. ERIC Documents Reproduction Service, Arlington, VA.

Catalog of free-loan educational films/video. St. Petersburg, FL: Modern Talking Picture Service.

Dukane Corporation, Audiovisual Division, St. Charles, IL. Publishes *Educational sound filmstrip directory*.

Educational film video locator of the consortium of university film centers and R. R. Bowker Company (3rd ed.). (1986). NY: Bowker.

Educators Progress Service, 214 Center Street, Randolph, WI. Publishes *Educators guides to free audio, video, films, filmstrips, etc.*

Free stuff for kids. (1984). Deephaven, MN: Meadowbrook Press.

Hitches, H. (Ed.). (1985). *America on film and tape: A topical catalog of audiovisual resources for the study of United States history, society, and culture*. Westport, CT: Greenwood Press.

Hunt, M. A. (Ed.). (1983). *A multimedia approach to children's literature: A selective list of films (and videocassettes), filmstrips, and records based on children's books* (3rd ed.). Chicago: American Library Association.

IBM InfoWindow courseware catalog. Marietta, GA: IBM Corporation.

Interactive Video. St. Louis, MO: Applied Video Technology.

Interactive videodiscs for education. Louisville, KY: Ztec Co.

Jeffrey Norton, Guilford, CT. Publishes *Videolog of video film* in various categories.

Laser Disc Newsletter. New York University, Suite 428, Hudson St., New York, NY 10014.

Libacher, J. (Ed.). (1985). *Feature films on 16mm and videotape available for rental, sale and lease* (8th ed.). New York: Bowker.

May, J. P. (1981). *Films and filmstrips for language arts: An annual bibliography.* Urbana, IL: National Council of Teachers of English.

McKee, G. (1983). *Directory of spoken-word audio cassettes.* New York: Norton.

MECC (Minnesota Educational Computing Corp.). *Videodiscs for education, a directory.* St. Paul, MN: Author.

Moore, N. R. (Ed.). (Biennial). *Free and inexpensive learning materials.* Nashville: Incentive Publishers, Inc., George Peabody College.

National AudioVisual Center, Capitol Heights, MD. Publishes *Media resource catalogs of documentary, feature, and instructional film.*

National Council of Teachers of English, Urbana, IL. Publishes annual *Bibliography of film and filmstrips for language arts.*

National Information Center for Educational Media (NICEM), P.O. Box 40130, Albuquerque, NM 87196. Publishes indexes to transparencies, slides, filmstrips, audiotapes and records, film and video, multimedia resources, and indexes of media by subject. Can also be accessed on-line.

National Video Clearinghouse, Syosset, NY. Publishes *Video source book.*

On cassette: A comprehensive bibliography of spoken word audio cassettes. (1985). New York: Bowker.

Optical publishing directory. Medford, NJ: Learned Information, Inc.

PBS video catalog. Alexandria, VA: PBS Video.

R. R. Bowker, New York. Publishes bibliographies and catalogs of spoken word audio cassettes, films, and other media, and *Educational film/video locator.*

Schwann *Record and Tape Guide* (monthly). Boston: ABC Schwann Publications.

Selecting instructional media; A guide to audiovisual and other instructional media lists. Littleton, CO: Libraries Unlimited.

Sullivan, K. (1985). *Films for, by, and about women, Series 2.* Metuchen, NJ: Scarecrow.

T.H.E. catalog, televised higher education: Catalog of resources. (1984). Boulder, CO: Western Interstate Commission for Higher Education.

The complete interactive video courseware directory. New Hyde Park, NY: Convergent Technologies.

The Great Plains national instructional television library catalog. Lincoln, NE: Great Plains National Instructional Television Library.

Video source book. (Annual). Computer-generated catalog of 18,000 video programs in entertainment, sports, fine arts, business, education. Syosset, NY: National Video Clearinghouse.

Videodiscovery catalog. Seattle, WA: Videodiscovery, Inc.

PRODUCERS AND DISTRIBUTORS OF AUDIOVISUAL MATERIALS

3M Audiovisual, Building 225-3NE, 3M Center, St.Paul, MN 55144

Allyn & Bacon AV Dept., 7 Wells Avenue, Newton, MA 02159

Ambrose Publishing Company (Time-Life Multimedia), 381 Park Avenue, Suite 1601, New York, NY 10016

American Audio Prose Library, 915 East Broadway, Columbus, MO 65201

American Museum of Natural History, Central Park West at 79th Street, New York, NY 10024

Argus Communications, 7440 Natchez Avenue, Niles, IL 60648

Art Now, Inc., 144 North 14th Street, Kenilworth, NJ 07033

Audio Book Company, Box 7111, Pasadena, CA 91107

Audio Visual Narrative Arts, Inc., Box 9, Pleasantville, NY 10570

Barr Films, 3490 East Foothill Boulevard, Pasadena, CA 91107

BFA Educational Media, 468 Park Avenue South, New York, NY 10016

Books on Tape, P.O. Box 7900, Newport Beach, CA 92060

British Broadcasting Corporation, 39 Baywood Ave., Toronto, ON

Broadcasting Foundation of America, 52 Vanderbilt Avenue, New York, NY 10017

Caedmon, HarperAudio, 10 East 53rd Street, New York, NY 10022

Communacad, The Communications Academy, 31 Center Street, P.O. Box 541, Wilton, CT 06897

Coronet/MTI Instructional Media, 108 Wilmot Avenue, Deerfield, IL 60015

Denoyer-Geppert Audiovisuals, 5235 Ravenswood Avenue, Chicago, IL 60640

Educational Corporation of America/Rand McNally, P.O. Box 7600, Chicago, IL 60680

Educational Images, P.O. Box 467, Lyons Fall, NY 13368

Educational Insights. 150 West Carob Street, Compton, CA 90220

EMC Productions, 300 York Avenue, St. Paul, MN 55101

Encyclopedia Britannica Educational Corporation, 425 North Michigan Avenue, Chicago, IL 60611

Evergreen Video Society, 213 West 35th Street, Second Floor, New York, NY 10001

Eye Gate Media, 3333 Elston Avenue, Chicago, IL 60611

Filmmakers Library, 133 East 58th Street, Suite 307, New York, NY 10022

Films for the Humanities, P.O. Box 2053, Princeton, NJ 08543

G. K. Hall Audio Publishers, 70 Lincoln Street, Boston, MA 02111

Great Plains National Instructional Television Library, Box 80669, Lincoln, NE 68501

Grolier Educational Corporation, Sherman Turnpike, Danbury, CT 06816

Hammond, Inc., 515 Valley Street, Maplewood NJ 07040

Harper and Row Media, 2350 Virginia Avenue, Hagerstown, MD 21740

Icarus Films, 200 Park Avenue South, Suite 1319, New York, NY 10003

Imperial International Learning, Box 548, Kankakee, IL 60901

Instructional Resources Corporation, 351 East 50th Street, New York, NY 10028

International Film Bureau, 332 South Michigan Avenue, Chicago, IL 60604

International Historic Films, P.O. Box 29035, Chicago, IL 60629

Learning Corporation of America, 1350 Avenue of the Americas, New York, NY 10019

Listening Library, Inc., 1 Park Avenue, Old Greenwich, CT 06870

McGraw-Hill Film Division, 674 Via de la Valle, Box 641, Del Mar, CA 92014 (Canada: McGraw-Hill Information Systems Company of Canada, 330 Progres Avenue, Toronto, ON MIP 2Z4)

Metropolitan Museum of Art, Educational Marketing, 6 East 82nd Street, New York, NY 10028

Modern Learning Aids, P.O. Box 1712, Rochester, NY 14603

Modern Talking Picture Service, 5000 Park Street North, St. Petersburg, FL 33709

Museum of Modern Art, 11 West 53rd Street, New York, NY 10019

National Audiovisual Center, 8700 Edgeworth Drive, Capitol Heights, MD 20743

National Audubon Society, 950 Third Avenue, New York, NY 10022

National Film Board of Canada, 1251 Avenue of the Americas, New York, NY 10020 (Canada: P.O. Box 6100, Station A, Montreal, Quebec H3C 3H5)

National Geographic Educational Services, 17th and M Streets, Washington, DC 20036

National Public Radio, 2025 M Street NW, Washington, DC 20036

National Video Clearinghouse, Inc., 100 Lafayette Drive, Syosset, NY 11791

Pacifica Foundation, 5316 Venice Boulevard, Los Angeles, CA 90010

PBS (Public Broadcasting Service), 1320 Braddock Place, Alexandria, VA 22314

RCA Educational Division, Front and Cooper Streets, Camden, NJ 08102

Scholastic Records, 730 Broadway, New York, NY 10003

Science Research Associates (SRA), 155 North Wacker Drive, Chicago, IL 60606

Silver Burdett Company, 250 James Street, Morristown, NJ 07690.

Society for Visual Education, Inc., 1345 Diversey Parkway, Chicago, IL 60614

Soundworks, 911 North Fillmore Street, Arlington, VA 22201

Spoken Arts, 310 North Avenue, New Rochelle, NY 10801

Sunburst Communications, 39 Washington Avenue, Pleasantville, NY 10570

TV Ontario, U.S. Sales Office, Suite 206, 143 West Franklin Street, Chapel Hill, NC 27514 (Canada: P.O. Box 200, Station Q, Toronto ON M4P 2T1)

United Transparencies, P.O. Box 688, Binghampton, NY 13902

Watershed Tapes, P.O. Box 50145, Washington, DC 20004

World Video, P.O. Box 3469, Knoxville, TN 37930

REVIEWS OF AUDIOVISUAL MATERIALS

Booklist (American Library Association)

Choice (Association of College and Research Libraries)

AFVA Evaluations (American Film and Video Association)

A-V/V PRO/FILES (Educational Products Information Exchange)

Curriculum Review (Chicago: Curriculum Advisory Services)

EPIE Reports

Film and Video News

Library Journal

Media and Methods

Media Review

Media Review Digest

School Library Journal

School Library Media Quarterly

Science Books and Films

Sightlines

Wilson Library Bulletin

REVIEWS OF INSTRUCTIONAL SOFTWARE

Some journals that review instructional software:

AEDS Journal

Arithmetic Teacher

Biology Teacher

Byte

Call–APPLE

Classroom Computer Learning

Compute!

Computers and the Humanities

Computers and People

Computers in Education

Computers in the Schools

Computers, Reading, and Language Arts

Computing Canada

Computing Teacher

Courseware Report Card

Educational Communication and Technology Journal

Educational Technology

Electronic Education

Electronic Learning

EPIE Reports

Exceptional Children

Family Computing

Hands On!

Interface: The Computer Education Quarterly

Journal of Biological Education

Journal of Computer-Based Instruction

Journal of Computers in Mathematics and Science Teaching

Journal of Courseware Review

Journal of Educational Computing Research

Journal of Educational Technology Systems

Journal of Instructional Development

Journal of Learning Disabilities

Logo Exchange

MacAPPLE

Microcomputers in Education

Micromath

Micro-Scope

Micro-SIFT

PC Magazine

PC World

Personal Computing

Perspectives in Computing

Pipeline

Popular Computing

Purser's Magazine

School Microware Reviews

Science Teacher

Software Review

Teaching and Computers

Tech Trends

Technical Horizons in Education Journal

TLC: The Educator's Guide to Personal Computing

SOFTWARE COMPANIES

There are scores of companies specializing in the production of instructional software. A useful list can be found in Vockell and Schwartz (1988).

ANNUAL DIRECTORIES OF COMPUTER COURSEWARE

Apple education software directory. Chicago: WIDL Video.

EPIE annotated courseware list. Water Mill, NY: EPIE Institute.

International microcomputer software directory. Fort Collins, CO: Imprint Software.

Microcomputer index. Santa Clara, CA: Microcomputer Information Services.

Microcomputer market place. New York: Bowker.

Microcomputer software catalog list. Portland, OR: Northwest Regional Laboratory.

Micro software solutions. Charsworth, CA: Career Aids, Inc.

Swift directory. Austin, TX: Sterling Swift.

Appendix D

Writing Poetry: A Curriculum

■ Aim ■

To develop in students an enhanced capacity and willingness to express themselves through poetry.

> **Poems are not clocks.** If we take them to pieces and put them together again, they may still give no reason at all why they tick. . . . However poems may differ on the surface, they have one important quality in common. They remain, as the painter Pablo Picasso said of all art, weapons of war against brutality and darkness.
>
> Charles Causley (1962, p. 11)

■ Rationale ■

In the world in which we live, poetry is in hiding, but it is everywhere to be found. Poetry is a part of people's lives from the cradle to the grave. Babies, if they are fortunate, hear lullabies in their earliest days. Parents and infants develop a private poetic language, in which words, and especially names, are often distorted to emphasize rhyme, repetition, onomatopoeia, and alliteration. Young children's games frequently involve rhymes, such as skipping rhymes, a lore almost entirely forgotten as children become adolescents and adults—and one becoming rarer in the TV culture. Perhaps all adolescents write poetry, at least in their heads. All of them know a great deal of poetry, in the form of the lyrics of hundreds of popular songs. Adults are influenced by advertising jingles, struck by the poetic eloquence of Martin Luther King, Jr. or Mario Cuomo, arrested by an eye-catching headline or the pithy title of a book or movie. They use catch-phrases in their conversation and construct their speech unconsciously to produce a certain cadence and musicality. Old people tend to remember poems learned in their youth and often revert to phrases and locutions long out of fashion. Their speech patterns slow down like the reducing ocean swell after a storm. Eventually, they are commemorated by those most succinct and lapidary pieces of poetry: the epitaphs on their gravestones.

"How do you get children to write"? asks Michael Carey (1989, p. 9). "By love—loving to write, loving to read, loving to share what they've written." Poetry provides a means for people to express what they know, feel, and experience with total authenticity. In reading the poetry of others, we can experience empathy, spiritual companionship, and affirmation of our own emotional re-sponses. In expressing ourselves in poetry, we can find joy, release, and reinte-gration of the divided and alienated self. It is sad that many students arrive at adolescence contemptuous of poetry, but it is tragic if they arrive at adulthood doing so. The purpose of this curriculum is, in the words of Douglas Anderson (1974, p. 235), not to teach, but to awaken—or perhaps to reawaken: all of us are born poets, and it is the culture that makes us prosaic. This curriculum is intended to provide adolescents with a mode of insight and expression that they will value for a lifetime.

▪ Definitions ▪

The only word requiring definition in this curriculum is "poetry." Unfortun-tely, it is a word that eludes definition, and especially any definition that seeks to distinguish it from prose. Juan Luís Borge maintained that the difference between poetry and prose was typographical. It may be wisest to allow learners to arrive at their own definition.

▪ Objectives ▪

Knowledge

1. Students will understand the range of verbal forms that comprise poetry. (critical)

2. Students will understand and internalize the importance of editing and revision in writing poetry. (important)

3. Students will develop and will be able to articulate some personal criteria by which they evaluate poetry. (important)

4. Students will develop a basic vocabulary for thinking about and discussing poetry. (desirable)

Skill

5. Students will develop their ability to interpret poetry. (critical)

6. Students will increase their competence and confidence in writing poetry. (critical)

Process

7. Students will read, listen to, discuss, and write a wide variety of poetry. (critical)

8. Each student will produce a work that links poetry with another medium. (desirable)

Experience

    9.   Students will interact with a practicing poet. (important)

   10.   Students will have the experience of expressing a significant idea, emotion, or experience in a poem that pleases them. (important)

Attitude

   11.   Students will develop increased enjoyment of reading poetry and confidence in their ability to understand it. (critical)

   12.   Students will enjoy listening to poetry. (critical)

   13.   Students will enjoy writing poetry and will develop confidence in and respect for their own poetic skills. (critical)

▪ The Students ▪

Poetry can be taught at any age. The principles will be the same, but the way in which it is taught will vary with the students. Eight-year-olds need different poems from twenty-year-olds. This curriculum is planned for adolescents between roughly the ages of 13 and 17. This is an age of powerful emotions, needs, and anxieties; of individuation; of questioning existing structures and authority; of outrage or cynicism at the contradictions in adult life; of loneliness and the conviction no one has ever had similar experiences; of increasingly abstract thought and idealistic principle; of the quest for meaning and a place in the world; of the need for new and significant relationships, for self-esteem and the respect of others. In other words, it is perhaps the poetic age par excellence. For the teacher of poetry, it is the primary window of opportunity. Those who emerge from this age with a stereotypical view of poetry are likely to maintain it indefinitely; those who develop an affinity for poetry are unlikely to lose it.

> *All my life I have been trying to learn to read, to see and hear, and to write.* It could be, in the grace of God I shall live to be eighty-nine, as did Hokusai, and speaking my farewell to earthly scenes, I might paraphrase: "If God had let me live five years longer I should have been a writer."
>
> Carl Sandburg (1960, pp. 13–14)

▪ Prerequisites ▪

Poetry is a universal language; there are therefore no prerequisites for this program.

∎ Preassessment ∎

There is no need for any formal pretest. However, a questionnaire, prior to or at the beginning of the program, could be used to provide the teacher with an indication of the attitudes and interests of the students. Here are typical questions that could be asked:

What is the best book you have ever read?

What is your favorite TV show?

What kind of music do you like best?

Who is your favorite musical artist or group?

What social issues are you interested in?

What is your favorite vocal?

What newspapers do you receive at home?

What parts of the newspaper do you usually read?

What magazines do you read?

Do you like writing letters?

Do you like writing stories?

What is a poem?

Have you ever written a poem?

How do you feel about poetry?

What picture comes to mind when you hear the word "poet"?

How do you feel about your ability to write poetry?

What would you like to get out of this course?

∎ Context ∎

Normally, a course on poetry would be taught in the context of an English, communications, language arts, or literature program. This curriculum is planned on the assumption that it would fit within such a context. There are clear advantages in this, as poetry can then be integrated with other forms of literature and communication. However, it may be pointed out that a course on poetry could also be taught in the context of a program in music, drama, art, history, or even physics. Or, it could be taught as an extracurricular program.

∎ Assessment ∎

Developing skill in writing poetry is not prerequisite to university admission or occupational certification. Its economic surrender value is nil. Indeed, a passion for poetry can be a passport to poverty. Several of the usual reasons for assessment, therefore, do not apply in this curriculum. The primary reasons for assessment in this context are two: (1) feedback to learners, to focus their attention, help them develop their abilities, and support their efforts; (2) evaluation of the effectiveness of the program in general, and specific aspects such as the sensitivity and responsiveness of the instruction, in order to improve the program in the future.

It is important that the teacher not become too attached to the attitude objectives of the curriculum. Students tend to resist anything they see as indoctrination. More appropriate may be such an approach as: Here is a kind of expression that many people find powerful and rewarding; we'll have a good look at it, so that you can decide whether there is anything in it for you.

Following are some suggestions for assessment. Assessment of asterisked objectives could be used for generating grades; assessment of other objectives is intended primarily for program evaluation.

1. Students will understand the range of verbal forms that comprise poetry.*

It should be possible to assess this understanding on the part of all students by monitoring student work and classroom discussion. More formally, students could be required to find and submit a piece of writing that both teacher and student agreed (a) was a poem, (b) lacked traditional rhyme, and (c) lacked traditional meter.

2. Students will understand and internalize the importance of editing and revision in the creation of poetry.*

Each student might be required to submit three drafts (early, middle, late) of a poem he or she has written. Student and teacher should agree that there is an increase in quality between each draft.

3. Students will develop and will be able to articulate some personal criteria by which they evaluate poetry.*

While this objective could be assessed informally in a small class by classroom or individual discussion, it could also be assessed by asking students, for example, to submit two poems of their choice, one that they like, and one that they want to criticize. Students are asked to state a number of elements (e.g., 2 or 3) they like and dislike in the poems chosen. Responses will have to be judged subjectively. "It rhymes" or "It doesn't rhyme" would probably not be acceptable praise or criticism. "I feel physically as if the top of my head were taken off" was a criterion cited by Emily Dickinson (Johnson, 1990, p. 6).

4. Students will develop a basic vocabulary for thinking about and discussing poetry.*

This objective should be arrived at incidentally, by use of relevant terms during class sessions. It could be assessed relatively easily by a selected-response test, such as a matching test, or by a constructed-response test, for example, by asking students to analyze a given poem and assessing the appropriateness of their use of literary terms.

5. Students will develop their ability to interpret poetry.*

This objective could be assessed by asking students to interpret one or more challenging poems. The criterion is not a "right" interpretation, but a response that is thoughtful, sensitive, or insightful.

6. Students will increase their competence and confidence in writing poetry.*

This objective can be assessed by monitoring growth of maturity and insight in the poems written by students in the course.

7. Students will read, listen to, discuss, and write a wide variety of poetry.*

These experiences constitute the content of the course. Students unable to participate in all or most sessions would need to satisfy the instructor that they had done an adequate amount of reading and writing out of class.

8. Each student will produce a work that links poetry with another medium.*

Work to be submitted could range from a single poem illustrated with a single drawing or photograph, to an audiotape or live performance of music and poetry or song, to a video or slide-tape program combining poetry and visual images. This exercise could appropriately be conducted in groups.

9. Students will interact with a practicing poet.*

This objective will be attained by all students who attend the poetry reading and interact with the poet. Students who are absent may be asked to attend another reading at which attendance for other students is elective.

10. Students will have the experience of expressing a significant idea, emotion, or experience in a poem that pleases them.

This objective could be evaluated by looking at the quality of poetry submitted by students.

Ask students to keep a poetry journal during the course, and analyze the quality of experience reported.

Students may be asked simply to submit a poem they have written that they like. Ideally, all students will be able to do so.

11. Students will develop increased enjoyment of reading poetry and confidence in their ability to understand it.

12. Students will enjoy listening to poetry.

13. Students will enjoy writing poetry and will develop confidence in and respect for their own poetic skills.

Here are some *suggestions for evaluation of attitudes:*

Note allusions made in and out of class by students to personal reading, writing, or listening to poetry; unprompted quotation or recital by students of poems or fragments from memory.

Review the quality of poetry written by students.

To assess confidence in understanding poetry, ask students to write a short critique or explanation of a challenging poem and observe both how much hesitation or anxiety they show in tackling the task and how adequately they critique or explain the poem.

Interview a sample of students.

Telephone a random sample of parents.

Unobtrusively check on the number of students (1) submitting poetry to the school magazine, local newspaper, poetry competition, and so on; (2) attending an after-class reading by a local poet; or (3) borrowing poetry records, tapes, and videos from the school or classroom library.

Invite students to continue to show the teacher poetry they write and monitor the number who do so.

Include questions on anonymous end-of-course evaluation sheets, for example—"How much do you enjoy reading/writing/listening to poetry: very much, somewhat, not at all"; or "About how many poems, over and above those assigned, have you read/written/listened to on your own this semester?" Include questions on specific aspects of the course to aid revision of the curriculum.

Ideally, to assess course effects, collect data both before and after the course.

To assess long-term effects, repeat all of these measures at intervals, for example, six or twelve months after the course ends.

▪ Grading ▪

It is recommended that, if possible, grading be in the form of written observations on student work and participation. It is most important that such comments emphasize the positive. Poetry is a very personal area. A single negative, destructive, or sarcastic observation on a student's effort may give that person a lifelong antipathy for poetry. Rejection slips are for hardened professionals, not for hopeful beginners.

If formal marks are required, they should be accompanied by written comments. The first nine objectives (asterisked) could be used to generate grades. In most cases, assessment of the objectives may either be on a scale or on a pass/incomplete basis.

▪ Instruction ▪

Sequence of instruction

There is no fixed sequence in which poetry should be taught. However, a few general suggestions may be made.

At the beginning, have students say what they think about poetry. Many students will have had negative stereotypes of poetry, often as the result of exposure to archaic, obscure, pretentious, or puerile poetry in earlier grades. "It's about boring things like flowers and love—mushy things," says a Grade 8 boy quoted by Georgia

Heard (1989, p. 13). "To me, poetry was a bunch of complex rhyming words, in a funny arrangement, that has some obscure meaning, written by a freelance weirdo" said another Grade 8 student with obvious poetic talent (Tsujimoto, 1988, p. 1). Allow students' past frustration and contempt to surface, and monitor this catharsis in an accepting and nonjudgmental fashion.

After reviewing preassessment data, ask students to bring to class examples of their favorite pop songs, gospel hymns, radio or TV commercials, anecdotes, or rock videos. Allow students to explore with other students what it is that they like about the examples chosen. In advance, obtain some examples of your own in different genres that provide good models for classroom discussion. Deal early with students' belief that poetry must rhyme and have a regular meter.

Provide each student with a notebook for use as a poetry workbook, ideabook, and journal. Ask students to record impressions, ideas, words, and dreams.

Begin to experiment with some easy exercises, such as asking students to build on incomplete statements, such as:

Yesterday _____, today _____.

I'd rather be a _____ than a _____.

If I were a _____, I would _____.

I remember _____.

I dream of _____.

By the time I'm 40, _____.

If I were a bird, _____.   (Cramer, 1981; Johnson, 1990)

Show an evocative drawing, cartoon, menu, object, poster, photograph, recipe, slide, or video clip and have students write a phrase or line that it suggests. Play word association games. Have students write two-word poems. Provide periods of silent writing. Use computers, if available, to allow students to experiment with format and typography of their own or other poets' work.

In the main part of the program, develop and nurture students' confidence in reading and writing poetry. Encourage students to write a little in their poetry workbooks every day, rather than a lot once a week. Be constantly supportive to students who lack confidence or continue to dislike poetry. Bring in professional poets, at a stage and for a purpose appropriate to their particular strengths. Choose poets who will be supportive of beginners' work and have them read, listen to, and comment on students' writing, as well as sharing and talking about their own work. Encourage students to share their writing, with partners, in small groups, in choral readings, or with the whole class. Have students practice revision on one another's work, which is always easier than revising one's own. Preread any poetry to be presented in public to ensure it will not embarrass the author or other students. Always obtain students' consent before presenting their work in public. If you have sufficient confidence and vulnerability, share your own work with students, particularly if you can illustrate the process of multiple revision.

Begin to show students some structural forms and features of poetry. Show examples of such forms as ballad, blank verse, chant, cinquaine, concrete poetry, diamante, epic, found poetry, haiku, hymn, limerick, lyric, sestina, sonnet, vilanelle, and so on, but avoid heavy analysis and do not allow formal structures to take precedence over informal ones. Help students discover some of the ways in which poets achieve effects through assonance, ambiguity, allusion, metaphor, understatement, and so on. Ensure exposure of students to as wide a range of poetry as possible, in the examples you share with them, in the classroom poetry library, and in the poetry you encourage them to read. In dealing with poetry in the classroom, avoid either analyzing it to death or adopting vacuous "What do you think?" approaches. Build poems collectively by free association. Avoid giving an impression that old poetry is better than new, or formal than informal, or obscure than understandable, or arcane than popular.

Provide as many fun experiences as possible; display students' poems in the classroom and hallway; have students recite their poetry outdoors; submit poems to the school magazine and local newspaper; put a poem in a bottle and throw it in the sea; take a field trip to a poetry coffee house reading; organize students individually or in groups to prepare an audiovisual poetry presentation.

Toward the end of the program, arrange for the participation of poets who can give supportive and professional feedback to students on their work and with whom they can discuss the craft of poetry. Have students complete an anthology of favorite poems that they dedicate to a particular person who is important to them. Try to ensure that all students produce some poetry of which they are proud. Arrange for students to use computer facilities to make professional-looking printouts of their work. Arrange to have students' work spiral bound in a booklet—it is particularly appreciated if the finished book is ready by Christmas. See if there is sufficient interest among students who want to continue working on poetry with the teacher or peers for an extracurricular poetry group. Let students know about local writing groups, poetry magazines, and competitions. Celebrate student work by bulletin board or hallway display; submission in poetry competitions or to poetry journals; classroom reading; reading over the PA system; at a school assembly, concert, or parents' evening; or on a call-in radio program.

▪ Strategies ▪

In addition to the strategies already mentioned, here are some suggestions.

Audiotape: Tape songs or poetry by folksingers, poets, students, or choral readings by the class.

Blind walk: Each student leads a blindfolded partner on a walk, encouraging the partner to use senses of hearing, smell, and touch.

Brainstorming: In whole class or small groups, students can brainstorm questions they want to ask a visiting poet, the last line of a poem, the reasons why poetry is unpopular, and so on.

Card-sort: Put a poem on cards that are jumbled and have groups of students rearrange them; each group is likely to arrive at a different final version.

Eavesdropping: Students listen to conversations in the hallway, cafeteria, school bus, and so on, and pick up snatches of poetry.

Epitaph: Ask students to compose their own epitaph.

Magazine: Have the students write, edit, and publish a class poetry magazine.

Meditation: Lead a meditation or visualization, endeavoring to quiet the chatter of the TV culture and allow some deep thought and images to emerge.

Movies: "Poetic" movies like *Elvira Madigan, Dr. Zhivago,* and *A Day in the Country* can be used to stimulate students' writing. In the movie *Breaker Morant,* for example, a tough Australian soldier composes a moving poem the night before his execution. A number of movies are available that depict the life and work of various poets.

Peer editing: Pair students carefully and ensure that groundrules of constructive criticism are understood.

Photographs: These may be used to stimulate or to illustrate student writing.

Portfolio: A portfolio of each student's writing should be built over the course of the unit.

Rhythm: Clapping, footstamping, drumming, or chanting can be used.

Video: Rock videos are good examples of the use of multiple media and of free association—sometimes of poetry.

▪ Individual Differences ▪

Poetic taste is highly idiosyncratic. Tastes will range widely in any classroom, both toward particular poetic form and content and toward poetry itself. Student self-confidence in the field of poetry can be expected to range from those who write poetry frequently and feel good about what they write to those who believe they could never write a line of poetry or have no desire to. Similarly wide variation can be expected in background, from students who have read widely in different poetic genres to those who have no recollection of voluntarily reading a poem. Intellectual, emotional, and social maturity will also vary, requiring an equivalent variety in the poetry chosen for the course.

Poetry is a wonderful vehicle for reaching marginalized students. Students who are shy and withdrawn, students with reading or learning disabilities, students with physical handicaps, students with behavioral difficulties—all can participate in reading and writing poetry. Poetry is a language that is available for young and old as they grapple with their loneliness, powerlessness, alienation, and heart-break, and celebrate their hopes, achievements, insights, and experiences.

Certain kinds of difference should be given special attention.

Culture.   Poems should be used in the unit by poets from different cultural groups, even if the class itself is relatively culturally homogeneous.

Gender.   Normally, the poems by male and female poets used in the course should be approximately equivalent.

Disability.   Handicapped or learning disabled pupils can excel in a poetry course. Students with reading difficulties can concentrate on oral and recorded work. Students with behavior problems can be encouraged to express their emotions in poetic form. Hearing impaired, visually impaired, and motor impaired students can participate fully in this unit.

Class.   Try to ensure that the poems chosen and the way they are treated vary in terms of their class assumptions and outlook.

Learning style.   Ensure that the unit does not focus exclusively on reading, listening, and writing, and hence disadvantage those learners who learn best by performance and active, kinesthetic learning. For some students, composing and performing rap music may be more appropriate than writing sonnets. Provision should be made in instruction for both high-anxiety (dependent) and low-anxiety (autonomous) students. Ensure that both those students who prefer to work in a quiet environment and those who need background music or the option of conversation can do so. There should be a mix of individual and group work. Illumination levels, seating arrangements, and time of day for the course need to be varied. Arrange to use all of the senses in teaching poetry: smell, taste, and touch, as well as reading and listening.

▪ Resources ▪

Materials

Consumables. Provide the following as required: spiral-bound notebooks for student journal and poetry workbook; photo album for best poems by students; audiotape and videotape; plenty of paper, including poster-size sheets and flip charts; felt-tip pens; art and other materials as needed for specific exercises.

Print. There should, if possible, be an extensive classroom library of poetry, including books, chapbooks, and anthologies.

Audio. A wide collection of audio records of poems should be available. Caedmon Records produces a wide list. A good collection of music records, especially currently popular songs, is desirable.

Video collection. A small collection of rock videos will be useful. Films on poetry and poets should be selected as appropriate.

[Note: Due to reasons of space and copyright, curriculum materials (e.g., poems) are not reproduced here. The success of this curriculum when implemented, however, will depend in part on its being accompanied by high-quality print and audiovisual materials that have been field tested for their appeal to target students and their potential for generating student and teacher enthusiasm. Use a lot of student work, and begin making a collection of student poetry (with permission) for future use.]

Teacher references

There are many excellent books on teaching poetry, several of which are inspiring as well as practical. The following represents a small selection:

Anderson, D. (1974).   *My sister looks like a pear: Awakening the poetry in young people.* New York: Hart Publishing Co.

Booth, D., & Moore, B. (1988).   *Poems please! Sharing poetry with children.* Markham, ON: Pembroke Publishers.

Carey, M. A. (1989).   *Poetry: Starting from scratch.* Lincoln, NE: Foundation Books.

Collom, J. (1985).   *Moving windows: Evaluating the poetry children write.* New York: Teachers & Writers Collaborative.

Dylan, B. (1987).   *Lyrics 1962-1985.* London: Cape.

Fader, D. (1969).   *Hooked on books.* New York: Pergamon.

Gensler, K., & Nyhart, N. (1978).   *The poetry connection: An anthology of contemporary poems with ideas to stimulate children's writing.* New York: Teachers & Writers.

Heard, G. (1989).   *For the good of the earth and sun: Teaching poetry.* Portsmouth, NH: Heinemann.

Johnson, D. M. (1990).   *Word weaving: A creative approach to teaching and writing poetry.* Urbana, IL: National Council of Teachers of English.

Koch, K. (1974).   *Rose, where did you get that red?: Teaching great poetry to children.* New York: Vintage Books.

Koch, K. (1980).   *Wishes, lies, and dreams: Teaching children to write poetry.* New York: Harper & Row.

McKim, E., & Steinbergh, J. W. (1983).   *Beyond words: Writing poems with children.* Green Harbor, MA: Wampeter Press.

McNeil, F. (nd). *When is a poem: Creative ideas for teaching poetry collected from Canadian poets.* Toronto, ON: League of Canadian Poets.

Powell, B. S. (1973). *Making poetry: Approaches to writing from classrooms 'round the world.* New York: Macmillan.

Tsujimoto, J. I. (1988). *Teaching poetry writing to adolescents.* Urbana, IL: ERIC Clearinghouse on Reading & Communication Skills; National Council of Teachers of English.

Equipment

Cassette player/recorder

Videocamera

VCR

Videoprojector, if available

Overhead projector

Slide projector

Facilities

Classroom space should be as flexible as possible, enabling furniture to be arranged as appropriate for class discussion, small-group work, individual work, viewing films or slides, arrangement in coffee-house design, and so on. Facilities needed outside the classroom will vary with the nature of out-of-class activities.

Personnel

Teacher. It is critical that the teacher be knowledgeable and enthusiastic about poetry. Ideally, he or she will be a writer as a well as a reader of poetry. This unit is designed to be taught by an instructor whose tastes in poetry are eclectic and who views poetry as deeply embedded in all aspects of life rather than restricted to narrow, literary, or academic forms. The teacher needs to have good skills of communication and organization. It is important that the teacher's attitude be positive, that he or she can develop rewarding relationships with adolescents, and that communication with and feedback to students be constructive and affirming.

Other teachers. There are likely to be other teachers in the school or system who have particular interests in poetry or are themselves poets and who could be called on for guest appearances or for advice. Teachers of the same students who are competent and willing to introduce some poetry into the teaching of their own subjects (for example, in history, music, or art) would serve a valuable integrating function.

Administrators. Approval of the building principal may be needed for guest poets, field trips, and so on. Administrators may be invited to attend performances of poetry. Poetry or presentations by students may be used in connection with parents' evenings, open houses, and so on, which is likely to be appreciated by administrators.

Parents.   The approach to poetry taken in this unit may disconfirm many parents' views, based on their own school experiences, of what poetry is. A note of explanation to parents (reviewed first by the principal) may help to explain the purposes of the unit. However, there may also be parents with special interests in poetry or who themselves write poetry and would be willing to discuss their interests or their work with students.

Poets.   It is important that students have direct contact with poets during the course. "Poets" in the context of this course includes songwriters, advertising copywriters, newspaper editors, political speechwriters, and so on. Poets can perform a vital function in reading and talking about their work, describing their working methods, and giving students feedback on their writing. To avoid stereotyping, it is best if the poets to whom students are personally exposed vary widely in such characteristics as personality, life style, age, and occupation. The National Endowment for the Arts in cooperation with state arts councils has since 1966 sponsored a Poets in the Schools program in all fifty states, and many state and local poets' organizations will facilitate school visits, readings, and critiques of student writing by poets.

Students.   Students are not only clients, but also resources. In any class of thirty adolescent students, there will be several who have tried their hand at writing poetry. (There will also usually be several who have highly stereotyped and negative ideas about poetry and poets.) Student potential should be used as widely as possible. Students can act as members of cooperative groups, edit one another's work, and research resources in the community. The more advanced students can serve as mentors, tutors, and role models for others. Students from other classes, especially older students, may be willing to visit the class to read their poetry, perform songs they have written, and so on.

Time

This unit is planned for a 3–5 week period, or 10–20 hours of instruction. Teacher preparation and out-of-class time could be substantial, at least for the first offering of the course. The amount of time students would commit out of class would vary with motivation. Highly motivated students could spend many hours. Less motivated students should not be compelled to spend time out of class on poetry, as it would be counterproductive.

Costs

Costs would vary substantially, depending on activities and availability of funds. Following are some high and low estimates.

	Low Estimate*	High Estimate
Videotape	0*	$ 100
Audiotape	0*	50
Video purchase	0*	500
Video rental	0*	50
Books	0*	500
Field trips	0	300
Guests: expenses	0	200
Guests: honoraria	0	500
Total	0	$2,200

* Assumes that all materials and equipment are already available, and that guests donate time.

■ Curriculum Adaptation ■

This curriculum is intended as a basic template that is adaptable to local needs. A local needs assessment could be conducted to ensure the appropriateness of the curriculum to the community. The curriculum should be adapted as necessary by local teachers or curriculum committees.

■ Curriculum Evaluation ■

When the initial curriculum document has been written or revised, it should be reviewed by the curriculum committee, by a sample of gatekeepers (e.g., influential teachers, parents, principals, consultants, superintendents, and school board members), and by as many specialists in curriculum planning, poetry, and poetry teaching as is appropriate and feasible. The "Curriculum Evaluation Guide" in Chapter 9 may be used for basic criteria. Necessary revisions should be made prior to pilot testing.

Pilot test

This curriculum could be pilot tested, piecemeal or totally, in a small number of classes, in a summer school program, in an enrichment class, in an extracurricular poetry club, in a community college writing class, or in an adult evening interest class.

Field test

A field test would involve a full tryout of the curriculum, involving a number of classes taught by qualified but typical teachers. It would be best for the course to be field tested with all kinds of classes: heterogeneously grouped, homogeneously grouped, special education, enriched, advanced placement, and so on, and at several different grade levels. Several different sites should be chosen for field testing, in order to provide maximum exposure of the innovation. Special attention should be paid to the compilation of a compendium of particularly effective poems and strategies for publication in the final document.

Program evaluation

Ideally, each time the curriculum is taught, whether under field test or regular conditions, it should be evaluated.

In evaluating the *effectiveness* of the curriculum, the basic questions are: How well was each objective achieved by how many students? What kind of attitudes resulted from the course? Long-term follow-up is recommended to assess enduring effects.

Equally important is the question, How much did people, students as well as teachers, like the program? The simplest way to find out is to ask them. Observations, visits, interviews, conversations, questionnaires, reading poetry produced in class, and many other means can be used as well.

Evidence should also be collected regarding other outcomes of the curriculum—by observation of students; by conversations with students, parents, and teachers; and by interviews with graduates and dropouts.

For planning a complete program evaluation, refer to the "Program Evaluation Guide" in Chapter 9.

▪ Implementation ▪

Approval

The necessary official approvals should be obtained before development or adaptation of the curriculum begins. This curriculum represents a "tuning up" of existing English/language arts/literature curricula in the poetry area. Unless controversial content is to be used, special permissions should not be necessary above the school level. Active support of principals, area chairs, and department heads is important. Support by central office personnel is almost always helpful.

It is also a good idea to conduct a needs assessment at the local level. On the basis of local findings, it may be desirable to modify aspects of the curriculum to meet local needs or interests. In addition to providing data on local resources, this will provide evidence of local support, interest, indifference, or opposition. Information of this kind is valuable at the implementation stage.

Consultation should not be only before and after design of the curriculum. The input of future users, that is, the teachers of English/literature/language arts who will implement the curriculum, should be sought throughout all phases of development or adaptation of the curriculum. Although not all teachers will take advantage of it, the opportunity to be involved in this decision making is important if a sense of ownership is to develop.

Support, in the form of practical advice, materials, and encouragement, must be available on-call to teachers who are piloting, field testing, or implementing the curriculum. Language arts consultants who are committed to the innovation can provide such support; so can teachers on the development and field testing teams.

Implementation of this curriculum by teachers should be voluntary. It is usually counterproductive to compel teachers to implement curricula against their will, and the result in this curriculum would almost certainly be an increase in student antipathy to poetry.

Diffusion

The curriculum should be pilot tested until all components are successful. It should then be field tested until the curriculum as a whole meets high standards of success. Successful field testing in several schools will go far to smooth the path of implementation.

The following means can be used to disseminate information, build support, and encourage additional teachers to implement the curriculum:

Presentations at professional development workshops by teachers who have successfully field tested the curriculum.

Videotapes of high points from classes using the curriculum, distributed to schools, shown at professional development or staff meetings, aired on local television stations, and so on.

Call-ins to local radio talk programs supporting the curriculum.

Write-ups in teacher magazines and local press.

Talk-up of the curriculum by successful implementers in staff meetings and informal settings.

Invitations to teachers to visit classrooms where the curriculum is successfully installed.

Organization and offer of peer coaching to teachers wishing to implement the curriculum.

Provision of release time to teachers to collect materials, meet with poets, attend conferences and workshops on poetry and poetry teaching.

Renewal

The curriculum should be reviewed on at least an annual basis to ensure its continued updating and improvement, the appropriateness of materials, and revisions needed in light of changes in student or teacher populations. It is a good idea for the teacher of this curriculum to keep an ideabook handy at all times to record positive events that occur and inspirations for the next offering of the course.

Appendix E

Curriculum Associations and Journals

ASSOCIATIONS

African Curriculum Organization, University of Ibadan, Ibadan, Nigeria

American Educational Research Association (Division B: Curriculum Studies), 1230 17th Street, NW, Washington, DC 20036, USA

Association for Supervision and Curriculum Development, 125 North West Street, Alexandria, VA 22314, USA

Association for the Study of Curriculum, School of Education, University of Durham, Leazes Road, Durham DH1 3JH, England

Australian Curriculum Studies Association, School of Education, Deakin University, Victoria 3217, Australia

Canadian Association for Curriculum Studies, c/o Canadian Society for the Study of Education, 14 Henderson Avenue, Ottawa, Ontario K1N 7P1, Canada

Curriculum Teachers Network, c/o Dale Lange, Department of Curriculum & Instruction, College of Education, University of Minnesota, Minneapolis, MN 55455-0208, USA

Professors of Curriculum, c/o Association for Supervision and Curriculum Development, 125 North West Street, Alexandria, VA 22314, USA

World Council for Curriculum and Instruction, School of Education, Indiana University, Bloomington, IN 47405, USA

JOURNALS

Curriculum Inquiry—Ontario Institute for Studies in Education, 252 Bloor Street West, Toronto, Ontario M5S 1V6, Canada

Curriculum—Association for the Study of Curriculum, School of Education, University of Durham, Leazes Road, Durham DH1 3JH, England

Curriculum—Projecto Multinacional de Desarollo Curricular y Capacitación de Docentes para la Educación Basica, Ministry of Education, Caracas, Venezuela

Educational Leadership—Association for Supervision and Curriculum Development, 125 North West Street, Alexandria, VA 22314, USA

Halaha uMaase bTichnun Limudim [Theory and Practice in Curriculum Planning]—Ministry of Education, Israel Curriculum Center, Jerusalem, Israel

Journal of Curriculum and Supervision—Association for Supervision and Curriculum Development, 125 North West Street, Alexandria, VA 22314, USA

Journal of Curriculum Studies—Taylor and Francis, 4 John Street, London WC1N 2ET, England

Journal of Curriculum Theorizing—53 Falstaff Road, Rochester, NY 14609, USA

WCCI Journal—World Council for Curriculum and Instruction, School of Education, Indiana University, Bloomington, IN 47405, USA

Note: A more complete listing of associations and journals may be found in Short (1991).

Appendix F

Feedback on End-of-Chapter Questions

CHAPTER 1

1. Almost any learning can be shown to have some value. If you learn the Tokyo telephone directory by heart, who knows when it might come in useful? But as there is never enough time or resources to teach everything of value, we need to decide what learnings have greatest present and future value for learners and teach these first.

2. AIDS education, smoking education, CPR, swimming, nutrition, and first aid are some survival curricula. You could also make a case for curricula dealing with such subjects as nuclear war, physical education, and self-concept as a protection against suicide.

3. Future well-being must also be considered, and this may involve some sacrifice of present happiness. The well-being of other people is also important. There are other values, such as freedom, which are not identical with happiness, but also worth pursuing.

4. A significant number of teenagers become parents, and for them and other students, it is important to know the significance of prenatal nutrition. It is much less costly to ensure good nutrition during pregnancy than to remediate infant malnutrition, the results of which affect mental as well as physical development.

5. On the basis of present and future learner needs; on the basis of what other sectors in society besides academics consider significant; on the basis of what assists social and personal, as well as intellectual development; on the basis of new intellectual developments not yet recognized as new disciplines or as part of old ones.

6. It is probably more important to listen sympathetically than to rush in with advice. However, you could suggest that she think or read about the basic needs and interests of learners at that age and stage, and which of these needs might best be met within the field of social studies, before deciding questions of content.

7. Among the many implications suggested by this finding are: curriculum does not need to replicate things that television does more

385

effectively; the unsocial nature of television watching implies a role for the school in enhancing social relations; people may need some help in developing skills of discrimination in television viewing; the school might see itself as having a role to provide a different image of the world than that fostered by commercially driven television programs.

8.   Most curriculum is based on what was considered important in the past, but the learners currently in school will live the rest of their lives in the future. Although we cannot predict the future, we need to make responsible forecasts in order to consider the trends and forces that will affect the context in which our students will utilize what they learned in school.

9.   The separation of art and science may be a false dichotomy; there are considerable similarities in the way great artists and scientists approach their work; planning is central in all of the arts; without competent planning, it is difficult for the artistic creativity of teachers to blossom in the classroom.

10.   However well-planned a curriculum, each teacher has to adapt it (i.e., replan it) for his or her students. The view that teachers merely implement externally planned curricula deprives teachers of professional autonomy and responsibility and reduces them to the status of functionaries or technicians.

CHAPTER 2 ───────────────────────

1 D   2 A   3 A   4 B   5 A   6 B   7 B   8 D   9 A   10 D

CHAPTER 3 ───────────────────────

1 C   2 A   3 C   4 C   5 C   6 C   7 D   8 C   9 D   10 B

CHAPTER 4 ───────────────────────

1 D   2 H   3 G   4 A   5 C   6 F   7 J   8 E   9 I   10 B

CHAPTER 5 ───────────────────────

1 F   2 F   3 T   4 F   5 T   6 F   7 T   8 T   9 T   10 F

CHAPTER 6

1. It disproves the notion that social class is always the major determinant of educational achievement.

2. The belief that expectations were already high enough and could not be raised successfully.

3. Cooperative classroom structures.

4. By an experiment, for example, installing excellent libraries in some ineffective schools and monitoring the results.

5. Learning-effectiveness research has now been conducted with adult learners in many different subjects and with similar results to those found in schools.

6. Among other possibilities, read, talk, and listen to your child.

7. It works because expectations influence behavior in many settings, and many students work to the standard set. It is limited in that it will be counterproductive if the expectations are set too high.

8. Some important study skills are: reading for meaning; effective listening; writing summaries or paraphrases; note taking; library skills; peer tutoring; preparing for tests; organizing study time.

9. As there is little commitment to what is learned, it will soon be forgotten.

10. Most people know how to compete without being taught how to do so; employers are generally looking for people who can work as effective team members; people learn better (and hence are better able both to cooperate and to compete) under cooperative conditions.

CHAPTER 7

1 A 2 B 3 A 4 A 5 C 6 A 7 B 8 C 9 B 10 A

CHAPTER 8

1. instruction
2. personnel
3. consumables
4. Montessori
5. noise
6. younger
7. responsibilities
8. ignored, omitted
9. foreign languages
10. operating

CHAPTER 9

1 B   2 D   3 C   4 B   5 A   6 A   7 A   8 C   9 D   10 D

CHAPTER 10

1.   Needs assessment helps to ensure that new programs are based on real and perceived local needs. It provides an opportunity for the community and interested parties to be consulted and feel involved. It informs curriculum developers of areas of support for and opposition to curriculum changes.

2.   A preferable approach would be one marked by respect, support, interest, involvement, accessibility, and autonomy.

3.   The principals of effective schools tend to spend most of their time visiting and observing classrooms; talking with teachers, students, and parents; studying curriculum and working with teachers on curriculum change; and teaching classes. (Effective principals also do paperwork, but they tend to do it at home in the evenings.)

4.   Some of the ways in which systems shoot themselves in the foot when trying to make curriculum change are: by giving teachers insufficient time, training, or resources to adapt to the change; by failing to show any intrinsic benefits of the change for teachers; by lack of good materials or suggestions for instruction or assessment accompanying the curriculum; by introducing changes that are too big or too numerous; by not involving teachers in designing the curriculum or the implementation; by providing for support from principals; and by insisting the change be introduced without modification.

5.   There is no real commitment to the change, so it will be at best only superficially implemented; because it does not meet local needs, there will be no long-term support for it, so when the incentive disappears, so will the innovation.

6.   The best people to advocate curriculum change are other teachers who have tried it out, like it, and have fully implemented it in their classrooms. The most effective methods will be face-to-face discussion, visits, observation in innovators' classrooms, videotapes of successful classes, and convincing evidence of student enthusiasm.

7.   If teachers are not allowed to modify a change, they may feel disempowered; they may feel that their professionality is not respected; they will be unable to adapt the curriculum to their own style or to the specific needs of their pupils; and the curriculum itself will not be able to evolve.

8.   At the end of the first cycle, the curriculum may not be fully in place; materials and strategies may not have been fully developed; resocialization of teachers or students will only be beginning; and it will be difficult to sort out the success of the program from the success of the implementation.

9. and 10.   There is no "right answer" to either of these questions.

References

Abbot, R. D., Wulff, D. H., Nyquist, J. D., Ropp, V. A., & Hess, C. A. (1990). Satisfaction with processes of collecting student opinions about instruction: The student perspective. *Journal of Educational Psychology, 82,* 201–206.

Abraami, P. D., d'Appollonia, S., & Cohen, P. A. (1990). Validity of student ratings of instruction: What we know and what we do not. *Journal of Educational Psychology, 82,* 219–231.

Ackoff, R. L., & Emery, F. E. (1972). *On purposeful systems.* London: Tavistock.

Adams, M. J. (1990). *Beginning to read: Thinking and learning about print: A summary.* Champaign, IL: University of Illinois at Urbana-Champaign, Center for the Study of Reading.

Adler, M. (1981). *Six great ideas: Truth, goodness, beauty, justice, equality, liberty: Ideas we judge by, ideas we act on.* New York: Macmillan.

Adler, M. (1982). *The paideia proposal: An educational manifesto.* New York: Macmillan.

Advisory Council for Adult and Continuing Education (1982). *Adults' mathematical ability and performance.* Leicester, UK: Author.

AERA, APA, & NCME (American Educational Research Association, American Psychological Association, & National Council on Measurement in Education) (1985). *Standards for educational and psychological testing.* Washington, DC: American Psychological Association.

AIDS. (1989). Statistics from the World Health Organization and the Center for Disease Control. *AIDS, 3,* 771–775.

Airasian, P. W. (1971). The role of evaluation in mastery learning. In J. H. Block (Ed.), *Mastery learning: Theory and practice* (pp. 77–88). New York: Holt, Rinehart & Winston.

Airasian, P. W. (1988). Measurement driven instruction: A closer look. *Educational Measurement: Issues and Practice, 7*(4), 6–11.

Airasian, P. W., & Terrasi, S. (1990). Test administration. In H. J. Walberg & G. D. Haertel (Eds.), *International encyclopedia of educational evaluation* (pp. 118–122). New York: Pergamon.

Alberta Education. (1978). *Program of studies for senior high schools.* Edmonton, AB: Author.

Alberta Education. (1985). *Junior high school curriculum: Problem solving: Challenge for mathematics.* Edmonton, AB: Author.

Alkin, M. C. (1991). Prototype evaluation. In A. Lewy (Ed.), *International encyclopedia of curriculum* (pp. 435–436). New York: Pergamon.

Allport, F. H. (1934). The J-curve hypothesis of conforming behavior. *Journal of Social Psychology, 5,* 141–182.

American Association for the Advancement of Science. (1989). *Science for all Americans: A project 2001 report on literacy goals in science, mathematics, and technology.* Washington, DC: Author.

American Psychological Association. (1974). *Standards for educational and psychological tests.* Washington, D.C.: Author.

American Psychological Association. (1988). *Thesaurus of psychological index forms.* Washington, D.C.: Author.

American School Health Association, Association for the Advancement of Health Education, and the Society for Public Health Education. (1989). *The national adolescent student health survey: A report on the health of America's youth.* Oakland, CA: Author.

Ames, C., & Archer, J. (1988). Achievement goals in the classroom: Students' learning strategies and motivation processes. *Journal of Educational Psychology, 80,* 260–267.

Ames, L. B., Gillespie, C., & Streff, J. W. (1972). *Stop school failure.* New York: Harper & Row.

Amigues, R. (1988). Peer interaction in solving physics problems: Sociocognitive confrontation and metacognitive aspects. *Journal of Experimental Child Psychology, 45*(1), 141–158.

Amundsen, R. (1912). *The South Pole.* London: John Murray.

Amundsen, R. (1927). *My life as an explorer.* New York: Doubleday.

Andersen, M. L. (1986). Changing the curriculum in higher education. *Signs: Journal of Women in Culture and Society, 12,* 222–254.

Anderson, C. L. (1986, April). *Where did we go wrong? An analysis of the way instructional systems development was mustered out of the army.* Paper presented at the Annual Meeting of the American Educational Research Association, San Francisco.

Anderson, D. (1974). *My sister looks like a pear: Awakening the poetry in young people*. New York: Hart.

Anderson, L. W. (1976). An empirical investigation of individual differences in time to learn. *Journal of Educational Psychology, 68,* 226–233.

Anderson, L. W. (1980, April). *New directions for research on instruction and time-on-task.* Paper presented at the Annual Meeting of the American Educational Research Association, Boston.

Anderson, R. D. (1983). A consolidation and appraisal of science meta-analyses. *Journal of Research in Science Teaching, 20,* 497–509.

Anderson, R. C., Hiebert, E. H., Scott, J., & Wilkinson, I. A. (1984). *Becoming a nation of readers: A report of the Commission on Reading.* Washington, DC: National Institute of Education.

Anderson, R. H., & Pavan, B. (1992). *Nongradedness: Helping it happen.* Lancaster, PA: Technomic.

Anyon, J. (1980). Social class and the hidden curriculum of work. *Journal of Education, 162*(1), 67–92.

Aoki, T., et al. (1977). *British Columbia social studies assessment.* Victoria, BC: British Columbia Ministry of Education.

Apple, M. W. (1979). *Ideology and curriculum.* Boston: Routledge & Kegan Paul.

Apple, M. W., & Jungck, S. (1990). "You don't have to be a teacher to teach this unit": Teaching, technology, and gender in the classroom. *American Educational Research Journal, 27,* 227–251.

Arias, O. S. (1987). Only peace can write the new history [Nobel lecture, 11 Dec 1978]. In *Les Prix Nobel en 1987* (pp. 257–263). Stockholm: Almqvist & Wiksell.

Aristotle. (1947). *Introduction to Aristotle* (R. McKeon, Ed.). New York: Random House.

Armbruster, B. B., & Anderson, T. H. (1991). Textbook analysis. In A. Lewy (Ed.), *International encyclopedia of curriculum* (pp. 78–81). New York: Pergamon.

Arnold, J. (1985). A responsive curriculum for emerging adolescents. *Middle School Journal*, 16(3), 14–18.

Aronowitz, S., & Giroux, H. A. (1985). *Education under seige: The conservative, liberal, and radical debate over schooling*. South Hadley, MA: Bergin & Garvey.

Asante, M. K. (1991). Afrocentric curriculum. *Educational Leadership*, 49(4), 28–31.

ASCD (Association for Supervision & Curriculum Development) Task Force on Business Involvement in the schools. (1989). Guidelines for business involvement in the schools. *Educational Leadership*, 47(4), 84–86.

Ashby, R., & Lee, P. (1987). Children's concepts of empathy and understanding in history. In C. Portal (Ed.), *The history curriculum for teachers* (pp. 62–88). London: Falmer.

Ashby, W. R. (1956). *Introduction to cybernetics*. New York: Wiley.

Ashton-Warner, S. (1979). *I passed this way*. New York: Knopf.

Asimov, I. (1982). *Isaac Asimov on numbers*. East Brunswick, NJ: Bell.

Association for Supervision and Curriculum Development. (1992). *Curriculum handbook*. Alexandria, VA: Author.

Ausubel, D. P. (1968). *Educational psychology, a cognitive view*. New York: Holt, Rinehart & Winston.

Ausubel, D. P. (1978). In defence of advance organizers: A reply to the critics. *Review of Educational Research*, 48, 251–257.

Ayers, W. (1989). "We who believe in freedom cannot rest until it's done": Two dauntless women of the civil rights movement and the education of a people [Review of *Fundi: The story of Ella Baker* and *Ready from within: Septima Clark and the Civil Rights Movement: A first person narrative*]. *Harvard Educational Review*, 59, 520–527.

Ayers, W., & Schubert, W. H. (1989). The normative and the possible: Values in the curriculum. *Educational Forum*, 53, 355–364.

Bacon, F. (1985). *The essayes or counsels, civill and morall* (M. Kiernan, Ed.). Cambridge, MA: Harvard University Press.

Bailey, T. (1991). Jobs of the future and the education they will require: Evidence from occupational forecasts. *Educational Researcher, 20*(2), 11–20.

Baker, D. (1990). *Gender differences in science: Where they start and where they go.* Paper presented at the Annual Meeting of the National Association for Research in Science Teaching, Atlanta.

Bangert-Drowns, R. L., Kulik, C. C., Kulik, J. A., & Morgan, M. T. (1991). The instructional effect of feedback in test-like events. *Review of Educational Research, 61,* 213–238.

Bangert-Drowns, R. L., Kulik, J. A., & Kulik, C. C. (1985). Effectiveness of computer-based education in secondary schools. *Journal of Computer-Based Instruction, 12,* 59–68.

Bangert-Drowns, R. L., Kulik, J. A., & Kulik, C. C. (1988). Effects of frequent classroom testing. Unpublished ms., Ann Arbor, MI: University of Michigan. (Cited in T. J. Crooks, 1988, The impact of classroom evaluation practices on students, *Review of Educational Research, 58,* 438–481.)

Bank, B. J., Slavings, R. L., & Biddle, B. J. (1990). Effects of peer, faculty, and parental influences on students' persistence. *Sociology of Education, 63,* 208–225.

Barker, B. (1986). *The advantages of small schools.* Las Cruces, NM: New Mexico State University. (ERIC Documentation Reproduction Service No. ED 265 988)

Barker, R. G., & Gump, P. V. (1964). *Big school, small school.* Stanford, CA: Stanford University Press.

Barnett, C. (1982). *The desert generals.* Bloomington, IL: Indiana University Press.

Barrow, R. (1988). Over the top: A misuse of philosophical techniques? *Interchange, 19*(2), 59–63.

Barth, R. S. (1990a). A personal vision of a good school. *Phi Delta Kappan, 71,* 512–516.

Barth, R. S. (1990b). *Improving schools from within.* San Francisco: Jossey-Bass.

Bates, J. A. (1979). Extrinsic reward and intrinsic motivation: A review with implications for the classroom. *Review of Educational Research, 49,* 557–576.

Bateson, M. C. (1989). *Composing a life.* New York: Atlantic Monthly Press.

Baudoux, C. (1988). De moins en moins de responsables féminines d'établissements scolaires au Québec: Les directrices adjointes du primaire. *Canadian Journal of Education, 13,* 465–478.

Bauman, Z. (1978). *Hermeneutics and social science.* New York: Columbia University Press.

Beard, R. M., & Pole, K. (1971). Content and purpose of biochemistry examinations. *British Journal of Medical Education, 5,* 13–21.

Beauchamp, G. (1983, November). *Curriculum and excellence in education: The role of theory and practice.* Paper prepared for a symposium in honor of Mauritz Johnson, State University of New York at Albany.

Becker, H. (1981). *Teacher practices of parent involvement at home: A statewide survey.* Paper presented at the Annual Meeting of the American Educational Research Association, Chicago, IL.

Becker, S. L., Burke, J. A., Arbogast, R. A., Naughton, M. J., Backman, I., & Spohn, E. (1989). Community programs to enhance in-school anti-tobacco efforts. *Preventive Medicine, 18,* 221–228.

Belenkey, M. F., Clinchy, B. M., Goldberger, N. R., & Tarule, J. M. (1986). *Women's ways of knowing: The development of self, voice, and mind.* New York: Basic Books.

Benbow, C. P., & Stanley, J. C. (1983). An eight-year evaluation of SMPY: What was learned? In C. P. Benbow & J. C. Stanley (Eds.), *Academic precocity, aspects of its development* (pp. 205–214). Baltimore: Johns Hopkins University Press.

Bergan, J. R., Sladeczek, I. E., Schwarz, R. D., & Smith, A. N. (1991). Effects of a measurement and planning system on kindergartners' cognitive development and educational programming. *American Educational Research Journal, 28,* 683–714.

Berk, R. (1988). Fifty reasons why student achievement gain does not mean teacher effectiveness. *Journal of Personnel Evaluation in Education, 1,* 345–363.

Berliner, D. C. (1986).   In pursuit of the expert pedagogue. *Educational Researcher*, 15(7), 5–13.

Berryman, C. (1973).   100 ideas for using the newspaper in courses in social science and history. *Social Education* 37, 318–320.

Bettelheim, B. (1960).   *The informed heart: Autonomy in a mass age.* New York: Free Press.

Bickis, U. (1992, February 14).   *Environmental quality.* Presentation at Queen's University Faculty of Education, Kingston, ON.

Biggs, J., & Collis, K. (1982). *Evaluating the quality of learning.* New York: Academic Press.

Biotechnology survey. (1988, April 30).   *The Economist*, pp. 3–18.

Bishop, J. H. (1989a).   *Incentives for learning: Why American high school students compare so poorly to their counterparts overseas.* Unpublished paper, Cornell University.

Bishop, J. H. (1989b).   Why the apathy in American high schools? *Educational Researcher*, 18(1), 6–10, 42.

Bishop, J. H. (1990a).   The productivity consequences of what is learned in high school. *Journal of Curriculum Studies*, 22(2), 101–126.

Bishop, J. H. (1990b, November).   *A strategy for inducing all Americans to give greater priority to learning.* Paper presented at the 18th Annual Urban Curriculum Leaders Conference, Scottsdale, AZ.

Black, P. J. (1968).   University examinations. *Physics Education*, 3(2), 93–99.

Blackie, J. (1963).   *Good enough for the children?* London: Faber & Faber.

Blase, J. J. (1987).   Dimensions of effective school leadership: The teachers' perspective. *Educational Administration Quarterly*, 24, 589–610.

Blatchford, P., Burke, J., Plewis, I., & Tizard, B. (1989).   Teacher expectations in infant school: Associations with attainment and progress, curriculum coverage and classroom interaction. *British Journal of Educational Psychology*, 59, 19–30.

Blishway, A., & Nash, W. R. (1977).   School cheating behavior. *Review of Educational Research*, 47, 623–632.

Block, J. H., Efthim, H. E., & Burns, R. B. (1989). *Building effective mastery learning schools.* New York: Longman.

Block, P. (1987). *The empowered manager.* San Francisco: Jossey-Bass.

Bloom, B. S. (1968). Learning for mastery. *UCLA Evaluation Comment,* 1(2), 1–12.

Bloom, B. S. (1976). *Human characteristics and school learning.* New York: McGraw Hill.

Bloom, B. S. (1981). *All our children learning: A primer for parents, teachers, and other educators.* New York: McGraw-Hill.

Bloom, B. S. (1984). The 2 sigma problem: The search for methods of group instruction as effective as one-to-one tutoring. *Educational Researcher,* 13(6), 4–16.

Bloom, B. S., Engelhart, M. D., Furst, E. J., Hill, W. H., & Krathwohl, D. R. (1956). *Taxonomy of educational objectives. Handbook 1: Cognitive domain.* New York: McKay.

Blum, A., & Grobman, A. B. (1991). Curriculum adaptation. In A. Lewy (Ed.), *International encyclopedia of curriculum* (pp. 384–388). New York: Pergamon.

Bobbitt, F. (1918). *The curriculum.* Boston: Houghton Mifflin.

Bobbitt, F. (1924). *How to make a curriculum.* Boston: Houghton Mifflin.

Bode, B. H. (1938). *Progressive education at the crossroads.* New York: Newson.

Boehnlein, M. (1987). Reading intervention for high-risk first-graders. *Educational Leadership,* 44(6), 32–37.

Bolgen, K. (1970). There are no hopeless children. *The Humanist,* 30(4), 14–22.

Bond, J. (1982). Pupil tutoring: The educational conjuring trick. *Educational Review,* 34, 241–252.

Boomer, G. (1982). *Negotiating the curriculum.* Sydney, Australia: Ashton Scholastic.

Booth, M. (1987). Ages and concepts: A critique of the Piagetian approach to history teaching. In C. Portal (Ed.), *The history curriculum for teachers* (pp. 22–38). London: Falmer.

Borgrink, H. (1987). *New Mexico dropout study, 1986–87 school year*. Santa Fe, NM: New Mexico State Department of Education. (ERIC Documentation Reproduction Service No. ED 303 289)

Botvin, G. J. (1986). Substance abuse prevention research: Recent developments and future directions. *Journal of School Health*, 56, 369–374.

Bouleau, C. (1963). *The painter's secret geometry: A study of composition in art* (J. Griffin, Trans.). New York: Harcourt, Brace & World.

Boyd, W. L. (1978). The changing politics of curriculum policy-making for American schools. *Review of Educational Research*, 48, 577–628.

Braddock, J. H., II. (1990). Tracking the middle grades: National patterns of grouping for instruction. *Phi Delta Kappan*, 71, 445–449.

Braddock, J. H., II., & McPartland, J. M. (1990). Alternatives to tracking. *Educational Leadership*, 47(7), 76–79.

Bradley, A. (1989, April 26). Top business heads say schools earn low grade. *Education Week*, p.5.

Brandt, R. (1987). On school improvement in Pittsburgh: A conversation with Richard Wallace. *Educational Leadership*, 44(8), 39–43.

Brief, R. S., & Bernath, T. (1988). *Indoor pollution: Guidelines for prevention and control of microbiological respiratory hazards associated with air conditioning and ventilation systems*. East Millstone, NJ: Exxon Biomedical Sciences.

Brinsley, J. (1627). *Ludus Literarius or the grammar schoole*. Quoted in M. Skilbeck, 1985, *School-based curriculum development*. London: Harper & Row.

British Columbia Ministry of Education. (1976). *Geology 12 curriculum guide*. Victoria, BC: Author.

Brody, L. E., & Benbow, C. P. (1987). Accelerative strategies: How effective are they for the gifted? *Gifted Child Quarterly*, 31, 105–109.

Brophy, J. (1987). Synthesis of research on strategies for motivating students to learn. *Educational Leadership*, 45(2), 40–48.

Broudie, H. S. (1961). Mastery. In B. O. Smith & R. H. Ennis (Eds.), *Language and concepts in education* (pp. 72–85). Chicago: Rand McNally.

Brown, D. S. (1988). Twelve middle-school teachers' planning. *Elementary School Journal*, 89(1), 69–87.

Brown, J. L. (1981). Defensive curriculum development. *Educational Leadership*, 39(2), 108–109.

Bryan, J. F., & Locke, E. A. (1967). Goal setting as a means of increasing motivation. *Journal of Applied & Social Psychology*, 51, 274–277.

Bryk, A. S., & Thum, Y. M. (1989). The effects of high school organization on dropping out: An exploratory investigation. *American Educational Research Journal*, 26, 353–383.

Buber, M. (1970). *I and thou* (2nd ed.). New York: Scribner.

Bullock, A. (1975). *A language for life: Report of the Committee of Inquiry into Reading and the Use of English*. London: Her Majesty's Stationery Office.

Bullough, R. V., Jr. (1987). Planning and the first year of teaching. *Journal of Education for Teaching*, 13, 231–250.

Bullough, R. V., Jr., Knowles, J. G., & Crow, N. A. (1989). Teacher self-concept and student culture in the first year of teaching. *Teachers College Record*, 91, 209–233.

Burlington Public Schools. (1985). *Burlington Art Curriculum, Grades K-8*. Burlington, MA: Author.

Burns, P. K. (1981). A quantitative synthesis of research findings relative to the pedagogical effectiveness of computer-assisted mathematics instruction in elementary and secondary schools. *Dissertation Abstracts International*, 42, 2946A.

Burns, R. (1955). *Poems and songs of Robert Burns* (J. Barker, Ed.). London: Collins.

Butler, R. (1988). Enhancing and undermining intrinsic motivation: The effects of task-involving and ego-involving evaluation of interest and performance. *British Journal of Educational Psychology*, 58, 1–14.

Cafferty, E. (1980). *An analysis of student performance based upon the degree of match between the educational cognitive style of the teachers and the educational cognitive style of the students*. Unpublished doctoral dissertation, University of Nebraska, 1980.

Cahan, S., & Cohen, N. (1989). Age versus schooling effects on intelligence development. *Child Development, 60,* 1239–1249.

Cairns, R. B., Cairns, B. D., & Neckerman, H. J. (1989). Early school dropout: Configurations and determinants. *Child Development, 60,* 1437–1452.

Calabrese, R. L., & Cochran, J. T. (1990). The relationship of alienation to cheating among a sample of American adolescents. *Journal of Research & Development in Education, 23,* 65–72.

California State Department of Education. (1986). *Handbook for physical education: Framework for developing a curriculum for California Public Schools, Kindergarten through Grade 12.* Sacramento, CA: Author.

California State Department of Education. (1987). *Science: Model curriculum guide Kindergarten through Grade 8.* Sacramento, CA: Author.

Calvino, I. (1988). *Six memos for the next millennium.* Cambridge, MA: Harvard University Press.

Cambourne, B., & Turbill, J. (1990). Assessment in whole-language classrooms: Theory into practice. *Elementary School Journal, 90,* 337–349.

Cameron, C., Politano, C., & Morris, D. (1989). *Buddies: Collaborative learning through shared experience.* North Vancouver, BC: Creative Curriculum.

Capon, N., & Kuhn, D. (1979). Logical reasoning in the supermarket: Adult females' use of a proper reasoning strategy in an everyday context. *Developmental Psychology, 15,* 450–452.

Capra, F. (1982). *The turning point.* New York: Simon & Schuster.

Carbo, M. (1990). Igniting the literacy revolution through reading styles. *Educational Leadership, 48*(2), 26–29.

Carey, M. A. (1989). *Poetry: Starting from scratch.* Lincoln, NE: Foundation Books.

Carlson, C. G. (1991). The parent principle: Prerequisite for educational success. *Focus, 26.* Princeton, NJ: Educational Testing Service.

Carmichael, H. W., Burnett, J. D., Higginson, W. C., Moore, B. G., & Pollard, P. J. (1985). *Computers, children, and classrooms: A multisite evaluation of the creative use of microcomputers by elementary school children.* Toronto: Queen's Printer.

Carnegie Foundation for the Advancement of Teaching. (1988). *An imperiled generation*. New York: Author.

Carraher, T. N., Carraher, D. W., & Schliemann, A. D. (1985). Mathematics on the streets and in the schools. *British Journal of Educational Psychology, 3*, 21–29.

Carroll, J. B. (1971). Problems of measurement related to the concept of learning for mastery. In J. H. Block (Ed.), *Mastery learning: Theory and practice* (pp. 29–46). New York: Holt, Rinehart & Winston.

Carter, J. (1990). Foreword. In I. Abrams (Ed.), *The words of peace: Selections from the speeches of the winners of the Nobel Peace Prize* (pp. 1–4). New York: Newmarket Press.

Case, R. (1973). Piaget's theory of child development and its implications. *Phi Delta Kappan, 55*, 20–25.

Case, R. (1991). The anatomy of curricular integration. *Canadian Journal of Education, 16*, 215–224.

Casey, W., Jones, D., Kugler, B., & Watkins, B. (1988). Integration of Down's syndrome children in the primary school: A longitudinal study of cognitive development and academic attainments. *British Journal of Educational Psychology, 58*, 279–286.

Cashion, M., & MacIver, D. (1988). In the opinion of low achievers: A study of low achievers in New Brunswick. *Education New Brunswick, 3* (June), 41–45.

Caspi, A., Elder, G. H., & Bem, D. J. (1988). Moving away from the world: Life-course patterns of shy children. *Developmental Psychology, 24*, 824–831.

Caswell, H. L., & Campbell, D. S. (1935). *Curriculum development*. New York: American Book Co.

Causley, C. (1962). *Poems of our time*. Leicester, UK: Salisbury Press.

Cave Brown, A. (1975). *Bodyguard of lies*. New York: Harper & Row.

Chapman, J. W., Lambourne, R., & Silva, P. A. (1990). Some antecedents of academic self-concept: A longitudinal study. *British Journal of Educational Psychology, 60*, 142–152.

Chen, C., & Stevenson, H. W. (1989). Homework: A cross-cultural examination. *Child Development, 60*, 551–561.

Chickering, A. W., & Gamson, Z. F. (1988). Seven principles for good practice in undergraduate education. *University Affairs, 29*(9), 3.

Chief Directorate of Schools, USSR Ministry of Education. (1987). The biology curriculum. *Soviet Education, 29*(5–6), 9–66.

Children's decline. (1992, January 3). *Globe & Mail,* p. A9.

Choppin, B. H. (1990a). Objective tests. In H. J. Walberg & G. D. Haertel (Eds.), *International encyclopedia of educational evaluation* (pp. 465–468). New York: Pergamon.

Choppin, B. H. (1990b). Correction for guessing. In H. J. Walberg & G. D. Haertel (Eds.), *International encyclopedia of educational evaluation* (pp. 345–348). New York: Pergamon.

Choppin, B. H. (1990c). Evaluation, assessment, and measurement. In H. J. Walberg & G. D. Haertel (Eds.), *International encyclopedia of educational evaluation* (pp. 7–8). New York: Pergamon.

Churchill, W. S. (1974). *Winston S. Churchill: His complete speeches. 1897–1963* (R. R. James, Ed.), Vol. 6. New York: Chelsea House.

Clark, C., & Yinger, R. J. (1980). *The hidden world of teaching: Implications of research on teacher planning.* East Lansing, MI: Michigan State University, Institute for Research on Teaching.

Clark, P. (1991). *A bibliography on curricular integration: Fundamental issues and approaches.* Burnaby, BC: Simon Fraser University, Tri-University Integration Project.

Clark, R. E., & Voogel, A. (1985). Transfer of training principles for instructional design. *Educational Communications and Technology Journal, 33,* 113–123.

Clark, T. A., & McCarthy, D. P. (1983). School improvement in New York City: The evolution of a project. *Educational Researcher, 12*(4), 17–24.

Clarke, M. (1991, February 24). Memo to politicians: Think of the troops on the ground. *Manchester Guardian Weekly,* p. 8.

Clay, M. M. (1987). Implementing reading recovery: Systematic adaptations to an educational innovation. *New Zealand Journal of Educational Studies, 22*(1), 35–58.

Clements, W. (1991, January).   Spectrum: Statistical lore for everyday living. *Globe & Mail Report on Business*, p. 84.

Cleveland, H., Mangone, G. J., & Adams, J. C. (1960).   *The overseas Americans.* New York: McGraw Hill.

Clift, R. T., Ghatala, E. S., Naus, M. M., & Poole, J. (1989).   Exploring teachers' knowledge of strategic study activity. *Journal of Experimental Education, 58,* 253–263.

Cochrane, J. (1981).   *The one-room school in Canada.* Toronto: Fitzhenry & Whiteside.

Cochran-Smith, M. (1991).   Word processing and writing in elementary classrooms: A critical review of related literature. *Review of Educational Research, 61,* 107–155.

Code of Fair Testing Practices in Education. (1988).   Washington, DC: Joint Committee on Testing Practices.

Coffman, W. E. (1971).   Essay examinations. In R. L. Thorndike (Ed.), *Educational measurement* (2nd ed.) (pp. 271–302). Washington, DC: American Council on Education.

Cohen, P. A., Ebeling, B. J., & Kulik, J. A. (1981).   A meta-analysis of outcome studies of visual-based instruction. *Education Communication and Technology Journal, 9,* 26–36.

Cohen, P. A., Kulik, J. A., & Kulik, C. C. (1982).   Educational outcomes of tutoring: A meta-analysis of findings. *American Educational Research Journal, 19,* 237–248.

Cohen, S. A. (1987).   Instructional alignment: Searching for a magic bullet. *Educational Researcher, 16*(8), 16–20.

Cohen, S. A., Hyman, J. S., Ashcroft, L., & Loveless, D. (1989, March).   *Comparing effects of metacognition, learning styles, and human attributes with alignment.* Paper presented at the annual meeting of the American Educational Research Association, San Francisco.

Cohen, S., Glass, D. C., & Singer, J. E. (1973).   Apartment noise, auditory discrimination, and reading ability in children. *Journal of Experimental Social Psychology, 9,* 407–422.

Coleman, J. S., Campbell, E. Q., Hobson, C. J., McPartland, J., Mood, A. M., Weinfeld, F. D., & York, R. L. (1966). *Equality of educational opportunity.* Washington, DC: Government Printing Office.

Coleman, P. (1986). School districts and student achievement in British Columbia: A preliminary analysis. *Canadian Journal of Education*, 11, 509–521.

Coleman, P., & LaRocque, L. (1990). *Struggling to be 'Good enough': Administrative practices and school district ethos.* New York: Falmer.

Coleman, P., Mikkelson, L., & LaRocque, L. (1991). Network coverage: Administrative collegiality and school district ethos in high-performing districts. *Canadian Journal of Education*, 16, 151–167.

Coleman, T. (1976, November 14). Survival of the fastest. *Manchester Guardian Weekly*, p. 20.

Coloroso, B. (1987). *Discipline: Winning at teaching* [Audiovisual kit]. Boulder, CO: Kids Are Worth It.

Comfort, R. (1990). On the idea of curriculum modification by teachers. *Academic Therapy*, 25, 397–405.

Comrey, A. L., Michael, W. B., & Fruchter, B. (1988). Obituary: J. P. Guilford (1897–1987), *American Psychologist*, 43, 1086–1087.

Conant, J. B. (1959). *The American high school today.* New York: McGraw Hill.

Conway, L. (1976). Classroom in the sky: A power trip for disadvantaged youth. *Phi Delta Kappan*, 57, 570–574.

Corcoran, T. B., & Wilson, B. L. (1987, September). Successful secondary schools. *Education Digest*, pp. 22–24.

Cornbleth, C. (1990). *Curriculum in context.* Bristol, PA: Falmer Press.

Cornfield, R. J., Doyle, K., Durrant, B., McCutcheon, K., Pollard, J., & Stratton, W. (1987). *Making the grade: Evaluating student progress.* Englewood Cliffs, NJ: Prentice-Hall.

Costa, A. L. (1989). Reassessing assessment. *Educational Leadership*, 1989, 46(7), 2.

Council on Medical Education. (1982). Future directions for medical education. *Journal of the American Medical Association*, 248, 3225–3239.

Counts, G. S. (1969). *Dare the school build a new social order?* New York: Arno Press.

Crain, R. L. (1984). *The quality of American high school graduates: What personnel officers say and do about it.* Baltimore, MD: Johns Hopkins Center for Social Organization of Schools.

Cramer, R. L. (1981). *Building concrete writing skills.* Duluth, MN.: Instructor Publications, Inc.

Cranton, P., & Smith, R. A. (1990). Reconsidering the unit of analysis: A model of student ratings of instruction. *Journal of Educational Psychology, 82,* 207–212.

Crawford, J. *Bilingual education: History, politics, theory, and practice.* (1989). Trenton, NJ: Crane Publishing.

Crichton, R. (1959). *The great imposter.* New York: Random House.

Criscuolo, N. P. (1982). Parent involvement in the reading program. *Phi Delta Kappan, 63,* 345–346.

Croll, P., & Moses, D. (1988). Teaching methods and time on task in junior classrooms. *Educational Research, 30*(2), 90–97.

Cronbach, L. J. (1983). Course improvement through evaluation. In G. F. Madaus, M. S. Scriven, & D. L. Stufflebeam (Eds.), *Evaluation models: Viewpoints on educational and human services evaluation* (pp. 101–115). Boston: Kluwer-Nijhoff.

Crooks, T. J. (1988). The impact of classroom evaluation practices on students. *Review of Educational Research, 58,* 438–481.

Crossen, C. (1991, December 7). Massaging statistics: The polls dance to anybody's tune. *Globe & Mail,* p. D5.

Crosswhite, F. J., Dossey, J. A., & Frye, S. M. (1989). NCTM standards for school mathematics: Visions for implementation. *Journal for Research in Mathematics Education, 20,* 513–522.

Cussons, R., & Hedges, H. (1978). *Volunteers in Halton schools.* Toronto: Ontario Institute for Studies in Education. Unpublished manuscript.

Cutler, A., & McShane, R. (1960). *The Trachtenberg speed system of basic mathematics.* Garden City, NY: Doubleday.

Daniels, L. (1991). *Integration and relevance*. Burnaby, BC: Simon Fraser University, Tri-University Integration Project.

Dar, Y., & Resh, N. (1986). Classroom intellectual composition and academic achievement. *American Educational Research Journal, 23,* 357–374.

Dauber, S. L., & Epstein, J. L. (1989, March). *Parents' attitudes and practices of involvement in inner-city elementary and middle schools.* Paper presented at the Annual Meeting of the American Educational Research Association, San Francisco.

Davis, F. B., & Diamond, J. J. (1974). The preparation of criterion-referenced tests. In C. W. Harris, M. C. Alkin, & W. J. Popham (Eds.), *Problems in criterion-referenced measurement* (pp. 116–138). Los Angeles: UCLA Center for the Study of Evaluation.

Day, E., & Shapson, S. (1988). A comparison study of early and late French immersion programs in British Columbia. *Canadian Journal of Education, 13,* 290–305.

De Landsheere, V. (1991). Taxonomies of educational objectives. In A. Lewy (Ed.), *International encyclopedia of curriculum* (pp. 317–327). New York: Pergamon.

Dempster, F. N. (1988). The spacing effect: A case study in the failure to apply the results of psychological research. *American Psychologist, 43,* 627–634.

Dennis, B. D. (1987). *Effects of small class size (1:15) on the teaching/learning process in grade two.* Unpublished doctoral dissertation, Tennessee State University.

Dennis–Yarmouth Regional School District. (1986). *Introductory Science.* Yarmouth, MA: Author.

DePaul, B. M., Tang, J., Webb, W., Hoover, C., Marsh, K., & Litowitz, C. (1989). Age differences in reactions to help in a peer tutoring context. *Child Development, 60,* 423–439.

Deutsch, R. (1977). *Mairead Corrigan, Betty Williams.* Woodbury, NY: Barron's.

DeVillaer, M. (1990). Client-centered community needs assessment. *Evaluation and Program Planning, 13,* 211–219.

Dewey, J. (1902). *The child and the curriculum and the school and society.* Chicago: University of Chicago Press.

Dewey, J. (1938). *Experience and education*. New York: Macmillan.

Dewey, J. (1975). *Moral principles in education*. Carbondale, IL: Southern Illinois University Press.

Dick, W., & Carey, L. (1990). *The systematic design of instruction* (3rd ed.). New York: Harper Collins.

Dolan, C. (1990, February 9). The educator-executive. *The Wall Street Journal Education Report*, p. R20.

Dole, J. A., Duffy, G. G., Roehler, L. R., & Pearson, P. D. (1991). Moving from the old to the new research on reading comprehension instruction. *Review of Educational Research, 61*, 239–264.

Doll, W. E., Jr. (1989). *Post-modernism's utopian vision*. Unpublished manuscript, Louisiana State University, Department of Curriculum and Instruction, Baton Rouge, LA.

Dorr-Bremme, D. W. (1991). Naturalistic evaluation. In A. Lewy (Ed.), *International encyclopedia of curriculum*. New York: Pergamon.

Dow, I. I., Whitehead, R. Y., & Wright, R. L. (1984). *Curriculum implementation: A framework for action*. Toronto: Ontario Public School Teachers Federation.

Doyle, W., & Ponder, G. A. (1978). The practicality ethic in teacher decision making. *Interchange, 8*(3), 1–12.

Drucker, P. F. (1969). *The age of discontinuity*. New York: Harper & Row.

Duignan, P. (1979, November). The pressures of the superintendency: Too many deadlines, not enough time. *Executive Educator*, pp. 34–35.

Dukas, H., & Hoffman, B. (Eds.). (1979). *Albert Einstein: The human side. New glimpses from his archives*. Princeton, NJ: Princeton University Press.

Dunn, K., & Dunn, R. (1987). Dispelling outmoded beliefs about student learning. *Educational Leadership, 44*(6), 55–61.

Dunn, R., Beaudry, S., & Klavas, A. (1989). Survey of research on learning styles. *Educational Leadership, 46*(6), 50–58.

Dunn, R., Deckinger, E. L., Withers, P., & Katzenstein, H. (1990). Should college students be taught how to do homework? The effects of studying marketing through individual perceptual strengths. *Illinois School Research & Development, 26,* 96–113.

Dunn, R., Dunn, K., & Price, G. E. (1989). *Learning style inventory.* Lawrence, KS: Price Systems.

Dunn, R., Gemake, J., Jalali, F., Zenjhausern, R., Quinn, P., & Spiridakis, J. (1990). Cross-cultural differences in learning styles of elementary-age students from four ethnic backgrounds. *Journal of Multicultural Counselling & Development, 18* (April), 68–93.

Dunn, R., Sklar, R. I., Beaudry, J. S., & Bruno, J. (1990). Effects of matching and mismatching minority developmental college students' hemispheric preferences on mathematics scores. *Journal of Educational Research, 83,* 283–288.

Durham College, Business Division. (1990). *Course outline for Accounting 295.* Oshawa, ON: Author.

Dye, J. S. (1989). Parental involvement in curriculum matters: Parents, teachers and children working together. *Educational Research, 31*(1), 20–35.

Eagly, A. H., & Johnson, B. T. (1990). Gender and leadership style: A meta-analysis. *Psychological Bulletin, 108,* 233–256.

Earl, T. (1987). *The art and craft of course design.* New York: Nichols.

Ebel, R. L. (1972). *Essentials of educational measurement.* Englewood Cliffs, NJ: Prentice-Hall.

Edmonds, R. (1979a). Effective schools for the urban poor. *Educational Leadership, 37*(1), 15–24.

Edmonds, R. (1979b). *A discussion of the literature and issues related to effective schooling.* St. Louis, MO: CEMREL.

Education Manitoba. (1981). *English language arts K-12 interim guide.* Winnipeg, MB: Author.

Egan, K. (1983). Children's path to reality from fantasy: Contrary thoughts about curriculum foundations. *Journal of Curriculum Studies, 15,* 357–371.

Egan, K. (1991). Relevance and the romantic imagination. *Canadian Journal of Education, 16,* 58–71.

Ehrenreich, B., & English, D. (1979). *For her own good.* New York: Anchor Books.

Eisner, E. W. (1969). Instructional and expressive educational objectives: Their formulation and use in curriculum. In W. J. Popham, E. W. Eisner, H. J. Sullivan, & L. L. Tyler (Eds.), *Instructional objectives* (pp. 1–31) (American Educational Research Association monograph series on curriculum evaluation, No. 3). Chicago: Rand McNally.

Eisner, E. W. (1989, March). *Imagination in human understanding.* Paper presented at the Annual Meeting of the World Council for Curriculum & Instruction, Orlando, FL.

Eisner, E. W. (1990). Who decides what schools teach? *Phi Delta Kappan, 71,* 523–526.

Eisner, E. W., & Vallance, E. (Eds.). (1973). *Conflicting conceptions of curriculum.* Berkeley, CA: McCutchan.

Elam, S. M. (1988). The second Gallup/Phi Delta Kappan poll of teachers' attitudes toward the public schools. *Phi Delta Kappan, 70,* 785–798.

Elam, S. M. (1990). The 22nd annual Gallup poll of the public's attitudes toward the public schools. *Phi Delta Kappan, 72,* 41–55.

Elam, S. M., Rose, L. C., & Gallup, A. M. (1991). The 23rd annual Gallup poll of the public's attitudes toward the public schools. *Phi Delta Kappan, 73,* 41–56.

Elia, J. S. I. (1986). *An alignment experiment in vocabulary instruction: Varying instructional practice and test item formats to measure transfer with low SES fourth graders.* Unpublished doctoral dissertation, University of San Francisco.

Elkind, D. (1988). From our President: Acceleration. *Young Children, 43*(4), 2.

Elliott, S. N., Sheridan, S. M., & Gresham, F. M. (1989). Assessing and treating social skills deficits: A case study for the scientist-practitioner. *Journal of School Psychology, 1989, 27,* 197–222.

Elmira City School District. (1987). *Instrumental Music Curriculum.* Elmira, NY: Author.

Emmer, E. T., Evertson, C. M., Sanford, J. P., Clements, B. S., & Worsham, M. E. (1984). *Classroom management for secondary teachers.* Englewood Cliffs, NJ: Prentice-Hall.

Ensminger, M. E., & Celentano, D. P. (1988). Unemployment and psychiatric distress: Social resources and coping. *Social Science and Medicine, 27,* 239–247.

Environmental Protection Agency. (1988). *The inside story: A guide to indoor air quality.* Washington, DC: US Product Safety Commission.

Epstein, J. L. (1986). Parents' reactions to teacher practices of parent involvement. *Elementary School Journal, 86,* 277–294.

Epstein, J. L. (1990). School and family connections: Theory, research and implications for integrating sociologies of education and family. In D. G. Unger & M. B. Sussman (Eds.), *Families in community settings: Interdisciplinary perspectives.* New York: Haworth Press.

Eraut, M. R. (1991). Defining educational objectives. In A. Lewy (Ed.), *International encyclopedia of curriculum* (pp. 306–317). New York: Pergamon.

Erb, T. (1987). What team organization can do for teachers. *Middle School Journal,* 18(4), 3–6.

Erdman, J. K. (1990). Curriculum and community: A feminist perspective. In J. T. Sears & J. D. Marshall (Eds.), *Teaching and thinking about curriculum: Critical inquiries* (pp. 172–186). New York: Teachers College Press.

Evans, E. D., & Engelberg, R. A. (1988). Student perceptions of school grading. *Journal of Research and Development in Education,* 21(2), 45–54.

Evertson, C. M., Emmer, E. T., Clements, B. S., Sanford, J. P., & Worsham, M. E. (1984). *Classroom management for elementary teachers.* Englewood Cliffs, NJ: Prentice-Hall.

Fader, D. (1969). *Hooked on books.* New York: Pergamon.

Falchikov, N., & Bond, D. (1989). Student self-assessment in higher education: A meta-analysis. *Review of Educational Research, 59,* 395–430.

Fanon, F. (1965). *The wretched of the earth.* New York: Grove Press.

Farkas, G., Sheehan, D., & Grobe, R. P. (1990). Coursework mastery and school success: Gender, ethnicity, and poverty groups within an urban school district. *American Educational Research Journal, 27,* 807–827.

Farrell, E., Peguero, G., Lindsey, R., & White, R. (1988). Give voice to high school students: Pressure and boredom, Ya know what I'm sayin'? *American Educational Research Journal, 25,* 489–502.

Farrell, G. E. (1989, March). *Curriculum development, implementation, and evaluation: A cross-cultural study of secondary schools in Australia, Canada, England, and the State of Georgia.* Paper presented at the Annual Meeting of the American Educational Research Association, San Francisco.

Farson, R. (1978). The technology of humanism. *Journal of Humanistic Psychology,* 18(2), 5–35.

Fay, B. (1987). *Critical social science: Liberation and its limits.* Ithaca, NY: Cornell University Press.

Feather, N. (Ed.). (1982). *Expectations and actions.* Hillsdale, NJ: Erlbaum.

Fehrman, P., Keith, R., & Reimers, T. (1987). Home influence on school learning: Direct and indirect effects of parental involvement on high school grades. *Journal of Educational Research,* 80, 330-337.

Feldhusen, J. F. (1989). Synthesis of research on gifted youth. *Educational Leadership,* 46(6), 6–11.

Findley, W. G., & Bryan, M. M. (1970). *Ability grouping 1970: Status, impact, and alternatives.* Athens, GA: University of Georgia, Center for Educational Improvement.

Fink, A., & Kosecoff, J. (1985). *How to conduct surveys: A step-by-step guide.* Beverly Hills: Sage.

Finn, C. E., Lightfoot, S. L., Greene, M., & Noah, H. J. (1989). National standards for American education: A symposium. *Teachers College Record,* 91, 3–30.

Finn, C. I. (1989, July 12). Made in Japan: Low-tech method for math success. *The Wall Street Journal,* p. A14.

Finn, J. D. (1989). Withdrawing from school. *Review of Educational Research,* 59, 117–142.

Finn, J. D., & Achilles, C. M. (1990). Answers and questions about class size: A statewide experiment. *American Educational Research Journal,* 27, 557–577.

Finn, J. D., Achilles, C. M., Bain, H. P., Folger, J., Johnston, J. M., Lintz, M. N., & Wood, E. R. (1990). Three years in a small class. *Teaching and Teacher Education,* 6, 127–136.

Finn, J. D., & Cox, D. (1992). Participation and withdrawal among fourth-grade pupils. *American Educational Research Journal,* 29, 141–162.

Flay, B. R. (1985). Psychosocial approaches to smoking prevention: A review of findings. *Health Psychology, 4,* 449–488.

Fleming, M., & Chambers, B. (1983). Teacher-made tests: Windows on the classroom. In W. E. Hathaway (Ed.), *New directions for testing and measurement, Vol 19: Testing in the schools.* San Francisco: Jossey-Bass.

Fletcher, J. D., Hawley, D. E., & Piele, P. K. (1990). Costs, effects, and utility of microcomputer assisted instruction in the classroom. *American Educational Research Journal, 27,* 783–806.

Flexner, A. (1910). *Medical education in the United States and Canada: Bulletin no. 4.* New York: Carnegie Foundation for the Advancement of Teaching.

Flinders, D. J., Noddings, N., & Thornton, S. J. (1986). The null curriculum: Its theoretical basis and practical implications. *Curriculum Inquiry, 16,* 323–342.

Flora, J. A., & Thoresen, C. E. (1988). Reducing the risk of AIDS in adolescents. *American Psychologist, 43,* 965–970.

Fogarty, R. (1991). *The mindful school: How to integrate the curricula.* Palatine, IL: Skylight Publishing.

Fort Worth Independent School District. (1989). *Grade One Social Studies.* Fort Worth, TX: Author.

Fortner, M. J. (1989). Educational programs and practices for academically able students in the United States, Japan, and Germany. *Roeper Review,* 11(4), 185–189.

Foshay, A. W. (1990). You and me and I and thou. In J. T. Sears & J. D. Marshal (Eds.), *Teaching and thinking about curriculum: Critical inquiries* (pp. 273–279). New York: Teachers College Press.

Foshay, A. W. (1991). The curriculum matrix: Transcendence and mathematics. *Journal of Curriculum & Supervision, 6,* 277–293.

Fowler, F. J. (1988). *Survey research methods.* Newbury Park, CA: Sage.

Fowler, R. H. (1989). Curricular reform in social studies: An analysis of the cases of Saskatchewan and British Columbia. *Canadian Journal of Education, 14,* 322–337.

Frase, M. J. (1989). *Dropout rates in the United States: 1988.* Washington: Office of Educational Research and Improvement.

Frederick, W. C. (1977).   The use of classroom time in high schools above or below the median reading score. *Urban Education, 11,* 459–464.

Fredericksen, N. (1984).   The real test bias: Influence of testing on teaching and learning. *American Psychologist, 39,* 193–202.

Freeman, D. J., & Porter, A. C. (1989).   Do textbooks dictate the content of mathematics instruction in elementary schools? *American Educational Research Journal, 26,* 403–421.

Freire, P. (1970).   *Pedagogy of the oppressed.* New York: Herder & Herder.

Freire, P. (1976).   *Education: The practice of freedom.* London: Writers and Readers Publishing Cooperative.

Freire, P., & Macedo, D. (1987).   *Literacy: Reading the word and the world.* South Hadley, MA: Bergin & Garvey.

French, W., et al. (1957).   *Behavioral goals of general education in high school.* New York: Russell Sage Foundation.

Frey, J. H. (1983).   *Survey research by telephone.* Beverly Hills: Sage.

Frick, T. W. (1990).   Analysis of patterns in time: A method of recording and quantifying temporal relations in education. *American Educational Research Journal, 27,* 180–204.

Frontier College. (1991).   *Frontier: Literacy.* Toronto: Author.

Frost, K. (1974).   Why 4000 people were fired. *Administrative Management, 35*(2), 54–55.

Frye, N. (1988).   *On education.* Markham, ON: Fitzhenry & Whiteside.

Frymier, J. (1988).   Understanding and preventing teen suicide: An interview with Barry Garfinkel. *Phi Delta Kappan, 70,* 290–293.

Fuchs, D., & Fuchs, L. S. (1986).   Test procedure bias: A meta-analysis of examiner familiarity effects. *Review of Educational Research, 56,* 243–262.

Fullan, M. G. (1982).   *The meaning of educational change.* New York: Teachers College Press.

Fullan, M. G. (1985).   Change processes and strategies at the local level. *Elementary School Journal 85,* 391–421.

Fullan, M. G. (1988). *What's worth fighting for in the principalship.* Toronto: Ontario Public School Teachers Federation.

Fullan, M. G. (1991a). *The new meaning of educational change.* New York: Teachers College Press.

Fullan, M. G. (1991b). Curriculum implementation. In A. Lewy (Ed.), *International encyclopedia of curriculum* (pp. 378–384). New York: Pergamon.

Fullan, M. G., Anderson, S. E., & Newton, E. E. (1986). *Support systems for implementing curriculum in school boards.* Toronto: Ontario Ministry of Education.

Fullan, M. G., Park, P. B., Williams, T. R., Allison, P., Walker, L., & Watson, N. (1987). *The supervisory officer in Ontario: Current practice and recommendations for the future.* Toronto: Ontario Ministry of Education.

Fuller, B. (1987). What school factors raise achievement in the third world? *Review of Educational Research, 57,* 255–292.

Fuller, R. B. (1970). *I seem to be a verb.* New York: Bantam Books.

Furstenberg, F. F., Brooks-Gunn, J., & Chase-Lansdale, L. (1989). Teenaged pregnancy and childbearing. *American Psychologist, 44,* 313–320.

Gagné, R. M. (1977). *The conditions of learning* (3rd ed.). New York: Holt, Rinehart & Winston.

Galluzzo, G. R. (1990, April). *Accessing public opinion on the purpose of schools.* Paper presented at the annual meeting of the American Education Research Association, Boston.

Gamoran, A., & Mare, R. D. (1989). Secondary school tracking and educational inequality: Compensation, reinforcement, or neutrality? *American Journal of Sociology, 94,* 1146–1183.

Garcia, E., Rasmussen, B., Stobbe, C., & Garcia, E. (1990). Portfolios: An assessment tool in support of instruction. *International Journal of Educational Research, 14,* 431–436.

Garner, R., Alexander, P. S., Gillingham, M. G., Kulikowich, J. M., & Brown, R. (1991). Interest and learning from text. *American Educational Research Journal, 2,* 643–659.

Gauldie, S. (1969). *Architecture: The appreciation of the arts.* London: Oxford University Press.

Gauthier, W. J. (1983). *Instructionally effective schools: A model and a process* (Monograph No. 1). Hartford: State of Connecticut, Department of Education.

Geiger, M. A. (1991). Changing multiple-choice answers: Do students accurately perceive their performance? *Journal of Experimental Education, 59,* 250–257.

George, W. C., & Denham, S. A. (1976). Curriculum experimentation for the mathematically talented. In D. P. Keating (Ed.), *Intellectual talent: Research and development* (pp. 103–131). Baltimore: Johns Hopkins University Press.

Ghent, W. (1990). *A ropes course curriculum.* Kingston, ON: Queen's University, Faculty of Education.

Gilligan, C. (1982). *In a different voice: Psychological theory and women's development.* Cambridge, MA: Harvard University Press.

Ginott, H. G. (1972). *Teacher and child: A book for parents and teachers.* New York: Macmillan.

Giroux, H. A. (1981). *Ideology, culture, and the process of schooling.* New York: Falmer.

Giroux, H. A. (1983). *Theory and resistance in education.* South Hadley, MA: Bergin & Garvey.

Giroux, H. A. (1988). *Teachers as intellectuals: Towards a critical pedagogy of learning.* Granby, MA: Bergin & Garvey.

Givens, C. J. (1988). *Wealth without risk.* New York: Simon & Schuster.

Gladstein, G. A. (1960). Study behavior of gifted stereotyped and nonstereotyped college students. *Personnel Guidance Journal, 38,* 470–474.

Glaser, R. (1967). Objectives and evaluation: An individualized system. *Science Education News,* June, 1–3.

Glass, G. V. (1978a). Standards and criteria. *Journal of Educational Measurement, 15,* 237–261.

Glass, G. V. (1978b). Integrating findings: The meta-analysis of research. In L. S. Shulman (Ed.), *Review of research in education, Vol. 5* (pp. 351–379). Itasca, IL: Peacock.

Glass, G. V., & Smith, M. L. (1978). *Meta-analysis of research on the relationship of class size and achievement.* San Francisco: Far West Laboratory for Educational Research and Development.

Glickman, C. D. (1990). Pushing school reform to a new edge: The seven ironies of school empowerment. *Phi Delta Kappan, 72,* 68–75.

Goldberg, M. F. (1991). Portrait of Reuven Feuerstein. *Educational Leadership, 49*(1), 37–40.

Goldenberg, C. N. (1987). Low-income Hispanic parents' contributions to their first-grade children's word-recognition skills. *Anthropology & Education Quarterly, 18,* 149–179.

Goldenberg, C. N. (1989). Parents' effects on academic grouping for reading: Three case studies. *American Educational Research Journal, 26,* 329–352.

Goldenberg, C. N. (1992). The limits of expectations: A case for case knowledge about teacher expectancy effects. *American Educational Research Journal, 29,* 517–544.

Good, T. L. (1983, April). *Classroom research: A decade of progress.* Paper presented at the annual meeting of the American Educational Research Association, Montreal.

Good, T. L., Reys, B. J., Grouws, D. A., & Mulryan, C. M. (1989). Using work-groups in mathematics instruction. *Educational Leadership, 47*(4), 56–62.

Goodlad, J. I. (1974). *Looking behind the classroom door.* Washington, OH: Jones.

Goodlad, J. I. (1983). A study of schooling: Some findings and hypotheses. *Phi Delta Kappan, 64,* 465–470.

Goodlad, J. I. (1984). *A place called school: Prospects for the future.* New York: McGraw Hill.

Goodlad, J. I., & Anderson, R. H. (1987). *The nongraded elementary school* (rev. ed.). New York: Teachers College Press.

Goodlad, J. I., & Oakes, J. (1988). We must offer equal access to knowlege. *Educational Leadership, 45*(5), 16–22.

Goodman, J. (1986). Teaching preservice teachers a critical approach to curriculum design: A descriptive account. *Curriculum Inquiry, 16,* 179–201.

Goodson, I. P. (1989). Curriculum reform and curriculum theory: A case of historical amnesia. *Cambridge Journal of Education,* 19, 131–141.

Gordimer, N. (1976). *Some Monday for sure.* London: Heinemann.

Gordon, T. (1974). *T.E.T., teacher effectiveness training.* New York: P. H. Wyden.

Gorman, W. J. (1989). Effective student evaluation. *Education Canada,* (Fall), 4–15.

Gorrell, J., & Cramond, B. (1988). Students' attitudes toward and use of written justifications for multiple-choice answers. *Educational and Psychological Measurement,* 48, 935–943.

Gottfried, A. E. (1990). Academic intrinsic motivation in young elementary school children. *Journal of Educational Psychology,* 82, 525–538.

Gottman, J. M., & Clasen, R. E. (1972). *Evaluation in education: A practitioner's guide.* Itasca, IL: Peacock.

Granville, W. C. (1962). *Color planning for hospitals and schools.* Chicago: Mobil Finishes Co. (ERIC Documentation Reproduction Service No. ED 000 492).

Green, E. E., Green, A. M., & Walters, D. (1971, October). *Biofeedback for mind-body self-regulation: Healing and creativity.* Paper presented at a Symposium on Varieties of Healing Experience, De Anza College, Cupertino, CA.

Greene, M. (1990). Realizing literature's emancipatory potential. In J. Mezirow & Associates, *Fostering critical reflection in adulthood: A guide to transformative and emancipatory learning* (pp. 251–268). San Francisco: Jossey-Bass.

Greenman, J. (1988). *Caring spaces, learning places: Children's environments that work.* Redmond, WA: Exchange Press.

Gross, N., Giacquinta, J., & Bernstein, M. (1971). *Implementing organizational innovations: A sociological analysis of planned educational change.* New York: Basic Books.

Grossman, P. L. (1989). Learning to teach without teacher education. *Teachers College Record* 91, 191–208.

Grugeon, E., & Woods, P. (1990). *Educating all: Multicultural perspectives in the primary school.* New York: Routledge.

Grumet, M. R. (1988). *Bitter milk: Women and teaching.* Amherst, MA: University of Massachusetts Press.

Guba, E. G., & Lincoln, Y. S. (1983). Epistemological and methodological bases of naturalistic inquiry. In G. F. Madaus, M. S. Scriven, & D. L. Stufflebeam (Eds.), *Evaluation Models: Viewpoints on educational and human services evaluation.* (pp. 311–333). Boston: Kluwer-Nijhoff.

Guilford, J. P. (1967). *The nature of human intelligence.* New York: McGraw Hill.

Gullickson, A. R. (1982). Teacher perspectives of their instructional use of tests. *Journal of Educational Research, 77,* 244–248.

Guskey, T. R. (1990). Cooperative mastery learning strategies. *Elementary School Journal, 91,* 33–42.

Guskey, T. R., & Easton, J. Q. (1983). The characteristics of very effective teachers in urban community colleges. *Community/Junior College Quarterly of Research & Practice, 7,* 265–274.

Guskey, T. R., & Gates, S. L. (1986). Synthesis of research on the effects of mastery learning in elementary and secondary classrooms. *Educational Leadership, 43*(8), 73–80.

Guskey, T. R., & Pigott, T. D. (1988). Research on group-based mastery learning programs: A meta-analysis. *Journal of Educational Research, 81,* 197–216.

Habermas, J. (1974). *Theory and practice.* London: Heinemann.

Hadaway, N. (1986, July 1). Any questions? [Letter to the editor]. *The Times* (London), p. 13.

Haft, H., & Hopmann, S. (1989). State-run curriculum development in the Federal Republic of Germany: Trends in the work and composition of commissions. *Journal of Curriculum Studies, 21,* 185–190.

Haladyna, T. M., Nolan, S. B., & Haas, N. S. (1991). Raising standardized achievement test scores and the origins of test score pollution. *Educational Researcher, 20*(5), 2–7.

Hall, C. W. L. (1982). *Needs assessment: A critical component in professional development planning and programming.* (ERIC Document Reproduction Service No. ED 223 710)

Hall, G. E., & Hord, S. M. (1987). *Change in schools: Facilitating the process.* Albany: State University of New York Press.

Hall, J. C. (1952). The effect of background music on the reading comprehension of 278 eighth and ninth grade students. *Journal of Educational Research, 45,* 451–458.

Hallam, R. N. (1970). Piaget and thinking in history. In M. Ballard (Ed.), *New movements in the study and teaching of history.* London: Temple Smith.

Haller, E. P., Child, D. A., & Walberg, H. J. (1988). Can comprehension be taught? A quantitative synthesis of "metacognitive" studies. *Educational Researcher, 17*(9), 5–8.

Hallinger, P., Bickman, L., & Davis, K. (1989, March). *What makes a difference: School context, principal leadership, and student achievement.* Paper presented at the annual meeting of the American Educational Research Association, San Francisco.

Hallinger, P., & Murphy, J. M. (1986). The social context of effective schools. *American Journal of Education, 94,* 328–355.

Hambleton, R. K. (1978). On the use of cut-off scores with criterion-referenced tests in instructional settings. *Journal of Educational Measurement, 15,* 277–290.

Hamilton, R. J. (1985). A framework for the evaluation of the effectiveness of adjunct questions and objectives. *Review of Educational Research, 55,* 47–85.

Hamner, W. C. (1974). Goal setting, performance, and satisfaction in an interdependent task. *Organizational Behavior & Human Performance, 12,* 217–230.

Hanna, G. (1989). Mathematics achievement of girls and boys in grade eight: Results from twenty countries. *Educational Studies in Mathematics, 20,* 225–232.

Hanuschek, E. A. (1986). The economics of schooling: Production and efficiency in public schools. *Journal of Economic Literature, 14,* 351–388.

Hanuschek, E. A. (1990). The impact of differential expenditures on school performance. *Educational Researcher, 19*(8), 45–51, 62.

Harari, H., & McDavid, J. W. (1973). Name stereotypes and teachers' expectations. *Journal of Educational Psychology, 65,* 222–225.

Harding, S. (1986). *The science question in feminism.* Ithaca, NY: Cornell University Press.

Hargreaves, A. (1989a, June). *Models of learning and the construction of curriculum*. Paper prepared for the annual meeting of the Canadian Society for the Study of Education, Quebec City.

Hargreaves, A. (1989b, June). *Contrived collegiality and the culture of teaching*. Paper presented at the annual meeting of the Canadian Society for the Study of Education, Quebec City.

Hartley, J. (1978). *Designing instructional text*. New York: Nichols.

Hartup, W. W. (1989). Social relationships and their developmental significance. *American Psychologist, 44*, 120–126.

Hatch, T., & Gardner, H. (1990). If Binet had looked beyond the classroom: The assessment of multiple intelligences. *International Journal of Educational Research, 14*, 415–429.

Hathaway, W. E., Hargreaves, J. A., Thompson, G. W., & Novitsky, D. (1992). *A study into the effects of light on children of elementary school age: A case of daylight robbery*. Edmonton, AB: Alberta Education.

Hawking, S. W. (1988). *A brief history of time: From the big bang to black holes*. New York: Bantam Books.

Hawkins, D. (1965). Messing about in science. *Science and Children, 5*(2), 5–9.

Hawkins, L. H. (1981). Studying air ionization and effects on health. *Building Services & Environmental Engineer, 3*(8), 11–13.

Haynes, N. M., Comer, J. P., & Hamilton-Lee, M. (1989). School climate enhancement through parental involvement. *Journal of School Psychology, 27*, 87–90.

Heard, G. (1989). *For the good of the earth and sun: Teaching poetry*. Portsmouth, NH: Heinemann.

Hechinger, G., & Hechinger, F. M. (1990). Child care in Scandinavia: An informal report. *Teachers College Record, 92*, 41–47.

Hedges, L. V. (1988). The meta-analysis of test validity studies: Some new approaches. In H. Wainer & H. Braun (Eds.), *Test validity*. Hillsdale, NJ: Erlbaum.

Heinich, R., Molenda, M., & Russel, J. D. (1989). *Instructional media and the new technologies of instruction* (3rd ed.). New York: Macmillan.

Heisenberg, W. (1974). *Across the frontiers.* New York: Harper & Row.

Hekman, S. J. (1990). Gender and knowledge: *Elements of a postmodern feminism.* Cambridge, UK: Polity Press.

Helmuth, H. (1972). Seats, desks, and students. *Orbit,* 13(1), 25–26.

Hendricks, M. (1990). Improving the recommendations from evaluation studies. *Evaluation & Program Planning,* 13, 109–117.

Hess, R. D., & Azuma, H. (1991). Cultural support for schooling: Contrasts between Japan and the United States. *Educational Researcher,* 20(9), 2–8, 12.

Hill, C. (1990). The growing up series: Films for today's child. *Blinkety Blink* (National Film Board of Canada), 4(2), 10–11.

Hirst, P. H. (1970). *The logic of education.* London: Routledge & Kegan Paul.

Hiscox, M. A. B. (1980). *The mathematical requirements of the pre-'A' level learner.* Nottingham, UK: Shell Centre for Mathematical Education, University of Nottingham.

Hlebowitsh, P. S. (1988). International school comparisons and the linkage to school reform. *High School Journal,* 72(1), 54–59.

Hodges, H. (1987). I know they can learn because I've taught them. *Educational Leadership,* 44(6), 3.

Hodges, H. (1990). *ASCD's International Polling Panel, 1990–1992, Resolutions survey: Executive summary.* Alexandria, VA: Association for Supervision and Curriculum Development.

Hoge, R. D. (1988). Issues in the definition and measurement of the giftedness construct. *Educational Researcher,* (Oct.), 12–16, 22.

Holdaway, D. (1984). *Stability and change in literacy learning.* Exeter, NH: Heinemann Educational Books.

Holmes, C. T. (1989). Grade-level retention effects: A meta-analysis of research studies. In L. A. Shepard & M. L. Smith (Eds.), *Flunking grades: Research and policies on retention.* London: Falmer.

Holmes, C. T., & Matthews, K. M. (1984). The effects of nonpromotion on elementary and junior high school pupils: A meta-analysis. *Review of Educational Research,* 54, 225–236.

Holmes, M., & Croll, P. (1989). Time spent on homework and academic achievement. *Educational Research*, 31(1), 36–45.

Holt, M. (1987). Are schools capable of making critical decisions about their curriculum? In N. Sabar, J. Ruddock, & W. Reid (Eds.), *Partnership and autonomy in school-based curriculum development: Policies and practices in Israel and England* (pp. 102–109). Sheffield, UK: University of Sheffield, Division of Education.

Hope, D. R., Smit, E. K., & Hanson, S. L. (1990). School experiences predicting changes in self-esteem of sixth- and seventh-grade students. *Journal of Educational Psychology*, 82, 117–127.

Hope, J. E. (1987). *Numeracy*. Regina, SA: Saskatchewan Education.

Hord, S. M., & Hall, G. E. (1987). Three images: What principals do in curriculum implementation. *Curriculum Inquiry*, 17(1), 55–89.

Hossler, D., & Stage, F. K. (1992). Family and high school experience influences on the postsecondary educational plans of ninth-grade students. *American Educational Research Journal*, 29, 425–451.

House, E. R. (1974). *The politics of educational innovation*. Berkeley, CA: McCutchan.

House, J. D., & Wohlt, V. (1991). Effect of tutoring on voluntary school withdrawal of academically underprepared minority students. *Journal of School Psychology*, 29, 135–142.

Houston, W. R. (1986). President's message. *Action in teacher education*, 7(4), ii.

Howe, M. J. A. (1989). Separate skills or general intelligence: The autonomy of human abilities. *British Journal of Educational Psychology*, 59, 351–360.

Huberman, A. M., & Miles, M. B. (1984). *Innovation up close: How school improvement works*. New York: Plenum.

Hugo, V. (1982). *Les Misérables*. New York: Penguin.

Hunter, J. E., & Schmidt, F. L. (1990). *Methods of meta-analysis: Correcting error and bias in research findings*. Newbury Park, CA: Sage.

Huntford, R. (1980). *Scott and Amundsen*. New York: Putnam.

Hurt, H. T., Scott, M. D., & McCroskey, J. C. (1978). *Communication in the classroom*. Reading, MA: Addison-Wesley.

Husén, T. (1985). The school in the achievement-oriented society: Crisis and reform. *Phi Delta Kappan, 66,* 398–402.

Hyde, J. S., Fennema, E., & Lamon, S. J. (1990). Gender differences in mathematics performance: A meta-analysis. *Psychological Bulletin, 107,* 139–155.

Idler, E. L., & Kasl, S. (1991). Health perceptions and survival: Do global evaluations of health status really predict mortality? *Journal of Gerontology, 46*(2), 555–565.

Inhelder, B., & Piaget, J. (1958). *The growth of logical thinking from childhood to adolescence.* New York: Basic Books.

International Council for Computers in Education. (1982). *Evaluator's guide for microcomputer-based instructional packages.* Eugene, OR: University of Oregon.

Irving, A. (1985). *Study and information skills across the curriculum.* London: Heinemann.

Jackson, P. W. (1992). Conceptions of curriculum and curriculum specialists. In P. W. Jackson (Ed.), *Handbook of research on curriculum* (pp. 3–40). New York: Macmillan.

Jackson, P. W. (Ed.). (1992). *Handbook of research on curriculum.* New York: Macmillan.

Jacobs, H. H. (Ed.). (1989). *Interdisciplinary curriculum: Design and implementation.* Alexandria, VA: Association for Supervision & Curriculum Development.

Jaggar, A. M. (1989). Love and knowledge: Emotion in feminist epistemology. In A. M. Jaggar & S. R. Bordo (Eds.), *Gender/body/knowledge: Feminist reconstructions of being and knowing* (pp. 145–171). New Brunswick, NJ: Rutgers University Press.

Jahoda, G. (1963). Children's concepts of time and history. *Educational Review, 15,* 87–104.

Jarvis, C. H., Whitehurst, B., Gampert, R. D., & Schulman, R. (1987, April). *The relation between class size and reading achievement in first-grade classrooms.* Paper presented at the annual meeting of the American Educational Research Association, Washington, DC.

Johnson, D. (1990). Parents, students and teachers: A three-way relationship. *International Journal of Educational Research*, 15, 171–181.

Johnson, D. M. (1990). *Word weaving: A creative approach to teaching and writing poetry*. Urbana, IL: National Council of Teachers of English.

Johnson, D. W., & Johnson, R. T. (1989). *Cooperation and competition*. Edina, MN: Interaction.

Johnson, D. W., & Johnson, R. T. (1990). Cooperative learning and achievement. In S. Sharan (Ed.), *Cooperative learning: Theory and research* (pp. 23–37). New York: Praeger.

Johnson, D. W., Johnson, R. T., & Holubec, E. J. (Undated). *Learning together and alone: Cooperative, competitive, and individualistic learning*. Minneapolis, MN: University of Minnesota Cooperative Learning Center.

Johnson, D. W., Johnson, R. T., Holubec, E. J., & Roy, R. (1984). *Circles of learning: Cooperation in the classroom*. Washington, D.C.: Association for Supervision and Curriculum Development.

Johnson, F. L., Brookover, W. B., & Farrell, W. C. (1989, March). *School personnel and students' view of parent involvement and their impact on students' academic sense of futility*. Paper presented at the annual meeting of the American Educational Research Association, San Francisco.

Johnson, R. T., & Johnson, D. W. (1981). Building friendships between handicapped and nonhandicapped students: Effects of cooperative and individualistic instruction. *American Educational Research Journal*, 18, 415–423.

Joint Committee for Educational Evaluation. (1981). *Standards for evaluation of educational programs, projects, and materials*. New York: McGraw Hill.

Jonassen, D. H., Hannum, W. H., & Tessmer, M. (1989). *Handbook of task analysis procedures*. New York: Praeger.

Jones, E. D., & Southern, W. T. (1988). *Chronological age at school entrance and the prevention of learning disabilities: Policy making and the misinterpretation of research*. Paper presented at the annual meeting of the Council for Learning Disabilities, San Diego. (ERIC Document Reproduction Service No. ED 202 580)

Jongsma, K. S. (1990). Training for reading recovery teachers. *Reading Teacher*, 44, 272–275.

Jorgenson, D. W., & Fraumeni, B. M. (1990). Investment in education. *Educational Researcher, 19*(8), 35–44.

Jorgenson, G. W. (1977). Relationship of classroom behavior to the accuracy of the match between material difficulty and student ability. *Journal of Educational Psychology, 69,* 24–32.

Joyce, B. R. (1987, March). *What do we know about expert teaching?* Paper presented at the annual meeting of the Association for Supervision and Curriculum Development, New Orleans.

Joyce, B. R., & Showers, B. (1982). The coaching of teaching. *Educational Leadership, 40*(2), 4–10.

Joyce, B. R., & Showers, B. (1985). Teacher education in India: Observations on American innovations abroad. *Educational Researcher, 14*(8), 3–9.

Juel, C. (1989). *The longitudinal study of reading acquisition (Grades 1–4).* Paper presented at the annual meeting of the National Reading Conferences, Austin, TX.

Kallison, J. M., Jr. (1986). Effects of lesson organization on achievement. *American Educational Research Journal, 23,* 337–347.

Kane, M. T., Kingsbury, C., Colton, D., & Estes, C. (1989). Combining data on criticality and frequency in developing test plans for licensure and certification examinations. *Journal of Educational Measurement, 26,* 17–27.

Kaplan, A. (1964). *The conduct of inquiry.* San Francisco: Chandler.

Kaplan, R. M., & Pascoe, G. C. (1977). Humorous lectures and humorous examples: Some effects upon comprehension and retention. *Journal of Educational Psychology, 69,* 61–66.

Karp, K. S. (1988). *The teaching of elementary school mathematics: The relationship between how mathematics is taught and teacher attitudes.* Unpublished doctoral dissertation, Hofstra University, Department of Administration and Policy Studies.

Karweit, N. L. (1985). Time spent, time needed, and adaptive instruction. In M. C. Wang and H. J. Walberg (Eds.), *Adapting instruction to individual differences* (pp. 281–297). Berkeley, CA: McCutchan.

Kearney, N. C., & Cook, W. W. (1961). Curriculum. In C. W. Harris (Ed.), *Encyclopedia of Educational Research* (pp. 358–365). New York: Macmillan and American Educational Research Association.

Keen, S. (1992). *Fire in the belly: On being a man.* New York: Bantam.

Kehoe, J. (1984). *A handbook for enhancing the multicultural climate of the school.* Vancouver: University of British Columbia.

Keith, T. Z. (1982). Time spent on homework and high school grades: A large-sample path analysis. *Journal of Educational Psychology, 74,* 248–253.

Keller, E. F. (1983). *A feeling for the organism: The life and work of Barbara McClintock.* New York: W. H. Freeman.

Keller, F. S., & Sherman, J. G. (1974). *The Keller Plan handbook.* Menlo Park, CA: W. A. Benjamin.

Kelly, B., Gerstein, R., & Carnine, D. (1990). Student error patterns as a function of curriculum design: Teaching fractions to remedial high school students and high school students with learning disabilities. *Journal of Learning Disabilities, 23,* 23–29.

Kelso Public Schools. (1990). *Physical Education Curriculum Guide.* Kelso, WA: Author.

Kemp, J. E., & Smellie, D. C. (1989). *Planning, producing, and using instructional media* (6th ed.). New York: Harper & Row.

Kemp, M. (1990). *The science of art: Optical themes in western art from Brunelleschi to Seurat.* New Haven: Yale University Press.

Kendall, F. E. (1983). *Diversity in the classroom: A multicultural approach to the education of young children* (Early Childhood Education Series).

Kennan, G. F. (1967). *Memoirs, 1925–1950.* Boston: Little, Brown.

Kennedy, J. F. (1966). *John F. Kennedy on education.* (W. T. O'Hara, Ed.). New York: Teachers College Press.

Kenney, A. M., & Orr, M. T. (1984). Sex education: An overview of current programs, policies, and research. *Phi Delta Kappan, 65,* 491–496.

Kerkhoff, A. C. (1986). Effects of ability grouping in British secondary schools. *American Sociological Review, 51,* 842–858.

Kerr, S. T. (1982). Innovation on command: Instructional development and educational technology in the Soviet Union. *Educational Communication and Technology, 30*(2), 98–116.

Kettle, M. (1990, April 15). Thatcher prefers learning by rote. *Manchester Guardian Weekly*, p. 21.

Keyser, D. J., & Sweetland, R. C. (Eds.). (1984–1986). *Test critiques* (Vols. 1–5). Kansas City, MO: Test Corporation of America.

Killings per 100 men. (1990, July 9). *Newsweek*, p. 7.

King, A. (1992). Comparison of self-questioning, summarizing, and notetaking-review as strategies for learning from lectures. *American Educational Research Journal, 29*, 303–323.

King, A. J. C. (1986). *The adolescent experience*. Toronto: Ontario Secondary School Teachers Federation.

King, A. J. C., & Peart, M. (1990). *The good school*. Kingston, ON: Queen's University.

King, M. L. (1965). The quest for peace and justice. *Les Prix Nobel en 1964* (pp. 246–259). Stockholm: Imprimerie Royale, Norstedt & Sonen.

Kirby, J. R., & Williams, N. H. (1991). *Learning problems: A cognitive approach*. Toronto, Kagan & Woo.

Klein, M. F. (1980). *State and district curriculum guides: One aspect of the formal curriculum* (I/D/E/A Study of Schooling Report No. 15). University of California at Los Angeles. (ERIC Document Reproduction Service No. ED 214 879)

Klein, M. F. (1989). *Curriculum reform in the elementary school: Creating your own agenda*. New York: Teachers College Press.

Kliebard, H. M. (1986). *The struggle for the American curriculum 1893–1958*. New York: Routledge & Kegan Paul.

Kliebard, H. M. (1989). Problems of definition in curriculum. *Journal of Curriculum and Supervision, 5*(1), 1–5.

Kline, M. (1974). *Why Johnny can't add: The failure of the new math*. New York: Vintage.

Knirk, F. G. (1987). *Instructional facilities for the information age*. Syracuse, NY: Syracuse University. (ERIC Documentation No. ED 296 734)

Knowles, M. S., & Associates (1984). *Andragogy in action: Applying modern principles of adult learning.* San Francisco: Jossey-Bass.

Koczor, M. L. (1984). *Effects of varying degrees of instructional alignment in post-treatment tests on mastery learning tasks of fourth grade children.* Unpublished doctoral dissertation, University of San Francisco.

Komisar, B. P. (1961). 'Need' and the needs-curriculum. In B. O. Smith & R. H. Ennis (Eds.), *Language and concepts in education* (pp. 24–42). Chicago: Rand McNally.

Konner, M. (1975). Relations among infants and juveniles in comparative perspective. In M. Lewis & L. A. Rosenblum (Eds.), *Friendship and peer relations* (pp. 99–129). New York: Wiley.

Kozma, R. B. (1991). Learning with media. *Review of Educational Research, 61,* 179–211.

Kubey, R., & Csikszentmihalhi, M. (1990). *Television and the quality of life.* Hillsdale, NJ: Erlbaum.

Kuh, G. D., et al. (1981). *Designing and conducting needs assessments in education.* Washington, DC: Office of Special Education and Rehabilitative Services.

Kulik, C. C., & Kulik, J. A. (1986, April). *Effects of testing for mastery on student learning.* Paper presented at the annual meeting of the American Educational Research Association, San Francisco.

Kulik, C. C., & Kulik, J. A. (1987). Effects of ability grouping on student achievement. *Equity & Excellence, 23*(1–2), 22–30.

Kulik, C. C., Kulik, J. A., & Bangert-Drowns, R. L. (1990). Effectiveness of mastery learning programs: A meta-analysis. *Review of Educational Research, 60,* 265–299.

Kulik, J. A. (1983). Synthesis of research on computer-based instruction. *Educational Leadership, 41*(1), 19–21.

Kulik, J. A. (1991). Findings of grouping are often distorted: Response to Allan. *Educational Leadership, 48*(6), 67.

Kulik, J. A., & Kulik, C. C. (1984a). Effects of accelerated instruction on students. *Review of Educational Research, 54,* 409–425.

Kulik, J. A., & Kulik, C. C. (1984b). Synthesis of research on effects of accelerated instruction. *Educational Leadership, 42*(2), 84–89.

Kulik, J. A., & Kulik, C. C. (1989). Meta-analysis in education. *International Journal of Educational Research, 13,* 221–340.

Kulik, J. A., Kulik, C. C., & Bangert-Drowns, R. L. (1985). Effectiveness of computer-based education in elementary schools. *Computers in Human Behavior, 1,* 59–74.

Kyi, A. S. S. (1991. *Freedom from fear and other writings.* New York: Penguin.

Lacville, R. (1990, September 23). Giving birth. *Manchester Guardian Weekly,* p. 24.

Ladd, G. W. (1990). Having friends, keeping friends, making friends, and being liked by peers in the classroom: Predictors of children's early school adjustment. *Child Development, 61,* 1081–1100.

Langland, W. (1966). *Piers the Plowman* (J. F. Goodridge, Trans.). New York: Penguin.

Lasswell, H. D. (1958). *Politics: Who gets what, when, how.* New York: Meridian.

Latham, G. P., & Yukl, G. A. (1975). Assigned versus participative goal setting with educated and uneducated woods workers. *Journal of Applied Psychology, 60,* 299–302.

Lavrakis, P. J. (1987). *Telephone survey methods: Sampling, selection, and supervision.* Newbury Park, CA: Sage.

Lee, E. (1985). *Letters to Marcia: A teacher's guide to anti-racist education.* Toronto, ON: Cross Cultural Communication Centre.

Lee, L. J., & Sampson, J. F. (1990). A practical approach to program evaluation. *Evaluation & Program Planning, 13,* 157–164.

Lee, V. E., & Marks, H. M. (1990). Sustained effects of the single-sex secondary school experience on attitudes, behaviors, and values in college. *Journal of Educational Psychology, 82,* 578–592.

Leithwood, K. A., & MacDonald, R. A. (1981). Reasons given by teachers for their curriculum choices. *Canadian Journal of Education, 6,* 103–116.

Leming, J., & Hollifield, J. (1985). Cooperative learning: A research success story. *Educational Researcher, 14*(2), 28–29.

Lepper, M. R., Greene, D., & Nisbett, R. (1973). Undermining children's intrinsic interest with extrinsic reward: A test of the "overjustification" hypothesis. *Journal of Personality & Social Psychology, 288,* 129–137.

Lerner, A. J. (1978). *The street where I live.* New York: Norton.

Levin, H. A., Glass, G. V., & Meister, G. R. (1987). Cost-effectiveness of computer-assisted instruction. *Evaluation Review, 11*(1), 50–72.

Lewy, A. (Ed.) (1991a). *International encyclopedia of curriculum.* New York: Pergamon.

Lewy, A. (1991b). Curriculum adaptation. In A. Lewy (Ed.), *International encyclopedia of curriculum* (pp. 440–441). New York: Pergamon.

Lezotte, L. (1983). *Research on effective schools* [Audiotape]. Washington, DC: Association for Supervision and Curriculum Development.

Lightfoot, S. L. (1983). *The good high school.* New York: Basic Books.

Lipka, J. M. (1989). A cautionary tale of curriculum development in Yup'ik Eskimo communities. *Anthropology & Education Quarterly, 20,* 216–231.

Lippmann, W. (1923). The great confusion: A reply to Mr. Terman. *New Republic, 33,* 145–146.

Lips, R., Salawu, H. T., Kamber, P., & Probert, S. D. (1987). Intermittent exposures to enhanced air-ion concentrations for improved comfort and increased productivity? *Applied Energy 28*(2), 83–94.

Literature survey reveals few changes in school reading lists (1989). *ASCD Update* 31(8), 3.

Little, J. W. (1981). *School success and staff development in urban desegregated schools: A summary of recently completed research.* Boulder, CO: Center for Action Research.

Little, J. W. (1982). Norms of collegiality and experimentation. *American Educational Research Journal, 19,* 325–340.

Lobel, R. E., & Levanon, I. (1988). Self-esteem, need for approval, and cheating behavior in children. *Journal of Educational Psychology, 80,* 122–123.

Lockhart, R. H. (1974). *Memoirs of a British agent.* London: MacMillan.

Lohrmann, D. K. (1988). AIDS education at the local level: The pragmatic issues. *Journal of School Health, 58,* 330–334.

Lorber, M. A., & Pierce, W. D. (1990). *Objectives, methods, and evaluation for secondary teaching* (3rd ed.). Englewood Cliffs, NJ: Prentice-Hall.

Louis, K. S., & Miles, M. B. (1990). *Improving the urban high school: What works and why.* New York: Teachers College Press.

Lozoff, B. (1989). Nutrition and behavior. *American Psychologist, 44,* 231–236.

Lueder, D. (1989). Tennessee parents were invited to participate—and they did. *Educational Leadership, 47*(2), 15–17.

Lukasiewicz, J. (1992, January 4). Attack predicted in 1925 [Letter to the editor]. *Globe & Mail,* p. D7.

Lundenberg, M. A., & Fox, P. W. (1991). Do laboratory findings on test expectancy generalize to classroom outcomes? *Review of Educational Research, 61,* 94–106.

Lynch, J. (1983). *The multicultural curriculum.* London: Batsford.

Mabbett, B. (1990). The New Zealand story. *Educational Leadership, 47*(6), 59–61.

Macdonald, J. B. (1977). Value bases and issues for curriculum. In A. Molnar & J. A. Zahorik (Eds.), *Curriculum theory* (pp. 10–23). Washington, DC: Association for Supervision and Curriculum Development.

MacKenzie, D. (1983). Research for school improvement: An appraisal of some recent trends. *Educational Researcher, 12*(4), 5–17.

Madaus, G. F. (1991). The effects of important tests on students: Implications for a national examination system. *Phi Delta Kappan, 70,* 226–231.

Madaus, G. F., & Kellaghan, T. (1992). Curriculum evaluation and assessment. In P. W. Jackson (Ed.), *Handbook of research on curriculum* (pp. 119–154). New York: Macmillan.

Madaus, G. F., Stufflebeam, D. L., & Scriven, M. S. (1983). Program evaluation: A historical overview. In G. F. Madaus, M. Scriven, & D. L. Stufflebeam (Eds.), *Evaluation models: Viewpoints on educational and human services evaluation.* Boston: Kluwer-Nijhoff.

Maheady, L., Harper, G. F., & Sacca, K. (1988). A classwide peer tutoring system in a secondary resource room program for the mildly handicapped. *Journal of Research and Development in Education, 21*(3), 76–83.

Maher, F. A. (1987). Toward a richer theory of feminist pedagogy: A comparison of "liberation" and "gender" models for teaching and learning. *Journal of Education, 169*(3), 91–100.

Malgady, R. G., Rogler, L. H., & Costantino, G. (1990). Hero/heroine modeling for Puerto Rican adolescents: A preventive mental health intervention. *Journal of Consulting & Clinical Psychology, 58,* 469–474.

Mandeville, G. K. (1988). School effectiveness indices revisited: Cross-year stability. *Journal of Educational Measurement, 25,* 349–356.

Mandeville, G. K., & Anderson, L. W. (1987). The stability of school effectiveness indices across grade levels and subject areas. *Journal of Educational Measurement, 24,* 203–216.

Mantzicopoulos, P., & Morrison, D. (1992). Kindergarten retention: Academic and behavioral outcomes through the end of second grade. *American Educational Research Journal, 29,* 182–198.

Margrabe, M. (1981). The library media specialist and total curriculum involvement. In N. W. Thomason (Ed.), *The library media specialist in curriculum development* (pp. 66–75). Metuchen, NJ: Scarecrow Press.

Markham, L. R. (1976). Influences of handwriting quality on teacher evaluation of written work. *American Educational Research Journal, 13,* 277–283.

Marquez, G. G. (1983, February 6). Nobel acceptance speech. *New York Times,* p. IV-17.

Marsh, H. W. (1990). Two-parent, stepparent, and single-parent families: Changes in achievement, attitudes, and behaviors during the last two years in high school. *Journal of Educational Psychology, 82,* 327–340.

Marsh, H. W. (1991). Failure of high-ability high schools to deliver academic benefits commensurate with their students' ability levels. *American Educational Research Journal, 28,* 445–480.

Martin, D., Kocmarek, I., & Gertidge, S. (1987). *A handbook for the caregiver on suicide prevention.* Hamilton, ON: Board of Education for the City of Hamilton.

Martin, J. R. (1985). *Reclaiming a conversation: The ideal of the educated woman*. New Haven: Yale University Press.

Martin, J. R. (1986). Redefining the educated person: Rethinking the significance of gender. *Educational Researcher, 15*(6), 6–10.

Maslow, A. H. (1959). Cognition of being in the peak experiences. *Journal of Genetic Psychology, 94,* 43–66.

Maslow, A. H. (1968). *Toward a psychology of being* (2nd ed.). Princeton, NJ: Van Nostrand.

Mason, C. L., & Kahle, J. B. (1988). Student attitudes toward science and science-related careers: A program designed to promote a stimulating gender-free learning environment. *Journal of Research in Science Teaching, 26,* 25–39.

Mason, J. (1982). *The environment of play*. West Point, NY: Leisure Press.

Mason, J. M., Anderson, R. C., Omua, A., Uchida, N., & Imai, M. (1989). Learning to read in Japan. *Journal of Curriculum Studies, 21,* 389–407.

McCaslin, M., & Good, T. L. (1992). Compliant cognition: The misalliance of management and instructional goals in current school reform. *Educational Researcher, 21*(3), 4–17.

McCord, C., & Freeman, H. P. (1990). Excess mortality in Harlem. *New England Journal of Medicine, 332*(3), 173–177.

McDade, L. A. (1987). Sex, pregnancy, and schooling: Obstacles to a critical teaching of the body. *Journal of Education, 169*(3), 58–79.

McDaniel-Hine, L. C., & Willower, D. J. (1988). Elementary school teachers' work behavior. *Journal of Educational Research, 81,* 274–280.

McDiarmid, G. L., & Pratt, D. (1971). *Teaching prejudice*. Toronto: OISE Press.

McEaney, J. E. (1990). Do advance organizers facilitate learning? A review of subsumption theory. *Journal of Research & Development in Education, 23,* 89–96.

McGaghie, W. C. (1991). Professional competence evaluation. *Educational Researcher, 20*(1), 3–9.

McGuffy, C. W. (1982). Facilities. In H. J. Walberg (Ed.), *Improving educational standards and productivity* (pp. 237–281). Berkeley, CA: McCutchan.

McIntyre, D. (1973). A guide to thermal comfort. *Applied Ergonomics, 4*(2), 66–72.

McKillip, J. (1987). *Need analysis: Tools for the human services and education.* Beverly Hills: Sage.

McKnight, C. C., Crosswhite, F. J., Dossey, J. A., Kifer, E., Swafford, J. O., Travers, K. J., & Cooney, T. J. (1987). *The underachieving curriculum: Assessing U.S. school mathematics from an international perspective.* Champaign, IL: Stipes.

McLaren, P. (1988). No light but rather darkness visible: Language and the politics of criticism. *Curriculum Inquiry, 18,* 313–320.

McLaughlin, G. H. (1969). SMOG grading: A new readability formula. *Journal of Reading, 12,* 639–646.

McLean, L. D. (1990). Time to replace the classroom test with authentic measurement. *Alberta Journal of Educational Research, 36*(1), 78–84.

McNeil, L. M. (1990). Reclaiming a voice: American curriculum scholars and the politics of what is taught in schools. *Phi Delta Kappan, 71,* 517–518.

Means, B., & Knapp, M. S. (1991). Cognitive approaches to teaching advanced skills to educationally disadvantaged students. *Phi Delta Kappan, 72,* 282–289.

Meece, J. L., Blumenfeld, P. C., & Hoyle, R. H. (1988). Students' goal orientations and cognitive engagement in classroom activities. *Journal of Educational Psychology, 80,* 514–523.

Mehran, M., & White, K. R. (1988). Parent tutoring as a supplement to compensatory education for first-grade children. *Remedial & Special Education, 9*(3), 35–41.

Men'shikov, V. (1991). Are we teaching any old thing, any old way? Thoughts on the curriculum of higher educational institutions. *Soviet Education, 33*(3), 37–50.

Messick, S. (1989). Validity. In R. L. Linn (Ed.), *Educational measurement* (3rd ed.) (pp. 13–103). New York: American Council on Education/Macmillan.

Miles, M. B., Saxl, E., & Lieberman, A. (1988).   What skills do educational "change agents" need? An empirical view. *Curriculum Inquiry*, 18, 157–193.

Miller, J. P., & Seller, J. (1985).   *Curriculum perspectives and practice.* New York: Longman.

Millman, J. (1989).   If at first you don't succeed: Setting passing scores when more than one attempt is permitted. *Educational Researcher*, 18(6), 5–9.

Milner, H. (1989).   *Sweden: Social democracy in practice.* New York: Oxford University Press.

Mitchell, J. V., Jr. (Ed.). (1983).   *Tests in print* (Vol. 3). Lincoln, NE: University of Nebraska Press.

Mitchell, J. V., Jr. (1985).   *The ninth mental measurement yearbook.* Lincoln, NE: University of Nebraska Press.

Mitchell, P. D. (1981, April).   *What does the discernible educational technologist need to know?* Paper presented at the Professional Educational Committee of the Association for Educational Communications and Technology, Philadelphia.

Mitgang, H. (1988).   *Dangerous dossiers: Exposing the secret war against America's greatest authors.* New York: Donald J. Fine.

Mitter, W. (1990).   Selection mechanisms for entry to higher education. In H. J. Walberg & G. D. Haertel (Eds.), *International encyclopedia of educational evaluation* (pp. 408–413). New York: Pergamon.

Molnar, A. (1990, February 9).   No business. *The Wall Street Journal*, p. R-32.

Montessori, M. (1964).   *The Montessori method.* New York: Schocken Books.

Moore, G. T. (1987).   The physical environment and cognitive development in childcare centers. In C. S. Weinstein & T. G. David (Eds.), *Spaces for children: The built environment and child development* (pp. 41–72). New York: Plenum.

Moore, S. (1976).   *The Stanislavski system.* Harmondsworth, England: Penguin.

Morris, D., Shaw, B., & Perney, J. (1990).   Helping low readers in Grades 2 and 3: An after-school volunteer tutoring program. *Elementary School Journal*, 91, 133–150.

Mortimore, P., & Sammons, P. (1987). New evidence on effective elementary schools. *Educational Leadership, 45*(1), 4–8.

Mortimore, P., Sammons, P., Stoll, L., Lewis, D., & Ecob, R. (1988). *School matters.* Berkeley, CA: University of California Press.

Mounts, N. S., & Roopnarine, J. L. (1987). Social-cognitive play patterns in same-age and mixed-age preschool classrooms. *American Educational Research Journal, 24,* 463–476.

Muller, R. (1978). *Most of all they taught me happiness.* New York: Doubleday.

Murchie, G. (1978). *The seven mysteries of life: An exploration in science and philosophy.* Boston: Hughton Mifflin.

Murphy, J. M., & Hallinger, P. (1988). Characteristics of instructionally effective school districts. *Journal of Educational Research, 81,* 175–181.

Murphy, J. M., & Hallinger, P. (1989). Equity as access to learning: Curricular and instructional treatment differences. *Journal of Curriculum Studies, 21,* 129–149.

Murphy, J. M., Weil, P., Hallinger, P., & Mitman, A. (1982). School effectiveness: A conceptual framework. *Educational Forum, 49,* 361–374.

Murtaugh, M. (1985). The practice of arithmetic by American grocery shoppers. *Anthropology & Education Quarterly, 16,* 186–192.

NAASP (National Association of Secondary School Principals). (1988). *Learning Style Profile.* Reston, VA: Author.

NAEYC & NAECS/SDE. (1991). Guidelines for appropriate curriculum content and assessment in programs serving children ages 3 through 8: A position statement of the National Association for the Education of Young Children and the National Association of Early Childhood specialists in State Departments of Education. *Young Children, 46*(3), 21–38.

National Assessment of Educational Progress. (1990). *Accelerating academic achievement: A summary of findings from 20 years of NAEP.* Princeton, NJ: Educational Testing Service.

National Association of Secondary School Principals. *Study skills kit.* Newtonville, MA: Author.

National Center for Educational Statistics. (1992). *American education at a glance*. Washington, DC: Author.

National Commission on Testing & Public Policy. (1990). *From gatekeeper to gateway: Transforming testing in America*. Chestnut Hill, MA: Boston College, Author.

National Council of Teachers of Mathematics, Working groups of the Commission on Standards for School Mathematics. (1989). *Curriculum and evaluation standards for school mathematics*. Reston, VA: National Council of Teachers of Mathematics.

National Council of Teachers of Mathematics, Commission on teaching standards for school mathematics. (1989). *Professional standards for teaching mathematics*. Reston, VA: National Council of Teachers of Mathematics.

National Reading Styles Institute. (1988). *Reading Style Inventory.* ® New York: Learning Research Associates.

National Research Council, Mathematical Sciences Education Board. (1989). *Everybody counts: A report to the nation on the future of mathematics education*. Washington, DC: National Academy Press.

National Research Council, Mathematical Sciences Education Board. (1990). *Reshaping school mathematics: A philosophy and framework for curriculum*. Washington, DC: National Academic Press.

Natriello, G., & Dornbusch, S. M. (1984). *Teacher evaluation and student effort*. New York: Longman.

Naylor, F. D. (1990). Student evaluation and examination anxiety. In H. J. Walberg & G. D. Haertel (Eds.), *International encyclopedia of educational evaluation* (pp. 125–127). New York: Pergamon.

New York City Board of Education. (1986). *Three, four, open the door*. New York: Author.

New York City Public Schools. (1991). *Children of the rainbow*. New York: Author.

New Zealand Department of Education. (1987). *The Curriculum Review: Report of the Committee to Review the Curriculum for Schools*. Wellington, NZ: Author.

Newman, R. S., & Goldin, L. (1990). Children's reluctance to seek help with schoolwork. *Journal of Educational Psychology, 82*, 92–100.

Newmann, F. M., & Thompson, J. A. (1987). *Effects of cooperative learning on achievement in secondary schools: A summary of research.* Madison, WI: University of Wisconsin, National Center on Effective Secondary Schools.

Nicholls, J. G., & Thorkildsen, T. A. (1989). Intellectual conventions versus matters of substance: Elementary school students as curriculum theorists. *American Educational Research Journal, 26,* 533–544.

Nicolson, N. (1986). *Napoleon 1812.* London: Weidenfeld & Nicolson.

Niemiec, R. P. (1985). The meta-analysis of computer-assisted instruction at the elementary school level. *Dissertation Abstracts International, 45,* 3330.

Niemiec, R. P., Blackwell, M. C., & Walberg, H. J. (1986). CAI can be doubly effective. *Phi Delta Kappan, 67,* 750–751.

Niemiec, R. P., & Walberg, H. J. (1985). Computers and achievement in the elementary schools. *Journal of Educational Computer Research, 1,* 435–440.

Nist, S. L., Simpson, M. L., Olejnik, S., & Mealey, D. L. (1991). The relation between self-selected study processes and test performance. *American Educational Research Journal, 28,* 849–874.

Noble, P. (1986, May). *Community survey: Needs assessment in Halton.* Lecture at curriculum seminar, Burlington, ON.

Noddings, N. (1984). *Caring: A feminine approach to ethics and moral education.* Berkeley: University of California Press.

Noddings, N. (1988). An ethic of caring and its implications for instructional arrangements. *American Journal of Education, 96,* 215–230.

Noddings, N. (1992). Gender and the curriculum. In P. W. Jackson (Ed.), *Handbook of research on curriculum* (pp. 659–684). New York: Macmillan.

Norcini, J. J., Shea, J. A., & Kanya, D. T. (1988). The effect of various factors on standard setting. *Journal of Educational Measurement, 25,* 57–65.

Nova Scotia Department of Education. (1978). *Law in high school curriculum guide.* Halifax, NS: Author.

Nutrition Canada. (1973). *Nutrition: A national priority.* Ottawa: Information Canada.

Oakes, J. (1985). *Keeping track: How schools structure inequality.* New Haven: Yale University Press.

Oakes, J. (1992). Can tracking research inform practice? Technical, normative, and political considerations. *Educational Researcher, 21*(4), 12–21.

Oakes, J., Gamoran, A., & Page, R. N. (1992). Curriculum differentiation: Opportunities, outcomes, and meanings. In P. W. Jackson (Ed.), *Handbook of research on curriculum* (pp. 570–608). New York: Macmillan.

Oakland, T., & Stern, W. (1989). Variables associated with reading and math achievement among a heterogeneous group of students. *Journal of School Psychology, 27,* 127–214.

OERI (Office of Educational Research and Improvement). (1990a). *Schools and staffing survey.* Washington, DC: Superintendent of Documents.

OERI (Office of Educational Research and Improvement). (1990b). *Beginning to read: Thinking and learning about print: A summary.* Washington, DC: Superintendent of Documents.

OERI (Office of Educational Research and Improvement). (1990c). *Bulletin.* (Fall/Winter). Washington, DC: Superintendent of Documents.

OERI (Office of Educational Research and Improvement). (1990d). *National education longitudinal study of 1988: A profile of the American eighth grader.* Washington, DC: Superintendent of Documents.

OERI (Office of Educational Research and Improvement). (1991). National assessment of educational progress 1990: National and trial state assessments in mathematics. *OERI Bulletin,* (Summer), 1–2.

OERI (Office of Educational Research & Improvement). (1992a, Spring). Smartline. *OERI Bulletin,* pp. 1, 4.

OERI (Office of Educational Research and Improvement). (1992b). *Dropout rates in the United States: 1990.* Washington, DC: Superintendent of Documents.

O'Farrell, L. (1990). Involving theatre professionals in the drama curriculum: Playwrights on playwriting. *Youth Theatre Journal, 4*(4), 3–6.

Offord, D., Boyle, M., & Racine, Y. (1990). *Ontario child health study: Children at risk.* Toronto, ON: Queen's Printer.

Olmstead, P. P. (1991). Parent involvement in elementary education: Findings and suggestions from the follow through program. *Elementary School Journal, 91,* 133–150.

Olson, J. (1979, April). *Images of the practitioner and curriculum change.* Paper presented at Invitational Conference on Images of the Teacher and Issues in Curriculum Change, Queen's University, Kingston, ON.

Olson, J. (1990, November). Virtue and the reformation [Review of *Curriculum and assessment reform*]. *CACS Newsletter,* pp. 5–6.

Olson, J. (1992). Trojan horse or teacher's pet? Computers and the teacher's influence. *International Journal of Educational Research, 17,* 77–85.

O'Neil, J. (1990, October). Findings of styles research murky at best. *Educational Leadership, 47,* 7.

O'Neil, J. (1991, June). Transforming the curriculum for students 'at risk'. *ASCD Curriculum Update,* pp. 1–2.

Ontario Ministry of Education. (1977). *English: Intermediate division curriculum guideline.* Toronto: Author.

Ontario Ministry of Education. (1986). *Curriculum Guideline, History and Contemporary Studies.* Toronto: Author.

Opfell, O. S. (1986). *The lady laureates.* Metuchen, NJ: Scarecrow Press.

Orpwood, G. W. F., & Souque, J-P. (1984). *Science education in Canadian schools.* Ottawa: Science Council of Canada.

Orr, J. B., & Flein, M. F. (1991). Instruction in critical thinking as a form of character education. *Journal of Curriculum & Supervision, 6,* 130–144.

Ostrow, D. G. (1989). AIDS prevention through effective education. *Daedalus, 118,* 229–254.

Owston, R. D. (1987). *Software evaluation: A criterion-based approach.* Scarborough, ON: Prentice-Hall.

Pallas, A. M., Natriello, G., & McDill, E. (1989). The changing nature of the disadvantaged population: Current dimensions and future trends. *Educational Researcher, 18*(5), 16–22.

Papanek, V. (1971). *Design for the real world.* New York: Pantheon Books.

Papert, S. (1980). *Mindstorms: Children, computers, and powerful ideas.* New York: Basic Books.

Parent Educator and Family Report, (1987), Jan-Feb.

Paris, S. G., Lawton, T. A., Turner, J. C., & Roth, J. L. (1991). A developmental perspective on standardized achievement testing. *Educational Researcher, 20*(5), 12–20.

Parker, G. (1986). *Year round schools.* Paris: Organization for Economic Cooperation and Development.

Parker, P. (1990, February 18) [Review of *The house of Nomura*]. *Sunday Times,* p. H5.

Parlett, M. R. (1991). Illuminative evaluation. In A. Lewy (Ed.), *International encyclopedia of curriculum* (pp. 420–424). New York: Pergamon.

Pea, R. D., & Sheingold, K. (Eds.). (1987). *Mirrors of minds: Patterns of excellence in educational computing.* Norwood, NJ: Ablex.

Pedersen, E., Faucher, T. A., & Eaton, W. W. (1978). A new perspective on the effects of first-grade teachers on children's subsequent adult status. *Harvard Educational Review, 48,* 1–31.

Peel, E. A. (1967). Some problems in the psychology of history teaching. In W. H. Burston & D. Thompson (Eds.), *Studies in the nature and teaching of history.* London: Routledge & Kegan Paul.

Pellicer, L. O., Anderson, L. W., Keefe, J. W., Kelley, E. A., & McCleary, L. E. (1990). *High school leaders and their schools. Volume II: Profiles of effectiveness.* Reston, VA: National Association of Secondary School Principals.

Peréz, A. P. (1985). *Christ in a poncho: Testimonials of the nonviolent struggles in Latin America.* Maryknoll, NY: Orbis.

Perrins, J. (1991). *Photography: Color printing* [unpublished curriculum]. Kingston, ON: Queen's University, Faculty of Education.

Peters, T. J. (1988). *Thriving on chaos.* New York: Knopf.

Peters, T. J., & Waterman, R. H., Jr. (1982). *In search of excellence: Lessons from America's best-run companies.* New York: Harper & Row.

Peterson, S. E., DeGracie, J. S., & Ayabe, C. R. (1987). A longitudinal study of the effects of retention/promotion on academic achievement. *American Educational Research Journal, 24,* 107–118.

Peterson, P., Wilkinson, L., & Hallinan, M. (1984). *The social context of instruction*. New York: Academic Press.

Phenix, P. H. (1986). *Realms of meaning: A philosophy of the curriculum for general education* (rev. ed.). New York: McGraw Hill.

Philadelphia School District. (1989). *Grade 3 science curriculum*. Philadelphia: Author.

Philip, T. (1989). The breaking of minds and bodies: Torture in the modern world. *Amnesty International Bulletin, 17*(1), 2–5.

Phoenix Union High School District. (1990). *World History/ Geography Curriculum Guide*. Phoenix, AZ: Author.

Piaget, J. (1976). *The psychology of intelligence*. Lanham, MD: Rowman & Littlefield.

Pinar, W. F. (1989). A reconceptualization of teacher education. *Journal of Teacher Education, 40*(1), 9–12.

Pinnell, G. S., Fried, M. D., & Estice, R. M. (1990). Reading recovery: Learning how to make a difference. *Reading Teacher, 43*, 282–295.

Pirie, S. (1981). *Mathematics in medicine: A report for the Cockcroft Committee*. Nottingham, UK: Shell Centre for Mathematical Education, University of Nottingham.

Pittman, R. B., & Haughwout, P. (1987). Influence of high school size on dropout rate. *Educational Evaluation & Policy Analysis, 9*, 337–343.

Pizzo, J. (1982). Breaking the sound barrier: Classroom noise and learning style. *Orbit, 13*(4), 21–22.

Plato. (1941). *The republic of Plato* (F. M. Cornford, Trans.). Oxford: Clarendon Press.

Plowden, E. (1966). *Children and their primary schools*. London: Her Majesty's Stationery Office.

Popham, W. J. (1986, April). *Instructional objectives: Two decades of decadence*. Paper presented at the annual meeting of the American Educational Research Association, San Francisco.

Popham, W. J. (1990). A twenty-year perspective on educational objectives. In H. J. Walberg & G. D. Haertel (Eds.), *International encyclopedia of educational evaluation* (pp. 189–194). New York: Pergamon.

Porter, A. C. (1989). A curriculum out of balance: The case of elementary school mathematics. *Educational Researcher, 18*(5), 9–15.

Posner, G. J. (1992, June). *Institutional roles of school subjects: How schools limit access to knowledge.* Paper presented at the annual meeting of the Canadian Association of Curriculum Studies, Kingston, Canada.

Posovac, E. J., & Carey, R. G. (1989). *Program evaluation: Methods and case studies* (3rd ed.). Englewood Cliffs, NJ: Prentice-Hall.

Pratt, D. (1971). *How to find and measure bias in textbooks.* Englewood Cliffs, NJ: Educational Technology Press.

Pratt, D. (1980). *Curriculum: Design and development.* New York: Harcourt Brace.

Pratt, D. (1982). A cybernetic model for curriculum development. *Instructional Science, 11,* 1–12.

Pratt, D. (1983a). Bias in textbooks: Progress and problems. In R. Samuda, J. Berry, & M. Laferriere (Eds.), *Educational implications of cultural diversity* (pp. 154–166). Toronto: Allyn & Bacon.

Pratt, D. (1983b). History in schools: reflections on curriculum priorities. *Historical Papers,* pp. 81–95.

Pratt, D. (1986a). Curriculum design as humanistic technology. *Journal of Curriculum Studies, 18,* 149–162.

Pratt, D. (1986b). On the merits of multiage classrooms. *Research in Rural Education, 3,* 111–115.

Pratt, D. (1987). Predicting career success in teaching. *Action in Teacher Education, 8*(4), 25–34.

Pratt, D. (1989). Characteristics of Canadian curricula. *Canadian Journal of Education, 14,* 295–310.

Pratt, D. (1990). System theory and curriculum. In T. Husén & N. Postlethwaite (Eds.), *International encyclopedia of education* (Supplementary Vol. 2) (pp. 637–640). Oxford: Pergamon Press.

Pratt, D. (1991a). Curriculum rationale. In A. Lewy (Ed.), *International encyclopedia of curriculum* (pp. 70–71). New York: Pergamon.

Pratt, D. (1991b). Cybernetics and curriculum. In A. Lewy (Ed.), *International encyclopedia of curriculum* (pp. 42–46). New York: Pergamon.

Pratt, D., & Common, R. (1986). The miseducation of Canadian educational administrators. *Canadian Administrator*, 25(5), 1–8.

Pratt, D., & Short, E. C. (In press). Curriculum management. In T. Husén & T. N. Postlethwaite (Eds.), *International encyclopedia of education* (2nd ed.). New York: Pergamon.

Pratt, M. (1987, February). *Life extension, fact or fantasy.* Paper presented at the annual meeting of the Pan-American Doctors Club, Huasca, Mexico.

Pratton, J., & Hales, L. W. (1986). The effects of active participation on student learning. *Journal of Educational Research*, 79, 210–215.

Prawat, R. S. (1991). The value of ideas: The immersion approach to the development of thinking. *Educational Researcher*, 20(2), 3–10.

Pring, R. (1973). Curriculum integration. In R. S. Peters (Ed.), *The philosophy of education* (pp. 123–149). London: Oxford University Press.

Psacharopoulos, G., & Loxley, W. (1982). *Diversification of secondary school curriculum study, guidebook.* Washington, DC: World Bank, Education Department.

Purpel, D. E. (1989). *The moral and spiritual crisis in education.* Granby, MA: Bergin & Garvey.

Puryear, J. B., & Lewis, L. A. (1981). Description of the interview process in selecting students for admission to U.S. medical school. *Journal of Medical Education*, 56, 881–885.

Putnam-Scholes, J. A. S. (1983, July). An epidemic of publicity. *Atlantic*, pp. 1–19.

Putting a dollar sign on life. (1967, January 21). *Business Week*, p. 87.

Pyle, W. H. (1913). Economical learning. *Journal of Educational Psychology*, 3, 148–158.

Quellmalz, E. S. (1990). Essay examinations. In H. J. Walberg & G. D. Haertel (Eds.), *International encyclopedia of educational evaluation* (pp. 510–515). New York: Pergamon.

Rabinovitz, M., & Schubert, W. H. (1991). Prerequisite knowledge. In A. Lewy (Ed.), *International encyclopedia of curriculum* (pp. 468–471). New York: Pergamon.

Rafferty, M. (1985). *Examinations in literature: Perceptions from nontechnical writers of England and Ireland from 1850 to 1984.* Unpublished doctoral dissertation, Boston College, Boston, MA.

Ramey, C. T., & Campbell, F. A. (1979). Compensatory education for disadvantaged children. *School Review,* 87, 171–189.

Ramey, C. T., & Smith, B. (1976). Assessing the intellectual consequences of early intervention with high-risk infants. *American Journal of Mental Deficiency,* 81, 318–324.

Ramsay, P., Sneddon, D., Grenfell, J., & Ford, I. (1983). Successful and unsuccessful schools: A study in southern Auckland. *Australian and New Zealand Journal of Sociology,* 19, 272–304.

Rathje, W., & Murphy, C. (1992). *Rubbish! The archaeology of garbage.* New York: HarperCollins.

Raudenbush, S. W. (1991a). Summarizing evidence: Crusaders for simplicity [Review of *Methods of meta-analysis: Correcting error and bias in research findings*]. *Educational Researcher,* 20(7), 33–37.

Raudenbush, S. W. (1991b). Review of methods of meta-analysis: Correcting error and bias in research findings. *Journal of the American Statistical Association,* 86(413), 242–244.

Redfield, D. L., & Rousseau, E. W. (1981). A meta-analysis of experimental research on teacher questioning behavior. *Review of Educational Research,* 3, 136–143.

Reid, D., & Dunkley, G. C. (1989). Weight control in the workplace: A needs assessment for men. *Canadian Journal of Public Health,* 80(1), 24–27.

Renault-Roulier, G. (1948). *Memoirs of a secret agent of Free France.* New York: McGraw Hill.

Reschly, D. J. (1988). Larry P.! Larry P.! Why the California sky fell on IQ testing. *Journal of School Psychology,* 26, 190–205.

Resnick, L. B. (1989). Developing mathematical knowledge. *American Psychologist,* 44, 162–169.

Rest, J., Power, C., & Brabeck, M. (1988). Obituary: Laurence Kohlberg (1927–1988). *American Psychologist,* 43, 399–400.

Rhys, W. T. (1979). Geography and the adolescent. In A. Floyd (Ed.), *Cognitive development in the school years* (pp. 249–261). New York: Wiley.

Rich, H. L., & McNelis, M. J. (1987). A study of academic time-on-task in the elementary school. *Educational Research Quarterly*, 12(1), 37–46.

Richardson, T. M., & Benbow, C. P. (1990). Long-term effects of acceleration on the social-emotional adjustment of mathematically precocious youths. *Journal of Educational Psychology*, 82, 464–470.

Robinson, G. E. (1990). Synthesis of research on the effects of class size. *Educational Leadership*, 47(7), 80–90.

Robinson, J. (1992). *Reflective evaluation: Working towards an appropriate Native teacher evaluation model in Labrador*. Unpublished M.Ed. thesis, Queen's University, Kingston, ON.

Rodriguez, J. J., Rodriguez, J. F., Rodriguez, D., Rodriguez, J. R., McGowan, E. B., & Esteban, M. (1988). Expression of the firefly luciferase gene in vaccinia virus: A highly sensitive gene marker to follow virus dissemination in tissues of infected animals. *Proceedings of the National Academy of Sciences USA*, 85(5), 1667–1671.

Rogers, C. (1969). *Freedom to learn: A view of what education might become*. Columbus, OH: Merrill.

Rogers, V. (1989). Assessing the curriculum experienced by children. *Phi Delta Kappan*, 70, 714–717.

Rossi, P. H., Freeman, H. E., & Wright, S. R. (1989). *Evaluation: A systematic approach* (4th ed.). Beverly Hills: Sage.

Roszak, T. (1986). *The cult of information: The folklore of computers and the true art of thinking*. New York: Pantheon.

Rothman, R. (1989). What to teach: Reform turns finally to the essential question. *Education Week*, 1(8), 10–11.

Rowan, H. (1978, January 8). Making more corn to grow. *Manchester Guardian Weekly*, p. 16.

Rudman, D. R., Feller, A. G., Nagraj, H. S., Gergans, G. A., Lalitha, P. Y., Goldberg, A. F., Schlenker, R. A., Cohn, L., Rudman, W. W., & Mattson, D. E. (1990). Effects of human growth hormone in men over 60 years old. *New England Journal of Medicine*, 323(1), 1–6.

Rugg, D. L., O'Reilly, K. R., & Galavotti, C. (1990). AIDS prevention evaluation: Conceptual and methodological issues. *Evaluation & Program Planning*, 13, 79–89.

Rugg, H., Bagley, W. C., Bobbitt, F., Bonser, F. G., Charters, W. W., Counts, G. S., Courtis, S. A., Horn, E., Judd, C. H., Kelly, F. J., Kilpatrick, W. H., & Works, G. A. (1926). The foundations and technique of curriculum-construction. In H. Rugg (Ed.), *Twenty-sixth yearbook of the National Society for the Study of Education. Part 2: The foundations of curriculum-making.* Bloomington, IL: Public School Publishing Co.

Rumberger, R. W. (1987). High school dropouts: A review of issues and evidence. *Review of Educational Research,* 57, 101–121.

Rumberger, R. W., Ghatak, R., Pouos, G., Ritter, P. L., & Dornbusch, S. M. (1990). Family influences on dropout behavior in one California high school. *Sociology of Education,* 63, 283–299.

Rury, J. L. (1988). The variable school year: Measuring differences in the length of American school terms in 1900. *Journal of Research and Development in Education,* 21(3), 29–36.

Russell, I. J., Caris, T. N., Harris, G. D., & Hendricson, W. D. (1983). Effects of three types of lecture notes on medical student achievement. *Journal of Medical Education,* 58, 627–636.

Rutter, M., Maughan, B., Mortimore, P., Ouston, J., & Smith, A. (1979). *Fifteen thousand hours: Secondary schools and their effects on children.* London: Open Books.

Ryan, R. M., Connell, J. P., & Deci, E. L. (1985). A motivational analysis of self-determination and self-regulation in education. In C. Ames & R. Ames (Eds.), *Research on motivation in education. Vol 2. The classroom milieu* (pp. 13–51). New York: Academia Press.

Ryle, G. (1949). *The concept of mind.* New York: Barnes & Noble.

Sabar, N. (1990, April). *The fall of the Berlin Wall: Implications for education.* Paper presented at the annual meeting of the American Educational Research Association, Boston.

Sabatier, R. C. (1989). AIDS Education: Evolving approaches. *Canadian Journal of Public Health,* 80 (May/June), Supplement 1, S9–S11.

Safty, A. (1988). French immersion and the making of a bilingual society: A critical review and discussion. *Canadian Journal of Education,* 13, 243–262.

Sajer, G. (1971). *The forgotten soldier.* New York: Harper & Row.

Salam, A. (1989). *Ideals and realities.* Teaneck, NJ: World Scientific Publishing.

Salend, S. J., & Sonnenschein, P. (1989).   Validating the effectiveness of a cooperative learning strategy through direct observation. *Journal of School Psychology, 27*, 47–58.

Sandburg, C. (1960).   *Harvest poems 1910–1960.* New York: Harcourt Brace.

Santrock, J. W. (1976).   Affect and facilitative self-control: Influence of ecological setting, cognition, and social agent. *Journal of Educational Psychology, 68*, 529–535.

Sarason, S. B. (1971).   *The culture of the school and the problem of change.* Boston: Allyn & Bacon.

Sarnacki, R. E. (1990).   Test-wiseness. In H. J. Walberg & G. D. Haertel (Eds.), *International encyclopedia of educational evaluation* (pp. 124–125). New York: Pergamon.

Satir, V. (1967).   *Conjoint family therapy: A guide to theory and technique.* Palo Alto, CA: Science & Behavior Books.

Scannel, D. P., & Marshall, J. C. (1966).   The effect of selected composition errors on grades assigned to essay examinations. *American Educational Research Journal, 3*, 125–130.

Scarborough Board of Education. (1990).   Reading recovery. *Research Speaks to Teachers, 25*(2), 1–2.

Schafer, R. M. (1975).   *The rhinoceros in the classroom.* Np: Universal Edition.

Scheerens, J., Vermeulen, C. J. A. J., & Pelgrum, W. J. (1989).   Generalizability of instructional and school effectiveness indicators across nations. *International Journal of Educational Research, 12*, 789–799.

Schlechty, P. C. (1990).   *Schools for the twenty-first century: Leadership imperatives for educational reform.* San Francisco: Jossey-Bass.

Schmidt, M., Weinstein, T., Niemiec, R., & Walberg, H. J. (1985, April). *Computer-assisted instruction with exceptional children: A meta-analysis of research findings.* Paper presented at the annual meeting of the American Educational Research Association, Chicago.

Schmuck, P., & Schmuck, R. (1990).   Democratic participation in small-town schools. *Educational Researcher, 19*(8), 14–19.

Schneider, B. H., Clegg, M. R., Byrne, B. M., Ledingham, J. E., & Crombie, G. (1989).   Social relations of gifted children as a function of age and school program. *Journal of Educational Psychology, 81*, 48–56.

Schoel, J., & Stratton, M. (1990). *Gold nuggets: Readings for experiential education*. Hamilton, MA: Project Adventure.

Schoggen, P., & Schoggen, M. (1988). Student voluntary participation and high school size. *Journal of Educational Research, 81*, 289–293.

Schön, D. A. (1983). *The reflective practitioner: How professionals think in action*. New York: Basic Books.

Schubert, W. H. (1980). *Curriculum books: The first eighty years*. Washington, DC: University Press of America.

Schubert, W. H. (1986). *Curriculum: Perspective, paradigm and possibility*. New York: Macmillan.

Schubert, W. H. (1988). *On mentorship: Examples from J. Harlan Shores and others through lenses provided by James B. Macdonald*. Paper presented at the Annual Bergamo Conference, Dayton, OH.

Schultz, T. (1989). Testing and retention of young children: Moving from controversy to reform. *Phi Delta Kappan, 71*, 125–129.

Schunk, D. H. (1984). Self-efficacy perspective on achievement behavior. *Educational Psychologist, 19*(1), 48–58.

Schunk, D. H. (1987). Peer models and children's behavioral change. Review of *Educational Research, 57*(2), 149–174.

Schwab, J. J. (1969). The practical: Arts of eclectic. *School Review, 79*, 493–542.

Schwab, J. J. (1970). *The practical: A language for curriculum*. Washington, DC: National Education Association.

Schwab, J. J. (1983). The practical 4: Something for curriculum professors to do. *Curriculum Inquiry, 13*, 239–265.

Scriven, B. (1975, November 7). Homo sedens: Theory and reality. *Times Educational Supplement*, p. 38.

Scriven, M. S. (1975). Education for survival. In K. Ryan & J. M. Cooper. *Kaleidoscope: Readings in education* (2nd ed.) (pp. 128–150). Boston: Houghton Mifflin.

Scriven, M. S. (1983). Evaluation ideologies. In G. F. Madaus, M. S. Scriven, & D. L. Stufflebeam (Eds.), *Evaluation models: Viewpoints on educational and human services evaluation* (pp. 229–260). Boston: Kluwer-Nijhoff.

Scriven, M. S., & Roth, J. L. (1978). *Needs assessment: Concept and application.* Englewood Cliffs, NJ: Educational Technology Publications.

Sealing, P. A. (1989). *Profile of child health in the United States.* Alexandria, VA: National Association of Children's Hospitals and Related Institutions.

Seeman, H. (1988). *Preventing classroom discipline problems.* Lancaster, PA: Technomic Publishing Co.

Seidman, S. A. (1980). A survey of schoolteachers' utilization of media. *Educational Technology,* (Oct.), 19–23.

Selmes, I. (1987). *Improving study skills.* London: Hodder & Stoughton.

Seymour, W. D. (1937). An experiment showing the superiority of a light-coloured "blackboard." *British Journal of Educational Psychology,* 7, 259–268.

Shakeshaft, C. (1987). *Women in educational administration.* Beverly Hills: Sage.

Sharan, S., Kussell, P., Herz-Lazarowitz, R., Bejarano, Y., Shulamit, R., & Sharan, Y. (1984). *Cooperative learning in the classroom: Research in desegregated schools.* Hillsdale, NJ: Erlbaum.

Sharpe, D. T. (1974). *The psychology of color and design.* Chicago: Nelson-Hall.

Shavelson, R. J., Baxter, G. P., & Pine, J. (1992). Performance assessments: Political rhetoric and measurement reality. *Educational Researcher,* 21(4), 22–27.

Shemilt, D. (1980). *History 13–16 evaluation study.* Edinburgh: Holmes McDougal.

Shemilt, D. (1987). Adolescent ideas about evidence and methodology in history. In C. Portal (Ed.), *The history curriculum for teachers* (pp. 39–61). London: Falmer.

Shepard, L. A. (1991). Interview on assessment issues with Lorrie Shepard. *Educational Researcher,* 20(2), 21–23, 27.

Shepard, L. A., & Smith, M. L. (1986). Synthesis of research on school readiness and kindergarten retention. *Educational Leadership*, 44(3), 78–86.

Shepard, L. A., & Smith, M. L. (1989). *Flunking grades: Research and policies on retention*. New York: Falmer.

Shepard, L. A., & Smith, M. L. (1990). Synthesis of research on grade retention. *Educational Leadership*, 47(8), 84–88.

Shor, I., & Freire, P. (1987). What is the "dialogical method" of teaching? *Journal of Education*, 169(3), 11–31.

Short, E. C. (1990). Challenging the trivialization of curriculum through research. In J. T. Sears & J. D. Marshall (Eds.), *Teaching and thinking about curriculum: Critical inquiries* (pp. 199–210). New York: Teachers College Press.

Short, E. C. (1991). International curriculum associations and journals. In A. Lewy (Ed.), *International encyclopedia of curriculum* (pp. 981–983). New York: Pergamon.

Short, P. M., & Spencer, W. A. (1990). Principal instructional leadership. *Journal of Research & Development in Education*, 33, 117–122.

Shrewsbury, C. M. (1987). What is feminist pedagogy? *Women's Studies Quarterly*, 15(3 & 4), 6–14.

Shymansky, J., & Kyle, W. C. (1988). A summary of research in science education: 1986. *Science Education*, 72, 245–373.

Sign of the times award. (1981). *Education Digest*, 66(9), 26.

Silberman, C. E. (1970). *Crisis in the classroom: The remaking of American education*. New York: Random House.

Silone, I. (1937). *Bread and wine*. New York: Harper.

Simmons, C., & Wade, W. (1988). Contrasting attitudes to education in England and Japan. *Educational Research*, 30(2), 146–152.

Simner, M. L., & Barnes, M. J. (1991). Relationship between first-grade marks and the high school dropout problem. *Journal of School Psychology*, 29, 331–335.

Simon, H. (1969). *The sciences of the artificial*. Cambridge, MA: MIT Press.

Sizer, R. (1986). *Horace's compromise: The dilemma of the American high school.* Boston: Houghton Mifflin.

Skeptical third-grader stumps Bush. (1991, March 12). *San Francisco Chronicle,* p. A9.

Skilbeck, M. (1985). *School-based curriculum development.* London: Harper & Row.

Slater, B. (1968). Effects of noise on pupil performance. *Journal of Educational Psychology, 59,* 239–243.

Slavin, R. E. (1986). Best-evidence synthesis: An alternative to meta-analytic and traditional reviews. *Educational Researcher, 15*(9), 5–11.

Slavin, R. E. (1987a). Mastery learning reconsidered. *Review of Educational Research, 57,* 175–213.

Slavin, R. E. (1987b). Making Chapter 1 make a difference. *Phi Delta Kappan, 69,* 110–119.

Slavin, R. E. (1987c). Ability grouping and student achievement in secondary schools: A best-evidence synthesis. *Review of Educational Research, 57,* 293–336.

Slavin, R. E. (1988a). Cooperative learning and student achievement. *Educational Leadership, 46*(2), 31–33.

Slavin, R. E. (1988b). Synthesis of research on grouping in elementary and secondary schools. *Educational Leadership, 46*(1), 67–77.

Slavin, R. E. (1989a). Research on cooperative learning: Consensus and controversy. *Educational Leadership, 47*(4), 52–54.

Slavin, R. E. (1989b). Achievement effects of substantial reductions in class size. In R. E. Slavin (Ed.), *School and classroom organization* (pp. 247–257). Hillsdale, NJ: Erlbaum.

Slavin, R. E. (1990). Achievement effects of ability grouping in secondary schools: A best-evidence synthesis. *Review of Educational Research, 60,* 471–499.

Slavin, R. E. (1991). Are cooperative learning and "untracking" harmful to the gifted? Response to Allan. *Educational Leadership, 48*(6), 68–71.

Slavin, R. E., & Karweit, N. L. (1984). Mastery learning and student teams: A factorial experiment in urban general mathematics classes. *American Educational Research Journal, 21*, 725–736.

Slavin, R. E., Karweit, N. L., & Madden, N. A. (Eds.). (1989). *Effective programs for students at risk.* Boston: Allyn & Bacon.

Smith, C. B. (1961). *A study of the optimum size of secondary school.* Unpublished doctoral dissertation, Ohio State University.

Smith, M. L. (1991a). Put to the test: The effects of external testing on teachers. *Educational Researcher, 20*(5), 8–11.

Smith, M. L. (1991b). Meanings of test preparation. *American Educational Research Journal, 28*, 521–542.

Smith, P. (1974). *The design of learning spaces.* London: Council for Educational Technology.

Smith, W. F., & Andrews, R. L. (1989). *Instructional leadership: How principals make a difference.* Alexandria, VA: Association for Supervision and Curriculum Development.

Sneider, C., & Pulos, S. (1983). Children's cosmographies: Understanding the earth's shape and gravity. *Science Education, 67*, 205–221.

Snow, R. E. (1989). Aptitude, instruction, and individual development. *International Journal of Educational Research, 12*, 869–881.

Soldier, L. L. (1989). Cooperative learning and the Native American student. *Phi Delta Kappan, 71*, 161–163.

Sommer, R. (1969). *Personal space: The behavioral basis of design.* Englewood Cliffs, NJ: Prentice-Hall.

Sommer, R. (1974). *Tight spaces: Hard architecture and how to humanize it.* Englewood Cliffs, NJ: Prentice-Hall.

Sosniak, L. A. (1991). Feasibility studies. In A. Lewy (Ed.), *International encyclopedia of curriculum* (pp. 438–440). New York: Pergamon.

South Carolina: A setting for values clash. (1991). ASCD Update, 33(7), 5.

Southern, W. T., Jones, E. D., & Fiscus, E. D. (1989). Practitioner objections to the academic acceleration of gifted children. *Gifted Child Quarterly, 33*, 29–35.

Sparks, G. M. (1983). Synthesis of research on staff development for effective teaching. *Educational Leadership, 41*(3), 65–72.

Spencer, H. (1911). *Essays on education.* London: Dent.

Spivak, M. (1974). Political collapse of a playground. In G. Coates (Ed.), *Alternative learning environments.* Stroudsberg, PA: Dowden, Hutchinson, & Ross.

Stake, R. E. (1971). Testing hazards in performance contracting. *Phi Delta Kappan, 52,* 583–589.

Stake, R. E. (1983, November). *Excellence, evaluation, and curricula.* Address at Excellence and the Curriculum: A Symposium in Honor of Mauritz Johnson, Albany, NY.

Stallings, J. (1980). Allocated academic learning time revisited, or beyond time on task. *Educational Researcher, 9*(11), 11–16.

Stallings, J. (1987). Are we evaluating what we value? *Action in Teacher Education, 9*(3), 1–3.

Stanley, J. C. (1976). Identifying and nurturing the mathematically gifted. *Phi Delta Kappan, 58,* 234–237.

Statistics Canada. (1987). *Characteristics of teachers in public elementary and secondary schools, 1985–1986.* Ottawa: Ministry of Supply & Services Canada.

Steers, R. M., & Porter, L. W. (1974). The role of task-goal attributes in employee performance. *Psychological Bulletin, 881,* 434–452.

Stein, M. K., Baxter, J. A., & Leinhardt, G. (1990). Subject-matter knowledge and elementary instruction: A case from functions and graphing. *American Educational Research Journal, 27,* 639–663.

Stevens, S. S. (1951). Mathematics, measurement and psychophysics. In S. S. Stevens (Ed.), *Handbook of experimental psychology* (pp. 1–49). New York: Wiley.

Stevenson, H. W., Lee, S.-Y., Chen, C., Lummis, M., Stigler, J., Fan, L., & Ge, F. (1990). Mathematics achievement of children in China and the United States. *Child Development, 61,* 1053–1066.

Stevenson, H. W., Lee, S.-Y., & Stigler, J. W. (1986). Mathematics achievement of Chinese, Japanese, and American children. *Science, 2331* (Feb.), 693–699.

Stewart, G. (1988). *Shutting down the national dream: A. V. Roe and the tragedy of the Avro Arrow.* Toronto: McGraw-Hill Ryerson.

Stiggins, R. J., & Bridgeford, N. J. (1985). The ecology of classroom assessment. *Journal of Educational Measurement, 22,* 271–286.

Stodolsky, S. S., Salk, S., & Glaessner, B. (1991). Student views about learning math and social studies. *American Educational Research Journal, 28,* 89–116.

Stonehill, R. M. (1992). The three phases of ERIC. *Educational Researcher, 21*(3), 18–22.

Stones, I. (1989). *Ergonomics for the office.* Hamilton, ON: Canadian Centre for Occupational Health & Safety.

Stringfield, S. C., & Teddlie, C. (1988, April). *Stability of findings in school effectiveness studies: Implications for the fine-tuning of practice.* Paper presented at the annual meeting of the American Educational Research Association, New Orleans.

Stufflebeam, D. L., McCormick, C. H., Brinkerhoff, R. O., & Nelson, C. O. (1985). *Conducting educational needs assessment.* Boston: Kluwer-Nijhoff.

Stufflebeam, D. L., & Webster, W. J. (1983). An analysis of alternative approaches to evaluation. In G. F. Madaus, M. D. Scriven, & D. L. Stufflebeam (Eds.), *Evaluation models: Viewpoints on educational and human services evaluation* (pp. 23–43). Boston: Kluwer-Nijhoff.

Suarez, L. M. (1991). Needs assessment studies. In A. Lewy (Ed.), *International encyclopedia of curriculum* (pp. 433–435). New York: Pergamon.

Sudlow, R. E. (1986, April). *What is an effective school?* Paper presented at the annual meeting of the American Educational Research Association, San Francisco.

Sugawara, O., Oshimura, M., Koi, M., Annab, L. A., & Barrett, J. C. (1990). Induction of cellular senescence in immortalized cells by human chromosome 1. *Science, 247*(4943), 707–710.

Sutton, R. (1991). Equity and computers in the schools: A decade of research. *Review of Educational Research, 61,* 475–503.

Swain, M., & Lapkin, S. (1983). *Evaluating bilingual education: A Canadian case study.* Acton, ON: Scholarly Book Services.

Swamy, A. N. (1987). *An analysis of students' conceptions of pressure-related gas behavior*. Dissertation Abstracts International, 47, 3386A.

Sweetland, R. C., & Keyser, D. J. (Eds.). (1984). *Tests: A comprehensive reference for assessment in psychology, education, and business* (2nd ed.). Kansas City, MO: Test Corporation of America.

Sylvan Learning Center.® (n.d.). Promotional material.

Tamir, P. (1990, April). *Effects of different curriculum process models on the outcomes*. Paper presented at the annual meeting of the American Educational Research Association, San Francisco.

Teddlie, C., Kirby, P. C., & Stringfield, S. C. (1989). Effective versus ineffective schools: Observable differences in the classroom. *American Journal of Education, 97*, 221–236.

Teitelbaum, P. (1989). Feminist theory and standardized testing. In A. M. Jaggar & S. R. Bordo (Eds.), *Gender/body/knowledge: Feminist reconstructions of being and knowing* (pp. 324–335). New Brunswick, NJ: Rutgers University Press.

Teresa, M. (1983). *Reflections, meditations, prayers*. San Francisco: Harper & Row.

Testone, A. Q. (1986). Effect of air ionization. *Evaluation Engineering, 25*(6), 78–89.

Thompson, J. L. (1983). *Learning liberation: Women's response to men's education*. London: Croom Helm.

Thorndike, E. L. (Ed.). (1919). *Educational psychology*. New York: Teachers College, Columbia University.

Thorndike, R. L. (1990). Reliability. In H. J. Walberg & G. D. Haertel (Eds.), *International encyclopedia of educational evaluation* (pp. 260–273). New York: Pergamon.

Thorpe, G. C. (1917). *Pure logistics*. Kansas City, MO: Franklin Hudson.

Tiberius, R. G., & Silins, H. (1980, July). *Individualizing the improvement of teaching*. Paper presented at the Sixth International Conference on Improving University Teaching, Toronto.

Tobin, K. (1987). The role of wait time in higher cognitive level learning. *Review of Educational Research, 24,* 69–95.

Tocher, M. M. (1991). *Ethnocultural minority parents and school perspectives: The quintessential kaleidoscope.* Master's thesis, Queen's University, Kingston, ON.

Tolstoi, L. (1967). *Tolstoi on education.* Chicago: University of Chicago Press.

Tom, A. R. (1984). *Teaching as a moral craft.* New York: Longman.

Tomchin, E. M., & Impara, J. C. (1992). Unraveling teachers' beliefs about grade retention. *American Educational Research Journal, 29,* 199–223.

Tougas, M. E. (1987, February). When a handicap isn't a hindrance. *Family Computing,* pp. 10–11.

Trachtenberg, D. (1974). Student tasks in text material: What cognitive skills do they tap? *Peabody Journal of Education, 52*(1), 54–57.

Trapani, C., & Getinger, M. (1990). Effects of social skills training and cross-age tutoring on academic achievement and social behaviors of boys with learning disabilities. *Journal of Research & Development in Education, 23,* 1–9.

Treisman, P. U. (1983). Improving the performance of minority students in college-level mathematics. *Innovation Abstracts, 5*(17), 1–5.

Tronto, J. C. (1989). Women and caring: What can feminists learn about morality from caring? In A. M. Jaggar & S. R. Bordo (Eds.), *Gender/body/knowledge: Feminist reconstructions of being and knowing* (pp. 172–187). New Brunswick, NJ: Rutgers University Press.

Tye, B. B. (1984). Unfamiliar waters: Let's stop talking and jump in. *Educational Leadership, 41*(6), 27–31.

Tyler, R. W. (1949). *Basic principles of curriculum and instruction.* Chicago, IL: University of Chicago Press.

Tyler, R. W. (1958). Curriculum organization. In N. B. Henry (Ed.), *The integration of educational experiences: The 57th yearbook of the National Society for the Study of Education* (pp. 105–125). Chicago: University of Chicago Press.

UNESCO (United Nations Educational, Scientific, & Cultural Organization). (1986). *The place of science and technology in school curricula: A global survey.* Paris: Author.

United Kingdom Department of Education and Science. (1975). *Acoustics in educational buildings*. London: Her Majesty's Stationery Office.

United Nations. (1959). *Yearbook of the United Nations*. New York: Author.

United States Department of Education. (1987). *What works: Research about teaching and learning* (2nd ed.). Washington, DC: United States Department of Education, Office of Educational Research and Improvement.

University of Illinois Survey Research Laboratory. (1982). *Telephone interviewer's general training manual*. Urbana, IL: Author.

Uphoff, J. K., & Gilmore, J. (1988). Pupil age at school entrance—how many are ready for success? *Educational Leadership, 43*(1), 86–90.

Vail, B. R. (1980, June). *Preparing parent volunteers for classroom work*. Paper prepared for the annual meeting of the Canadian Society for the Study of Education, Montreal.

Vajda, S. (1989). *Fibonacci and Lucas numbers and the golden section: Theory and application*. New York: Halstead.

Van Creveld, M. (1977). *Supplying war: Logistics from Wallenstein to Patton*. Cambridge: Cambridge University Press.

Van Houte Wolters, B. H. A. M., Kerstjens, W. M. J., & Verhagen, P. W. (1990). The use of color to structure instructional texts. In S. Dijkstra, B. H. A. M. Van Houte Wolters, & P. C. Van Der Sijde (Eds.), *Research on instruction: Design and effects* (pp. 79–91). Englewood Cliffs, NJ: Educational Technology Publications.

Van Nord, J. E. (1991). Study skills. In A. Lewy (Ed.), *International encyclopedia of curriculum* (pp. 537–540). New York: Pergamon.

Van Til, W. (1989). Restoring honor to the teaching profession. *Contemporary Education, 60,* 178–183.

Vandell, D. L., & Mueller, E. C. (1980). Peer play and friendships during the first two years. In H. C. Foot, A. J. Chapman, & J. R. Smith (Eds.), *Friendship and social relations in children* (pp. 181–208). New York: Wiley.

Vann, A. (1979). Can principals lead in curriculum development? *Educational Leadership, 36*(6), 404–405.

Vasari, G. (1987). *Lives of the artists, Vol. 1*. New York: Viking Penguin.

Vernon Public Schools. (1986). *Science curriculum guide, the middle school of the Town of Vernon, Grades 6–8*. Vernon, CT: Author.

Vichniak, I. (1988, August 8). UN's horror catalogue on child slavery. *Manchester Guardian Weekly*.

Vockell, E., & Schwartz, E. (1988). *The computer in the classroom*. Santa Cruz: Mitchell.

Walberg, H. J. (1984a). Families as partners in educational productivity. *Phi Delta Kappan*, 65, 397–400.

Walberg, H. J. (1984b). Improving the productivity of America's schools. *Educational Leadership*, 41, 19–27.

Walberg, H. J. (1985). Homework's powerful effects on learning. *Educational Leadership*, 42(7), 76–79.

Walberg, H. J., & Fowler, W. J., Jr. (1987). Expenditure and size efficiencies of public school districts. *Educational Researcher*, 16(7), 5–13.

Walberg, H. J., & Haertel, G. D. (1990). Preface. In H. J. Walberg & G. D. Haertel (Eds.), *International encyclopedia of educational evaluation* (pp. xvii–xxvii). New York: Pergamon.

Walberg, H. J., & Rasher, S. P. (1979). Achievement in 50 States. In H. J. Walberg (Ed.), *Educational environments and effects* (pp. 353–368). Berkeley, CA: McCutchan.

Walker, W. L. (1988). Educational reform: Putting children at risk for no purpose. *Contemporary Education*, 60(1), 27–28.

Wallace, T., & Walberg, H. J. (1991). Parental partnerships for learning. *International Journal of Educational Research*, 15, 3–145.

Washburne, C. W. (1925). Burk's individual system as developed at Winnetka. In G. M. Whipple (Ed.), *Adapting the schools to individual differences: National Society for the Study of Education 24th yearbook, Part 2* (pp. 77–82). Bloomington, IN: Public School Publishing Co.

Waugh, R. F., & Punch, K. F. (1987). Teacher receptivity to systemwide change in the implementation stage. *Review of Education*, 57, 237–254.

Webb, R. A. (1974). Concrete and formal operations in very bright 6- to 11-year-olds. *Human Development, 17,* 292–300.

Weber, J. M. (1987). *Strengthening vocational education's role in decreasing the dropout rate.* Columbus, OH: Ohio State University, National Center for Research in Vocational Education. (ERIC Documentation Reproduction Service No. ED 284 062)

Webster's New Collegiate Dictionary. (1973). Springfield, MA: G. & C. Merriam Co.

Webster, A. (1984). *The educative process.* Unpublished manuscript, Massey University, Palmerston North, New Zealand.

Webster, W. J., & Olson, G. H. (1988, April). *Causes and correlates of school effectiveness.* Paper presented at the annual meeting of the American Educational Research Association, New Orleans.

Weich, J., & Leichner, P. (1988). Analysis of changing answers on multiple-choice examinations for a nation-wide sample of Canadian psychiatric residents. *Journal of Medical Education, 63,* 133–135.

Weinstein, C. E., Goetz, E. T., & Alexander, P. A. (Eds.). (1988). *Learning and study strategies: Issues in assessment, instruction, and evaluation.* New York, NY: Academic Press.

Weinstein, C. S. (1979). The physical environment of the school: A review of the research. *Review of Educational Research, 49,* 577–610.

Weinstein, C. S., & David, T. G. (Eds.). (1987). *Spaces for children: The built environment and child development.* New York: Plenum.

Weir, W., & May, R. B. (1988). Environmental context and student performance. *Canadian Journal of Education, 13,* 505–510.

Weisner, T. S., & Garnier, H. (1992). Nonconventional family life-styles and school achievement: A 12-year longitudinal study. *American Educational Research Journal, 29,* 605–632.

West, C. K., Farmer, J. A., & Wolff, D. P. (1991). *Instructional design: Implications from cognitive science.* Englewood Cliffs, NJ: Prentice-Hall.

What do our 17-year olds know? (1990, September). *ASCD Curriculum Update,* pp. 4–5.

Whipple. G. M. (Ed.). (1925). *Adapting the schools to individual differences: National Society for the Study of Education 24th yearbook, Part 2.* Bloomington, IN: Public School Publishing Co.

White, E. E. (1888). Examination and promotions. *Education, 8,* 519–522.

White, K. R., Taylor, M. J., & Moss, B. D. (1992). Does research support claims about the benefits of involving parents in early intervention programs? *Review of Educational Research, 62,* 91–125.

White, P. (1990). Friendship and education. *Journal of Philosophy of Education,* 24(1), 81–91.

Whitehead, A. N. (1967). *The aims of education.* New York: MacMillan Free Press.

Whitehead, M. (1990). Meaningful existence, embodiment and physical education. *Journal of Philosophy of Education, 24,* 3–13.

Whitehurst, G. J., Falco, F. L., Lonigan, C. J., Fischel, J. E., DeBaryshe, B. D., Valdex-Menchaca, M. C., & Caulfield, M. (1990). Accelerating language development through picture book reading. *Developmental Psychology, 24,* 552–559.

Wichita Public Schools. (1987). *Elementary Physical Education Curriculum.* Wichita, KS: Wichita Public Schools, Curriculum Services Division.

Willems, E. P. (1965). *Participation in behavior settings in relation to three variables: Size of behavior settings, marginality of persons, and sensitivity of audiences.* Unpublished doctoral dissertation, University of Kansas.

Willett, J. B., & Singer, J. D. (1991). From whether to when: New methods for studying student dropout and teacher attrition. *Review of Educational Research, 61,* 407–450.

Willett, J. B., Yamashita, J. J., & Anderson, R. D. (1983). A meta-analysis of instructional systems applied in science teaching. *Journal of Research in Science Teaching, 20,* 405–417.

Willms, J. D., & Chen, M. (1989). The effects of ability grouping on the ethnic achievement gap in Israeli elementary schools. *American Journal of Education, 97,* 237–257.

Wilms, O. H. (1986). *An analysis of the implementation of an art program in an indigenous culture: With particular reference to the Six Nations Reserve, Hosweken.* Unpublished doctoral dissertation, University of Toronto.

Wilson, B. L., & Corcoran, T. B. (1988). *Successful secondary schools: Visions of excellence in American public education.* New York: Falmer.

Wilson, C. W., & Hopkins, B. L. (1973). The effects of contingent music on the intensity of noise in junior high home economics classes. *Journal of Applied Behavior Analysis, 6,* 269–275.

Wilson, R. J., & Rees, R. (1990). The ecology of assessment: Evaluation in educational settings. *Canadian Journal of Education, 15,* 215–227.

Windham, D. M., & Chapman, D. W. (1990). *The evaluation of educational efficiency: Constraints, issues, and policies.* Greenwich, CT: Jai Press.

Winters, M. (1990). The development and design of curriculum guides: A look back and look forward. *CASCD Journal,* (Winter), 3–11.

Winters, M. (1992). *Curriculum development at the local level.* Alexandria, VA: Association for Supervision & Curriculum Development.

Wisconsin Department of Public Instruction. (1985). *A guide to curriculum planning in health education.* Madison, WI: Author.

Witkin, B. R. (1984). *Assessing needs in educational and social programs.* San Francisco: Jossey-Bass.

Wittgenstein, L. (1961). *Tractatus logico-philosophicus.* London: Routledge & Kegan Paul.

Wolf, R. M. (1990). Questionnaires. In H. J. Walberg & G. D. Haertel (Eds.), *International encyclopedia of educational evaluation* (pp. 374–378). New York: Pergamon.

Wolfle, J. (1988). Adolescent suicide—An open letter to counsellors. *Phi Delta Kappan, 70,* 294–295.

Wood, H. B. (1990). *An autobiographical bibliography* (unpublished document).

World Health Organization. (1988). *World health statistics annual, 1988.* Geneva: Author.

World Health Organization. (1990). *World Health Statistics Annual 1990.* Geneva: Author.

Worthen, B. R. (1990). Program evaluation. In H. J. Walberg & G. D. Haertel (Eds.), *International encyclopedia of educational evaluation* (pp. 42–47). New York: Pergamon.

Wright, W. J. (1991).   The endangered black male child. *Educational Leadership*, 49(4), 14–16.

Wringe, C. (1988).   *Understanding educational aims.* London: Unwin Hyman.

Wurtman, R. J. (1975a).   The effects of light on man and other mammals. *Annual Review of Physiology*, 37, 467–483.

Wurtman, R. J. (1975b).   The effects of light on the human body. *Scientific American*, 233(1), 69–77.

Wutchiett, R., Egan, D., Kohaut, S., Markman, H., & Pargament, K. (1984).   Assessing the need for a needs assessment. *Journal of Community Psychology*, 12(1), 53–60.

Yager, R. E., & Penick, J. E. (1986).   Perceptions of four age groups toward science, classes, teachers, and the value of science. *Science Education*, 70, 355–363.

Yates, A., Gray, F. B., Misiaszek, J. I., & Wolman, W. (1986).   Air ions: Past problems and future direction. *Environment International*, 12, 99–108.

Yeomans, E. (1921).   *Shackled youth: Comments on schools, school people, and other people.* Boston: Atlantic Monthly Press.

Yerushalmi, Y. H. (1991).   *Freud's Moses: Judaism terminable and interminable.* New Haven, CT: Yale University Press.

Zeller, R. A. (1990).   Validity. In H. J. Walberg & G. D. Haertel (Eds.), *International encyclopedia of educational evaluation* (pp. 251–259). New York: Pergamon.

Zimbardo, P. G. (1977).   *Shyness.* New York: Harcourt Brace.

Acknowledgments

Figure p. 1   "School bus arriving" (pencil) by Amy Pero (age 6).
                      Reproduced by permission of the artist.

Figure p. 12   © Amnesty International

Figure p. 24   © The Eaton Collection, Archives of Ontario

Figure p. 31   © Glen Dines

Figure p. 35   "The Sunset" (watercolor) by Stephen Cardeiro (grade 2).
                      Reproduced by permission of the artist.

Figure p. 39   © The Nobel Foundation

Figure p. 46   © John Dempsey

Figure p. 57   © Ken Heyman

Figure p. 65   "Puppe Victory" (pointillism) by Tina Karvinen (grade 10).
                      Reproduced by permission of the artist.

Figure p. 73   © Nouvelles Images S.A. Editeurs et S. Baker 1990

Extract   Kent, K. (1985). "A Successful Program of Teachers
       p. 74   Assisting Teachers." *Educational Leadership* 43, 3: 30–33.
                      Reprinted with permission of the Association for Supervision
                      and Curriculum Development. Copyright © 1985 by ASCD.
                      All rights reserved.

Figure p. 84   © Punch/Rothco

Extract   Eisner, E.W. (1969). Instructional and expressive educational
       p. 87–88   objectives: Their formulation and use in curriculum. In W.J.
                      Pophjam, E.W. Eisner, H.J. Sullivan, & L.L. Tyler (Eds.),
                      Instructional Objectives (American Educational Research
                      Association monograph series on curriculum evaluation,
                      No. 3). Chicago: Rand McNally

Figure p. 89   © The Nobel Foundation

Figure p. 101   "Sally" (tempera) by Blair White (grade 1). Reproduced by
                      permission of the artist.

Figure p. 103   © Harley Schwardron

Figure p. 112   © Rapho Agence de Presse Photographique

Extract   John Blackie. (1963). Good enough for the children.
      p. 123   London: Faber & Faber, pp. 15–16.

Figure p. 133   © The Nobel Foundation

Figure p. 149   "Moose on the Run" (stencil on ink) by Beth Desveaux
                      (grade 8). Reproduced by permission of the artist.

Figure p. 156   © George Abbott/Phi Delta Kappan

Figure p. 158   © John Drysdale 1988

Figure p. 165   © The Nobel Foundation

Figure p. 166   © The Nobel Foundation

Figure p. 168   "My Family" (crayon) by Tracey Steele (age 6). Reproduced
                      by permission of the artist.

Figure p. 179   © The Nobel Foundation

Case study   University of Chicago Press, American Journal of
      p. 182–83   Education, and C. Teddlie, P.C. Kirby & S. Stringfield.

Figure p. 192   © Nouvelles Images S.A. Editeurs et J. Niepce-1989

List   p. 208–09   Summary of points from: Johnson, D.W., Johnson, R.J., &
                      Holubec, E.J. (Undated). Learning together and alone:
                      Cooperative, competitive, and individualistic learning.
                      Minneapolis, MN: University of Minnesota Cooperative
                      Learning Center.

Figure p. 214   © Glenn Bernhardt

Figure p. 219   "Boy Praying" (pencil) by Rosemary Pratt (grade 11).
                      Reproduced by permission of the artist.

Figure p. 220   © The Nobel Foundation

Figure p. 222   © Tony Saltzman

Extract   From "I know they can learn because I've taught them,"
      p. 226   *Educational Leadership* (1987) 44(6), p. 3. Helene Hodges,
                      Director of Research and Information, ASCD.

Figure p. 250   © Gang Feng Wang

Figure p. 256   "Pancake Day" (pencil) by Laura Babcock (grade 1). Reproduced by permission of the artist.

Figure p. 277   © Frank Cotham / Phi Delta Kappan

Figure p. 281   © The Nobel Foundation

Figure p. 285   Sturgeon Creek Regional Secondary School, Photography Department. Program developed by Bill Cann, history teacher.

Extract p. 288   Cecilia Hill and National Film Board of Canada

Figure p. 296   "Elephant" (paper cutout) by Amy Bjerknes (grade 8). Reproduced by permission of the artist.

Figure p. 297   © The Nobel Foundation

Figure p. 302   © 1989 Randy Glasbergen

Figure p. 305   Rodney Jones. Used by permission of Harcourt Brace, Inc.

Figure p. 320   "School bus leaving" (pencil) by Gregory Snider (age 6). Reproduced by permission of the artist.

Figure p. 321   © The Nobel Foundation

Figure p. 322   © Ford Button / Phi Delta Kappan

Figure p. 327   © Times Newspapers Ltd.

Extract p. 353–57   Joint Committee on Standards for Educational Evaluation, Standards for Evaluation of Educational Programs, Projects, and Materials. (1986). McGraw-Hill Inc. Used with permission of McGraw-Hill.

Index of Names

(Page numbers in parentheses indicate entries in the reference list.)

Index of Subjects

Feedback Sheet

I would be most grateful for feedback from users of this text. As François Mitterand, President of France, once said, "I enjoy praise, but I learn more from criticism." If you have any corrections, recommendations for improvement, suggestions for additions or deletions, or additional examples of ideas discussed in this book, I would be very interested in hearing from you.

Please cut out or photocopy this page and send to:
David Pratt, c/o Education Department,
College Division, Harcourt Brace College Publishers
301 Commerce Street, Suite 3700
Fort Worth, TX 76102, USA.

_____

_____

_____

_____

_____

_____

_____

_____

_____

Use additional pages if necessary.

Your name and address:

_____

_____

_____

Thank you!